KU-760-470

 Fish, Reptiles, and Amphibians 194–199

 The Weather and Natural Phenomena 259–266

 Media 328–332

 Insects 200–206

 Time and the Seasons 267–273

 Sounds 333–340

 Trees 207–214

 Astral Bodies 274–278

 Messages and Communication 341–347

 Flowers 215–222

 Landscapes 279–285

 Magic 348–353

 Fruits and Vegetables 223–229

 Cityscapes and Buildings 286–294

 Monsters and Mythical Creatures 354–361

 Fire 230–236

 Schools and the Workplace 295–300

 Social, Family, and Work Gatherings 362–367

 Earth 237–243

 Colors and Shapes 301–311

 Puzzles and Mysteries 368–373

 Air 244–250

 Numbers 312–316

 Sport, Games, and Entertainment 374–382

 Water 251–258

 Travel and Journeys 317–327

 Erotica 383–389

THE SECRET LIFE OF
DREAMS

This book belongs to

Aïsha Makki

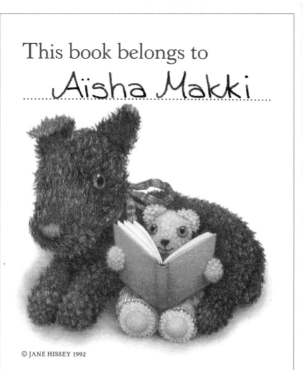

© JANE HISSEY 1992

THE SECRET LIFE OF
DREAMS

Decoding the Messages
from Your Subconscious

Clare Gibson

THUNDER BAY
P·R·E·S·S
SAN DIEGO, CALIFORNIA

TABLE OF CONTENTS

Introduction 6

1 The Archetypes 18

2 Religion and Spirituality 25

3 Family Members 33

4 People 41

5 Positive Emotions 48

6 Ambition and Success 54

7 Negative Emotions 62

8 Anxiety and Frustration 68

9 Conflict 77

10 Loss 85

11 Positive Actions 93

12 Negative Actions 99

13 Birth 108

14 Childhood 116

15 Marriage 123

16 Death 129

17 Authority Figures 137

18 The Body 143

19 Clothing and Adornments 154

20 The Home 162

21 Food and Drink 171

22 Animals 177

23 Birds 187

24 Fish, Reptiles, and Amphibians 194

25 Insects 200

26 Trees 207

27 Flowers 215

28 Fruits and Vegetables 223

29 Fire 230

30 Earth 237

31 Air 244

32 Water 251

33 The Weather and Natural Phenomena 259

34 Time and the Seasons 267

35 Astral Bodies 274

36 Landscapes 279

37 Cityscapes and Buildings 286

38 Schools and the Workplace 295

39 Colors and Shapes 301

40 Numbers 312

41 Travel and Journeys 317

42 Media 328

43 Sounds 333

44 Messages and
Communication 341

45 Magic 348

46 Monsters and
Mythical Creatures 354

47 Social, Family,
and Work Gatherings 362

48 Puzzles and Mysteries 368

49 Sports, Games,
and Entertainment 374

50 Erotica 383

Keeping a Dream Diary 390

Bibliography 396

Acknowledgments & Photo Credits 396

Index 397

Thunder Bay Press
An imprint of the Advantage Publishers Group
5880 Oberlin Drive, San Diego, CA 92121-4794
www.thunderbaybooks.com

Copyright © 2003 Saraband (Scotland) Ltd.

Copyright under International, Pan American, and Universal Copyright Conventions. All rights reserved. No part of this book may be reproduced or transmitted in any form or by any means, electronic or mechanical, including photocopying, recording, or by any information storage-and-retrieval system, without written permission from the publisher. Brief passages (not to exceed 1,000 words) may be quoted for reviews.

All notations of errors or omissions should be addressed to Thunder Bay Press, editorial department, at the above address. All other correspondence (author inquiries, permissions) concerning the content of this book should be addressed to Saraband, The Arthouse, 752–756 Argyle Street, Glasgow G3 8UJ, Scotland (hermes@saraband.net).

ISBN 1-59223-101-2

Library of Congress Cataloging-in-Publication Data available upon request.

Printed in China

1 2 3 4 5 07 06 05 04 03

Für Marianne Gibson. Wer sonst?

EDITOR: Sara Hunt
ART & PRODUCTION EDITOR: Deborah Hayes
ASSOCIATE EDITOR: M. Jane Taylor
PRODUCTION ASSISTANT: Kerry Ryan

INTRODUCTION

"Dreaming permits each and every one of us to be quietly and safely insane every night of our lives," as *Newsweek* quoted the sleep researcher and psychiatrist William Dement saying in 1959, but are our dreams really the stuff of madness? Not according to the ancient Egyptians, Greeks, and Romans, or to the recorders of the Judeo–Christian Bible, who all believed that dreams are divinely inspired, as did—and do—countless indigenous cultures. And not in the view of the groundbreaking psychologists Freud and Jung either, who also argued that dreams should not be dismissed as meaningless because they are often profoundly illuminating manifestations of our unconscious fears and hopes, fundamental instincts and drives, and, indeed, of our true personalities.

As bizarre as the dream scenarios in which we find ourselves night after night may seem when we look back at them from a waking perspective, most dream analysts believe that many are transmitting serious messages from our unconscious to our conscious minds, inner communications that, if heeded, have the potential to set us on a richer, and more fulfilling, path in waking life. If we are to reap the riches of our own unconscious minds, however, we must first learn to understand the secret life of dreams.

Below: While napping recharges flagging energy levels, it appears that dreaming helps to maintain mental health.

The Hows and Whys of Sleep

Sleep is so crucial to our health and well-being that we are believed to spend about a third of our lives sleeping. And it is when we consciously relinquish control of our bodies and abandon ourselves to sleep that the unconscious mind comes to the fore, giving rise to dreams. Although the purpose of neither sleep nor dreams is yet fully understood, the pioneering work that Nathaniel Kleitman, Eugene Aserinsky, and William Dement carried out at the University of Chicago's Department of Physiology's sleep laboratory during the 1950s provided the first scientific breakthrough into understanding what happens to us while we are sleeping. This was an important foundation that subsequent researchers have built upon in giving us an increasingly clear picture of the nocturnal activities of the mind.

After you have settled yourself in bed, have turned out the light, and are drowsily drifting off in the direction of dreamland, your body and brain undergo radical changes that make them markedly different from their waking state. Once you have started to doze, sleep researchers believe that you rapidly progress through four stages of slow-wave sleep that form the basis of a cycle that repeats itself four or five times over an eight-hour period of sleep.

To start with, both your body and brain become increasingly relaxed, your heartbeat slows, as does your

breathing, and your eyes start to roll from side to side. During this first stage, you are neither fully conscious nor completely unconscious and could quickly become wide awake again if disturbed. At this point of light sleep, you are in the hypnagogic state (and shortly before waking up you are in a similar condition, called the hypnapompic state), when you may experience muscular spasms called myoclonic jerks; hallucinations and distorted images may float before your closed eyes; and you may hear disembodied voices.

During stage two, your eyes continue to roll, your breathing and heart rate become ever slower, your blood pressure drops, your brain activity decreases, and you are increasingly oblivious to the noises of the outside world (although you could still be woken relatively easily).

Having entered the third stage of sleep, you are now sleeping soundly, and it would be difficult to rouse you. The speed at which your heart is beating drops still further, as does your breathing rate and body temperature.

Next, you enter a type of deep slumber known as nonrapid-eye-movement (N.R.E.M.), or orthodox, sleep, when your brain is operating at its slowest. With your brain now released from the demands of the conscious mind, it is able to take stock of your body and releases a growth hormone to repair damaged tissues and stimulate growth, while the immune system goes to work on attacking any viral or bacterial infections that may have breached the body's defenses during the day. It is also thought that your brain's hippocampus records memories of the events of the day during this stage of sleep. It would now be quite difficult to wake you, and although you may suffer an attack of the night terrors, get up and sleep-walk, or dream nebulous, thought-based dreams, you will rarely be able to recall any such nocturnal experiences. If your alarm clock regularly jerks you into wakefulness during this stage, you may believe that you never dream at all.

This slow-wave sleep cycle lasts for about ninety to one hundred minutes, and at the end of stage four you move back through the cycle again, through stages three and two, to one, at which point you enter a phase named rapid-eye-movement (R.E.M.), or paradoxical, sleep. Now your brain waves speed up, your heartbeat and breathing become faster and more irregular, your blood pressure rises, you may have an erection if you are a man, and your eyes dart rapidly around behind your eyelids (which is why R.E.M. sleep is so named), although your body is otherwise in a state of paralysis to ensure that you do not injure yourself by acting out your dreams. (If you happen to wake while you are thus temporarily paralyzed, you may feel that something malevolent is preventing you from moving, which may explain the supposed succubus and incubus dreams of yore and, in more recent times, so-called "alien abductions.") Indeed, most of the dreams that we remember occur during R.E.M. sleep, when the brain's cortex is firing on all cylinders. After around ten minutes of R.E.M. sleep, you enter stages two, three, and four again, and continue to move backward and forward through the sleep cycle in this way during the course of the night. As the cycle progresses, however, each R.E.M. phase becomes increasingly longer, with the last—whose duration is around thirty to forty-five minutes—containing your longest, most visual, vivid, and active dreams. Of all of your dreams (and you may have had a great number during four or so periods of R.E.M. sleep), these are the ones that you are most likely to recall on waking.

Research indicates that while N.R.E.M. sleep is vital for physical rest, repair, and recuperation, dream-packed R.E.M. sleep is crucial to our psychological well-being, and perhaps even our sanity. Indeed, Dement concluded that if a subject was deprived of R.E.M. sleep one night—when he or she would exhibit unmistakable signs of sleep-deprivation, ranging from concentration and memory impairment through irritability to paranoia, during the day—the next night he or she would spend more time in R.E.M. slumber, apparently in compensation. This begs the questions, do we sleep to dream, and why do we dream? These issues have intrigued humans for millennia, and although numerous theories have been put forward in explanation, a conclusive, scientifically proven answer remains elusive. And while there is validity in the theory popularized by British molecular biologist Francis Crick (of D.N.A. fame) that dreaming enables the brain to sift though the events of the previous day, filing away the recollection of significant occurrences and jettisoning trivial memories to prevent the brain from becoming burdened with an overload of unimportant information, most researchers believe that dreaming fulfills a profound emotional human need.

Ancient and Indigenous Cultures' Perceptions of Dreams

Ancient literature and art are teeming with references to dreams. Although the Babylonian poem the *Epic of Gilgamesh* (which is thought to date from around 1760 B.C.) contains perhaps the oldest documented dreams, those that are described in the Judeo–Christian scriptures are the most accessible to us, and therefore the best known. Many of these biblical dreams are unambiguously described as revelations from God. In Genesis 28:10–17, for example, it is told that Jacob was dreaming of angels ascending and descending a ladder reaching up to heaven when the Lord appeared by his side and promised him and his descendants the land on which he was lying. Some biblical dreams are admonitory, however, as is made clear in Job 33:15–16: "In dreams, in visions of the night, when deepest sleep falls upon men, while they sleep on their beds, God makes them listen, and his correction strikes them with terror." Certain Old Testament dreams puzzled those who dreamed them, notably King Nebuchadnezzar, whose dream of a tree flummoxed him, as well as his "magicians, exorcists, Chaldeans, and diviners," until Daniel explained that the tree symbolized the king himself (Daniel 4). Many psychologists today would reach a similar conclusion, and would also agree with Joseph's explanation that in his dream of the sun, moon, and eleven stars (Genesis 37:9–11), the sun represented his father, the moon, his mother, and the stars, his eleven brothers. (Biblical dreams are too numerous to be discussed fully here, so if you are interested in reading more for yourself, consult Genesis 20:3–8 for Abimelech's dream; Genesis 40:8–19 for Pharaoh's butler and baker's dream; Genesis 41:1–36 for Pharaoh's own dream; Daniel 2:1–45 for another of Nebuchadnezzar's dreams; and Matthew 1:20–24 for Joseph's dream.)

Most of the world's religions, including Hinduism and Islam, similarly credit dreams with profoundly revelatory or prophetic qualities: according to Buddhist lore, for instance, Queen Maya became aware that she had conceived a son (the future Buddha) when she dreamed of a white elephant descending into her womb.

The Bible makes it clear that the dreams related within its pages were divine messages that were intended to inform, reveal, predict, warn, or chastise, an explanation for dreams that was shared by the polytheistic ancient Egyptians, Greeks, and Romans. As well as regarding many dreams as oracles from their gods, these people furthermore believed that dreams had healing powers, and therefore tried to incubate (see page 13) curative dreams at sanctuaries attached to the temples of their gods of medicine including Imhotep and Serapis in Egypt, Asclepius in Greece, and his counterpart

Above: Papyruses dating from around 2000 B.C. indicate that the ancient Egyptian system for interpreting dreams is the oldest on record.

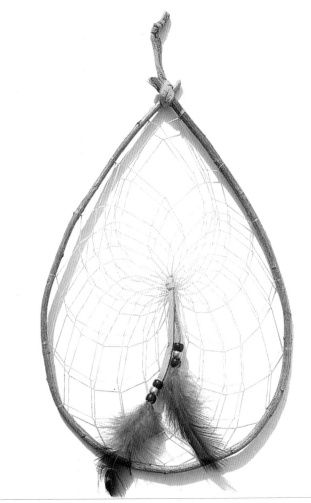

Above: The Native American dreamcatcher is said to trap bad dreams in its web until first light dissolves them, good dreams passing through its central hole into the sleeper.

Aesculapius in Rome in the hope of invoking divine aid, the resulting dreams then being interpreted by dream specialists. In common with the ancient Babylonians, they also made a distinction between positive dreams, which they believed emanated from essentially human-friendly gods—that is, as long as they were properly propitiated—and nightmares, which were thought to be omens inflicted on sleepers by malevolent demons (and the Babylonians paid the priests of Mamu handsomely to intercede with their goddess of dreams in an attempt to prevent such dreams from becoming a reality).

For millennia, dreams have therefore been accorded supernatural significance by most of the world's spiritual traditions, but there are certain cultures to which the phenomenon of dreaming is fundamental, both to their sense of identity and to the regulation of their society. Indeed, the Australian Aborigines believe that the Australian landscape, along with the creatures and plants that inhabit it, was created by their supernatural ancestors (some of which were human, others animals, and yet others hybrid creatures) upon waking from their slumber during the "Dreaming," or the "Dreamtime" (*altjiranga* or *alcheringa*). Not only did these ancestors lay down the rules and rituals by which Aboriginal life should be lived, but it is also said that they established a mystical connection between their descendants and their totem animals and plants before returning to their sleeping state. Many African and Native American tribes cherish remarkably similar totemic creation myths, and, what's more, often believe that dreams provide a direct conduit to their ancestors' wisdom. Dream-pooling plays a crucial role in such societies, when tribal members may gather together for the specific purpose of collectively incubating a dream focusing on a tribal issue, then listen to each other recount the dreams that they have had, ponder possible interpretations, and if any dream seems particularly important, or a pattern of dreams can be discerned, tailor tribal policy to the dreamland message. Like many modern dream interpreters, other Native American tribes believe that dreams express our deepest, and most hidden, desires. Another view of dreaming that is shared by some modern-day dream researchers is held by the Inuit of Hudson Bay, among other people, who are convinced that the soul leaves the body and goes wandering while the dreamer is sleeping.

Early Dream Interpreters

Historians credit the ancient Egyptians with being the oldest culture to develop a regularized system of dream interpretation, which generally accorded with the contrary-dream theory (which holds that a positive dream heralds a downturn in waking fortunes, while a nightmare foretells an improvement in the dreamer's real-life circumstances). It seems, however, that it was the ancient Greeks who first delved deeper into the possible reasons why humans

Above: Raphael's fresco *The School of Athens* (1509–10) portrays Plato and Aristotle (center) surrounded by other legendary Greek thinkers (Heraclitus is depicted in the foreground, leaning on his elbow).

dream, in doing so proposing a variety of theories suggesting that dreams are internal communications rather than messages from an external source.

Most of these dream theorists—or those whose thoughts survive, at least—were philosophers, the earliest being Heraclitus (*c.* 544–483 B.C.), who observed, "The waking have one world in common; sleepers have each a private world of their own." In commenting that "The virtuous man is content to *dream* what a wicked man really *does*," Plato (*c.* 427–347 B.C.) may have anticipated Freud in proposing a wish-fulfillment explanation for dreams, while his pupil Aristotle (384–322 B.C.) may have preceded Jung's theory of the collective unconscious by speculating that, because people's dreams have similar themes, they may arise from a shared source. Aristotle also emphatically rejected the prevalent classical idea that dreams were divine oracles, stating in his work *De Divinatione Per Somnum (On Divination Through Sleep)* that "most so-called prophetic dreams are to be classed as mere coincidences . . ." And it was the "father of medicine," the Greek physician Hippocrates (*c.* 460–377 B.C.), who first advanced the view that some dream-world symbols reflect the condition of the dreamer's body (a deluge of water denoting an excess of blood, for

instance), and should therefore be regarded as valuable diagnostic tools. Perhaps the most influential dream theorist of this age was a Roman, however, namely Artemidorus (A.D. 138–180), the author of *Oneirocriticon (The Interpretation of Dreams)* and the first dedicated dream researcher to focus on symbolism and common types of dreams. Artemidorus's broad conclusion was that, while dreamland symbols can have general meanings, their personal significance to the dreamer has to be taken into account when interpreting dreams, along with the dreamer's personality and individual circumstances.

Although the early Christian Church fathers respected dreams as the bearers of potentially illuminating spiritual insights, the advent of the Middle Ages and the increasingly repressive control of the Roman Catholic Church (which regarded dreams as the devil's work) over Western society put a halt to any serious attempt to study dreams. With the waning of the restrictive influence of the Church during the eighteenth century, however, members of the German Romantic Movement turned their attention to their dreams in a quest to explore the free expression of human feeling and individuality, in doing so identifying the unconscious as the source of their dreams. Thereafter, there was a general revival of interest in the meaning of dreams during the nineteenth century, mainly as a result of the publication of countless popular dream dictionaries like Raphael's *Royal Book of Dreams* of 1830 (by the English astrologer Robert Cross Smith), although such publications were essentially frivolous guides characterized by their fortune-telling flavor.

The Freud-Jung Revolution

With the publication of *Die Traumdeutung (The Interpretation of Dreams)* in 1900, the Austrian psychoanalyst Sigmund Freud (1856–1939) dropped a bombshell that shocked the genteel society of the Belle Epoque era to the core, the reverberations of its impact spreading rapidly throughout the Western world. And the reason for the frisson of outrage that initially greeted his book in a relatively prudish age was its conclusion that our dreams are wish-fulfillment fantasies that have their origins in our infantile urges, especially our sexual desires.

According to Freud, the human mind has three components: the id, the primitive, unconscious mind; the ego, the conscious mind, which regulates or represses the id's "antisocial" instincts with a kind of self-protective defense mechanism because it considers them disturbingly contrary to social norms; and the superego, the conscience that, in turn, modifies the ego. Freud believed that the id is governed by the pleasure principle (which seeks to gratify ever-present unconscious needs), and that the instincts that the ego, which operates under the reality principle in trying to satisfy the conditions imposed by the outer world, works the hardest to repress are the sexual drives that we first experience in infancy. The id is in the ascendant while we are dreaming, when it expresses the urges that the ego (which relaxes its censorship while we are sleeping) represses when we are conscious. These are expressed as symbols, the theory being that if the wishes that underlie these symbols were portrayed literally, they would be understood by the ego, which would immediately be shocked into wakefulness, when it would again repress them. If a dream is to be successfully interpreted, its manifest content (that is, the symbols that the dreamer recalls appearing in the dream on waking) must be stripped of its various disguises to reveal its latent content, or the drives that the symbols represent. The way that Freud advocated achieving this goal was by using free association, or spontaneously voicing the responses that immediately spring to mind when certain key words relating to the dream are pronounced, thereby trying to elude the censorship of the ego at the same time as tapping into the id's thought processes, which, after all, generated the dream in the first place. This process, Freud believed, could give an enlightening insight into the nature of the dreamer's unconscious instincts, and notably his or her libido.

"I was never able to agree with Freud that the dream is a 'façade' behind which its meaning lies hidden—a meaning already known, but maliciously, so to speak, withheld from consciousness. To me dreams are a part of nature, which harbors no intention to deceive, but expresses something as best it can, just as a plant grows or an animal seeks food as best it can." So wrote Freud's former colleague, the Swiss analytical psychologist Carl Gustav Jung (1875–1961), in his posthumously published book *Memories, Dreams, Reflections* (1962). Although Jung had originally been an enthusiastic supporter of Freud's ideas, and the two men collaborated closely for a number of years, Jung's increasing disagreement with certain Freudian theories caused their relationship to end shortly before World War I. As well as his rejection of the Freudian "dream-as-a-façade" viewpoint, Jung felt that there was far more behind dreams than simply the expression of sexual desires, furthermore sensing that the contents of the unconscious were not merely determined by personal experience, but were shared with all other humans. He subsequently evolved his theory of the collective unconscious, which he described as a storehouse of inherited patterns of experiences, instincts, and memories common to humankind that are expressed in dreams in the form of universal images or symbols, which he called archetypes. Jung believed that we have inherited our collective unconscious and its archetypes from our instinct-influenced primeval ancestors, and that "their origin can only be explained by assuming them to be deposits of the constantly repeated experiences of humanity" (*On the Psychology of the Unconscious*, 1917). And because, according to Jungian theory, the psyche consists of the personal unconscious and the collective unconscious (with the conscious mind making up the trio of psychic components), when we encounter a mystifying symbol in dreamland, it is crucial to decide whether it relates to our personal experience or is instead an archetype. Many archetypes are familiar to us through our knowledge of religious symbolism, myths, legends, and fairy tales. This is why Jung proposed that it is the dreamer, who knows him- or herself better than anyone else can, who is best equipped to interpret his or her dreams, but by direct, not free, association because, as Jung put it, "Free association will bring out all of my complexes, but hardly ever the meaning of a dream. To understand the dream's meaning, I must stick as close as possible to the dream images." (*The Practical Use of Dream-analysis*, 1931). By this, Jung meant concentrating on the symbol alone as you list all of the qualities with which you associate it.

But why does the unconscious mind screen archetypal symbols on the dream screen? Jung believed that it is for purposes of psychic self-regulation by the self (our core, or essential, identity), in order to promote healthy development and eventually bring the conscious and unconscious minds into a state of perfect equilibrium or psychic wholeness, which he called individuation. Because the unconscious (be it personal or collective) can only express itself fully in dreams, it autonomously strives to compensate for the influence that the conscious mind wields over us when we are awake by conveying symbolic dreamland messages that reflect our current progress in life. These messages bring repressed or neglected urges to the fore, offer guidance, or warn us that we are straying from the path, or destiny, that would ultimately lead to fulfillment. But, as Jung explained, before we can benefit from the intuitive wisdom of the personal or collective unconscious, we must consciously strive to understand its symbolic language and become familiar with its visual vocabulary.

Some Other Influential Dream Theorists

Although the revolutionary theories of Freud, and particularly Jung, have become seminal to dream interpretation, the work of later psychologists has elaborated on the possible purpose of dreams, as well as proposing alternative methods of decoding them.

As the originator of the inferiority-complex theory, it is perhaps not surprising that the Austrian "individual psychologist" Alfred Adler (1870–1937) believed that dreams are on the one hand concerned with wish fulfillment because they enable the individual

dreamer to attain the superiority, or power, in the dream world that is denied to him or her in waking life, and, on the other, with problem solving. As far as Adler was concerned, "The purpose of dreams must be in the feelings they arouse." He went on to say in *What Life Should Mean to You* (reprinted in 1962), "We must arrive at the conclusion that dreams are an attempt to make a bridge between an individual's style of life and his present problems without making new demands of the style of life. The style of life is the master of dreams. It will always arouse the feelings that the individual needs."

Fritz Perls (1893–1970), the noted Gestalt psychologist, devised an often effective method of making sense of a baffling dream, namely by adopting a noninterpretive interviewing technique. Perls, who believed that dreams project hidden aspects of our personalities, advocated placing two chairs opposite each other, one earmarked for you and the other for the dream. While sitting in "your" chair, he suggested that you address the "dream's" chair and ask a character or object that featured in the dream what it was trying to say. Then you should swap chairs and try to adopt the dream's mindset before answering your question, moving to and fro between the two chairs in this way until your answers have clarified the meaning of your dream.

The American dream specialist Gayle Delaney also advised using an interviewing technique, but in this case addressing the questions directly to yourself (or else asking someone else to quiz you). The queries in Delaney's list include the following. How did the dream make you feel? What was the dream setting, and can you connect it with your waking life? Who were the people in your dream, and what are they like in the waking world? Were there any objects in your dream, and, if so, can you describe them? How do each of these aspects of your dream relate to your waking life? What occurred in the dream, and does it remind you of anything that has happened in real life?

The interpretive hints given in this book are a fusion of all of these groundbreaking theories and techniques, but especially those of Jung and Freud.

Dream Types

Anthropological researchers have concluded that the dreamland experiences of ancient and indigenous cultures fall into four general categories: "big" dreams that have collective importance to the dreamer's society; prophetic dreams; healing dreams; and "little" dreams that have relevance to the dreamer alone. Twenty-first-century dreamers have many more types of dreams, however, some of which are outlined below.

Cathartic Dreams By immersing us in a dream that evokes an extreme emotional reaction, the unconscious gives us the opportunity to express, and thus relieve, pent-up feelings that we may feel unable to vent in the waking world.

Contrary or Compensatory Dreams In a contrary or compensatory dream, the unconscious depicts the dreaming self in a completely different situation to that within which we find ourselves during the day. If your waking hours are filled with feelings of grief following the death of a loved one, for example, your dream may compensate for your depression by immersing you in a light-hearted atmosphere. Your unconscious may alternatively give you a personality transplant, so that if you are shy, you may revel in the novelty of being super-confident in dreamland. Such dreams are believed to compensate for, or balance, a waking life or personality that has become distinctly skewed in one direction, and may also be advocating incorporating the lifestyle or personal characteristic that your dream highlighted into your waking life.

False Awakenings You may have experienced a false awakening during the night if you awoke in the morning convinced that the events that were played out in your dream really happened because your memory of them is so powerful. Researchers believe that many reported sightings of ghosts are due to false awakenings, which happen when you are actually still asleep, but believe, in your slumbering state, that you are awake.

Above: You may successfully incubate a dream of a special someone if you concentrate on visualizing your loved one's face before drifting off to sleep.

Incubated Dreams Incubated dreams sometimes occur when you have set your conscious mind on experiencing a particular dream—perhaps to help you to solve a waking problem—the theory being that your unconscious then responds to your conscious suggestion after you have fallen asleep. It is believed that you can encourage such dreams by meditating on your chosen subject or problem, or, if you are hoping to dream of a person, by studying his or her photograph; by visualizing the dream; or by repeating a short sentence describing the nature of the dream that you want to have, or by asking for the answer to your problem, immediately before going to sleep.

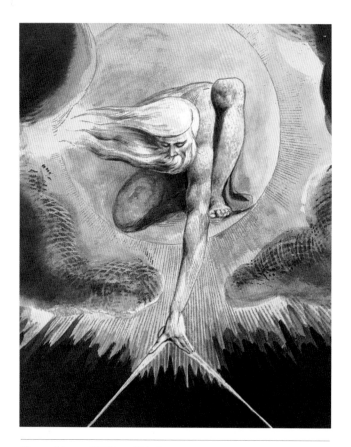

Above: Many of William Blake's visionary prints, such as *The Ancient of Days* (1794), were created using a dream-inspired technique that he termed "illuminated printing."

Inspirational Dreams Many great works of art, music, and literature have stemmed from inspirational dreams, when the unconscious makes us a gift of a creative idea. The mystical work of the English poet and artist William Blake (1757–1827) was reportedly inspired by his dreams, for example, as were the paintings of many Surrealist artists, the books of such authors as Robert Louis Stevenson (1850–94), and the compositions of musicians like Guiseppe Tartini (1692–1770).

Literal Dreams Literal, factual, or processing dreams are action replays of your recent experiences in the waking world. Although they usually have little symbolic significance, by reviewing the day's occurrences they may sometimes throw light on a previously unrecognized aspect of the dreamer's situation. External stimuli, such as a telephone that is really ringing, can also be incorporated into literal dreams.

Lucid Dreams While you are sleeping, you may sometimes become aware that you are dreaming. Your conscious realization may have been triggered during R.E.M. sleep either because something about your dream struck you as being ludicrous or because the crescendo of terror that you experienced during a nightmare reached an intolerable peak. It takes time and practice to avoid waking up, but it is possible to train yourself to become a lucid dreamer, when, armed with the rational powers of your conscious mind, you may be able to face the monsters that give you nightmares and expose them as being nothing more dangerous than your own fears. You may also be able to control the course of your dreamland experiences to a certain extent, perhaps in order to enjoy wish-fulfillment dreams.

Mutual Dreams Although they are rare, mutual dreams occur when two people dream the same dream, sometimes even meeting up in dreamland. Such shared dreams may either arise spontaneously or can be incubated. If you have agreed to share a dream with someone you know (and the best results are achieved by people who are emotionally or physically close), you should decide on the dreamland location together and should both then visualize that setting before going to sleep.

Nightmares Nightmares are dreams that distress or terrify us, and usually arise when we are feeling anxious or helpless through being exposed to a stressful situation or hostile person in the waking world. Such deeply unpleasant dreams, which occur during R.E.M. sleep, are often recurring, but once we have consciously identified the nightmares' trigger and have then rationally confronted and worked through the unresolved fears and anxieties that it arouses in us, they will usually eventually cease.

Night Terrors Night terrors are related to nightmares, but because they strike during stage four of slow-wave sleep, we rarely remember what so terrified our dreaming selves, although we are nevertheless left with an overwhelming sense of dread.

Out-of-body Experiences Many researchers dismiss the notion that the mind, consciousness, soul, or spirit has the ability to leave its body and travel through space, yet such experiences have been well documented, even if they are not understood. Also known as astral travel or projection, out-of-body experiences (O.B.E.s) are believed to occur during sleep, as well as at times of physical or emotional trauma (and especially during near-death experiences, or N.D.E.s).

Past-life Dreams If your dream was set in a historical setting, some analysts would say that you relived an actual past-life experience or a previous incarnation, or else assumed the identity of one of your ancestors. Most professional analysts dispute the existence of past-life, or far-memory, and genetic dreams, however.

Physiological Dreams Physiological, or body, dreams reflect the actual state of the dreamer's body,

---

Below: Some people believe that they experience out-of-body experiences while sleeping, when a silver cord may connect the slumbering body to the traveling spirit.

so if, for example, you became dehydrated during the night, you may have had a physiological dream in which you were parched with thirst. Such dreams may sometimes highlight the onset or progress of a more serious physical condition, when they are usually recurrent.

Precognitive Dreams Did Abraham Lincoln (1809–65), the sixteenth president of the United States, really foresee his death a few days before his assassination, when he dreamed of being told that the president had died? Although they are the subject of heated controversy (and most dream researchers dismiss them as either coincidences or the expression of unconscious knowledge), true precognitive, prophetic, or clairvoyant dreams anticipate real-life events that the dreamer has no way of predicting (even unconsciously). It seems that such dreams are more prevalent among people with highly developed psychic abilities, but are nevertheless extremely rare. If you believe that you have had a dream of this nature, make sure that you record and date it so that you have proof of your dream should it really come true.

Problem-solving Dreams If you went to sleep mulling over a problem, you may have found that you woke with the solution running through your brain. This probably happened because you had already unconsciously solved your problem, and sleeping on it gave your unconscious the opportunity to reveal the answer that had eluded your conscious mind, perhaps in the form of a problem-solving dream. Indeed, many inventions originated in dreamland after their inventors had consciously failed to make a crucial breakthrough, including the chain-stitch sewing machine that the American inventor Elias Howe (1819–67) patented in 1846, which was prompted by his dream of Africans carrying spears with eye-shaped holes in their flattened tips, which his waking mind translated into sewing-machine needles. James Watt (1736–1819), the Scottish engineer and inventor of the steam engine, dreamed of molten metal falling from the sky and shaping itself into balls, which gave him the idea for drop-cooling and hence ball bearings. Other famous problem-solving dreams include that of the German chemist August Kekulé von Stradonitz (1829–96), who, while in the hypnagogic state, dreamed of a snake swallowing its tail, resulting in a "eureka!" moment when he realized that the ring theory explains the molecular structure of benzene.

Recurring Dreams Recurring dreams typically plague dreamers when they are consciously worried about an ongoing waking situation, when they are suffering from a phobia, or when they have repressed, rather than resolved, the memory of a traumatic event. When the trigger state of affairs comes to an end in the waking world, so, usually, do the dreams. If, however, they stem from an underlying phobia or trauma, it is thought that the purpose of the unconscious in continuing to expose a dreamer to the cause of his or her horror is to force him or her to haul the memory to the forefront of the conscious mind, to consider it rationally, and to try to come to terms with it. After this, the dream should gradually become less frequent before, it is hoped, finally disappearing. If you suffer from recurring dreams, remember that your unconscious is trying to help, not torment, you, and that it will continue to try to drum home its message until you consciously receive it, acknowledge it, deal with the problem that prompted it, and thus release yourself from its grip.

Safety-valve Dreams If you had a dream in which you hit your annoying colleague with a satisfying "thwack!," you may have had a safety-valve dream. According to Freud, the unconscious makes us a present of these dreams when we need to let off steam by forcibly expressing pent-up emotions or desires, but are unable to do so in the real world due to a perceived need to behave in accordance with convention.

Below: Safety-valve dreams enable us to express in the safe environment of dreamland the violent emotions that we consciously suppress while we are awake.

Above: If you spend your waking hours worrying about making ends meet, and came across a stash of cash in dreamland, you almost certainly had a wish-fulfillment dream.

Telepathic Dreams In a typical telepathic dream, someone known to the dreamer appears in dreamland accompanied by a powerful sense of distress, after which the dreamer later learns that that person experienced a real-life crisis (such as the sudden onset of an illness, an accident, or even death) at the precise time that he or she had the dream. It is thought that telepathic transference, or meetings of minds—when the dreamer receives a powerful emotional message signaled by the transmitter, who may not have been aware of communicating in this way—occur between people who have a close emotional connection.

Wish-fulfillment Dreams By fulfilling our fantasies in dreamland—whether we long to be millionaires, to be admired by others, to be irresistibly desirable, or just to go on vacation—the unconscious is compensating us for an unsatisfying waking existence.

How to Use This Book

The fifty chapters that follow encompass the entire spectrum of dream themes, from those that arouse strong emotional responses like happiness and excitement, anxiety, or anger, to those that puzzle you by focusing on something as mundane as a kitchen or a computer, an apple or a television—or even something entirely abstract, such as a color or shape. The chapters follow a logical, sequential pattern, but as you probably already know, logic is the strength of the conscious mind, while the unconscious, or dreaming, mind works in mysterious ways, preferring to communicate by subtly intuitive, random, and symbolic means. This is why the messages embedded in our dreams can be so difficult to decipher—that is, until you have cracked the code by learning their secret language—and this book will give you the key with which to gain access to your unconscious mind's wealth of wisdom.

The first step in interpreting your dream is to look up the situation in the index and refer first to the emboldened page number(s), which will be the most specific reference(s) to your dream theme. Remember to try to think laterally, or "outside the box," and the book will initiate you into the techniques of this approach through the symbolic icons that you will find at the end of certain paragraphs. Each icon refers you to a chapter that is linked to the subject that you looked up to start with. The key to these icons is located on the endpapers at the beginning and end of the book for ease of reference, and the icons appear prominently in the margins of each page.

If, for example, you dreamed that you were running, you'll find a possible explanation for your dream in Chapter 6, whose theme is ambition and success, but you'll also be referred to Chapter 49, in which the meaning of sports-related dreams is explored, as well as to Chapter 8, on anxiety, in which the act of running to escape when pursued is discussed. In those chapters you'll find further ideas to help you to gain a deeper understanding of your dream, and consequently also of yourself. If these primary meanings do not explain your dream adequately, refer back to the index and look up the more tangential references listed there until you find a situation that most resembles your dream.

THE ARCHETYPES

The maternal woman who comforts you, the white-haired wise old man, the jeering prankster: your unconscious mind may often cast these and other archetypal characters or images to play a leading, and sometimes perplexing, role in the screenplay of your dreams. You may never have encountered these characters during your waking life, but they are a part of your psyche—the collective unconscious—and are therefore familiar to your dreaming self. What do they mean?

Many archetypes are, of course, familiar to us on a conscious level because they populate the realms of myth, legend, spirituality, and fairy tale. We know the Merlin of Arthurian legend, Christianity's Virgin Mary, and her opposite, Snow White's wicked stepmother. We are familiar with the dastardly Joker in Hollywood's Batman movies. Yet these characters are not random inventions: as archetypes, they are ancient, universal, and enduring personifications of our most basic human instincts and urges.

When you encounter these archetypes in your dreams, you will rarely experience an indifferent reaction to them. The first key to unlocking the mystery of the message they bear is your instinctive response. Do they make you feel deeply threatened, gloriously inspired, unbearably frustrated, or imbued with a profound sense of well-being? Always remember, when an archetypal character or image features in your dream, it has sprung from the deepest level of *your* brain; *your* unconscious mind has conjured it up for a positive purpose. You will find more archetypal images within the pages of this book, too, many of which are aspects of those detailed below.

The Persona

Did you dream of putting on a face mask, of altering your appearance with cosmetics, or of donning a disguise? If so, this dream probably concerns your persona. We all have a persona, and usually more than one.

Rather like the masks that the thespians of ancient Greece wore to convey their characters' personalities to the audience, the persona's wardrobe of masks comprises the various "faces" that we consciously present to different audiences—be they family members, friends, colleagues, or strangers. We wear these masks in order to show ourselves off in the most positive light and to thus become accepted, liked, admired, or even acclaimed. Your persona is not, however, the real "warts and all" you. And depending on the context of the dream and how it felt to you, your unconscious mind may either be

warning you that your persona is in conflict with your true self or advising you to adopt a different persona in order to help you achieve your heart's desire.

The Shadow

Did you dream of someone of the same gender as you, perhaps a stranger, or maybe someone you know, who behaved in a way that you found repulsive, hateful, shocking, brutal, or somehow repellently primitive, so much so that your instinctive response was one of overwhelming loathing? If so, you may have encountered your shadow, which, although the polar opposite of the persona that your ego has so carefully and consciously constructed, is nevertheless part of your psyche.

A useful indicator of your shadow's character is a quality that you particularly despise in others, such as cowardice, boastfulness, pessimism, or violent tendencies. Because the conscious mind does such a good job of repressing the shadow in your waking life, its only outlet is the dream world. When your shadow appears, it is trying to tell you that it is time to acknowledge, and perhaps even consciously embrace, that part of yourself that was highlighted so negatively in your dream. Remember that although your ego is prejudiced against it, your shadow qualities are not necessarily bad, and that transporting them from the darkest recesses of your dreaming mind into the light of your waking hours may enhance your creativity and *joie de vivre*.

The Anima and the Animus

Did someone of the opposite sex play a leading role in the dramatic action of your dream, or arouse deep feelings of yearning, attraction, or admiration? If so, your slumbering self may have witnessed the appearance of your anima (if you are a man) or animus (if you are a woman), a character who may be a stranger to your conscious mind, but is nevertheless your "soul image." (In fact, two of the meanings of the Latin words *anima* and *animus* are "soul" and "mind.") This does not, however, mean that your anima or animus is a mirror image of your conscious personality; it is the reverse. This is one of the reasons why the anima and animus manifest themselves as a member of the opposite sex. This is also why, if you are a cautious, rational man, your anima may assume the character of a spontaneous, sentimental woman—or, if you are an indecisive, retiring woman, your animus may take the form of a resolute, independent man.

Opposite: Do you have a regal persona in your dream, or do you don the mask of a superhero? **This page, clockwise from left:** This shadow figure might appear to you as an exaggerated form of the dark side of your personality; a youthful, exuberant girl might be the dream anima of a conventional man; this confident dream businessman represents the animus of a reticent woman.

Above: Carefree optimism and youthful potential are characteristics of the princess archetype. **Below, right:** The mother archetype is loving and nurturing. **Opposite:** Circe, the sorceress who lured Odysseus into danger, embodies the witch whose appearance in your dream indicates selfishness.

They may be latent, but we all possess both masculine and feminine qualities. A man's anima is the blueprint for his feminine side; originally based on his mother, it eventually expands to encompass the qualities of all of the women whom he has come to know in life. In the same way, although a woman's animus (which represents her masculine characteristics) is initially modeled on her father, the men who subsequently enter her life also have a bearing on it. Depending on the nature of these flesh-and-blood influences, particularly the appropriate parent, the animus or anima may be either positive or negative in character. (Their various aspects are outlined below.

For more on the animus, see "The Masculine Principle"; for the anima, see "The Feminine Principle.") Both may be symbolized by people you know, by mythological, legendary, or spiritual characters, or by objects that in some way represent masculinity or femininity to you.

By introducing your animus or anima to a dream, your unconscious mind is trying to tell you that you need to balance, or compensate for, those attitudes that dominate your conscious mind or behavior. If you are a man, it may be signaling that you have been ignoring your emotional, intuitive, or empathetic impulses, for instance, and if you are a woman, that you should try to become more intellectually focused, practical, or confident. Heeding your soul image will not only help you to develop into a more content and well-rounded individual, but will also strengthen and improve your relationships with members of the opposite sex.

The Feminine Principle

The myriad attributes and complexities that make up the feminine principle are embodied by the archetype of the great mother, or Mother Earth. This archetype is the symbol of the "complete" woman, within whom the four primary qualities of womanhood (the maternal instinct, romantic inclinations, practical intelligence, and spiritual intuition), each of which have a positive and negative aspect, coexist in perfectly balanced harmony. Such a woman is a rarity in life, however, for one quality will usually predominate. Whether you are a woman or a man (for whom the feminine archetype may have taken the form of your anima), take special note of the female figure—be it a person, a creature, a quality, or an object—who made such an impression on your sleeping self. She carries a message from your unconscious that you should remedy an imbalance, thereby potentially transforming your life for the better.

The **mother**, the first feminine archetypal figure (who represents instinct), is symbolized by an idealized mother figure, such as Christianity's Virgin Mary, who is selfless, nurturing, caring, and comforting. Kind and empathetic, it is her unconditional love and reassurance that we long for in times of adversity. If you dream of her, ask yourself whether you need to develop these motherly qualities within yourself. The other face of this archetype is the **terrible mother**, the mother's dark side, within whom the maternal qualities have undergone a nightmarish transformation. Typified by the cruel stepmother of fairy tales, she is intent on dominating, criticizing, undermining—even devouring—those whom, in a normal relationship, she should love unselfishly. If you dream of her, ask yourself: is someone (and it may even be you) having a damaging, suppressive effect on you by being overly stifling or selfish?

The second feminine quality is that of sunny emotions, innocent romantic yearnings, and youthful hopes and desires, whose embodiment is the fairy-tale **princess**, the unspoiled heroine who is destined to fall in love with her own handsome prince and live happily ever after. That is, unless she morphs into the **siren** or seductress, the Lorelei character of German legend whose voracious sexual appetite and irresistible lure spell the doom of countless hapless men. A dream princess may be telling you to rediscover the carefree optimism of your youth, while a dream siren may be warning you to jettison your selfishness and work on becoming more mature in your relationships.

The **amazon** represents the third feminine quality, that of intellect and practicality. She is the professional woman who competes successfully in a man's world, although a romantic partner and children are often notably absent from her private life. The amazon's dark side is the **huntress**, the woman who hunts for men much as a tigress stalks her prey, only to spit them out and throw them away when they have served her purpose. If you dream of the amazon, ask yourself if your obsession with your career is wrecking the potential fulfillment that you might enjoy if you had a rich emotional life. If you dream of the huntress, question whether you are using or misleading your romantic partner or unconsciously avoiding deepening your emotional commitment.

The final feminine archetype is the **priestess**, the personification of spirituality and intuition, the wise woman of folklore, not quite at home in this world and somewhat aloof, who seems to have channeled a higher power that she uses for the collective good. Although the **witch**, her negative aspect, shares the priestess's powers, she uses them coldly, calculatingly, and destructively to advance her own aims. If either of these archetypes appears to you during a dream, ask yourself, on the one hand, whether you are working with integrity toward a common cause, or whether, on the other hand, your selfish, manipulative motives and methods will alienate others and ultimately leave you feeling isolated.

The Masculine Principle

The masculine principle is symbolized by the great father, or the wise old man. In his person, the male qualities of authority, idealistic potential, virility or physical power, and spiritual insight are harmoniously combined. Each of these qualities—in both their positive and negative aspects—manifests itself as an archetypal figure. And if one of these archetypes appears to you in a dream, whether you are a man or a woman (for whom the masculine archetype may have assumed the role of your animus), ask yourself whether it is highlighting an aspect of yourself or your behavior that you need to address.

The **father** is the ideal male parent, characterized in fairy tales by the good king who has ultimate authority over his realm and rules it justly and benevolently, thereby commanding the respect of all. A staunch protector of the weak and a generous provider to the needy, he uses his authority positively—unlike his shadow, the **ogre**. The ogre is embodied by the corrupt policeman, who relishes exercising the unlimited powers his position has granted him by gratuitously meting out overly harsh punishment, regardless of whether the punishment is deserved. Because he will not tolerate dissent or insubordination, the dream ogre represents a threat to your individuality from a powerful authority; the dream father, on the other hand, may simply be regarded as a role model.

If the father represents authority, his son, the fairy-tale **prince**, represents the questing nature of the hopeful and idealistic young man who seeks to clarify his purpose in life by gaining knowledge and experience. Will he fulfill his positive potential? Or is he doomed to become his dark side: an irresponsible **wastrel** and philanderer, whose total lack of intellectual or moral purpose and whose desire for immediate sensory gratification sends him drifting aimlessly through life, taking his pleasures where he finds them? A dream that features the young prince may be encouraging you to loosen the bonds of adulthood and recapture some of your youthful idealism, while dreaming of a wastrel may be a warning that it's time to grow up and behave more responsibly.

The third aspect of the masculine principle is the *warrior*—the hero—the mature man whose aggression, courage, great physical strength, and determination have enabled him to prove himself on the battlefield and who never shirks from confronting further challenges. His appearance in your dreams points toward the need to take decisive action, be it to promote your aims in your working life or to further your social aspirations. The warrior's negative counterpart is the *villain*, the ubiquitous bad guy who features in so many of Hollywood's movies, the baddie who at best unashamedly cons the gullible and vulnerable and, at worst, resorts to violence to release his frustrations. The message that he conveys is usually unambiguous: think and behave in the opposite fashion!

The *high priest* represents masculine spirituality. A solitary, hermitlike figure, he possesses a penetrating wisdom that seems to emanate from another, higher realm. Although a loner, he can be regarded as a spiritual guide, guru, or mentor. The high priest will use his powers and knowledge to guide those whom he judges worthy of his help, just as Merlin assisted King Arthur in Arthurian legend. His counterpart, the *black magician* (although equally knowledgeable and accomplished) is consumed by his lust for power and uses his dark arts to further his own ends only.

The black magician is not concerned with positive concepts such as unselfishness and morality. If you dream of either of these figures, question your motives, or those of the person whom you identify with the high priest or black magician: are they ultimately altruistic and benevolent or selfish and malevolent?

Above: Merlin represents the high priest, or your spiritual guide in the dream world.
Opposite: This young man embodies the prince archetype; his appearance in your dream may be a reminder that you should nurture your idealism rather than succumbing to cynicism.
Overleaf: Three aspects of the trickster: a clown, a Greco-Roman satyr, and a coyote—the trickster figure of innumerable Native American legends. The dream trickster's behavior points out the moral of your dream's story.

The Trickster

Did a clown do his utmost to steal the limelight in your dream through sleight of hand or wounding mockery? Or did you watch someone suddenly transform himself into someone, or even something, else? Clowning, playing pranks, throwing insults, anarchical behavior, and shape-shifting are all hallmarks of the trickster. This wild, juvenile, egotistical maverick, the rebel without a cause who acts entirely on impulse, is in a state of happy amoral thrall to his own physical appetites. The trickster delights in overturning the status quo and mocking the staid and respectable qualities that we consciously prize.

Personified in myth by the Greco-Roman gods Hermes and Mercury and by the Norse Loki, in literature by Br'er Rabbit and Reynard the Fox, and in colloquial expression by the phrase "monkeying around," this irritating attention-seeker is nevertheless worthy of your attention. The trickster represents that part of your unconscious self that feels—often justifiably—obliged to sabotage your most earnest conscious efforts. Ask yourself, for example, whether you can truly be proud of your attitudes and achievements, or whether you have started to become complacent, staid, pretentious, or downright vain. Do you, in fact, need a good dose of shaking up, lightening up, or taking down a peg or two? If you heed the messenger, the trickster's influence may transform your waking life into a more honest, happy, and carefree one.

RELIGION AND SPIRITUALITY

When interpreting any dream of a religious or spiritual nature, it is crucial to take your own beliefs (or lack of them) into consideration. A dream of Christ will obviously have personal significance to a devout Christian, yet may puzzle or worry a Muslim or atheist dreamer. If you dream of a figure or aspect of a spiritual belief that you hold, it is likely that your unconscious mind is reminding you to think or behave in accordance with the tenets of your faith when addressing a problem in your waking life. A dream that features a facet of a belief system that is alien to yours may seem less clear-cut, but the key to its interpretation lies in what that figure or object represents to you. For example, if you associate Buddha with serenity, then by summoning up Buddha, your dreaming mind may be signaling that you need to find some mental or spiritual calmness.

Gods and Goddesses

Did you dream that you were seduced by a breathtakingly beautiful goddess of love, or that you were paralyzed with fear when caught in the sights of a vengeful warlord with supernatural powers? If so, your dreaming self may have conjured up a divine archetype to transmit a message to your conscious mind—whether or not you can identify the erotic seductress as Venus or the fearsome warrior as Mars.

The characteristics of the gods and goddesses that populate the pantheons of many religions, living or dead, transcend the divides of time, culture, and geography. Take, for instance, such mighty sky gods as the Canaanite Ba'al, the Greek Zeus and Roman Jupiter, the Celtic Taranis, the Vedic Indra and Hindu Vishnu, the Germanic Donar, and the Norse Thor, all linked by their propensity to hurl thunderbolts as a sign of their divine displeasure. Such gods are similar because they are archetypal figures, embodiments of universal and unvarying human emotions and behavioral patterns. This is why your dreaming self will recognize what these divine archetypes represent—be it love, aggression, jus-

A dream of the Norse god Thor can have many interpretations. As a representative of the warrior archetype, his appearance in your dream may suggest that an aggressive male in your life is riding roughshod over you. As a hurler of thunderbolts, he may warn that you are in danger of receiving a stunning bolt from the blue.

Left: In Judeo-Christian belief, the prophet Jeremiah is noted for his doom-and-gloom-laden prophesies. Did his appearance in your dream warn of an impending disaster, or has your unconscious mind cast someone as a Jeremiah figure? **Below right:** If you are a Muslim, dreaming of Muhammad may be a signal to heed the teachings of the Prophet.

tice, jealousy, anger, or another profound energy—even if you can't identify the particular god or goddess who featured so prominently in your dream.

Many deities fall into one of the archetypal categories outlined in Chapter 1, so first refer to this chapter to see if you can identify your dream deity's role and consequently understand his or her divine message. Then consider the raw energy that the god or goddess embodies, and how it relates to your life. For instance, if you are a man who dreamt you were being seduced by the goddess of love, ask yourself if your dream Venus came to you in response to your need for sexual satisfaction. Or, if you are a woman who has dreamt of the vengeful warlord, do you find your aggressive male boss so intimidating that your fear is compromising your performance?

The Supreme Being

We each have our own, different conceptualization of the "supreme being." For some, it may be the almighty God of Judeo-Christian or Islamic tradition; for others, it may be nature's eternal life force;

while still others may believe it to be the state of perfect enlightenment. However you envisage or understand its nature is, perhaps, less significant to interpreting its appearance in your dream than is your recognition of its transcendent, universally controlling, divine power, as well as your feelings of insignificance in relation to it.

If you dream of the supreme being at a time when your life appears to be spiraling out of your control, your unconscious mind may be begging for illumination and guidance from the highest spiritual level. Alternatively, it may be a message that you need

to examine, and possibly rectify, your current motives and morals. A more prosaic interpretation may be that someone who has authority over you—this could be your school teacher or an employer—is either "playing God," or that your reverence for him or her is excessive and is perhaps totally misplaced.

Prophets and Perfect Beings

If you are a Jew who dreamed of either the Messiah or an Old Testament prophet, a Muslim to whom Muhammad appeared, a Christian who witnessed Christ, or a Buddhist who received a vision of Gautama Siddhartha while you were sleeping, your dream encounter will probably have affected you deeply.

The fact that your dreaming mind has summoned up a figure of the utmost spiritual importance to you indicates that you may have reached a crisis point in your life, and that you may feel anxious about making a crucial decision that will have an irrevocable bearing on your future. Alternatively, do you have something on your conscience that will not let you rest easily? Do you feel embarrassed about an aspect of your behavior

itual purity that lifts them far above the flawed world of humanity. Indeed, their otherworldliness and sanctity is often represented both in dreams and in art by such devices as angelic wings, symbols of transcendence, and by haloes or auras of light, signifying holiness and divine illumination.

Although we may not be able to achieve such an ideal state of spiritual perfection, such characters embody positive qualities, both general and more specific, to which we can at least try to aspire.

Sometimes, the message they imparted can be relatively mundane. For instance, if you are familiar with Christian lore and dream about Saint Matthew, one of the New Testament apostles and the patron saint of tax collectors, your unconscious mind may simply be sending you a reminder that it's time to file your tax return. Yet, because Matthew was a martyr, it may be pertinent to consider whether his appearance in your dream means that you are feeling exploited by someone.

Regardless of their religious affiliation, angels and saints are traditionally considered to be messengers, or intermediaries, between the supreme being and humans. Did your dream angel bear a warning about some transgression of thought or deed? If so, consider whether you need to adopt a more moral stance on something in light of the angel's communication.

Did you feel blessed by a message from your guardian angel as you slept? If so, your unconscious mind may be telling you that your instincts about some issue—perhaps about a big decision— are good and that righteousness is on your side. In addition, because angels inhabit a more elevated, rarified realm than we, their manifestation in dreams may open a conduit to a higher level of spiritual awareness. If the significance of the angel's appearance still remains unclear, try meditating on your dream; you may find that the fog of confusion lifts, giving your conscious mind a new aspect.

toward someone? Or is your life lacking a spiritual dimension? Whether you are yearning for divine guidance or whether you know, deep down, that you need to change something about you for the better, heeding the message that your spiritual role model embodies will help you to reach the decision that is ultimately best for you. And if you dream of a leading figure of a religion that you do not share, do not dismiss the apparition as a "false prophet," for, despite their disparities of detail, all religious figures represent facets of the universal truth.

Angels and Saints

Depending on your religion or spiritual beliefs, you may have dreamt of an angel or a saint, a bodhisattva or an immortal, an avatar or an arhat, all perfect beings that possess a level of spir-

Devils and Demons

If you dreamed of the devil or his evil minions, it does not mean that you are bound for hell. None of us is perfect: we all possess the potential to tread a malevolent or immoral path through life (although some of us are better able to resist the lure of this hazardous course). If you are pondering a difficult decision, ask yourself if your dream devil was a caution from your conscience that you are in danger of succumbing to false temptation, of taking that one significant step that will set you on the path to ultimate unhappiness. Alternatively, your conscience may be bothering you. Do you regret some aspect of your behavior in the past ? If so, the devil of your dream may continue to plague you until you right the wrong.

It may be, however, that a dream of the devil is warning of an external threat, rather than of a threat that lurks within you. Have your raw instincts (which, after all, work in tandem with your unconscious, dreaming mind) picked up negative vibes from someone? If so, it may be advisable to take your instinctive response seriously and to be on your guard when dealing with that person.

Opposite page: A profound desire for illumination and guidance, or perhaps perfect truth, may be indicated by a dream in which Christ or Buddha appears. **Above:** Angels are said to act as messengers between the divine realm and the human world, and a dream angel may therefore bring a communication from a higher spiritual plane. The appearance of an angel or similar spiritual intermediary in a dream is a reminder that you should not ignore a moral or troubling issue you may have been avoiding in waking life. **Left:** Dreaming of a devil or hellish imp, or of behaving devilishly, is usually a warning, be it from your conscience or your instincts.

Heaven and Hell

Dreaming of being in heaven or hell reveals either your current state of mind (are you finding life especially heavenly or hellish at the moment?) or your hopes or fears for the future. Such dreams can, therefore, be reflective, escapist (if your dream heaven was the polar opposite of your current situation), or admonitory (if you are wracked with guilt about something that you've done or are tempted to do). But these sorts of dreams relate to your waking life in the earthly realm and are not predictive of where you'll actually spend the afterlife—that is, if you believe in life after death.

Spiritual Authorities

Rabbis, popes, cardinals, and bishops, priests and priestesses, lamas, gurus, mullahs, monks and nuns—all represent spiritual authority, and they may unsettle us if they appear in our dreams. Unless the message he or she imparted was unambiguously positive, it is likely that you were discomforted by your encounter with such a character, and herein lies the key to interpreting your dream. Were you uneasy because he or she provided an unwelcome

Opposite: A graphic dream of the descent into hell means that you are repressing feelings of guilt over an aspect of your actions or intentions. **Right:** Buddha taught the path to nirvana, or the state of freedom from all earthly desires. Dreaming of being in spiritual heaven reflects how you currently perceive your waking life.

reminder of a neglected moral responsibility toward someone (maybe even yourself)? Have you deviated from the straight and narrow and, if so, are you harboring feelings of guilt? Or are you unconsciously yearning to be

shepherded back into spiritual line? Although these are profoundly difficult questions to ask yourself, addressing your answers by taking positive action will ultimately transform your sense of spiritual well-being.

Religious Ceremonies and Accouterments

The setting, ceremonial, and any accouterments should all be taken into account when dissembling the components of a religious or spiritual dream, for each of these elements contributes toward its meaning. Although their primary significance will usually accord with any religious teachings that you have absorbed, certain interpretations are universal.

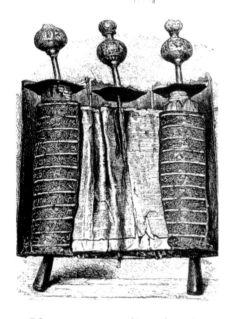

If you were reading, hearing, singing, or chanting the words of sacred scriptures in your dream, your unconscious mind may be signaling your desire to receive a definitive answer or truth. Although your question may not be of a spiritual nature, it is nevertheless likely that you feel the need of guidance from a higher authority. Similarly, if you were praying in your dream, your invocation may reflect a feeling of powerlessness and a desperation for divine assistance.

If you were a member of a dream congregation or participated in, or witnessed, a religious rite, your dream reaction is paramount. Depending on your current situation, the feeling of being comforted, or uplifted, or blessed could either denote your joy at being in harmony with a prevailing moral code or, alternatively, a deep-rooted desire to fall in line with the attitudes and beliefs of the rest of the flock. If your reaction was one of rejection or rebellion, however, your unconscious mind may be urging you to assert your individuality, which is perhaps being stifled by the strictures of a collective belief system.

The use of candles and chalices is common to many systems of religious and spiritual belief, but these are also ancient and power-ful symbols in their own right. The candle's flame signifies enlightenment, be it of the mind or spirit. So, if your dream scene was illuminated by candlelight, this may indicate your hope of "seeing the light." Chalices enclose the water of life or, in the case of the Holy Grail, the blood of Christ—both agents of sacred healing and renewal. Because it holds out the hope of mystical transformation, a chalice is a symbol of destiny. Take special notice of the appearance of your dream chalice: was it a golden vessel studded with gems or a humble glass beaker? The chalice reflects how you see yourself and, as such, indicates the difficulty of your quest to achieve your highest potential.

Center left: If a religious book or manuscript, sacred scriptures or laws, such as the Torah, featured in your dream, you may be seeking a clear-cut and authoritative answer to a weighty problem that has been troubling you. You should pay attention to this problem before it becomes more intractable. **Above:** A dream chalice symbolizes the potential to undergo a mystical transformation and therefore represents your spiritual destiny (should you choose to seek it). **Left:** Spiritual or intellectual enlightenment is the message that the unconscious mind highlights when it sets the dream stage with burning candles. The flame is also a sign of purity and a symbol of new or eternal life because it represents regeneration.

FAMILY MEMBERS

You may wake up feeling either deeply troubled or profoundly reassured after having had a dream that featured a member of your family, especially if he or she was your father or mother. How your waking mind reacts to your dream relation is often linked with your feelings for him or her in the real world, which is why examining your relationship in light of the aspect highlighted by your unconscious is the first step to take when analyzing such a dream. If you remain baffled, however, the next step is to consider whether the dream character could have been an archetypal figure that your dreaming mind summoned up under the guise of a convenient family member. If you decide that this is probably the case, the message that your dream may have been relaying will probably relate to your own emotions, attitudes, or behavior, indicating that you should project your analytical searchlight inward rather than outward.

Your Parents

During your formative years, and for a significant part of your life, it is likely that you were both physically and emotionally dependent on your parents or, if either or both of them were absent during your childhood years, on an alternative mother or father figure. Most of us become gradually less reliant on our parents as we tread the path through adolescence to adulthood, yet vestiges of our early emotional dependency usually remain with us, be it on a conscious or an unconscious level. And because our parents, or parental figures, wielded such enormous influence over us during the long period when our personalities were in the process of developing and we were gradually learning to recognize and assert our increasing individuality and independence, our feelings toward them remain intense.

The dreams that you have of your mother or father may have a variety of interpretations, ranging from the clear and straightforward to the opaque and complex. All, however, hinge on how you perceive your emotional interaction with them, particularly when you were a child and they were the all-powerful centers of your universe.

As the gentle, loving, and nurturing mother of Christ, the Virgin Mary embodies the selfless qualities of the ideal mother. If your mother treated you as though you were the precious center of her universe and you dreamed of being cherished and comforted by her, your dream reflects your mother–child relationship, but may also indicate that you are in need of some tender, loving care.

Did your mother appear in your dream to give you a comforting hug and words of encouragement, and was she warm and loving toward you while you were growing up? If so, your dream may simply be confirming the importance of the maternal role that she has played in your life, perhaps also indicating that you are feeling insecure and in need of some validation and unconditional love. Or did you dream that your father chided you about your recent performance at work, and do you have uncomfortable memories of him admonishing you for not studying harder at school or for poor grades? If so, your dream may simply be underlining your own dissatisfaction at not having met the standards that your father instilled in you. When your dream parents are true to their actual characters, the message imparted is usually clear and can be taken at face value.

But did your dreaming mind perversely cast your emotionally withdrawn, even hurtful, mother as an angel of compassion, love and understanding? Or did your gentle father, who never disciplined you when you were a child, shock your dreaming self by aggressively chastising or punishing you? Dreams in which parents behave completely out of character can be extremely unsettling—sometimes deeply upsetting—because they turn what we have come to regard as accepted truths on their heads. Such dreams may have little to do with your real-life parents, however, and far more to do with unresolved aspects of yourself or your life situation that you have never fully (if at all) acknowledged or addressed, but perhaps need to

Left: If you felt that your mother disliked and resented you when you were growing up, but she laughed, cuddled, and cosseted you in your dream, you may be in need of mothering. Below: If your father abstains from alcohol in actual life, but your dream portrayed him as a hopeless drunk, your unconscious may be telling you that acknowledging his human flaws would be liberating. Opposite, top: Could your dream father have been encouraging you to "get on your bike" and become more independent? Opposite, bottom: If your puritanical mother astonished you in a dream by letting her hair down and having fun, did you feel shocked or delighted?

in order to find emotional peace or fulfillment. In such instances, your unconscious mind may have conjured up a parental archetype either to bring the neglected issue to your attention or, alternatively, to warn you of an authority figure who presents a threat to your individuality. So ask yourself: could the ideal mother of your dream have been telling you that you need to "mother" yourself or someone close to you? Or consider this: maybe your dream ogre doesn't represent your father after all, but your over-controlling boss, who is doing his utmost to stifle your individuality and undermine your confidence by bullying and belittling you.

Do either—or both—of your parents regularly feature in your dreams? If so, the frequency of their appearance indicates that they continue to play a crucial role in your life. Their behavior in your

dream may, however, indicate that you are too dependent on one or other of them—or on both—than is healthy at this stage in your life. Did your kindly, teetotaler mother horrify you in your dream by drunkenly hurling abuse at you, something that she has never done, and you're convinced she'd never do, in life? By ridiculing a much-venerated mother in such a way, the dream may be signaling that you have chosen to ignore her human foibles (and none of us is perfect) and have put her on a pedestal of perfection. There are two issues to consider here. Firstly, would regarding your mother more objectively give you some welcome emotional independence? And, secondly, although you may consciously never have acknowledged it, would you secretly feel liberated if your mother really did behave in a less straight-laced way, thereby allowing you to interact on a more equal basis? Alternatively, does your father, perhaps a stickler for discipline who ruled your childhood with a rod of iron, often re-

enact his authoritarian behavior in your dreams? If so, have you become obsessively fixated on that part of his character that you most resent about him? Or could his unrelenting dream criticism reflect your low sense of self-esteem or self-confidence? Whether or not your parent's behavior in life mirrors that in the realm of sleep, such negative dreams often raise the question of whether it's time for you to become more independent and to strike out on your own, regardless of what your parents may think of the wisdom of your life choices.

Was it your behavior toward a parent that you found particularly upsetting in a dream? Did you dream of murdering your father while in the grip of an uncontrollable rage? Or did you stand in front of your mother and vehemently list all of the qualities that you hate in her? If so, fear not, because you're unlikely to do the same in waking life. Such dreams are usually nothing more than either a safety valve that enables you to express feelings of anger that you have been consciously suppressing, or an indication of your need to rebel, to break irrevocably free from parental control and to take charge of your destiny. Dreaming of being prostrate with grief at your father or mother's funeral can sometimes send a similar message, but may also be an emotional dress rehearsal staged by your unconscious mind to prepare you for the devastation that you will feel when your parent really does die.

Finally, if a satisfactory explanation underlying a dream of your mother or father continues to elude

you, refer to Chapter 1. It may well be that your anima (if you are a man who dreamed of your mother) or animus (if you are a woman in whose dream your father featured) or, indeed, another archetypal figure may have disguised itself as your parent.

Your Grandparents

If you dreamed of either of your grandparents, or perhaps even of a great-grandparent whom you never knew, he or she may have imparted a direct message to your dreaming self that may either have comforted or worried you. If, like many children, you regarded your grandparents, or a specific grandparent, as someone on whom you could always rely for unconditional affection and encouragement (particularly if your relationship with your parents was fraught), their appearance in your dreams may be reassuring. Your dream grandparent may have appeared to remind you of the happy times that you shared and, if you believe in the afterlife, may enjoy again.

Apart from reflecting a nostalgic yearning for the security of childhood and tight-knit familial bonds, dreaming of either of your grandparents may indicate that you are unconsciously crying out for their loving guidance, born of a lifetime's experience, as you dodge your way past life's dilemmas and pitfalls. But if you don't associate the grandparent of whom you dreamed with a sage and impartial source of wisdom, ask

yourself whether he or she could have been an archetype in disguise, especially the priestess (or wise old woman) or priest (or wise old man). Whoever you identify your dream grandparent as, heeding the advice he or she has given will help to set you on the path that is right for you.

Indeed, even if your dream ancestor's message was unclear, the very appearance of a family elder usually indicates that you should look to the past for a solution to some problematic aspect of your current circumstances. The key could either be a lesson learned from an actual event that has passed into family lore (which may have parallels with the problem that you are facing) or, alternatively, an ancestral trait that you have inherited, which you may be able to view more objectively in someone else.

Left: When grandparents appear in your dreams, they usually do so in response to your unconscious need for some wise advice that you know you can rely on. Perhaps something that happened during their lifetime has a direct bearing on a dilemma that you are currently facing. **Right:** If you regard your grandparents as a source of love and laughter, dreaming of them may serve to hearten and encourage you during times of difficulty.

Your Siblings

Because they are of the same generation, our interaction with our siblings is usually less burdened by the search—even battle—for individuality and independence that often complicates our relationships with our parents. That having been said, the conflict engendered by sibling rivalry frequently looms large between brothers and sisters. And although this conflict typically lessens as the years pass, vestiges of childhood jealousy or antipathy may resurface in the dream world.

A dream in which your brother or sister is cast in a negative light may, therefore, denote unresolved and corrosive childhood feelings toward that sibling. If a bullying brother tormented you in your dream as he did when you were growing up, for instance, your unconscious may be telling you that

it's high time you took your courage in both hands and confronted him, thereby breaking the pattern. Taking a less clear-cut example: your real-life sister, a goody two-shoes whose unfailing kindness has always irked you, may persist in

infuriating your dreaming self with her saintly patience. If so, your powerful reaction may indicate that, not only should you begin to respect her compassionate qualities for the sake of your relationship, but you may even benefit from adopting these qualities yourself.

But what if you are an only child, yet dream of having a sister? Or what if your brother behaves completely out of character in the screenplay of your dream? Such dreams may have nothing to do with family at all, but may instead point to an aspect of yourself. If, for example, your dream sister offended you by her appalling rudeness, your dream may be highlighting your feelings of guilt about your own discourtesy to a certain person. Alternatively, such a dream may advocate being more assertive in your dealings with someone, even if your conscious mind balks at the thought because you associate assertiveness with rudeness (in which case your dream sister may actually be your own shadow). Similarly, if your selfish brother's behavior was extremely noble and brave in your dream, your sleeping mind may be setting you an example to emulate.

If your dream casts someone you know, but who is unrelated to you, in the role of a sibling, it usually indicates that you cherish brotherly or sisterly feelings for him or her, with all of the undertones of rivalry or platonic love that such a relationship entails.

A final issue to consider in any dream relating to a sibling is whether he or she represents an archetype, be this a prince or wastrel, a princess or siren, or, indeed, any of the other faces of the archetypal masculine and feminine principles. For the characteristics and messages of these archetypes, see Chapter 1.

Sons and Daughters

Most parents are hypersensitive—indeed, often even deeply intuitive—where their children are concerned, although this may be on a more unconscious than conscious level. If you are a parent, the most likely explanation for any dream that features your child is therefore a straightforward one. If you dreamed that your son was in danger, for example, it simply means that you are worried about his safety, and perhaps with good cause. Equally, a dream in which your daughter accuses you of not understanding her usually indicates that your unconscious (if not your conscious) mind has become increasingly, and uncomfortably, aware that you have indeed been brushing aside her opinions and that you should perhaps try harder to see certain issues from her point of view.

If you dreamed that you were a parent, but you are actually childless, your dream may be a form of wish fulfillment. Or, your dream offspring may instead represent progeny of the non-flesh-and-blood variety.

Alternatively, but more unusually, a dream son or daughter may represent one of the many archetypes that are facets of the masculine and feminine principles, so if the meaning of your dream continues to elude you, consulting Chapter 1 may provide an answer.

Opposite page: Dreams of your brothers or sisters may often bring unresolved issues of sibling rivalry bubbling up to the surface of your conscious mind. The unconscious mind also occasionally uses a brother or sister figure to highlight a quality within yourself that it would be helpful to address. **This page:** If you are a parent and dream of your child, you can usually take the dream at face value. If, however, you are childless, your dream child may refer to a cherished idea or project.

Your Extended Family

Any dream that features a family member can frequently be taken at face value, in that it may simply reflect your feelings toward, or relationship with, the person in question. But, if you are unable to make a satisfactory interpretation based on your real-life feelings or relationship, it may be that your unconscious mind has drawn a parallel between an aspect of your own character (or that of someone unrelated to you) and the dream relation. This may be particularly true if he or she is a member of your extended family.

If you are finding it difficult to analyze the meaning of your dream, it may be that your unconscious has cast a masculine or feminine archetype in the role of your relation, in which case Chapter 1 may provide enlightenment. As a guideline, ask yourself if your dream aunt has more in common with the archetypal amazon or huntress than with your mother's sister, or if your dream uncle may have been the warrior or villain disguised as the familiar face of your father's brother. Similarly, a dream niece may be a manifestation of the princess or siren, while the prince or wastrel may have assumed the identity of your dream nephew.

Archetypes may also invade your dreams in the guise of in-laws or step-relations—the terrible mother as a mother-in-law or stepmother, for instance, or the ogre figure as a father-in-law or stepfather. A negative dream about a parent-in-law or step-parent usually indicates the feelings of insecurity and, to a certain extent, rivalry, that arise when an alien authority figure enters your life through marriage. Such feelings are quite natural: after all, by marrying your mother or your father, your step-parent has acquired a measure of authority over you and, however benevolent their intentions may seem, you may nevertheless feel that your individuality is under threat. Engineering a tactful confrontation may put an end to any such troubling repetitive dreams, but be warned that the repercussions may be seismic outside the safety of the dream world.

Being Orphaned or Adopted

Dreaming of being either an orphan or an adopted child usually indicates that your relationships with members of your actual family have instilled a sense of loss or rejection in you.

Because people are designated orphans when both of their parents have died, dreaming of having lost your parents (and this applies if they are still alive, too)

may denote that you feel deprived of the unconditional love and support that is associated with ideal mother and father figures. In other words, you may feel condemned to navigate your course through life alone, without adequate levels of support.

Dreaming of being adopted indicates that you feel like an outsider in relationship to your family circle, be it because your relatives have somehow excluded you or because you seem to have little in common with them. Do you feel that your family has collectively rejected you (a feeling that may be compounded by the assumption that you were given up for adoption by your "birth parents")? Or do you consider yourself to be at odds with the rest of your family? Either way, such a dream may suggest the need to create a surrogate family (and maybe your friends could fulfill such a role) within which you feel accepted, loved, and secure.

Dreaming of being orphaned, abandoned, or adopted denotes a fundamental insecurity about your position within your family circle. Such dreams suggest that you feel somehow rejected or excluded by your nearest and dearest and that you should perhaps turn to your friends for the emotional support and loving acceptance you crave.

Night after night, we watch an ever-changing cast of characters interact with each other, as well as with ourselves, in the screenplay of our dreams. Many of these characters, such as our relations (see the chapter on family members) and our friends, are well known to us in our waking life. Others, like celebrities and royalty, we are familiar with only through their regular appearance in newspapers and magazines or on television and cinema screens. Strangers, and people whose importance in the dream world is more defined by their occupation—or lack of it— than their "civilian" identities, often loom large, too. Each of these types of people throws light on some aspect of our lives, be it our actual relationships, our hopes and worries, or facets of our personalities.

Your Friends

Did your closest friend, whom you see almost daily, put in a nocturnal appearance in your dream? If so, and if he or she behaved or communicated with you in the same easy manner that characterizes your relationship in the waking world, it's safe to assume that the dream merely reflects the important part that he or she plays in your life. The same interpretation applies if your friend has moved away and face-to-face contact is rare, although such a dream may additionally be signaling that he or she has been on your mind and that a reunion may be long overdue.

If, however, your dream highlighted or exaggerated a characteristic or behavioral quirk in your friend, it may indicate one of two things. If, for instance, your friend's attitude toward life is generally happy-go-lucky, but he pushed this tendency to its limits in your dream by behaving with such reckless abandon that you felt terrified, there are two probable explanations. Firstly, although his devil-may-care attitude may appeal to you in day-to-day life, your unconscious mind may be telling you that his lack of caution is actually making you feel uneasy. Alternatively, is it possible that your dream is warning you that it is *you*, rather than your friend, who is the reckless one? Indeed, the dreaming mind tends to project aspects of ourselves onto our nearest and dearest, the purpose of such transference being to make us aware of something that we

either don't recognize in ourselves or that we would prefer not to. Either way, your fearful reaction in your dream indicates that someone's recklessness, be it your friend's or your own, may have dangerous consequences.

Dreams in which friends— people who, after all, you like and trust—suddenly turn on you in anger, or even with murder in mind, are particularly troubling. Perhaps you woke up sweating after a dream in which your best

Left: A dream of a long-lost friend may be urging you to renew contact. **Above:** If your friend behaved recklessly in your dream, does he or she have a quality that makes you uneasy and that your dreaming mind exaggerated?

friend was doing her utmost to suffocate you. If so, it may be that your unconscious is warning you that you are in danger of being "smothered" by her neediness, and that her dependence on you is threatening your own independence. Indeed, such negative dreams or nightmares involving friends often signify that your relationship is not all that it seems, and considering your friend's behavior, both in your dream and in life, as well as your dream reaction, will provide the key to the problem.

Strangers and Aliens

Unlike dreams in which friends behave out of character, when strangers make guest appearances in our dreams, we are unhampered by all the emotional baggage of friendship when trying to work out their significance. Yet far from being simply a random encounter, the stranger's manifestation in your dream may, in fact, have been a deliberate attempt by your unconscious to tell you something of major significance.

Dream strangers generally represent an aspect of your character or of a relationship that you either haven't consciously acknowledged or that you have neglected. This is why they appear unfamiliar, or "strange," to you. How these mystery strangers look—threatening or vulnerable, unattractive or angelic, for instance—and behave, along with your reaction to them, will give you important clues as to the nature of the problem area.

If you're female, did you dream that an unfamiliar man approached you and requested that you accompany him on a trip? It may be that the stranger was your animus, and that his message was that you should explore the adventurous, masculine side of your personality that yearns to see the world. Similarly, if you are a man, did you dream that you witnessed an unknown woman being hit by an automobile and that she begged you to tend to her injuries? Your anima may be signaling that someone in your life has been hurt (not necessarily physically) and that you should draw on your caring, feminine qualities with which to help her. Are you a man who dreamed of a cringing, cowardly man, whom you didn't recognize, but whose spinelessness aroused deep disgust in your dreaming self? This may have been your shadow trying to draw your attention to a testing situation in your waking life from which you may unconsciously feel the need to run (and maybe you indeed should).

Left: If you are a woman, a Pied Piper figure may be your animus encouraging you to strike out for pastures new. **Above:** In the dream world, spacemen or visitors from other planets signify alien forces. Although you may initially find them alarming, communicating with them will make them seem less threatening. **Right:** Waking life offers many opportunities for chance encounters that have no significance, but the strangers who appear in your dreams have been specifically cast by your unconscious to send you a message.

If dream strangers represent a facet of your personality, any spacemen or extraterrestrials whom your sleeping mind beams down into your dreams usually indicate that you are feeling threatened by "alien" forces or influences. Starting a dialog with them, however difficult this may initially be, and thereby coming to understand them, should allay your fears of the unknown. The same applies if you dreamed of a foreigner dressed in his or her national costume and speaking an unfamiliar tongue. ☆

Celebrities and Royalty

At some level, when we gaze at photographs of famous people, most of us wish we could be like those visions of extraordinary beauty (such as Marilyn Monroe or Audrey Hepburn, if we are women) or those celebrated icons of manliness (such as John Wayne or Clint Eastwood, if we are men). The same holds true if a celebrity graced your dream with their stellar presence. Whether you yearn to be as good-looking, rich, or powerful as the star who descended from unattainable heights into your dream world, or whether you simply have a crush on them, such dreams are frequently the wish-fulfilling response of your unconscious to your desires.

As well as giving you temporary gratification and a sheen of reflected glamor (perhaps in compensation for your self-consciousness about your personal appearance or your humdrum life), your dream celebrity may also have served a more profound purpose. The celebrity may have been acting as your anima (if you are a man) or animus (if you are a woman). He or she may, for example, have highlighted a personal quality that either you greatly admire and would like to possess or that is pertinent to a current situation you

are in. If you dreamed of Nelson Mandela, for instance, would you like, or do you need, to cultivate within yourself the virtues of compassion, patience, and tolerance for which he is renowned? It may also be that you cherish a deep-rooted, but unfulfilled, longing to change direction in life and that your dreaming mind has summoned up an eminent representative of your heart's desire to inspire you and encourage you to follow your dreams. If you secretly yearn to be a musician (maybe you dream of sharing center stage with Bruce Springsteen, and of together sending the crowd wild), then perhaps it is time for you to consider pursuing your vision. 🎭

Being singled out by a celebrity in your dream—no doubt to the envy of your dream friends, who suddenly see you with new, admiring eyes—furthermore suggests that you feel that you are somehow undervalued or taken for

than the city streets, that you are heading for, or that you have starved a part of your personality into a state of destitution.

The clue often lies in either the beggar's identity or request. Was it your disheveled wife who begged coins from you in the street? If so, ask yourself whether you have

Opposite: Dreams that star icons of wisdom, dignity, or leadership signify either wish fulfillment or the need to develop a latent quality within yourself. **Left:** If a vagrant accosted you in your dream, take note of what he or she wanted. **Below:** Dreaming of people who have opted for an alternative lifestyle may reflect your yearning to adopt a more unconventional way of life.

granted by those around you. Dreaming of meeting a royal personage, be it a king, queen, prince, or princess, has particular significance in this regard because it indicates that you desire recognition, respect, or admiration. And who better to fulfill your craving than someone who is universally acknowledged as being of the highest social standing? The dream redresses the balance, but only for a few minutes, and only in the dream world, yet because it signals a low sense of self-esteem, if you heed the message and take steps to boost your self-confidence, its legacy may be lasting.

Beggars and Drifters

If dream celebrities and royalty represent your aspirations, then their polar opposites—beggars, hobos, and vagrants—usually send a caution that unless you change some aspect of your life, you, too, could lose everything and end up tramping the streets. Although such dream characters may warn of impending monetary losses—even outright bankruptcy—this meaning is generally only pertinent if your financial situation in the real world is giving you cause for concern. The more typical explanation is either that it is "lonely street," rather

driven her into such an impoverished state by not giving her enough affection and emotional support. Or did you dream that an unknown beggar accosted you on your way home from work, but instead of entreating you for money, pleaded with you to give him a book? If so, it may be that you have been so busy furthering your career (here symbolized by the money) that you have been neglecting your essential need for academic stimulation and learning (represented by the book). Ignoring the beggar's entreaty in your dream signifies your outright refusal to "feed" your undernourished intellect, yet your consequent feelings of guilt may tell you that this was the wrong response and that you should be more sympathetic should you encounter the beggar again. Giving in to his plea, on the other hand, indicates that you are unconsciously aware of the importance of taking positive action.

Dreaming of people for whom traveling is a life choice rather than the only option sends a different message. Perhaps you dreamed that you were standing by the window and watching a convoy of gypsy caravans pass by, and that you wondered where it was headed, and you felt tempted to hitch up your wagon and join it. In this case, you should consider whether your life has become too staid and settled and whether you would welcome a more unconventional, uninhibited, free, or adventurous existence.

People at Work

When the main point of interest about someone in your dream was his or her occupation or profession, there is usually a good reason why your unconscious mind has highlighted that particular activity or job. The message may just be a straightforward one that you instinctively understand: dreaming of watching an artist at work may, for instance, reflect your unconscious frustration at being prevented from expressing your creativity. Your unconscious mind may be encouraging you to release the artist within. If the explanation eludes you, however, trying a little free association may help you to see the light. Perhaps you dreamed of a soldier. If so, ask yourself which qualities you associate with military personnel. If discipline is the first quality that springs to mind, consider whether your life is either too disciplined or not disciplined enough (your dream reaction to the soldier, such as dislike or admiration, should help you to decide which).

Some occupations have certain general connotations in the language of dreams that may help you to decipher their relevance to a particular facet of your life.

Accountants and book-keepers deal with matters of financial regularity and are also noted for their objective, analytical skills. Dreams in which they appear may be warning you either to manage your finances better or to adopt an unemotional and systematic approach when attempting to resolve a problem. A dream in which a scientist plays a part similarly suggests that you need to adopt a strictly reasoned and impartial investigative stance in response to a challenge in your waking life.

Members of the medical profession, such as doctors and nurses, are concerned with diagnosing and treating health problems. Their appearance in your dream may therefore reflect a worry about some aspect of your health (in which case it is probably advisable to make an appointment with your doctor, who may set your mind at rest). Alternatively, they may signal that you need to take better care of yourself before you run your body into the ground and become vulnerable to ill-health. Nurses, in particular, often indicate that you are in need of some emotional attention and care.

Salespeople sell things. Was it you who was trying to make the sale? If so, consider the nature of the product, the identity of the customer, and his or her response to your salesmanship. If you were demonstrating a vacuum cleaner to your boss and her reaction was positive, your unconscious may be urging you to pitch your big idea (perhaps how to make your office truly paperless) to her in waking life. If someone else was the dream salesperson, ask yourself who is attempting to sell you what, and whether you really want to commit yourself to that sort of "purchase."

The purpose of waiters, porters, and maids is to serve people. Did your dream cast you in one of these roles, and did you hate being treated as a servant? It may be that you feel that your services—be it at work or in your domestic arena or personal life—are being exploited by someone who has assumed too much control over you (and if your dream boss was known to

you, ask yourself whether it could be that person). If, however, someone you know was the service-provider and you treated him or her unkindly, perhaps it is *you* who is taking unfair advantage of that person's willingness to help. Alternatively, it may be that your duties in life are becoming overwhelming and that you simply wish that someone would step in and relieve you of some of your workload.

Opposite, left to right: If someone's occupation was of significance in your dream, it is usually pertinent to an area of your life. A lawyer denotes the need to behave "lawfully," a fireman may be urging you to douse the flames of anger that are burning you up, while an artist may be telling you to give rein to your talent for painting. **Left:** Waiters are employed to serve people. Do you feel that you are at everyone else's beck and call, or are you treating someone as a "hired help"? **Below:** Dreams featuring soldiers or armed guards indicate that you would benefit from developing a more disciplined approach to waking life.

♡ POSITIVE EMOTIONS ♡

Dreams in which we feel imbued with pure joy are less common than those in which we are riven by feelings of anxiety and perplexity. The relatively scarce manifestation of positive emotions in the dream world is perhaps explained by the constant difficulties inherent in living life in the real world and our consequent worries about the stability of our relationships, domestic situation, or professional circumstances. Yet while these concerns are often mirrored by anxiety dreams, the unconscious sometimes gives the conscious mind solace by conjuring up scenarios in which we feel deeply contented, loved, and secure, or even experience exhilarating feelings of release and freedom. If life seems particularly grim at the moment and a shrill alarm call has torn you from such a night-time idyll, your unconscious mind was therefore probably trying to comfort and encourage you with a compensatory or wish-fulfillment dream.

Happiness and Contentment

If you dreamed that you were unreservedly happy or profoundly content, and if this characterizes your overall response to the world around you when you're awake, lucky you! Most of us are, however, beset by niggling doubts or worries about aspects of our working or home lives and relationships. And if something is giving you cause for concern, yet your dreaming self luxuriated in a rosy glow of contentment, there is one of two possible explanations. The first is that your unconscious mind is trying to hearten you and enhance your sense of wellbeing in compensation for your conscious unhappiness or discontentment. Alternatively, your unconscious may be presenting you with the key to real-life happiness. Try to recall the source of your dream contentment: was it a person, an action, a conversation, a sensory experience, or something else? Once you have identified exactly what gave you such pleasure, consider

whether the dream was fulfilling a wish that is unrealistic in waking life, or whether the attainment of your heart's desire may actually be possible, that is, should you decide to pursue it.

Left, above, and opposite: Whether you dreamed that your life was filled with love and laughter, something made you jump for joy, or you luxuriated in the warm embrace of your significant other, the purpose of your unconscious may have been to comfort and hearten you at an unhappy or difficult time in your waking life.

Left: Dreams that remind you of the heady, early days of your romance are a reminder to rediscover your passion. **Below:** If you were surprised to find yourself courting a colleague in your dream, could you unconsciously be nurturing seeds of love within your heart? **Opposite:** Witnessing a dream betrothal denotes a yearning to be loved and cherished.

Love and Tenderness

If you basked in the euphoria of being in love, the first step to take when interpreting your dream is to ask yourself who, or what, aroused such feelings in you. If it was your partner, whom you adore, your dream is simply reaffirming your enduring love for him or her. If, however, the first flush of romance has long since past, it may be that your dreaming mind is reminding you of the overwhelming love that you once felt, continue to feel—albeit at a more unconscious than conscious level—and could quickly rekindle. That is, if you set your conscious mind to work on fanning the flames of your ardor.

You may, however, have been unsettled by a dream in which you were in love with someone whom, in waking life, you regard as nobody more significant than a colleague or neighbor. Or perhaps you do indeed feel drawn to that person, but are trying to quash your interest because you regard it as being inappropriate. This type of dream may be very unsettling, especially if you're already in a stable relationship or your dream soul mate is somehow otherwise forbidden fruit. But, uncomfortable as it may be to admit to yourself, it is important to consider whether your unconscious has homed in on your attraction to that person—an attraction that your conscious mind has maybe suppressed. If you decide that this is the case, your dream was probably giving rein to your repressed desires in a safe environment within which no actual damage can be inflicted on anyone. Alternatively, it may be that your unconscious has highlighted genuine seeds of love. If you are footloose and fancy free and your dream causes you to see the object of your sleeping mind's desire in a new, amorous light, it may be time to acknowledge, and then think about expressing, your feelings for that person.

Did you dream that you witnessed two other people's touching love for each other and felt envious or excluded? Or, alternatively, did you dream that you were bathed in the warming love of a friend, acquaintance, or family member? Such dreams often express a deep-rooted need for the unconditional affection, comfort, and support that we enjoy when we are the objects of love, be it platonic or otherwise. As variations on the compensatory, wish-fulfillment theme, these dreams may signal that your levels of self-esteem and self-worth are running on low and require refueling with the reassuring, confidence-boosting love of those close to you.

Finally, if you dreamed of being in love with someone—and it may be anyone you know—but your feelings weren't reciprocated, the message is straightforward. Are you uncertain of how the focus of your dreaming affection really regards you in waking life, and are you fearful of being rejected?

Release and Freedom

A dream may sometimes give us such an exhilarating sense of release, liberation, or freedom, that waking up to the realization that it was just a dream dooms us to deal with the day's demands feeling crushed by a cloud of disappointment.

Perhaps you were thrilled to the core in your dream when you discovered your ability to fly, testing your new-found skill by soaring and swooping effortlessly through the air. Or perhaps you lazed indolently in a sunlit, flower-strewn meadow without a care in the world, or strode out of your school or office for good, without a backward glance or single regret. Whatever your dream, the euphoric buzz that you experienced is unlikely to be matched in the waking world. This is because such dreams are typically wish-fulfilling, escapist fantasies to which your unconscious mind has treated you in an

Below and right: Dreams in which we break away from the chains that inhibit our freedom of mind or action often reward us with a blissful feeling of release. A dream of flying high or floating free holds out the tantalizing promise of liberation in the real world, but only after you've released the real you by striking off the shackles that bind you.

attempt to compensate for the dreariness and drudgery of your day-to-day life.

Do you feel that the limitations of your life have pushed you into a corner from which there is no escape? Do you feel that you have ended up trapped in a claustrophobic relationship, or are others' ceaseless demands stealing your precious free time, sapping your energy, and stifling your individuality? In short, do you crave the release of a more unpredictable, stimulating, and rewarding existence or relationship that would give you the freedom to be yourself? Your dream is urging you to find a more fulfilling alternative to your current situation. And unless either your circumstances change of their own accord or you yourself strike off the shackles of other people's expectations and step out in a direction of your own choosing, you will probably be condemning yourself to many more bitter awakenings.

⚘ AMBITION AND SUCCESS ⚘

Be they professional or personal, short- or long-term, we all have ambitions in life that we consciously set our hearts and minds on achieving. The dreaming mind also plays a role in helping us to attain our cherished goals by periodically presenting us with progress reports on our success to date. Some of these updates take the form of simple wish-fulfillment dreams: winning the lottery or celebrating a stellar promotion, for instance. Yet because the unconscious mind has a tendency to use confusing symbols and to send contrary messages, others can be more difficult to decipher. It is nevertheless important to try to interpret such dreams because they usually contain a pertinent observation or warning that has not yet become apparent to your conscious mind.

Running, Climbing, and Jumping

Running, climbing, and jumping are all actions that are associated with moving forward, or with making physical progress, in waking life. Their significance in dreams has little to do with physical advancement, however, but instead reflects how well you are doing in your quest to achieve your ambitions. This is why it's helpful to take careful note of a number of aspects of your dream when attempting to analyze it. What exactly was the goal toward which you were running, climbing, or jumping? Did you become tired or breathless or did your body perform effortlessly, like a well-oiled machine? Were you competing against the clock or rivals? Were there any obstacles in your path? Did you reach your

Right: The dreaming mind uses vigorous actions like jumping as a metaphor for your progress through life or toward a particular goal. You may have seen yourself "jumping ahead" (as in this image) or "falling short" of your target.

destination? If so, did you feel triumphant? Or were you disappointed by your sense of anticlimax?

The answers to these questions about your dream will help you to assess your progress and to identify any hindrances or hurdles obstructing your passage, also giving you an inkling of how you'll feel, be it ecstatic or somewhat let down, when you eventually achieve your aim.

If you dreamed of racing against rivals—and maybe also the clock to achieve a personal, national, world, or Olympic record—and you are currently employed, your dream almost certainly relates to your career (it's not for nothing that working life is often called a "rat race"). The clock represents the time pressure that you feel you are under, and the record represents the level of the attainment on which you have set your sights. Whether your fellow competitors were unknown to you or whether they were real-life colleagues, they represent your competition in the race to win a professional prize—be it enhanced admiration, status, or money—on which you have set your heart. These are the people whom you—consciously or unconsciously—have identified as being a real threat to your chances of becoming "number one." Feeling as though you were flying as you ran toward the finish line indicates that you are cruising toward your goal with ease. Keeping pace with your

Left: Did your unconscious portray you passing the baton successfully in the relay race of life, or did you fumble the exchange and ruin your team's chances of success? And who were your team mates? **Below:** In dreamland, hurdles symbolize the obstacles that hinder your progress. Did you tackle them with ease, or did they bring you down?

When we climb something, we are moving slowly upward toward a definite objective. In the dream world, what you are climbing denotes the scale of the task on which you are focused. Your destination—if it is the summit—signifies the apex of your personal aspirations, which is likely to be attaining a higher professional, social, or spiritual status.

In your dream, were you climbing a ladder, a flight of stairs, a hill, or a mountain? A ladder may

rivals signifies that you are doing relatively well, but suggests that you could fall behind at any moment. Finally, struggling to catch up with the pack ahead warns that you may fail to make the grade. If you recognized your dream rivals, were they running in front of you, behind you, or abreast of you? Their position in relation to your dreaming self will tell you how you perceive them to be performing—be it better, worse, or at the same level as you.

Was the dream race a marathon? If so, it suggests that your working life has become an exhausting slog. But, if you completed the marathon, this grueling stage of your career may at last have come (or be coming) to an end. Indeed, whatever the race, winning it indicates that you unconsciously believe that you have the potential

to achieve your aim, while losing it denotes either a lack of confidence in your abilities or warns that someone else may beat you to this particular goal.

denote the "corporate ladder," with each rung representing a step toward your ultimate goal (as, indeed, may each step of a flight of stairs). Your dream ladder may alternatively be a phallic symbol, with connotations of masculine drive, power, and mastery—qualities that you may need to adopt if you are to get to the

top. A hill signifies a harder and longer challenge than those presented by ladders and stairs, while climbing to the peak of a mountain represents the ultimate test of your agility, strength, and stamina. Did you literally face an uphill struggle in your dream? If so, how did you tackle it? With confidence and patience, or with fear and a sense of defeatism? Did you keep the pinnacle in your sights, or was it shrouded in mist? Did fallen rocks obstruct your progress? Did you have a climbing companion? If so, did you work together as a team or did he or she prove a liability?

Examining such aspects of your dream will tell you more about the nature of your approach to achieving your goal, about the problems or people that are helping or hindering your progress, whether you have lost sight of your target, and, as a result of all of these considerations, your chances of success.

Finally, did you reach the object of your ascent and feel on top of the world? If so, your dreaming mind is encouraging you by telling you that you have the ability to re-enact your achievement in that aspect of your real life in which you harbor ambitions. Did you reward yourself by admiring the view from your high vantage point? If so, the landscape, and perhaps even the people, that you looked down upon will tell you what you have distanced yourself from, or left behind, in life. If your goal eluded you, however, and you turned to retrace your steps, the message may be that your aim is either unrealistic or too daunting to attain.

We jump, or leap, from one position to another either to clear a hurdle in our path or to get from A to B more swiftly. If you found yourself jumping in your dream, your unconscious mind was probably drawing a parallel with some aspect of your waking life. By depicting

Opposite and left: In dreams, mountains denote the daunting scale of the task ahead of you. Did you succeed and find yourself "on top of the world"? **Below:** Dreams of a triumphant graduation day reflect many students' heart-felt wishes.

your dreaming self executing a perfect jump, for instance, your unconscious may be signaling that you have made, or are considering making, a quantum leap, perhaps in the form of a significant decision. If, however, you stumbled and fell, your dream may be warning you that you have either made the wrong choice or are in danger of doing so.

Celebrating Personal Achievements

If you are a student and dreamed of being dressed in a gown and mortarboard as you stepped proudly onto a stage to receive a diploma or degree, with the sound of tumultuous applause ringing in your ears, it is likely that you enjoyed a wish-fulfillment dream. In the dream world, at least, you have fulfilled your expectations and your reward is the recognition, praise, admiration, and respect of your clapping audience. Although such a dream should not be taken as a promise that your wish will be fulfilled in actual life, it does, however, suggest that you feel that your performance merits its just reward (and maybe the examiners will concur!).

Left: Goal! Unless you are actually a keen soccer player, your dream is commending you for having scored a different sort of goal during your waking hours. **Below:** Dreaming of receiving medals of honor denotes a desire for your qualities or actions to be recognized by the highest appropriate authority.

Perhaps you dreamed that you scored the winning goal or hit a vital home run in a professional sporting contest. If you are actually a soccer or baseball player, your dream is similarly concerned with wish fulfillment. But what if you are a hopeless athlete? What does your dream mean then? In such instances, it is likely that your unconscious mind is rewarding you for having done well at something that you may not consider very significant in waking life, highlighting your achievement by immersing you in the warmth of the feel-good factor. It could, for example, be commending you for your personal contribution to a large team project, a contribution that may have been a deciding factor in the project's eventual success.

Alternatively, your dream may have portrayed you being invested with the highest honor that your country can bestow for bravery on the field of battle, or maybe you won a Pulitzer Prize for literature. If you are a soldier or writer, the dream may have been fulfilling your desire for your skills to be acknowledged as being of the highest order and your wish to receive a commensurate reward from the highest appropriate authority. If your profession is far removed from these areas of endeavor, however, it may again be that your dreaming mind is telling you that you deserve great credit for something that you have done, perhaps a selfless or courageous action or an inspired letter that you wrote recently. Dreaming of receiving a Pulitzer Prize for literature may, on the other hand, be encouraging you to pursue your interest in writing and to develop, at long last, those ideas for a novel that you've never gotten around to committing to paper. You may have the potential to be a best-selling author, your dreaming mind is trying to tell you, but you'll never know unless you set down your opening words. If you have artistic inclinations and dream of creating a brilliant painting or sculpture that receives universal acclaim, your unconscious may similarly be urging you to explore your latent artistry.

The Spoils of Success

Diplomas, trophies, medals, and other prizes and awards are symbols of having been successful— even outstanding— in a particular field of expertise. If you dream of receiving any of these tangible tokens of recognition, it is likely that your unconscious mind is compensating you for a lack of reward or respect for your efforts in waking life. The type of prize that you dreamed about may give you a clue about what you've accomplished that you feel merits reward. If your dreaming self is honored with a Nobel peace prize, for instance, could it be that you've managed to engineer a truce between feuding members of your family (yet no one has thanked you for, let alone acknowledged, your efforts)?

Did you dream that you were the focus of attention in a solemn ceremony in which a laurel wreath or glittering crown was placed on your head or a lush garland was draped around your neck? If so, your dream indicates that you crave, or feel you deserve, to be acknowledged as being pre-eminent, or head and shoulders above the rest, be it professionally or socially (the type of ceremony should tell you which). Such a dream can therefore fall into the compensatory, wish-fulfillment category, but may also, to a certain extent, be literal. If you dreamed of being crowned, for example, have you indeed been recently rewarded for a big achievement?

Have you recently received a promotion that you have worked long and hard to secure (and that perhaps gives you authority over a number of people)? If so, your unconscious may have been drawing your attention to the responsibility that you, as a newly crowned "monarch," have for your "subjects."

Were you delighted to have been presented with a bouquet or gift in your dream? If so, take note of both the giver and the nature of the flowers or present. The giver may be someone in whose love or affection you already feel secure. But if the giver is simply an acquaintance, your unconscious may be alerting you to the esteem in which he or she may hold you—a high level of regard that you may intuitively have recognized, but that comes as a surprise to your conscious mind. Bouquets are traditionally given to mark an achievement, birthday, or anniversary, or else as a lavish token of love. Is your dreaming mind compensating for other people's lack of recognition of a personal milestone that you have achieved in waking life? Or do you wish that

Left and below: In the dream world, being presented with a trophy or rosette suggests that you are yearning to be acknowledged and fêted as the best in an area of endeavor with which you are preoccupied. **Below:** Did your dream bouquet make up for one that was unforthcoming in waking life?

Below and right: A chest spilling over with treasure and wads of money both symbolize valuable assets in dreams, but not necessary financial ones. **Opposite:** If you gave a stellar performance in your dream and were rewarded with rapturous applause, your unconscious may have been compensating for others' refusal to appreciate or celebrate your waking talents.

a loved one would be more demonstrative? Alternatively, because metaphorical bouquets are also the antonyms of brickbats, are you feeling wounded that compliments have not been forthcoming for something you've done that, in your opinion, deserves praise? But what could it signify if the flowers have wilted? Is the giver's admiration for you dying? And if you were the grateful recipient of a gift, ask yourself whether it may represent a gift in the sense of a talent or skill. If you were given an expensive fountain pen, for example, could the giver have been encouraging you to put pen to paper, to make use of your poetic or literary "gift"?

If you woke up from a most agreeable dream in which you basked in the glory of fame and fortune, ask yourself what pleased you the most. If you relished being the focus of adulation, it may be that you crave attention and admiration, either for what you consider to be your sterling personal qualities or for the expertise that you believe you possess in a certain area of your professional life.

A dream of being famous usually reflects a need for increased recognition and respect from those around you, but may also be a heartening, wish-fulfillment message from your unconscious to keep believing in your ability to secure a hotly desired aim in life. If, however, your dreaming self was less concerned with being glorified and more gratified by having acquired a fortune, be it in the form of money, jewels, or other valuable assets, your unconscious was sending you an entirely different message. Such a dream is likely to have been of a simple compensatory, wish-fulfillment nature if your financial position is currently precarious (buy that winning lottery ticket and solve all your financial worries in an instant!) or if you feel that you deserve a pay raise.

However, symbols of riches such as cash and precious metals or stones often represent things of intrinsic value, but not necessary monetary worth. Trying some free association may help you to identify what such assets mean to you on a nonmaterialistic level. Does "gold" signal a "heart of gold" to you? If so, whose? Is someone a "gem"? Could your cache of treasure have represented the people you treasure? Or could it be the "treasury" of knowledge, experience, or ideas that lies within you yourself? Are you blessed with a "wealth" of friends? Do you associate money with power, freedom, desirability, or a measure of personal "worth"? Do you believe that money can buy you happiness? Pondering such questions should help you to identify the secret message embedded in your dream, and if it casts a new light on what's really important to you, you may in turn find yourself questioning the long-term value of your previous goals, aspirations, and ambitions.

NEGATIVE EMOTIONS

When we dream that we are incandescent with rage, transfixed by fear, made poisonous by jealousy, wracked with guilt, or awash with grief, we awake with relief to the realization that it was just a dream. In the morning hours, we try to banish from our minds the negative emotions that tormented us in the dream world. The conscious mind usually employs this protective strategy successfully—that is, unless something in our waking life recalls the dream, causing those uncomfortable memories to come flooding back. We may try hastily to shut them out again, only to be plagued by a similarly unsettling dream a few nights later. This vicious cycle is caused by conflict between the conscious and unconscious minds. Underlying the dream, which will often be a recurring one, is a real problem or fear that the conscious mind has suppressed as being too painful or too difficult to face up to. This effort to suppress the problem or fear is undermined by the unconscious mind's counterstrategy of sending us the dream in an attempt to make us try to recognize, confront, and thus resolve whatever it is that the conscious mind has buried.

Because the language of the unconscious is symbolic, you may find it difficult to identify what triggered your upsetting dream. In this case, consulting chapters 8 (Anxiety and Frustration), 9 (Conflict), 10 (Loss), 12 (Negative Actions), and 16 (Death) for specific types of dreams that arouse negative emotions within us may provide the key.

Hostility and Anger

Certain individuals may often provoke feelings of hostility in us during waking life. If you bristled with dislike when your cocky colleague breezed into your dream, just as you do in the office, your unconscious is probably just mirroring your conscious antipathy. Alternatively, you may be feeling defensive about a threat that you feel that individual poses to you, and you may be unconsciously preparing yourself to mount a counterattack. But, if someone of the same sex as you—perhaps someone you know, perhaps not—instantly switched your dream self into hostile mode through his or her offensive behavior or demeanor, consider whether that person could have been your shadow. Ask yourself what about him or her so repelled you. Because the unconscious mind sometimes projects those characteristics or qualities that we consciously dislike in ourselves—and have therefore suppressed, but nevertheless still possess—onto someone else in our dreams, your unconscious may be sending you a signal that you should acknowledge this consciously suppressed aspect of yourself and come to terms with it.

Many things anger us in waking life, but we can rarely afford the luxury of letting off emotional steam by exploding with rage, for fear of unleashing dramatic and far-reaching consequences. A dream in which you saw red and reacted with unbridled fury to someone or something may, therefore, have had a safety-valve purpose—allowing you to give vent to your anger in the secure environment of the dream world. Another possibility is that your dreaming mind was warning you that you are close to the edge and that your suppressed rage is becoming so overwhelming that you may soon lose control in waking life. If, on consideration, you feel that this is indeed the case, try to remember who, or what, provoked your anger in your dream, and especially what so aggrieved you. Did you express your fury vocally? If you did, a vital clue to your agitation may lie in the words that you shouted.

Horror and Fear

If you wrenched yourself out of a nightmare in which you were overcome by panic, horror, or fear, what terrified you? Was it being attacked by a horde of giant, hairy spiders, and are you actually arachnophobic? Or were you in an airplane that was spiraling downward, out of control, and are you afraid of flying in waking life? If so, such a dream may simply be reflecting

your phobia. And as appalling as the dream may have been, your unconscious mind's intention was not to torture you, but rather to encourage you to confront (and

thus eventually conquer) your fear. If you have a recurring dream of this nature in which you gain some level of consciousness while experiencing it, try to urge your dreaming self not to run away from the spiders, but instead to take control and stand and face them. You may find the dream consequences more benign than you'd imagined and dreaded, which will ease your fear and may even put an end to the dream once and for all.

The cause of other fear-inducing dreams are sometimes less clear-cut, however. Did you dream, for example, that you were overcome by a feeling of dread while you were getting dressed in preparation for visiting a friend, someone whom you like and trust

Opposite: Dreams allow us to express the hostility that we bottle up when we are awake. **Left:** The unconscious sometimes depicts our fears in monstrous form, as shown in this Victorian illustration. **Below:** Could your dream vampire have represented a vitality-sapping friend? Or did you see a vampire movie last night?

in waking life? Such a dream may indicate that there is something about him or her that you fear at an unconscious level. Think carefully about your friend and about your relationship and try to draw parallels between what occurred in your dream. Does your dream help you to identify something about him or her that you feel threatened by? It may be, for example, that you have noticed that your friend has a tendency to copy your style of dressing—a habit that you may find flattering in waking life, but that you may unconsciously feel is threatening your individuality.

Or perhaps you dreamed that you were being pursued by a hideous monster, could run no farther, and were about to fall victim to its razor-sharp claws. The monster symbolizes something that you fear, which, unless you find a way of dealing with it in waking life, threatens to consume you. Try to work out what the monster may represent—it may be a predatory lover, a dragonlike teacher or step-parent, or your own feelings of jealousy—and then, armed with this insight, find a way of fighting back and thus banishing your fear.

Jealousy and Rejection

"The green-eyed monster" is a term that is used to denote jealousy, and if you dreamed that you were jealous of someone (whether or not you assumed such a monstrous form), the message is usually straightforward: something about that person makes you feel inadequate. If you can identify what it is, heed the message from your unconscious that you need to come to terms with your feelings of deficiency in that respect. If you are envious of her appearance or his charm, for instance, ask yourself if this is a quality that you should be nurturing in yourself. An alternative is to try to detoxify your feelings by accepting that, while you admire that particular personal quality, you possess many other strengths and virtues that more than make up for your self-perceived failing in this area. If, however, you dreamed that someone was jealous of you, it is likely that you have unconsciously detected that he or she harbors hostile feelings toward you.

If you are in a secure relationship, but dreamed that your partner left you for someone else, your unconscious is simply reflecting your feelings of insecurity about the strength and consistency of his or her love for you. Don't take it as an omen, that is, unless your relationship has actually hit a rocky patch or you believe that he or she is having an affair, in which case your dreaming mind is probably mirroring your waking fear of rejection.

If you dreamed that you did the rejecting, however, there are a number of possible explanations. One is that your unconscious is reinforcing your conscious feelings for that person in your dream; another is that it is alerting you to the negative emotions that that individual arouses in you

(of which you are not yet consciously aware). On the other hand, it may be that your dreaming self rejected your shadow, which represents a quality lurking within you that your conscious mind finds repellent. If so, what was it? A further possibility is that the person whom you rejected represents a demand on your time and energy that you feel you can no longer cope with, or else a viewpoint or characteristic that you find offensive.

Opposite: Subconscious insecurity can trigger a dream in which you are madly jealous.
Below: If, like Eve, you gave in to temptation in your dream, your unconscious may have been fulfilling your deepest desires.

Temptation and Guilt

Did your dream lead you into temptation? Are you happy in a settled relationship, but dreamed that you succumbed to the sexual charms of an irresistible stranger? Dreams like this reflect and fulfill profound unconscious desires,

65

needs, and urges that the conscious mind has tried to suppress with perhaps varying degrees of success. If they repeatedly recur, it would be advisable to acknowledge the problem area—for example, sexual frustration—and then to try to work on resolving it in waking life.

If you gave in to a temptation that your conscious mind brands as being a crime against morality, it is likely that you felt guilty upon waking up, underlining the need to face and deal with the issue that your dreaming mind has highlighted. As well as cheating on loved ones, further scenarios that typically make us feel guilty—be it in the real or dream world—are when we cheat someone out of something, when we behave badly toward someone, or when we commit a moral transgression or even a crime. Perhaps you dreamed that you secretly sabotaged a friend's career plans, that you snubbed your helpful neighbor, or that you stole your own child's allowance. The message of all of these guilt dreams is that your conscience is troubling you about some aspect of your behavior in your relationship with the person concerned—whether you're consciously aware of it or not. Are you, perhaps, envious of your friend's talents and do you fear being eclipsed by her success? Are you abusing your neighbor's unfailing helpfulness by never returning the favor? Are you depriving your children of something, not necessarily money, to which they have a right?

Perhaps you woke up, appalled, from an awful dream in which you had robbed a bank, you were caught red-handed, stood before a judge feeling contrite and guilty, and were then sentenced to death. In such instances, the unconscious mind has conjured up the most dramatic scenario possible in an attempt to alert your conscious attention to something that you should be feeling guiltier about. In telling you to mend your ways, it uses symbols of crime, authority, and punishment to ram the message home (the execution sentence

emphasizing the need to put an end to your guilt-inducing behavior and to turn over a new leaf). When decoded, you may realize that such a dream is signaling that you're feeling guilty about some minor financial transgression (maybe your bank credited some money that wasn't yours to your account, and you've kept quiet about the error). Whatever your transgression, you may find that you will need to put it right in order to gain peace of mind.

stricken with intolerable unhappiness in your dreams, however, your unconscious may be giving graphic expression to feelings of general depression, and the dreams are likely to continue unless you acknowledge your depression and perhaps seek help.

Opposite, left: If you were humiliated as a dunce in your dream, are you afraid that you are out of your depth? **Opposite, right:** Dreams often warn that greed isn't good, as the legend of the gold-obsessed King Midas of Phrygia cautions. **Left and below:** Dreams provide an outlet through which to release feelings of overwhelming sadness and despair.

Sadness and Tears

If, when you dreamed, you were swamped by feelings of sadness and you wept uncontrollably, it is likely that you have indeed had cause for grief in waking life, but that you have buried your feelings rather than put yourself through the pain of working them through. Your unconscious may, therefore, have been providing a vital outlet for your sadness. You may have found that shedding floods of dream tears was cathartic, and you may have woken feeling melancholy, yet also unburdened.

If you grieved for someone you love who has actually died, your dream can be taken at face value, while if you dreamed that you were deeply saddened at failing to achieve an aim on which you had set your heart, you may still be mourning a lost opportunity. Although it may take some time, thinking through such issues rationally, in the cold light of day, will often help you to come to terms with them. If you constantly find yourself crying and

ANXIETY AND FRUSTRATION

Dreams of being engulfed by feelings of anxiety or frustration are among the most common—and disturbing—of experiences in the dream world. To a greater or lesser extent, we are all plagued by such dreams, particularly at times of exceptional stress in our waking lives. The stress may be due to an important test, exam, or interview, a looming dental or medical appointment, or even a more insidious fear of failing in our careers or relationships. It may play itself out in dreams of falling, of being pursued, paralyzed, or confined, of missing a vital connection, of being frustrated by a machine's refusal to function, or of finding ourselves inappropriately clothed or—worse still—naked in public. Whether or not we can consciously identify the cause, these dreams all stem from deep-rooted worries about our self-perceived inadequacies or external threats to our emotional security in our waking life.

Whenever you have a dream like this (and it may be a recurring one), try to pinpoint exactly what caused you the most anxiety or frustration, because this may provide the key to unlocking the root of your fear. Knowledge is power, as they say, and once you have consciously grasped the core message that your unconscious has sent to your dreaming self, you will be empowered to confront your fear and, as a result, to at least find ways of managing it, if not conquering it completely.

Testing Situations

If you are a student who is facing an important test or exam in real life, did you have a stressful dream that the dreaded day had dawned? Perhaps you found yourself sitting at a desk feeling totally unprepared and, as you read the test, you were consumed by a rising sense of panic and you realized that you were unable to answer the questions. If so, your dream is merely expressing your fear of failing the test (although your unconscious may also be warning you that you need to study harder). Or, are you an adult whose examination days are long past and, yet, you were horrified to find yourself stuck in such a dream scenario? In this case, the test is probably a metaphor for a testing situation that you are facing in your professional life, while your dream reaction mirrors your waking lack of confidence. Have

you been put to the test at work, perhaps a promotion to work toward, a challenge that you feel ill equipped to meet?

The same fear-of-failure explanation applies to other types of dream tests. These can include driving tests, interviews, auditions, and presentations—particularly if one is pending in your waking

JUNIOR HIGH SCHOOL

life. The subtle difference in these cases is the presence of an "audience," even if it consisted of only one person. Who was questioning you, evaluating your performance, or judging you in your dream? Was it someone, or more than one person, to whom you feel you need to prove your worth in real life? An audience's response is rarely positive within anxiety dreams, and you may have been laughed at or subjected to a tirade of criticism. Can you remember what you were humiliated for, charged with, or accused of? If so, ask yourself whether your critics may have had a point. Also consider whether your merciless evaluators could have represented self-critical aspects of yourself. If so, do you either tend to judge yourself too harshly, thereby lowering your self-confidence, or, alternatively, do you consciously

close your ears to your inner critics even though their comments, while admittedly hurtful, may actually be helpful? Finally, were you dismayed when you started stammering as you addressed your audience? If so, this may underline your feelings of uncertainty.

Opposite: If you dreamed of being transported back to school to take a crucial exam, you may be facing an equally testing challenge or ordeal in adult life. **Above:** If your mind went blank when you read the questions on your dream exam paper, you may be afraid of failing an important test of your character or abilities.

A related dream theme is sitting in trepidation in front of the doctor or lying helpless in a hospital bed or the dentist's chair, dreading what's about to happen to you. If you have in fact scheduled a medical or dental appointment or are due to go into the hospital in the real world, this anxiety dream reflects your concern about what you may learn, or what is likely to unfold.

Depending on what happened, it may also be that your unconscious has set up this dream scenario as a rehearsal to build up your courage. Another possible explanation, especially if there is no such appointment in your diary, is that your unconscious is telling you that you should face an unavoidable ordeal (not necessarily one connected with your body) with fortitude. Alternatively, it may be that you are unconsciously aware of a problem with your health or teeth that requires professional attention and that your dreaming mind is signaling the need to consult your doctor or dentist.

Falling

Many of us have dreams of falling, and some types of falling dreams can be attributed to a straightforward phobia or physical cause. If, for example, you suffer from vertigo and dreamed of swaying dizzily as you stood at a great height looking down to the ground far below, your dream may merely be mirroring your conscious phobia of heights. Or, as you were dropping off to sleep, did you dream that you were walking along a path and that you suddenly stepped into nothingness? In this case, your sleeping body probably underwent a muscular spasm that is known as a myoclonic jerk, a physical action that sometimes occurs during the hypnagogic state before you are fully asleep, to which your unconscious reacted while you slept by incorporating it into your dream.

The falling dreams that cause us the most anxiety are those that the unconscious mind uses to draw our attention to our insecurity and fear of losing control, failing, or "falling down," in some area of our lives, be it at school, work, or home. You may, for instance, have dreamed that you were teetering on the edge of a cliff or skyscraper, absolutely terrified that you would fall off and plummet into oblivion. When interpreting your dream, the geographical feature or structure on which you were standing represents the high expectations that you have for yourself, or that others have for you. Although you

may have fulfilled these expectations in waking life, you may still fear that you will no longer be able to stay on top of them. The structure's nature or appearance is, however, less symbolically significant than your fear of falling off it. That is, unless your dreaming mind re-created the office building you actually work in—then its significance is clear: you are frightened of failing in your career and of your professional pride "coming to a fall." Otherwise, ask yourself what you are afraid of falling from. Grace, favor, power, or the professional or social position that you have worked so hard to secure? Or is there something, perhaps a relationship, to which you are resolutely clinging because you are petrified of letting go of it?

What happened next in your dream? Did you manage to edge away from danger, thereby gingerly regaining control of the situation? If so, your unconscious may be signaling that you have the ability to do just that in waking life. Or did you fall? If so, did you wake up in mid-flight or did you reach the ground? Dreaming of falling can be equated with losing control, of "letting yourself down," a sensation that is often so terrifying that your conscious mind steps in to rescue you by waking you up. Yet if you did hit the ground, you were probably surprised to find little, if any, harm done, indicating that even if you do "fall" from your current elevated position, the result may be less damaging than you'd antici-

pated. In all instances, your unconscious is trying to push you to identify the source of your fear and to try to find a solution to it, even if it means lowering your aspirations or accepting your failings.

Being Pursued

Did you awake with a dry mouth, your heart pounding, and thoughts of escape flooding your mind after a dream in which you were being chased or hunted down by someone or something? If so, who or what were you fleeing from? Was it someone you know? Or was it a nameless or faceless pursuer, a hideous monster, or a ferocious animal? The answer will tell you whether you feel threatened by a person (or the situation that he or she represents) in your life, or

Opposite: In dreamland, towering mountains represent our lofty aspirations; dreaming of falling denotes a fear of failure. **Below:** Dreaming of being pursued by a ravening bear may warn that you are inadvisably suppressing a basic urge.

whether the source of your fear lies within you yourself.

If you know the person who was chasing you (or, alternatively, the corporate body or sphere of life, such as finances, that he or she represents), try to work out why you may be feeling threatened by him or her in the real world. For example, perhaps you dreamed that your sweet-natured girlfriend, now transformed into a wild, screaming harpy, chased you relentlessly for mile after exhausting mile, and you some-

how knew that she was going to eat you if she caught you. This dream may denote your fear of being pressurized into making a commitment to your girlfriend—perhaps marriage—because you suspect that she would try to dominate you and consume your individuality. Or maybe your pursuer was the owner of the local store, who lets you buy goods on credit, and you've been "forgetting" to pay off your debt in waking life. In this instance, your unconscious may have been highlighting your suppressed feelings of guilt about neglecting to fulfill your obligation. Alternatively, if you were being chased by someone you work with, or are acquainted with, it may be that your unconscious has detected his or her feelings of hostility toward you and is sending you a graphic warning to be on your guard.

If, however, you didn't recognize the person who was chasing you, it is possible that he or she represents an aspect of yourself that you are anxious to escape, particularly if the pursuer's appearance repulsed you and if he or she was of the same sex. Could that tormentor have been your shadow? If so, what frightened you the most about him or her? Was it his or her neediness? Greed? Lust? Your unconscious may be telling you that it is precisely this quality within yourself that you should acknowledge and come to terms with.

Maybe a werewolf or other monstrous being was hunting you down, or perhaps the predator was a man-eating tiger. Again, such nonhuman pursuers usually symbolize an internal fear or need

rather than an external threat. They generally represent an aspect of your "animal," or instinctual, nature—perhaps aggression—that you may have been suppressing in waking life, but that it may be healthier to give controlled rein to. If, however, the werewolf or monster had the face of someone you know, maybe it is that person's "monstrous" urges that terrify you.

Left: Dreaming of being forced to wear a straitjacket reflects frustration about restrictions on your freedom in waking life. **Opposite, top:** If you dreamed of a dream ball and chain, what is shackling you and weighing you down in life? **Opposite, below:** Confinement dreams raise issues of constraint and powerlessness in the real world.

Whoever it is, or whatever you decide your pursuer stands for, remember that he, she, or it represents an unsolved problem, and that stopping, turning, and facing up to it, be it in the real or dream world, will neutralize its menace.

Hindrances and Paralysis

During dreams of being chased, we may be running as hard as we can, only to find ourselves despairingly facing an impasse. This is the unconscious mind's way of telling us that we have come to a "dead end," that there is no way of escaping the fears that pursue us. Equally, our flight may be hampered if we become trapped in quicksand, enter a minefield, or are burdened by carrying an ever-increasing weight on our shoulders, all of which denote being held back by forces, and perhaps dangerous ones, beyond our control. Sometimes, however, our dreaming selves may sabotage our escape attempts by becoming completely paralyzed, being simply unable to move as we see, or sense, the pursuer coming ever nearer. Maybe you've had just such a dream, in which, to your horror, you find yourself suddenly rooted to the spot and powerless to move, although you know that it's crucial to regain the use of your legs in order to flee.

There are a number of possible explanations for this distressing dream scenario. It may be, for instance, that you are suffering from emotional paralysis in the face of a situation that requires a drastic decision, such as whether to break off your relationship with your girlfriend or else to go down the marriage route (see above). Identifying who, or what, was chasing you, and perhaps the place of safety for which you were headed, may help you to decide whether this is indeed the case. Alternatively, as may be its purpose in conjuring up a dream impasse, your unconscious may be reflecting your feelings of powerlessness and/or hopelessness regarding an apparently unsolvable problem in your waking life. Does something, or someone, make you feel as though you are wedged in between a rock and a hard place?

There is also a physical cause for such dreams, however, known as sleep paralysis. Particularly during R.E.M. sleep, the stage of sleep during which dreams are the most prevalent, the brain shuts down the body's nerve impulses, notably to the limbs (although not to the eyeballs), to prevent us from literally acting out the screenplay of our dreams and thus endangering ourselves. You may be dreaming of playing football, hitting your brother, or lighting a fire, but your brain has ensured that you are physically incapable of doing so in response to your dream's suggestion. Should you regain a measure of awareness during sleep paralysis (which is unusual, but does happen), your unconscious mind may then mirror your physical paralysis in your dream.

Being Confined

Did you dream that you were locked up in a cell or cage, or immobilized by ropes or chains? If so, you probably felt immensely frustrated, which is not really surprising because it was probably frustration that engendered the dream in the first place. Dreams of being imprisoned or restrained usually send a signal that you are feeling frustrated because something, or someone, in your life is preventing you from acting freely and from realizing your potential or ambitions.

Did you see your captor in your dream? If so, could he or she be the person who is "boxing you in"? Are you living by someone else's rules? Or are you feeling "locked into," or trapped within, some situation, relationship, or responsibility, from which you feel there is no escape? In such instances, it is likely that your unconscious is highlighting your feelings of powerlessness in an attempt to urge you to break free, be it from a deadening job, a rela-

Being Late

You may have run as fast as your legs could carry you in your dream, constantly checking your watch in a fever of anxiety in case you missed the bus, only to see it pull away from the bus stop ahead of you. Unless you soon have to make a journey in waking life and the details of the trip are weighing on your mind, then dreams of arriving too late to catch a bus or train, or to keep an appointment, often signify your frustration and anger at having missed an important opportunity that would have taken you to the next staging post in life. Was someone responsible for holding you up? If so, do you blame him or her for hindering your progress in some aspect of your waking life? Such dreams may also warn that you are becoming worn out, whether mentally or physically— or both—especially if you dreamed that you were too tired to summon up the extra spurt of energy that would have enabled you to hop on to the vehicle.

tionship that is stifling your individuality, or a depressingly regular commitment to a neighbor. And if you were gagged, it is probable that you feel that someone, or something, has taken away your freedom of speech.

Alternatively, it may be that you have constructed a cage around yourself, that your imprisonment is self-inflicted, or that your bonds are self-administered, in order to protect yourself from the potential emotional hurt that may result from being true to your nature. Could your prison cell or restraints represent your own inhibitions? If you feel that this may be the case, maybe it's time

to break loose and enjoy a taste of freedom. Another possible explanation is that you are nervous of making a life-changing decision, preferring instead to maintain the status quo rather than risk failure. By depicting your dreaming self in prison or bound and fettered, your unconscious mind is telling you that this is no way to live and that you should break out of your self-imposed captivity by taking that first heady, albeit initially frightening, step toward freedom.

If you had a dream like this, ask yourself if you are frustrated at having missed the "bus" or "boat," and, if so, ask yourself what that bus or boat may represent. Was it a career opportunity or a date that you failed to make with someone whom you found attractive? Buses and boats are also public vehicles, so do you feel that others are forging ahead and leaving you behind?

Machinery Malfunction

Little is more frustrating in waking life than a machine or piece of electrical equipment on which you rely breaking down or malfunctioning. If, in your dream, your computer crashed or your automobile shuddered to a halt, you were probably just as furious as your waking self feels when faced with such a setback. But why did your unconscious infuriate you with such a dream?

There is a choice of two probable answers. The first is that your dreaming mind is warning you that you are failing to keep your computer or automobile in tiptop order in waking life, and that disaster may soon strike unless you install an antivirus software program in your computer or take your automobile to be serviced. The second answer may, however, refer to you—the computer or automobile may be a metaphor for an aspect of yourself that is in danger of going wrong. The computer, for example, may denote your mind: could it be that you are in some way exposing it to invasion by an infection, perhaps a poisonous idea? Could the automobile symbolize your

own energy, or "drive"? Are you in danger of running out of "fuel"? Are you out of control, or are you stalling in life? And, if a piece of electrical equipment blows a fuse, are you equally close to exploding with fury and frustration?

Being Inappropriately Clothed or Naked

Do you still cringe with embarrassment at the memory of a dream in which you witnessed a wedding in the midst of a crowd of people wearing smart clothes, looked down, and then realized with horror that you were dressed for the beach? Or maybe you were mortified to find yourself at a party wearing formal evening dress, while everyone else was wearing casual clothing? Dreaming of being inappropriately clothed often indicates that you feel out of place. Be it socially or at work or school, dreaming of being underdressed generally signifies that you fear that you are falling short of other people's standards,

while dreaming of being over-dressed often suggests that you may have misplaced feelings of superiority. Because we generally select our apparel in order to fit in with what those around us are wearing, such dreams, therefore, usually denote insecurity about your social position and how other people regard you.

Alternatively, perhaps you dreamed that you ventured into a packed store to shop for groceries and suddenly realized that you weren't wearing any clothes at all! If you've experienced this dream scenario, did you feel deeply ashamed and humiliated? Or did you rather enjoy the disapproval of the people who witnessed your nudity? Or were you the only one aware of your nakedness?

The clothes that we wear are an aspect of the persona, or social mask, that we don in our dealings with others, so that, when we are naked, all artifice and pretension is stripped away, enabling others to see us as we really are, or our true selves. Your unconscious may

Opposite, top: If you dreamed of a dungeon, were you responsible for your own incarceration? **Opposite, below:** The fear of being late induces great anxiety. **Above:** A locked computer represents your "blocked" mind: are you in denial? **Left:** Have your energy reserves become dangerously depleted?

Below: Dreaming of feeling blissfully liberated when naked in clothed company hints that you shouldn't be afraid to expose the real you to the scrutiny of others.

have cast you in this situation for a variety of reasons. If you stood shrinking in the middle of a jeering crowd, it may be warning you that you feel exposed and vulnerable under the spotlight of other people's scrutiny. In this case, you may be worried that you are regarded as an object of ridicule and derision, either because you suspect that you may be making a fool of yourself or because you fear that the real you is somehow flawed. Do the people with whom you work or socialize make you feel inadequate? Are you afraid that, if you lower your defenses and behave naturally, they'll reject you? What is it that you are afraid of exposing about yourself?

If, however, you felt liberated by your nudity and you didn't care who saw you, your dreaming mind may be telling you that it's time to cast off the restrictions, inhibitions, and pretences (but not your garments!) with which you have clothed yourself. Your unconscious may be encouraging you to feel free to reveal to others who you really are. And, if you were the only one who noticed your nudity, your unconscious is probably encouraging you to "expose" yourself by indicating that, because no one will bat an eyelid, it's safe to do so.

CONFLICT

Unlike violence, which can often be unilateral, or one sided, conflict requires at least two people or forces, representing diverging opinions or ideologies, to be in opposition, each striving, be it verbally or physically, to impose their will on the other. Conflict can take many forms—an argument or fight, disobedience, mutiny or rebellion, or a battle or war, for instance—while the ammunition used may range from wounding words to lethal weapons.

The unconscious mind depicts such dramatic clashes to try to shock you into recognizing a simmering conflict in your own life. You may not be fully aware of the conflict—be it a disagreement with a particular person, a career path or job with which you are unhappy or incompatible, or even a conflict within yourself, perhaps regarding a decision that needs to be taken. Try to work out what your dream conflict symbolizes, and to identify what each participant represents in your waking life. This knowledge will give you a clearer understanding of the problematic issues besetting you and, consequently, the key to resolving them.

Wars of Words and Fisticuffs

If you dreamed that you had a heated quarrel with someone, who was that person? If you know him or her, is your relationship scratchy or harmonious in waking life? It may be that your dream merely mirrors your real-life antipathy toward him or her, his or her antipathy toward you, or your mutual dislike of each other. You may not yet be consciously aware of your aversion to that individual, or of the anger that you may arouse in him or her. In such instances, and especially if it was you who instigated and dominated the argument, your dream may have had a safety-valve purpose, giving you an outlet through which to release your feelings of grievance or aggression. Alternatively, your unconscious mind may have been alerting your conscious self to that person's feelings of hostility toward you.

If, however, having considered the nature of your relationship, you believe it to be congenial, with no negative undercurrents, it may be that the person with whom you were arguing represents an aspect of yourself—an interpretation that is even more likely if your adversary was a stranger. What did he or she look like, and can you remember what the argument was about and who accused whom of what? For example: perhaps you are a conventional man who dreamed that you quarreled with an unknown teenager, and that the youth accused you of being a staid stick in the mud, to which you countered that at least you were making something of your life. Your dream self may actually have been arguing with that youthful, uninhibited part of yourself that yearns to be liberated from the restrictions of work and family, perhaps even restrictions that you have imposed

Left: Dreams of physically fighting with someone usually allude to a personal conflict or feelings of hostility in waking life.

What happened next? Did your verbal sparring escalate into a physical fight? If it did, the dream may denote both the intensity and the difficulty of your ongoing struggle, whoever it may be with—either yourself or someone else. Did you overpower your opponent, or did his or her superior strength constrain and subdue you? And how did your disagreement finally end? Was it amicable, or were both of you stalking off in opposite directions in a huff? A peaceful conclusion indicates that you may be able to settle the conflict (whether it is raging within yourself or between you and another individual), while the events of the dream may point toward the most effective way of doing so—perhaps through surrender or compromise. If the dream argument wasn't settled, however, that area of conflict in your life is likely to be a continuing source of problems.

Disobedience, Mutiny, and Rebellion

The common strand that links disobedience, mutiny, and rebellion is conflict with an authority figure, such as a parent, corporate body, or government. If you were disobedient, mutinous, or rebellious in your dream, whose authority were you flouting? If it was your mother or father, it is probable that you unconsciously feel the need to assert your individuality and to loosen, or even sever, the parent–child bond that may be preventing you from living your life according to your own rules. Alternatively, your unconscious may simply have been giving vent to your feelings of resentment toward that parent in the safe environment of the dream world.

Perhaps you dreamed that your boss ordered you to do something that you considered wrong, or that you were so overworked that her latest demand was the final straw,

on yourself. Did the teenager's accusation strike home in your dream, so much so that it stayed with you and you found yourself reluctantly musing on it after you awoke? Could the dream teenager have had a point? Are you guilty as charged? Have you become set in your ways, and would you welcome a little more freedom or variety in your life?

and you flatly refused to comply. A dream like this may reflect your mounting anger or exhaustion in the face of the demands being made of you in your job, something of which you may be unaware because your conscious attention is focused on trying to stay on top of your workload. Did you feel liberated by your refusal? If so, maybe it's time either to ask for a transfer so that you can escape your tyrannical boss, or to leave your soul-destroying job and find a new position in which you are valued.

An alternative explanation for dreams like these, particularly if you were in revolt against a faceless entity, is that you are rebelling against some part of yourself, whose control you unconsciously

wish to break free of. Try to remember what you rebelled against in your dream and why, and then to draw a parallel with your waking life. If you led a rebellion against the Inland Revenue Service in protest of its nationwide

issuance of extortionate tax demands, for example, could you be "overtaxing" yourself in waking life? Or, if you revolted against an authoritarian dictator, could you be unconsciously protesting against a restrictive regime that you have imposed on yourself?

Opposite, top: Titian's David and Goliath. Did you dream that you overcame an apparently more powerful opponent, or that a youthful combatant felled you? Such dreams may refer to a conflict or power struggle in your workplace or a simmering argument with a family member. **Opposite, below:** If you were involved in a mutiny in your dream, do you long to rebel against your authoritarian boss? **Above:** Going on strike in your dream may reflect feelings of exhaustion and frustration in your working life. **Left:** If you found yourself arm-wrestling in your dream, are you engaged in a real-life battle of wills?

Battles and Wars

Like arguments and disobedience, battles and wars embody conflict, sometimes between warring aspects of oneself—perhaps between the instinctive urges of the unconscious and the rational control of the conscious mind, as may be suggested if the battle was waged between "savages" and an ultramodern fighting force. Which army did you belong to? If it was the "savages," your dreaming mind may be signaling that your true allegiance lies with your heart (that is, your instincts), but, if it was the modern army, it may be telling you that your inclination is to follow the rule of your head (or your conscious mind). If you witnessed the outcome in your dream, or admired any winning maneuvers, the identity of the victorious army and the nature of its successful tactics may give you an indication of how best to resolve the conflict within yourself.

Although they may represent enmity between two individuals, too, because they are fought on such a massive scale, with innumerable combatants massed against each other, dreams of battles and wars may also point to an explosive disagreement brewing up between groups of people in your life. If you dream of armies at war (and again, try to identify both them and their respective causes), it may denote increasing tensions between two

Opposite: If a battle was raging in your dream, whose side were you on, and whose army were you fighting against? **Left:** An armed soldier in full war cry is the embodiment of aggressive enmity. **Below:** Could your dream war have symbolized a clash of opinions, or were you painfully reliving a traumatic wartime experience?

opposing camps within your family or workplace, for instance, perhaps over the terms of a recently disclosed will or an impending change in working practices. Could your dreaming mind be warning you that you will soon become embroiled in such a conflict? If so, your dream may have indicated whose side you will take or whether you would prefer to act as a peacemaker.

If, however, you are (or were) a soldier who saw action on the field of combat, it may be that your experiences were so traumatic that they have returned to haunt you, perhaps in the form of distressing recurring dreams. In this case, seeking professional counseling may help you to lay your ghosts to rest.

Weaponry and Military Hardware

During the course of your dream fight or battle, did you see swords flashing, daggers, knives, or bayonets thrusting, guns smoking, bullets flying, cannons blazing, or bombs exploding? Whenever the dreaming mind highlights weaponry and devastating military hardware, it does so for one of four significant reasons. One is to underline straightforward feelings of hostility, antipathy, or aggression toward someone (maybe you). The second possibility is that this is a warning that you may soon need to take drastic defensive measures against

Were you wielding the weapon in your dream? If so, who was your target? Someone you know (in which case, consider the three possible interpretations outlined above), or a stranger? If it was the latter, the fourth explanation may be particularly pertinent. Is it possible that your victim represents an aspect of yourself that you'd like to "kill off"? If so, what is it? Your victim's appearance, demeanor, and reaction to being threatened may provide you with the

Opposite: A dream explosion's searing heat and billowing black clouds of smoke graphically parallel the damaging consequences of exploding with pent-up fury. **Left:** In legend, only Arthur could draw Excalibur from its stone, so demonstrating his rightful kingship. This type of dream symbolizes justice prevailing, or spiritual authority. **Bottom:** Guns are often phallic symbols in the secret life of dreams. **Below:** Explosives may hint at someone's possession of explosive information or "dynamite."

Swords often feature in religion, mythology, and legend, being wielded, for instance, by heroic figures of Christianity (like saints Michael and George, to subdue evil forces in the form of dragons).

someone or something that presents a very real threat to you.

The third interpretation is, perhaps, less obvious. Because, according to Freudians, weapons (which are usually hard, straight, long, and penetrating) are phallic symbols, a man who dreams of using a weapon, especially against a woman, is expressing an unconscious urge to gain sexual mastery over his intended victim. On the other hand, if a woman dreams of being menaced with a weapon, her dream is reflecting either her sexual insecurity regarding men generally, or a perceived sexual threat from a specific male.

answer, which may, for instance, be cowardice, treachery, or dangerous behavior.

As well as being phallic objects, certain types of weapons have other symbolic meanings that may help you to decipher the message of your dream.

As such, they may represent spiritual protection and the triumph of good over evil, an association that is underlined in Christian belief by their crosslike shape. Swords can also denote kingship, as exemplified by King Arthur's sword, Excalibur, and may consequently denote the highest level of authority. Because they are double-edged weapons, however, swords can equally be negative symbols of malevolent power. Although the lance shares much of the sword's symbolism, its explicitly phallic shape often points to sexual issues when it features in a dream.

They may be similar in shape and purpose to swords, but daggers and knives are both significantly shorter and less redolent with symbolism. Their appearance in dreams, especially when used against the dreamer, generally signifies a threat from someone—in the case of daggers, perhaps of being "stabbed in the back," or being confronted with a dangerous, precarious, or decisive situation (such as when one is on a "knife's edge").

Bayonets are thrusting weapons that are used in conjunction with guns, and their symbolism in dreams may denote extreme danger, a desire for total mastery, or the sexual impulse, either aimed at

someone else or directed against the dreamer him- or herself. If a male dreamer is toting a gun, the unconscious may have selected this weapon to denote his sexual performance, and if he then fires a "blank," concerns about failing virility and impotence may be indicated. But, because one can also feel impotent in other areas of life, and not just in bed, a misfiring gun may reflect general feelings of powerlessness.

Bullets, cannonballs, and bombs all explode on detonation or impact. If you dreamed of any of these types of ammunition, did you fire or detonate

them, or were they used against you? If it was the former, your dreaming mind may be warning you that you are in danger of exploding with anger or frustration, and your dream target may tell you who, or what, is aggravating your aggression. Alternatively, could an explosive situation be building up in a relationship or in the workplace? And, if your firepower ran out, could this dream scenario be referring to your lack of

"ammunition" in a conflict in your waking life?

Like spears, arrows can, again, have phallic connotations, but may also refer to "Cupid's arrow," or being smitten by romantic, rather than sexual, love. Were you the arrow's target, or were you taking aim at someone else? Did the arrow score a bull's eye or fall short of its target? Was it a "poisoned arrow"? Because arrows are also used symbolically to point the way, an alternative explanation is that your unconscious pulled an arrow from its quiver to direct you along the correct path, perhaps relating to an impending decision or life choice.

Top left: Because it is long, hard, and thrusting, a dream lance may allude to the penis.
Above: If you dreamed of a bomb, are you currently on a short emotional fuse and in danger of detonating with burning anger?
Center: A dream arrow may refer to being smitten by Cupid's arrow and falling in love.
Left: Bullets often signify verbal firepower in the context of dream conflicts.

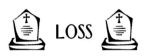

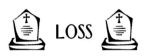 LOSS

Many types of dream imbue us with an aching sense of loss: dreams of being abandoned or bereaved, for instance, or those that take us back to a happier past or even a faraway homeland. Many such dreams are literal, in that they reflect our feelings of grief and regret about traumatic events that have actually befallen us. Others, however, may be a metaphor for something that is missing in our lives, be it companionship, direction, or even a sense of identity, while still others warn that we are in danger of losing something dear or important to us. However upsetting or frustrating they may be, such dreams are not meant to torment us, but are usually sent by our unconscious minds to enlighten, and thus strengthen, us.

This chapter covers just some aspects of loss, but remember that there are many others, too. In the dream world, you may, for instance, lose weight, teeth, hair, or looks, your sense of sight, smell, hearing, taste, or feeling, a body part, or even your life. You may furthermore lose your balance, your virginity, your innocence, a baby, your head or your mind, your freedom, or your self-control. Clocks may lose time, and games may be lost, while your possessions may be lost to a catastrophe or crime. The significance of such losses in dreams is discussed within the relevant chapters.

Abandonment and Redundancy

Anxiety dreams in which loved ones abandon us, leaving us feeling lost, bereft, and helpless, hark back to an archetypal childhood fear of being abandoned by our parents, people on whom our younger selves depended utterly for both emotional and physical nourishment—indeed, for our very survival. As adults, this profound terror of being deserted may manifest itself in dreams of being abandoned or rejected by our partners or friends.

If you had a dream like this, it may reflect your feelings of insecurity about the strength of the

Right: Dreams of being abandoned by loved ones tap into a childhood fear of being deserted by our parents, on whom we were totally dependent—for love and emotional security, as well as food and shelter.

love and regard that the person (or group of people) who abandoned you in your dream has for you in waking life. Although such dreams usually express a normal human fear of exclusion from an emotionally sustaining relationship, it may be that your unconscious mind has indeed detected a cooling in the warmth of your partner or friend's feelings for you. In this case, your dream may be alerting you to the need to start shoring up your relationship in order to ward off this worse-case scenario. If, however, your partner really did leave you, or your friend suddenly withdrew his or her friendship, and you found yourself reliving your pain in your dream, it is likely that you haven't resolved your abandonment issues. Could the message of your dream have been that you should take action to confront this loss, put the past behind you, start thinking positively, and take control of your life?

If you dreamed that you were fired from your job, laid off, or otherwise "let go" by your employer, you may have felt similarly abandoned, shunned, or cast adrift. If you are actually feeling uncertain about the regard in which you are held at work, the dream may merely have been mirroring your insecurity. Alternatively, could your dream have a parallel with your sense of uselessness (not necessarily in your job) in some area of your life? Perhaps your children have grown up and left home and you feel unneeded as a parent, for instance. But if you have real reason to fear losing your job, perhaps due to the prevailing dismal economic climate, your dreaming mind may be highlighting the importance of preparing yourself for just such a disaster—both emotionally and by laying practical contingency plans. But, if you actually lost your job and the experience returns to haunt you in your dreams, it may be that you still haven't fully come to terms with your feelings of rejection. If this is the case, your dreaming mind may be urging you to work through your feelings so that you can move on in life.

Or did you dream that, after the initial shock of having been

This page and opposite: Although recurring dreams of funerals can underline feelings of emotional devastation following a bereavement, by repeatedly exposing us to our pain, they gradually help us to come to terms with our loss, thereby dulling the excruciating rawness of our initial grief.

deserted—be it by a partner, friend, or employer—you felt somehow liberated and started behaving "with abandon"? Your unconscious may have been hinting that, far from being a catastrophe, the severance of your ties with your dream deserter in waking life would give you some welcome freedom.

Bereavement, Loneliness, and Farewells

Did you wake up sobbing after having had a dream in which you were bereaved? If so, have you actually been bereaved, and did you dream of your departed loved one? Such dreams, which are a common reaction to the death of our nearest and dearest, are the unconscious mind's way of

trying to help us to work through our grief and eventually to accept our loss. They can also be cathartic experiences because they often allow us to express our unhappiness and anger more graphically and dramatically than we feel able to in the real world (particularly if we fear upsetting those around us). In this sense, these dreams can give us a feeling of release, but they may also be comforting, especially if you conversed with the person who has died in the dream, or if you felt somehow reassured that he or she had gone to a better place.

But what if you were grieving in your dream for the death of someone who is still alive? Who was that person? If it was someone who is actually ill, or whose life hangs in the balance, it may be that your unconscious was trying to prepare you for the worst

by giving you an opportunity to rehearse how you would feel in the event of his or her death. It may also be that your dreaming

mind highlighted something—maybe your love and gratitude—that you wish to impart to your loved one before it is too late, something that you would bitterly regret leaving unsaid before he or she died. Indeed, many bereavement dreams reflect our guilt and sadness at having neglected our responsibilities to a deceased person, or having failed to repair a rift while he or she was still alive. Perhaps your dead mother upset you deeply in your dream by accusing you of not having visited her enough. In the case of a dream like this, your mother's voice is likely to have been that of your conscience, urging you to acknowledge, resolve, and learn from your self-perceived failing.

Right: If you dreamed of a family waving a fond farewell to a relative departing for a new life, perhaps you're ready to fly the nest yourself.
Below: A dream of a young hero bidding his wife a fond farewell before setting off to war may indicate that you are tired of your safe domestic life and long for excitement.

If, however, you dreamed of mourning the death of someone, maybe a friend, who is in good health, it's unlikely that your dream presaged their actual death (that is, unless their occupation is a dangerous one, carrying an unusually high risk to life and limb). In such a dream, your unconscious mind may have used your friend as a symbol of some-

thing to which you'd be advised to put an end in waking life. What is it about you, or your life, that your friend could have rep-

resented? Overdependence or recklessness, perhaps? It may also be that your friend represents a quality, one that you associate with him or her, that you feel has departed your life. What could it be? Fun? Insight? Relaxation? Alternatively, you may fear—perhaps with good reason—that he or she will soon terminate your friendship, spelling the death of your relationship and leaving you feeling bereaved. Finally, and particularly if you have quarreled with your friend in real life, your dream may have been drawing your conscious attention to the need for resolution and closure, be it by settling the conflict within your own mind or between the two of you.

Whoever the deceased was, dreams of being bereaved sometimes bring issues of loneliness to the fore, whether or not you are consciously aware of them. If, for example, your partner's attention is currently focused exclusively on work and you feel deprived of his or her time or affection in the real world, your feelings of loneliness may surface during your sleep (for example, you may dream of being a widow or widower). Indeed, such a dream may also be pointing to an emotional distance that you may believe to be temporary, but that, if left unbridged, could end up being permanent. But what if you simply dreamed of being lonely? If so, your dream may be a literal one, the purpose of your unconscious (in highlighting your current isolation) being to prod you into reconnecting with those around you, be it your family, friends, or coworkers. Humans are fundamentally sociable animals, and perhaps you have become more emotionally withdrawn, or even physically isolated, than is healthy. If you work from home, for example, such a dream may be urging you to make a conscious effort to get out and about more. Conversely, if your home, work, and social life is hectic and you dreamed that you enjoyed a period of solitude, it may be that you need just that in waking life.

Dreams of bidding someone a final farewell often have a similar significance to dreams of bereavement. If you were parting from someone whom you know in your dream, ask yourself whether your relationship may be coming to an end or whether it's time to take your leave of some facet of your life that you connect with that person.

Nostalgia and Homesickness

Did your dreaming mind transport you back into your past? If so, did you wake with a sense of loss and yearning, or with a profound sense of relief that it was only a dream? The dreaming mind usually takes us back in time for one of two purposes. One is to compensate for our unhappiness or dissatisfaction in our waking life, when it comforts us by reminding us of the happy times that we have enjoyed, our nostalgia thereby giving us hope that we might experience an equally carefree period again.

If, however, you were disturbed to find yourself reliving an unhappy period of your past in your dream, it is likely that you have not come to terms with it. Perhaps you have preferred to try to banish the unhappy memory from your mind, rather than consciously confronting and resolving whatever it was that made you miserable. By sending you the dream, your unconscious is signaling that this is the wrong approach, however, and that you should face up to your painful memories and, by doing so, lay your demons to rest.

Perhaps you were awash with homesickness in your dream, having found yourself far away from your loved ones and longing to

Above: If you dreamed that you returned to your childhood past, when your days were suffused with sunshine and emotional warmth, you may have been deeply upset to awake to the cold light of day. By immersing you in a dream like this, your unconscious was probably trying to compensate for the trials and tribulations that have been heaped on your adult shoulders.

return to the safety and comfort of your home or homeland. If so, did your feelings of loss relate to your present domestic circumstances or to those of your past? And what, in particular, did you miss? The answer will tell you what your unconscious has identified as being lacking in the real world. It could be the security of close family bonds, or something about your past home life that meant a lot to you, but that you feel you have now lost—perhaps your childhood innocence—or, in the case of your homeland, a sense of belonging.

Opposite: Life is a long and winding road, and if you found yourself disastrously lost in the landscape of your dream, your unconscious may have been highlighting your loss of direction in the real world. **Above:** Did your dream show someone steadfastly following the "right track" to overcome adversity? Perhaps your subconscious is preparing you to face up to an uncomfortable but unavoidable solution to a problem you've been unsure how to tackle.

Getting Lost

As you progressed through your dream, did you panic at the sudden realization that you'd become hopelessly lost? If so, your unconscious mind may have been highlighting your loss of direction in waking life and, by implication, the need to get back on the "right track." Ask yourself in what sense you may have "lost your way." It may be, for example, that you are confused about how best to proceed in a relationship or along a career path. Alternatively, your dreaming mind may have been warning that you have started to lose your sense of identity, your innate knowledge of exactly who you are and where you are headed in life. Identifying the problem area, and then considering your options carefully, should help you to decide the best way forward.

Losing Something

Did you dream that you looked down at your wrist and realized with a start of regret that you'd lost your favorite bracelet? If so, you may indeed have noticed during your waking hours that the clasp is loose, in which case your dream could have been underlining the need to have it

replaced before you incur the loss of the bracelet in real life. Similarly, if you have actually lost something and your dream depicts you finding it again, it is worth checking the location highlighted in your dream because you may be unconsciously aware of the item's whereabouts, even though it has slipped your conscious mind. Such dreams sometimes also warn that you are becoming distracted and have started to lose your powers of concentration, focus, and your ability to manage the minutiae of life.

If, however, you dreamed that you lost, and were searching for, something that has no immediate significance to you, your unconscious may have conjured up your dream loss as a symbol of something that is missing from your life. If you were searching for a key, for example, is a solution to a pressing problem eluding you? Or

could it be the key to self-knowledge? If you found the key in your dream, it is likely that the answer will soon become clear, but if you didn't, the solution will probably be some time coming, if at all. If you remain mystified as to the meaning of your dream, trying a free-association exercise may help you to decipher the lost object's symbolism, which may be love, potential, or any other quality that would give you fulfillment.

Debts and Bankruptcy

If you dreamed that you were in debt and on the verge of financial disaster—or, worse still, that you were actually bankrupt—your unconscious may have been reflecting your worries about your real-life monetary situation and magnifying the need to take urgent action. There are alternative explanations for dreams of debts and bankruptcy, however, which have little to do with the loss of money.

A dream debt, for instance, may sometimes denote a "debt of honor" or a favor that you should

Left and below: If you dreamed of bankruptcy or destitution, could your unconscious be warning that you are in danger of becoming morally bankrupt or emotionally destitute, or are you heading for professional ruin?

repay to someone. To whom are you indebted, and for what? You may, for instance, feel indebted to a neighbor for taking care of your house while you were on vacation, or to your partner for standing by you during a recent period of hardship. Such dreams often indicate feelings of guilt, so perhaps it's time to repay your "debt" in waking life.

Dreams of going bankrupt and ending up a pauper often refer to the potential loss of cherished nonfinancial resources or personal qualities—perhaps your talents, looks, or family values—that give you the power and strength to move through life with confidence and pride. If you were disturbed by such a dream, ask yourself what your lost riches could symbolize. The love of your friends and family (are you risking all that you hold dear by being sexually promiscuous)? Your integrity and self-respect (are you in danger of becoming morally bankrupt)? Your physical vigor (are your energy reserves about to start running on empty)? Whatever you decide your loss represents, heeding the warning of your dream and taking the appropriate remedial steps may avert a real-life emotional, physical, or professional crash.

⚖ POSITIVE ACTIONS ⚖

Positive actions generally feature less prominently in dreams than their negative counterparts, but when they do, their purpose may be to set us an example to emulate during our waking hours. By portraying acts of bravery in a dramatic dream scenario, the unconscious may be underlining the need to be equally courageous in confronting a difficult situation in the real world. It may even be telling us that we need to save ourselves from something that poses a dangerous threat to our own safety (be it emotional or physical). Dreams in which mercy, charity, and assistance play a conspicuous part may similarly highlight qualities that we would be wise to apply to our relationships or current circumstances, while dreams of tenderly embracing or touching someone may help us to clarify our true feelings for that person. Finally, when we see ourselves undertaking useful or creative activities in dreamland, the underlying message may be that taking similarly positive action will enable us to move forward in certain areas of our lives.

Bravery and Rescue

Did you wake from a dream of dashing bravery, in which someone assumed the role of a knight in shining armor, riding to the rescue by courageously fighting off danger? If so, who was the hero or heroine? Was it you, someone you know (or at least know of), or a stranger? Who did he or she rescue, and from what?

Was the star of your dream a person (perhaps a mentor or partner) whom you regard as your actual, or potential, protector or "savior" in waking life? If so, then your unconscious may have been either underlining your reliance on that individual or hinting at the crucial part that he or she could play in coming to your defense. Otherwise, it is likely

Left: If you dreamed that you were rescued from a fate worse than death by a mighty hero, do you wish that a strong-armed protector would extricate you from a difficult situation that is currently threatening your security at work?

that your dreaming mind has summoned up a heroic archetype. When you are facing a testing situation in the real world, your unconscious may try to demonstrate the best course of action by screening a dramatic parallel in the cinema of your dreaming mind. By casting a superhuman being, a celebrity or movie star, or even you yourself as the hero or heroine of the piece, and by directing him or her to perform daring, altruistic, or courageous deeds with complete fearlessness, your unconscious is prompting you to admire these qualities and, consequently, to employ them in your waking life. 🎭 👼 🤝

This dream strategy is intended to inspire, enthuse, and encourage you to be similarly decisive and brave when confronting a challenge in the real world, even if its nature is, as yet, unclear to

you. If this is the case, ask yourself who the hero or heroine rescued (maybe it was you, a terrified child, or your family pet). Also consider who, or what, he or she was battling in your dream (a force of nature, someone with whom you are familiar, a monster, or a ferocious animal, perhaps). Identifying what they could represent or symbolize with reference to your own life may enlighten you. In short, ask yourself what in (or about) your life needs rescuing, what is threatening it, and how best to save it—the clues will lie in your dream. And if, as your dream's starring character rode off into the sunset, he or she gave you a parting piece of advice, heed it well. It is likely to provide you with insight and guidance.

Mercy, Charity, and Assistance

Maybe you woke from a dream with a sense of sheer disbelief that someone (was it you?) had behaved with mercy or charity to

Left: If you are floundering in a chaotic sea of emotions, you may be yearning to see signs of a lifeguard who could set you down on solid foundations. **Below:** A dream of a heroic figure, such as Liberty leading the French people in revolution, may inspire you to rebel against a repressive authority in waking life. **Opposite:** By depicting the Statue of Liberty, your dream may be urging you to be compassionate, perhaps by undertaking charitable work.

a character whom you'd identified as being a out-and-out scoundrel or trickster—perhaps by releasing an incorrigible criminal from captivity or by showering money on a professional conman.

Although you may have thought the person who behaved with mercy or charity in your dream to have been gullible or naïve, it is likely that you also felt a sneaking sense of admiration for the decency or trust in human nature that he or she displayed. In such instances, it is possible that your dreaming mind devised this scenario to draw your attention to the need to rise above your negative tendencies to distrust and condemn and, instead,

to recognize (and perhaps even adopt) such higher values as selflessness and good faith. This message is particularly pertinent if the benefactor resembled such archetypal figures as the mother or father, high priest or priestess, or, if it was you, you felt somehow uplifted by your act of mercy or charity. If, for instance, you are feeling disgusted with your sister because you know that she is cheating on her husband, or you are fed up with bailing out your chronically penniless friend, your unconscious may be urging you to consider how much she actually means to you, despite her faults. Perhaps it's time to show some understanding, rather than jeopardize your relationship by perpetuating your judgmental or accusatory stance. 🎭

If, however, someone behaved with mercy or charity toward you, and you were overwhelmed with gratitude because you felt unworthy of such kindness, it may be that you are feeling guilty about your behavior or attitude toward someone in the real world and you yearn for forgiveness (and thus absolution). Who showed you clemency or compassion in your dream, and what were you forgiven for? Or, what were you given that you so desperately needed?

Did you dream that your colleague gave you practical assistance in your dream, or that you did a friend a favor in some way, be it by lending her money or by supporting him in an argument? If so, your dream may have been a literal one that reflects the current status quo within your relationship, in that you may rely on your colleague's help to cope at work or else that your friend depends on you to deal with life's little difficulties. Alternatively, the dream may have had an advisory purpose, prompting you either to seek assistance when dealing with a certain problem or to give help where it is currently needed.

Embracing and Touching

Did you dream that you gave someone a tender hug and kiss, with no ulterior motive, but just to express your affection? Or that you enjoyed having your shoulders massaged, not because it gave you sexual pleasure, but sim-

Above: Did you dream of a valiant soldier rescuing his wounded colleague from the field of battle? If so, are you hoping that a strong ally will come to your rescue in a vicious workplace conflict? **Left:** A dream kiss may reveal tender feelings you didn't realize you had for someone, or a longing for greater emotional intimacy if you are feeling isolated. **Opposite, above:** The delightful caress of your loved one in the dream world is usually a simple reflection of your love and trust in your partner. **Opposite, below:** A dream massage may highlight the need to be relieved of the stresses and strains of waking life.

ply because it made you feel relaxed and infused with a sense of wellbeing? If so, the dream embrace denotes your fondness for that person, whether or not you are consciously aware of the warmth of your feelings (and his or her identity may have surprised you!), be they of love, friendship, or admiration. Depending on the circumstances of the dream and that person's situation in real life, your gesture could also have been prompted by sympathy and a desire to comfort. ♡

Your dream massage, on the other hand, could have been signaling your yearning for physical contact or emotional intimacy if this is lacking in your life at present, or else your feeling of luxuriating within a trusting relationship with someone (maybe your partner, if he or she was giving you the massage) with whom you communicate well. Alternatively, by portraying you in a blissfully relaxed state, your unconscious may have been highlighting the need to wind down and pamper your mind, body, or both. 👄

Useful Activities

Did you dream that you took up jogging—and enjoyed it—or that you embarked upon a project to sew a patchwork quilt, or threw yourself into a frenzy of spring-cleaning? When the unconscious mind depicts you engaged in activities like these, it may be indicating the need to take similar action in waking life. Is your

Below: A dream featuring people sewing industriously at a patchwork project may be encouraging you to join together separate aspects of your life or character, or simply to value teamwork and companionship instead of always "going it alone."

lifestyle mainly sedentary, for example, and are the pounds starting to pile on? If so, by portraying you running for recreation, your dreaming mind may have been setting you a health-promoting example that you'd benefit from emulating during your waking hours. Or, if you love sewing, but have been too busy with other things to indulge your passion, your unconscious may have been urging you to take time out of your busy schedule to pursue the hobby that gives you such enjoyment. And if you were spring-cleaning, could your house actually do with being spruced up and reorganized from top to bottom?

An alternative explanation, particularly if you are unable to draw a parallel between the dream and real worlds, is that your unconscious was speaking in symbols. If the message conveyed by your dreaming mind (by showing you working out, for example) eludes you, ask yourself what you need to exercise. Could it be your mind, your patience, or your self-control? Or could your patchwork templates and blocks have represented disparate sections of your life that you'd be well advised to connect in order to create a harmonious whole? Would a little industriousness, self-application, and attention to detail be helpful at this stage in your life? Or has your general outlook become cynical, and is it your mental attitude, rather than your home, that requires freshening up? Do you need to make sweeping changes in your life or to throw away the detritus from your past that is obstructing your view of the present? If you can make the connection, your dream is likely to have hinted at the solution. 🏠

NEGATIVE ACTIONS

As disturbing as they are, dreams in which the action focuses on negative actions are rarely predictive, so don't worry that their horrifying circumstances are about to be replayed in the real world. They are not, however, meaningless. But what could your unconscious mind's purpose have been in inflicting a dream on your sleeping self that aroused such intense feelings of terror, disgust, guilt, or helplessness? What can it have been thinking?

Your unconscious is part of you, not a separate entity, so the answer may become clearer if you rephrase the question: what can *you* have been thinking? Dreams of violence, attack, ambush, and abduction usually reflect feelings of hostility or controlling tendencies that you may have repressed or unconsciously recognized in someone else during your waking hours, while dream rapes may denote being forced to give way to another's will. By depicting words or acts of deceit and deception, the unconscious may be pointing out that someone is cheating (perhaps you) in the real world, and dreams of crime and punishment may bring feelings of guilt to the fore. And although they may not always be caused by human behavior, dreams of accidents and catastrophes are, nevertheless, further examples of negative actions whose disastrous consequences may warn of the need to take urgent remedial action in an area of your life that is about to collapse into devastation and chaos.

Violence and Attack

Unless your dreaming mind is replaying something that actually happened to you (when it is probably encouraging you to be brave in confronting the memory of the traumatic event that befell you, and thus to come to terms with it), dreams in which aggression escalates into violence usually denote your mounting hostility toward someone, if you were the aggressor, or your fear of some kind of imminent attack in the real world, if you were the victim.

Did you dream that you were arguing with someone who refused to accept your point of view, and that you suddenly saw red and launched a frenzied attack on that person? If so, who provoked your violent outburst? If it was someone—maybe your teenaged daughter—who is driving you to distraction through her contrariness in waking life, it is likely that your unconscious mind conjured up this dream scenario as a safety valve through which to release your escalating frustration and anger. These feelings

Right: A dream in which you saw someone threatened with violence may have reflected your feelings of helplessness when confronted by the hostility of someone you know during your waking hours. Or perhaps you have behaved aggressively yourself?

may also tend to prompt dreams in which you inflict violence on someone who wields real-life power over you—perhaps your mother, teacher, or boss—whose dominance you resent, but feel powerless to resist during your waking hours. Such dreams may, therefore, be compensatory scenarios in which you can reverse your real situation by forcibly asserting yourself in dreamland, and thereby assuming control over the resented authority figure. Although dreams such as these may be manifestations of wish fulfillment, your unconscious may also have been urging you to make a stand in waking life, particularly if the dream outcome was in your favor.

Even if you weren't rebelling against an authority figure, a desire for control and power is nevertheless implied by a dream in which you acted violently toward someone. When interpreting such a dream, it's crucial to consider whether your target could have represented an aspect of yourself, particularly if your victim was a stranger. Could your

unconscious have projected an archetypal figure onto the dream screen to bear the brunt of your anger and, if it did so, why? If, for example, you dreamed that the intolerable bragging of a person of the same sex caused you to fly into such an uncontrollable rage that you physically attacked him or her, could you have been trying to quash your own tendency to boast? And if you felt disconnected or unmoved—neither remorseful nor relieved—by your violence, the probability that you are striving for some measure of self-control is underlined.

But what could it have meant if you were the victim of violence in your dream? If your attacker was familiar to you, the straightforward answer may be that you are aware, at some level, of his or her overwhelming antipathy, or else that you somehow distrust that person. In this case, your unconscious could be preparing you to withstand an attack (usually psychological or emotional rather than physical) in waking life. Alternatively, you may feel that

you are currently under an actual attack from someone. Are you feeling victimized by some individual? There are, however, a number of other explanations for dreams like these.

If you are a woman who dreamed of being physically assaulted by a man whom you know in the real world, for instance, it may be that your unconscious was alerting you to his sexually predatory nature, or your fear of his intentions toward you. But if you are a man, dreaming of being attacked by a male colleague may reveal your unconscious recognition of his determination to metaphorically thrash you in your career, or else your dread of this happening. Whatever your sex, a malevolent female assailant may have represented the terrible mother or huntress archetype, while a fearsome male aggressor may have

represented the archetypal ogre or villain. In either case, try to identify the "terrible mother," "huntress," "ogre," or "villain" of whom you are so afraid, be it consciously or unconsciously, in waking life.

If, however, your dream attacker was not a human, but an animal, its significance probably relates to a problem within yourself, rather than an external threat. The type of animal, and what you associate it with, is an important factor in the interpretation of your dream. Because the unconscious often uses beasts to symbolize aspects of our "animal" nature, it may be that you have so neglected, or even denied, a basic human urge or instinct, that you have provoked its symbolic representative to attack you in your dream in a desperate bid

Opposite, top: If your dream depicted you in front of a firing squad, are you being victimized? **Opposite, bottom:** Who provoked you to lash out with your fist in a dream scene? **Above:** Was the woman in your dream a manifestation of the archetypal terrible mother? **Right:** This dream assault by owls and bats denotes anxiety.

for survival. If you are a man who dreamed of being charged by a bull, for example, and you equate this animal with rampant sexuality, has your sex life dwindled into nothingness, or have you been repressing your sexual urges? If so, it is probably time to take the bull by its horns and to reacquaint yourself with your sexuality.

Were you left battered and bruised, injured, or wounded by your dream assailant? If so, your unconscious may have added another layer of meaning to your dream. A dream of being kicked in the derrière by your partner or friend may have been a metaphorical "kick in the ass" from your unconscious—something that you may unconsciously feel that you

deserve. Although it may have bruised your pride, if you have been feeling guilty about your recent laziness, it may have given you just the motivation you needed to get up off your butt. More serious dream injuries, on the one hand, can be a stark warning of the approach of physical danger, or, on the other hand, may imply that you are suffering an emotional hurt, perhaps inflicted by the person who wielded the weapon in your dream. Can you identify who has wounded you, stabbed you in the back, or rendered you incapable in real life? Because weapons have phallic significance, a penetrating wound may alternatively refer to a sexual experience or dread, especially if you are female. Finally, if you watched blood pouring from your wound in a dream, it may be that you feel that you are being drained of all your vigor and strength, be it emotional or physical, or that you are being "bled dry" financially. Again, the identity of your attacker may reveal the person who is sapping your vital energy.

Ambush and Abduction

Although violence may occur in instances of ambush and abduction, it is usually either incidental or accidental, the motives for such negative actions having less to do with causing physical hurt and being more concerned with preemption, possession, and the establishment of total mastery over a target or targets.

Did you dream that, after lying in wait for your neighbor as she walked home from work, you leapt out from behind a bush, overpowered her after a brief struggle, and then took her captive? If so, does she know something about you that you fervently wish would remain a secret? Because ambush implies the preemption of a likely negative outcome, it may be that the dream scenario was reflecting your desperation to head off personal humiliation. Alternatively, is there something that you envy about her in waking life? Her striking appearance? Her affluent lifestyle? Her popularity? If this is the case, your unconscious mind may have been signaling

Opposite, bottom: A dream of being devoured by your father may have reflected his tendency to suppress your individuality in the waking world. **Opposite, top:** If you dreamed of an ambush, what scenario are you desperate to head off in real life? **Below:** A woman's dream of being physically violated may denote her fear of being humiliated or forced to act against her will.

your desire to "capture" the quality that you admire in her and make it your own. Another explanation for a dream like this is that you hunger for complete power over your abductee, and that you long to make her a slave to your will and desires.

If, however, *you* were ambushed or abducted in your dream, the meaning is reversed. Who staged the ambush? If it was a coworker, for example, could he be trying to sabotage your plan to win a promotion? Who seized you against your will in your dream? If it was your new boyfriend, have you been perturbed by the dominant tendencies that he's started to display, and are you now beset by anxieties that he is aiming to take complete control of your life and to restrict your freedom of action? Dreams of abduction may also highlight worries about being forced to leave your comfortable routine or cozy circle of family and friends. (If, for instance, you are agonizing over whether to accept or reject an opportunity to move away from your hometown or job, your unconscious may be trying to shock you into staying.) Finally,

and particularly if the circumstances are unspecific, dreams of ambush or abduction may be warning that you are on the verge of ceding control of your life—but to whom, or what, only you will be able to work out.

Rape

If you dreamed that you were raped, you are probably trying to forget your awful dream experience as quickly as possible. Before you succeed in banishing the memory from your mind, however, it may be helpful to take a moment to try to identify your dream rapist and to ask yourself why your unconscious may have subjected your sleeping self to such a degrading ordeal.

If you have actually been raped, your unconscious may be urging you to resolve your feelings of violation by confronting you with a replay of the trauma that befell you. If, however, you have never had to submit to a sexually bru-

tal assailant, one of two possible explanations may be pertinent. The first is that your dream was a literal warning, particularly if you are female. Is there actually a predatory person circling you in your life who sets your inner alarm bells screaming "potential rapist!"? The alternative explanation, particularly if your dream rapist was someone who you are certain presents no sexual threat (but who may be a bully or intrusively inquisitive), is that you fear him or her assuming total domination over you and forcing you to do something (although nothing sexual) against your will. Whatever your gender, if you dreamed that your sister raped you, for example, it may merely reflect your perceived position of weakness in a battle of wills. Perhaps you are currently embattled over who should look after your aged parent, and you dread the possibility of your sister taking advantage of your vulnerabil-

ity, gaining the upper hand, and thereby making you go along with her wishes. And if you are a man who dreamed of being raped by another man, someone you know, either explanation may again apply, although your dream may be reinforcing your feelings of powerlessness, humiliation, and shame at having to acquiesce to his (nonsexual) demands in waking life. Is it time to start asserting yourself and fighting back?

If you are a man who dreamed of raping a woman, it may be that something about her—perhaps her arrogance—makes your hackles rise, and that your dream is expressing your urge to punish her for constantly putting you down by "putting her in her place" and forcing her to submit to your superiority. Although an element of sexual attraction may be a factor in such a dream, the more important issue is an urgent need to gain mastery over someone who has somehow rejected you. Recurring dreams of this nature are a different matter, however, pointing as they do to dangerously violent urges that may soon spill over into the real world, in which case professional counseling is strongly advised.

Finally, if you were appalled to see someone else being raped in your dream, but were unable to intervene, the message is probably that you feel powerless to stop the rapist (did you recognize him?) from taking brutal advantage of the victim (who was she?) during your waking hours.

Deceit and Deception

Were you perturbed to hear someone telling barefaced lies or cheating someone out of something in dreamland, or, worse still, was the liar or cheat actually you? Dreams of deceit and deception are often literal cautions that you are either being duped by someone or are feeling guilty about not having been entirely honest in real life.

If you dreamed that your friend, for instance, said something that you knew to be an outright lie and you were outraged at her audacity, your dream may have been highlighting your growing awareness of her duplicity in waking life. But if you were telling the lie and felt remorseful as a result, your conscience may have been rebuking you and urging you to make amends for having behaved similarly, or else for having perpetrated another act of dishonesty, during your waking hours. Alternatively, and particularly if the dream persistently returns to haunt you, are you currently "living a lie"? If you think that this is the case, your unconscious is probably underlining the need to be true to yourself. Dreams involving fraud, forgeries, and other forms of cheating (including on a partner) send the same messages.

Crime and Punishment

Did you awake from a dream in which you committed a crime and then were punished for your actions? If so, you probably felt greatly relieved to return to your crime- and punishment-free waking life, yet you may have been troubled by a lingering emotion that evoked how you felt in your dream. What was that emotion? Was it guilt or burning anger about the injustice that was done to you? If you can iden-

Opposite, top: If your friend was cheating during a dream poker game, is he also deceiving you during your waking hours? **Opposite, bottom:** A judge's gavel is a symbol of justice. **Right:** If you dreamed that you held up a driver at gunpoint, your frustration level is becoming a problem. **Below:** A dream of being hauled into custody by men in uniform hints at feelings of guilt about having committed a real-life transgression against society.

tify the feeling, it is likely that you have found the key to unlocking the secret of your dream. If you felt shamefaced about committing your dream crime, for instance, you are probably feeling guilty about a wrong that you have done, or are considering doing, in waking life. Although you may have repressed your feeling of culpability during your waking hours, by conjuring up a scenario in which you were exposed to it, your unconscious may have been trying to force you to acknowledge your transgression, to set the wrong right, and thereby gain peace of mind.

But what did your dream portray you doing? Defrauding or inflicting violence on someone (if so, see above), committing the ultimate crime of murder, or stealing something? Dreams of stealing from another person, be it by means of burglary, robbery, or deception, generally signal that you are envious of something with which that individual is blessed—perhaps wealth, beauty, or popularity—something that

you'd like to possess yourself. So ask yourself who you were robbing, and of what. Because we are usually emotionally far removed from the owners of department stores, dreams of shoplifting generally focus on a petty transgression or theft. Have you, perhaps, been appropriating office supplies for your own use? If you were a blackmailer, however, then your unconscious may have been cautioning you that "emotional blackmail" is the wrong approach when trying to persuade someone to comply with your wishes.

Whatever your dream crime, if you were caught in the act, held up your hands, and then found yourself awaiting punishment, your conscience was probably signaling its disapproval of your behavior, while your unconscious may have been warning that your real-life "crime" is about to be discovered and that you are in dan-

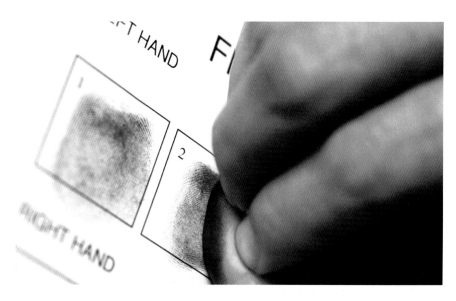

ger of being punished for it. Who punished you in your dream? If the person was known to you, it was probably someone toward whom you harbor remorseful feelings. If it was a nameless judge, you may be feeling guilty about flouting some kind of authority (maybe parental, maybe moral, or perhaps the rule of the law) in waking life. And if a howling lynch-mob descended on you, have you committed a crime against society by repeatedly fare-dodging or failing to scoop your dog's poop?

Alternatively, if you dreamed that you were accused of a crime that you didn't commit and that you were wrongfully chastised, despite your protestations of innocence, do you feel that someone is punishing you unfairly? Have you, for example, been given the cold shoulder by your boyfriend because he believes that you are having an affair, even though there is no doubt of your faithfulness in your own mind?

When your punishment was pronounced, were you shocked by its severity because it seemed out of all proportion to your wrongdoing? If so, rather than portraying a literal *quid pro quo*, your dreaming mind is likely to have indicated the depth of your feelings of unconscious guilt: the more draconian the punishment, the more terrible you feel

about your transgression. Were you whipped in your dream? If so, does your sorry "ass" deserve it? Or do you feel like a whipped dog, be it due to your contrition, or because life (or else the individual who was beating you in dreamland) has dealt you some hard blows? If your dream depicted you being restrained, imprisoned, or sentenced to death, consult the

chapters on anxiety and frustration, or death.

Did you dream that you were an accessory to a crime, although you didn't commit it yourself? Dreams like these may denote your feelings of guilt about colluding with something that you know is morally wrong. Is it time to blow the whistle, or at least remonstrate with the perpetrator? If, however, someone you know committed a crime against you in your dream, and you are struggling to decipher the code used by your unconscious, enlightenment may come if you ask yourself if he or she has somehow committed (or is about to commit) a wrong against you. For instance, if you dreamed that your brother stole an object that was your pride and joy, could your dream have reflected your resentment that he has "stolen" your girlfriend in real life?

Accidents and Catastrophes

Did you dream that you were driving along the highway when your automobile suddenly spun hopelessly out of control and plowed into pedestrians and other traffic at top speed? If so, your unconscious mind may actually have detected a mechanical problem and may be alerting you to the need to have your vehicle's

steering and brakes checked. Alternatively, your unconscious may have been commenting anxiously on the course of your life: have you been living in the "fast lane"? And, as a result, are you in danger of "losing control," suffering a physical or emotional "crash," and "coming to the end of the road"? Or have you set yourself on a "collision course"? If so, whom did you hit in your dream accident (was it a colleague with whom you have had a dramatic difference of opinion?), and was anyone else involved in the fallout (perhaps a friend or a mutual coworker who tries to keep the peace)?

If you dreamed of an accident in the home or of an airplane crash, try to think along the same lines. What is potentially unsafe within your house, or what sort of disaster could be about to befall your family? Are you "flying too high," or could your optimism regarding a pet project be misplaced and unrealistic?

Although dreams of witnessing natural disasters or catastrophes that are not of human making—such as raging brushfires, volcanic eruptions, devastating floods, or suffocating landslides or avalanches—point to a less specific source of danger, they may nevertheless warn that you are about to be engulfed in disaster (as a result of which you may suffer emotional devastation). Only you will be able to decipher the symbolism of your dream catastrophe, but its warning should certainly not be ignored. And if the message from your unconscious continues to

Opposite, top: If you were fingerprinted in your dream, were your guilty feelings surfacing? **Opposite, bottom:** Do you feel that you are being treated like a scapegoat in the real world? **Below:** A dream of an automobile wreck may have been warning that someone you know drives dangerously, or else that your waking life is spinning out of control.

elude you, employing free association may provide clarification. Are you about to burn up or explode with repressed anger, become flooded with negative emotions, or else be buried under the burdens of life? But if you felt strangely liberated, rather than devastated, by the disaster that befell you, could it be that you would unconsciously welcome such a catastrophic catalyst because, although terrifying, it would transform your life for the better?

Whatever happened in your dream, did you emerge relatively unscathed? And did you manage to rescue anyone from the scene of the accident or catastrophe? If so, your unconscious was indicating that you have the strength to overcome a disaster in life, while the person whom you saved may denote what is worthy of saving in your life, on the one hand, or, on the other, what is in desperate need of salvaging. A child may, for instance, symbolize your innocence or developing potential, an older person may represent your maturity or wisdom, while your partner could represent love and trust.

🕊 BIRTH 🕊

When the unconscious summons the themes of pregnancy, birth, and babies into our dreams, it usually does so for one of three reasons. If you are pregnant, or hoping to conceive in the near future, the dream may be mirroring your actual situation, with all of the hopes and fears that bringing a child into the world entails. Otherwise, the dream may have been fulfilling profound yearnings. If procreation in the real world is not at the forefront of your conscious mind, however, then it may be that its unconscious counterpart is trying to reacquaint you with the "baby" within. This could be either an aspect of yourself that is utterly dependent on others for emotional or physical sustenance, or the part of yourself that longs to be given life or to be reborn. But if this explanation doesn't apply, your gestating dream baby may symbolize your "brainchild," perhaps an idea or project that you have conceived and are longing to carry safely to term before joyfully introducing it to the wider world.

Conception and Pregnancy

Did you awake from a dream in which you discovered that you were pregnant? If so, were you overjoyed, apprehensive, or appalled? If you are a woman and are trying to conceive, your unconscious may have been fulfilling your waking-life hopes in the dreaming world (although, because the dream may also have been a literal response to the presence of an actual fetus, your dream may soon come true). An apprehensive reaction to a dream like this may, on the other hand, be reflecting your waking uncertainty about the possibility of conceiving. It could be, for instance, that your partner is eager to start a family, while you're not so sure (or would at least prefer to wait a while). And if you were horrified by your dream conception, it may be that you really don't want a baby, but you fear that you may have conceived one accidentally (and your unconscious may have been try-

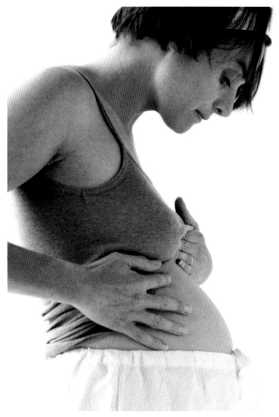

Left: By depicting your pregnancy, your unconscious may have been giving you the opportunity to rehearse how you would feel if you were actually an expectant mother. **Below:** Pregnancy dreams sometimes highlight the need to nurture your "brainchild." **Opposite:** Are you hoping that your dream of pregnancy will come true?

you are too young (or otherwise ill equipped) to start a family—is that your unconscious has presented you with a pregnancy scenario in order to give you the opportunity to experience how you might feel should you find yourself in this situation (and perhaps thereby allaying your feelings of anxiety and giving you confidence that you could cope with a baby).

There is, however, an entirely different interpretation for dreams of conception and pregnancy, and one that is especially pertinent to male dreamers. Is it possible that the dream pregnancy or fetus had nothing at all to do with parenthood, but instead represented the fertilization of a concept, or the sprouting of a creative seed, within your mind or someone else's? If you were pregnant in your dream, were you struck by a brilliant idea recently, and have you been mulling over how best to develop its stellar possibilities in order to bring it to triumphant fruition? In your dream, were you sailing through pregnancy, or were you plagued by morning sickness? Your state of well-being in your dream may have reflected your feelings of confidence or anxiety about how well your "brainchild" is developing.

ing to shock you into taking better precautions). Men who dream of their partner conceiving or being pregnant may, similarly, be giving unconscious expression to their own wishes, ambivalence, or apprehension about becoming a father.

If you are a woman, a dream of being farther along in pregnancy may, again, be concerned with either wish fulfillment or your real-life circumstances. Indeed, many expectant mothers dream of observing or communicating with their unborn child as it develops in the womb, which might be an unconscious method of bonding with their baby while they await its birth. An alternative explanation for dreams like these—particularly if you feel that

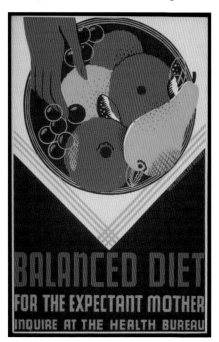

Abortions, Miscarriages, and Stillbirths

Whether or not you are actually a pregnant woman, a dream of having an abortion, a miscarriage, or a stillbirth probably left you feeling traumatized and bereft. And if you are expecting a baby in real life, your dream must have been a nightmare. Although it is, of course, possible that your dream miscarriage or stillbirth hinted that your unborn child isn't developing as it should, it is far more likely that your unconscious was simply playing back your natural feelings of anxiety on the dream screen (in which case, you'd benefit from consciously trying to calm your fears).

However, most dreams of this nature (particularly if the dream abortion, miscarriage, or stillbirth dominated a man's dream) refer to a concept that you have conceived—an idea that your unconscious is warning may be, or should be, doomed to failure, leaving its potential unrealized. If your dream portrayed an abortion, how did you react? Were you so distressed that you tried to stop the termination? If so, your dreaming mind may have been warning you that someone (could you identify the dream abortionist?) is determined to intervene in order to prevent your cherished plans from becoming a reality. If, however, you were relieved by the abortion, your unconscious may have been signaling the advisability of aborting the idea that is developing in your mind. Perhaps you conceived the idea carelessly and it

is consequently flawed, or maybe you would be overwhelmed by the burdens of responsibility should you allow the idea to progress all the way to full term. Alternatively, could the dream abortion have denoted something about which you feel guilty—perhaps something that you colluded in creating, such as a dubious plan of action—and could your unconscious have been trying to tell you to "kill off" whatever it is that is causing you such anxiety?

Although a dream that focuses on a miscarriage will frequently convey a similar message, consider the possibility that it may have denoted a "miscarriage of justice," especially if your sleeping self burned with anger rather than being grief-stricken. Could your dream have been mirroring your conscious rage that your colleague, and not you, was rewarded with a promotion for the success of a project that you'd conceived and, indeed, regarded as "your baby"?

In some respects, stillbirths are more tragic than abortions and miscarriages, not least because the baby may have been carried to term and may have been perfectly formed, the only element missing being that vital spark of life. A stillborn baby may again sym-

bolize a concept, but often represents a talent that you possessed, but that died (for whatever reason—be it malnutrition, neglect, or a crucial defect) before you could show it off to the world in all its glory.

Birth and Babies

Are you an expectant mother who dreamed of going into labor and giving birth to your baby at long last? If so, and the dream birth was easy, the purpose of your unconscious in bringing forward your due date was probably to hearten you and fulfill your

Above: An empty cradle may symbolize the loss of a baby. **Right:** If you dreamed of a young mother, your unconscious may have been responding to your curiosity about how you would cope with motherhood. **Opposite:** Whether the reference was to your baby or "brainchild," dreaming of your healthy offspring indicates that it is developing well.

fervent wish that all will go well. If your dream labor was difficult, however, it almost certainly reflects your inevitable anxieties, and your dreaming mind may have put you through this unpleasant dummy run in order to force you to confront your fears, thereby strengthening and preparing you for the testing event ahead. But when you gave that final push and your offspring emerged, were you astonished to see that you'd given birth to a kitten rather than a human baby? Again, dreams like these often simply mirror your worries about giving birth (in this case hinting that the prospect is causing you to "have kittens"). And, if you are a prospective father in the real

world, your birth dream may similarly have been depicting your hopes and fears for the welfare of your partner and unborn child.

If you are a woman who dreamed of having a baby, but aren't actually pregnant, your unconscious may have been reflecting your wish to have a child in due course. An alternative interpretation, which applies as much to men as to women dreamers, is that the birthing process denotes the imminent entrance of a fully formed idea, plan, or project into your real-life world—something that will no longer be a figment of your imagination, but will have a life of its own, while your own life will never be the same again.

Did the dream delivery go smoothly, or was it protracted and

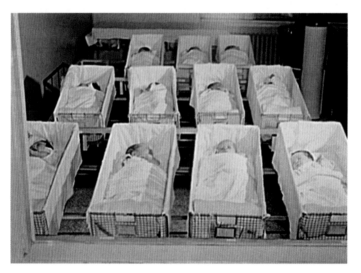

difficult? The answer may indicate the likely ease, or otherwise, of making your "brainchild" a reality. Or did your dream home in on a particular aspect of the birth—the umbilical cord, for

Left: The message being signaled by a dream in which you helped your baby to stand upright is that it won't be long before it stands on its own two feet. **Below:** Was your dream baby the fruit of your body or your imagination? **Bottom:** In dreams, multiple births often denote your various personal qualities.

example? If the cord was wrapped around the baby's neck in your dream, it may warn that your "brainchild" is in danger of being "strangled at birth," or, if it was safely severed, that your mental offspring has been cut free and is now independent of you. Perhaps you labored in vain, without being rewarded by the sight of your newborn. In this case, your unconscious may be indicating that your waking efforts to bring your project to its culmination, although strenuous in the extreme, will not be fulfilled, or, at least, not quite yet.

Whatever else happened in your dream, did you find yourself the proud parent of a bouncing baby? Unless your unborn child's arrival is imminent in the real world, such a dream is again likely to have referred to a cerebral creation, a budding talent, or something full of potential that has just made its debut in life. (And if you had two, or even more, babies in your dream, they may symbolize

twin ideas or personal aspects, which, although related, are nevertheless subtly different and distinct, such as your musical and dramatic talents.)

Babies are demanding individuals who need constant attention, and your unconscious may, by implication, have been signaling that you will have to nurture and care for your "brainchild" lavishly if it is to thrive, and if your dream baby was premature, this message is underlined. If you found yourself having to look after someone else's offspring in your dream, have you been left nervously "holding the baby" during your waking hours? Maybe your father's away on business, you've been left in charge of the family firm during his absence, and you're worried about the respon-

sibility that's been placed on your shoulders, for example. And how did the baby behave? Did it gurgle happily or scream incessantly? A contented infant may denote that you are fulfilling the needs of your "brainchild" (or someone else's), while a distressed baby in

your dream may indicate that your new idea, project, or ability is being left neglected.

If you were horrified by a dream in which you lost, or even injured, your baby, it may be that you fear that your self-perceived shortcomings will result in a similar fate for the still tender fruit of your imagination (or hard work) in the waking world. If, however, the baby was actually your young child, it is quite likely that your dream was highlighting your current state of mind. Have you been overwhelmed by the demands of parenthood and are you feeling increasingly unable to cope? If so, your unconscious was probably giving rein to your feelings of guilt about failing to be the perfect parent (at least in your own mind), depending on the circumstances of the dream, perhaps also highlighting your frustration and desperate craving for a little more time to yourself.

Finally, if a likely answer eludes you when interpreting a dream like this, a further possibility to consider is whether the dream newborn (particularly if it was you yourself) may have represented your own "inner child." Perhaps it represented that side of you that longs for the comfort of receiving unconditional love and emotional nourishment, the

Above and left: Did you relish holding a baby in your dream, or did the weight of your responsibility make you feel anxious?

part of you that would like to start, or relive, life all over again. Or perhaps it represented a latent aspect of your personality or talent that has matured to the extent that it is ready to launch itself into your waking life.

Fostering and Adoption

Did you dream that you fostered or adopted a baby, that you ecstatically welcomed him or her into your home, and that you simply couldn't do enough for the new addition to your family? If you are actually contemplating fostering or adopting a child, your dream was almost certainly ful-

filling your yearnings (albeit only during your sleep). But if nothing is farther from your mind, the purpose of your unconscious may have been to shine a spotlight on the profound satisfaction that you would derive from being allowed to shower someone with love and take care of his or her every desire or need. Has an object of affection been woefully lacking from

your life? Do you need to find an outlet (not necessarily a child, but perhaps a partner, relative, friend, pet, or even a charitable activity) through which to release your dammed-up urge to love and care for someone selflessly?

Alternatively, if you dreamed of fostering or adopting a person whom you know in waking life, your unconscious may have been hinting at your desire to be given the right or permission to lavish affection on that individual or somehow to formalize your devotion to him or her. If you dreamed that you fostered your adored teenaged nephew,

for example, in whose progress you are vitally interested, would you welcome being asked to act as his mentor?

Above: If you dreamed of being reborn, do you yearn for the opportunity to make a fresh start in life? **Left and below:** Dreams of fostered or adopted children may reflect a frustrated desire to lavish love on a special someone.

Baptisms and Naming Ceremonies

Did you dream that you attended an infant's naming ceremony or baptism? If so, your unconscious may simply have been recalling a similar event that you recently witnessed in waking life, or else one that is impending. An alternative explanation is that the baby who was being named or baptized in your dream represents a concept or idea that is about to be, or maybe already has been, formally presented to an appreciative audience. Perhaps you have long been considering setting up your own company, for example, in which case your unconscious may be telling you that the time is now right to fill in the necessary paperwork and go public, and that "your baby" will receive an enthusiastic response. (If you can remember what the child was called, your unconscious may even have presented you with a wonderful name for your company!)

In the Christian religion, the focus of baptisms and christenings, be they of babies, children, or adults, is the washing away of original sin and the start of a new life as a member of the Christian community. If you are a practicing Christian, your dream may, therefore, have been denoting your wish either to be "reborn" yourself, or, depending on who was being christened or baptized, your desire for someone else to undergo a transformation that would redirect him or her down

the right path in life. The reference may not have been to spirituality, but perhaps to negative thoughts or a damaging lifestyle. If you were being baptized in your dream, it may be, for instance, that you have been feeling depressed in waking life and have become a slave to health-abusing habits. If this is the case,

Above: In the world of dreams, naming ceremonies, baptisms, and christenings all hint that your child, or perhaps your "brain-child," is ready to be accepted by the community at large.

your unconscious may have been urging you to draw a line under this miserable and self-destructive phase of your life—to transform your mindset radically, to make positive changes to your lifestyle, and consequently, to emerge "reborn" as a more healthy person, in mind, body, and spirit. Finally, did godparents feature in your dream, and were they people you know? If so, your unconscious may have been telling you that if you turn to them for help, they will readily support you in your new life.

CHILDHOOD

In the secret language of the unconscious, a dream child, whether or not it is you, almost always represents the child within—usually the carefree young innocent that you once were and, perhaps, would like to be again. Dreams in which a child (or a childhood symbol, such as a toy) plays a leading role therefore often signal that your waking circumstances are troubling and weighing you down. In many cases, these dreams mean that it's high time either to restore the balance by allowing yourself to have some fun, or to adopt a simpler, less adult, perspective on life. Alternatively, such dreams may be alerting you to your childish behavior in the real world, thereby urging you to mend your ways.

Childhood is the time when our personalities form, when we become increasingly socialized, and when we learn many of the fundamental rules of life. Therefore, a dream in which you find yourself revisiting a place or scenario from your childhood may be pointing to a lesson that you absorbed (or one that you failed to grasp) at that time, and this may have a useful bearing on your current situation.

Children

Did you dream that you had reverted to your five-year-old self and that you were contentedly sitting on your grandmother's lap, sucking your thumb as you listened to her reading a bedtime story? A dream like this can have two likely explanations. The first is that reviewing happy childhood memories in dreamland expresses your nostalgia for a time when life was full of fun and frolics (your only worry being how to avoid eating the disgusting broccoli that the grownups insisted was so good for you).

The alternative, however, may be more concerned with your present feelings of insecurity and confusion. By reminding you how loved and secure you once felt, and how simple life was when you were five, your dream may have been comforting you, thereby compensating for your adult unhappiness. If you are facing a difficult decision, the dream may

also have been highlighting your desire for guidance by focusing on your grandmother—someone who may have wanted the best for you, who was a font of homespun wisdom, and whose advice was untainted by ulterior motives. Consider, too, whether your unconscious could have cast the archetypal figure of the wise old woman, or priestess, in the role

of your grandmother. (Indeed, when any of your relations figure in your dreams of childhood, do not discount the possibility that they represent archetypes rather than your actual kin.)

Above: If you dreamed that you were a child safe and happy in the arms of your parents, you are subconsciously yearning for the security of your early years.

If your dream did not evoke specific memories of your childhood, or if a strange boy or girl played the starring role, your unconscious may similarly have summoned up an archetype—that of the child within. Whether your "inner child" was portrayed by you

or another actor on the dream stage, he or she may have represented the part of you that either never grew up (remaining true to your childlike attitudes), or that you've banished from your waking life (but longs for read-

mission). Your unconscious may, therefore, have been highlighting your own immature conduct in the real world, on the one hand, or else your yearning to recapture the innocence of childhood, on the other. The clues will lie in the dream child's behavior.

If, for example, a small boy bullied an even smaller girl in your dream, causing her to dissolve into helpless tears, could your unconscious have been drawing a parallel with the bully's cruelty and how you are currently treating someone (maybe a junior colleague) in real life? Did you find, as a child, that you were able to force others to submit to your will with your fists, and are you con-

tinuing to employ similarly abusive tactics (albeit psychological instead of physical) to this day? If so, now that your unconscious has drawn your conscious attention to your behavior, do you feel proud or ashamed of yourself? But if you were the bully's victim in your dream, is someone in your life, perhaps a vindictive neighbor, making you feel like a vulnerable, abused, and powerless child? Or if you dreamed that a two-year-old's temper tantrum drove you to distraction, could your dreaming mind have been comparing the toddler's hysteria with your own tendency to fly into a childish rage when you don't get your way during your waking hours? Alternatively, if a little girl was happily playing make-believe with her dolls in your dream, could it be that you long to return to your optimistic, childhood state of mind, before the realities of life shut down numerous avenues of opportunity, when the power of imagination made all things possible?

Above: A dream of finding yourself a child again, and of having a wonderful time dressing up, may have been encouraging you to have more fun in your adult life. **Top and right:** All dream toys may either advocate or warn against childish behavior, but dolls usually symbolize a particular person in your waking world. How you treated the doll in the context of your dream reveals your feelings for that person.

There are a number of further interpretations for dreams in which children feature, depending on the identity of the child and your response to him or her. If you dreamed of your actual child, your unconscious is likely to have been portraying your waking hopes or fears for him or her. But if you are childless, dreamed of romping with a band of laughing children, and hope to start a family in waking life, your dream probably falls into the wish-fulfillment category.

Alternatively, if your miserable childhood returns to haunt you in your dreams (which may be recurring), your unconscious may be forcing you to relive your former unhappiness in an attempt to make you confront the source of your distress, and, armed with a new weapon—your adult understanding—to come to terms with what happened to you, put it behind you, and move on.

Finally, just as a baby can symbolize a "brainchild" in dreams, a child may represent the progress of "your baby," be it a project, talent, or idea. Was your dreaming

Left: Pleasant dreams of your schooldays indicate relief from your recent worries. **Right:** Do you need to exert more control over your child or your "brainchild"? **Below and opposite:** Are you suppressing the rebellious or carefree feelings expressed by these dream teenagers?

self pleased to see him or her developing normally, or did you have cause for concern?

Teenagers

They may be adolescents, but teenagers are still children—that is, until they reach the latter teenage years. Although their significance in dreams is often similar to that of dream children, their appearance usually has less to do with innocence and powerlessness and more to do with youthful attitudes and behavior

(both good and bad) as well as the choices that teenagers face when they are about to cross the threshold from childhood into the adult world.

Is it many decades since you were a teenager, yet you dreamed of being transported back in time, thereby regaining your youthful looks, vigor, and outlook? If so, you may be mourning the loss of precisely those qualities as a consequence of aging, or you may be regretting not having made the most of your potential and the opportunities that beckoned at a time when (as you now realize, with the benefit of hindsight) the world was your oyster.

Rather than mirroring your nostalgia, however, your unconscious may have been urging you to adopt a younger attitude to life, particularly if your dream teenager was unknown to you. If you are a woman who dreamed of an adolescent girl, what did you admire about her? Her infectious good humor? Her enthusiasm? Her ambition? If you are a man who dreamed of a male teenager, what struck you about him? His "can-do" attitude? His idealism? His trusting nature? Whichever the quality, consider the possibility that this aspect of yourself has become withered and faded over the years, but that working on redeveloping

it may reap dividends in real life— not least by restoring your *joie de vivre*. And if you are a man who dreamed of the good-humored girl, or if you are a woman to whom the "can-do" young man appeared while you were sleeping, you may have been visited by your anima (if you are male) or animus (if you are female), bearing a similar message.

You may, however, have been thoroughly unsettled by a teenager's behavior in your dream. Perhaps he or she was rude to you and obstinately refused to listen to your dreaming self's sweet voice of reason. Just as the unconscious shines a spotlight on undesirable childish actions for an admonitory purpose, so it frequently highlights instances of teenage willfulness and petulance to try to jolt you into recognizing such behavior in

yourself. Have you been ungraciously closing your ears to the advice of someone who is trying to help you (perhaps an authority figure, such as a parent or a teacher) because you regard winning a perceived battle of wills to be more important? If so, could you be cutting off your nose to spite your own face? If you are the parent of a teenager and this dream scenario reenacts the events of day-to-day life, it is most likely that your dream was simply a literal one. But if your dream teen, who was not your offspring, really wounded your pride by ridiculing your achieve-

Left: A dream cheerleader highlights youthful enthusiasm—are you envious of this? **Above:** Do you regret abandoning your teenage hobbies? **Opposite:** Dream childhood environments, activities, and playthings may either encourage a more carefree outlook or warn against behaving childishly.

ments and values, you may have received a nocturnal visit from the ever-infuriating archetypal trickster. Which of his accusations stung you the most? Was it your supposedly stupid obsession with keeping up appearances? If so, could he have been right? Should you loosen up a little and let people see you as you really are?

Childhood Activities and Environments

The messages transmitted by dreams of childhood toys, activities, and environments are generally two sides of the same coin; one encouraging, the other discouraging, depending on how you felt in your dream. If, for example, you dreamed that you were busy having a wonderful time playing with a toy train, your dream may have been reminding you of the pleasure to be had from occa-

sionally letting your hair down and doing nothing more useful than playing (be it childish or adult games). This may be particularly true if the pursuit of fun and relaxation has been sorely lacking from your life recently. However, if you became bored with your dream toy and you have indulged yourself lately during your waking hours by buying all manner of entertaining, but pointless, gadgetry, your unconscious may have been urging you to put away childish things (which don't give you real satisfaction anyway) and to spend your time more productively.

While the appearance of toys in dreams can reflect your desire for a more carefree, less responsible, existence, or warn of the need to grow up in some respect, sometimes also pointing to

your nostalgia for your lost childhood, dolls may have special significance. Because they are modeled on the human form, and because children often endow them with characters, your dreaming mind may have used a doll to symbolize someone in your life, much as psychotherapists coax children to reveal the events of traumatic experiences by asking them to reenact them with dolls. Because this reverses the balance of power in the real world, it is an exercise in transference that usually reveals negative emotions about the person whom the doll represents—and if you stuck pins into your dream doll, these feelings are underlined. So if you dreamed of taking your anger out on a doll, who are you really furious with?

If you dreamed that you found yourself in a schoolyard, surrounded by a crowd of exuberant children, were you exhilarated by their rough and tumble? Or did you feel disdainful of their games? If you thoroughly enjoyed yourself in

your dream, your unconscious may have been signaling your suppressed need to have fun. But if you felt aloof from the shrieking children running around you, it may instead be that you'd prefer to play no part in the immature enthusiasm or behavior currently being exhibited by a group of people—perhaps your colleagues—in waking life.

Above and right: If your dreaming mind recreated your kindergarten, or a birthday party that you attended as a child, can you remember a lesson that you learned there? The importance of being considerate to your playmates, perhaps, or of not depriving the others of a slice of the cake by being too greedy? And does this lesson have relevance to your waking behavior? Childhood feelings, from happiness to humiliation, are so intense that incidents in our waking life can trigger memories that have long been buried.

Did you dream of being back at kindergarten or elementary school, or in some other environment that you strongly associate with your childhood? If so, it may be that your unconscious transported you back in time to that place in an effort either to remind you of a valuable lesson that you learned (or else failed to heed) there. Did your kindergarten teacher, for example, constantly impress on you the need to be kind to your fellow tots, and have you been treating your friends inconsiderately recently? Alternatively, if you dreamed that you were more concerned with goofing around with your buddies at school than pleasing your exasperated teacher, and that you got poor grades as a result, is this a pattern that echoes your behavior during your adult life? By reminding you of this cause and effect, could your unconscious have been urging you to break this pattern, to stop employing immature strategies in an attempt to make yourself popular, and instead to start applying yourself to furthering your career?

MARRIAGE

In the secret life of dreams, things are not always quite what they seem. So, while dreaming of a proposal, engagement, wedding, or marriage may indeed have temporarily fulfilled your waking matrimonial wishes (or else emphasized your doubts about making such a lifelong commitment), one of two other interpretations may be more relevant to your current situation. The first is that your unconscious may have used the proposal or wedding as a metaphor for an entirely different form of commitment—one that is unromantic in the extreme, such as your commitment to your career or to a financial obligation. The second is more abstract still, in that your dreaming mind may have conjured up the marriage scenario to indicate the need to bring together two opposing aspects of your personality—perhaps the masculine and feminine qualities that each of us possess—to create a harmonious union.

Dreams of unfaithfulness and divorce can be deeply unsettling, particularly if you believe your relationship to be rock solid in real life. You may be relieved, therefore, to know that these dreams (like those described above) may not reflect the actual state of your marriage or partnership. Instead, your unconscious may have been bringing to the fore anxious, guilty, or escapist feelings—emotions that, again, may not refer to your romantic or domestic situation at all, but to a platonic friendship or professional association.

Proposals and Engagements

If you are a woman, were you thrilled by a dream in which your ideal man got down on one knee, declared his undying love for you, asked you to be his wife, and then slipped a sparkling diamond ring onto your trembling finger? If so, and the man of your dreams is actually the man whom you long to marry in waking life, your unconscious was almost certainly mirroring your conscious wishes—just as it may have been if you are a man who dreamed of proposing marriage to your girlfriend, to whom you are truly devoted.

But what if you are already a married woman or man who dreamed that you were taken aback when a person who is known to you in the real world, or else a stranger, pleaded with you to spend the rest of your life with him or her? Thinking very carefully about whatever you associate this person with, or what your dream suitor could represent, may help you to decode the message of this perplexing dream. The proposal is most likely to have denoted a significant commitment that you may be being asked to make, while the person pressing his or her suit may symbolize the nature of that commitment. So if, for example, your closest friend proposed to you in your dream, what is it to which he'd like you to commit in the real world? Could it be the year off work that he's been trying to persuade you to take so that the two of you can backpack around the world together? Or if you decide that your dream stranger reminded you of a businesswoman and you're considering a job offer in waking life, could your admirer have represented the company that wants to hire you? Your dreaming reaction to the proposal—be it joyful

If you dreamed of receiving a marriage proposal and being presented with a dazzling engagement ring, do you hope that your dream will come true in the real world?

acceptance or instant rejection—should give you an inkling about how you really feel about committing yourself to that extended vacation or accepting the position.

As for the dream engagement ring, in both the real and dream worlds it is a symbol of the recipient's commitment to entering into a contract, just as a wedding ring denotes the wearer's love for the giver, and his or her intention of remaining true. (Incidentally, both rings are worn on the third finger of the left hand, which was traditionally believed to be connected to the heart.) In your dream, did you wear the ring with delight? Did you refuse it? Or, having accepted it, did you later struggle to tug it off and be free of the burden of your commitment?

Weddings and Marriage

Did you find yourself earnestly pledging your troth, for better or for worse, to a bride or bridegroom in front of a rapt and moist-eyed congregation in your dream? How did you feel as you uttered those solemn wedding vows, and to whom did you make them? If you are actually engaged to be married, or else wish that you were (and, on waking, longed for your dream to come true), your unconscious may have been indulging you by depicting your heartfelt hopes. This may be especially true if your dream bride or groom was the person whom you love and desire, or else a glamorous celebrity with whom you are currently obsessed, during your waking hours.

Or did you dream that you found yourself overcome by a mounting sense of panic as you walked down the aisle? Did you feel that you were walking reluctantly toward a dead end? And, in your dream, did the awful realization dawn on you that being tied to your dream bride or groom for a lifetime was the last thing in the world that you wanted? If you are actually engaged to be married, your dreaming mind may have put you through

such a graphic rehearsal in an attempt to make you aware of your misgivings about getting married and to examine them in the cold light of day. It may be, for instance, that you are being pressured into marriage in real life, but, having being swept along by the frantic pace of the wedding arrangements, have managed to suppress your doubts. If this is the case, your unconscious was probably urging you to acknowledge your qualms (at least to yourself, if not also to your intended) and either come to terms with them or call off the wedding. In symbolic terms, the altar before which you were standing in your dream denotes sacrifice. Are you in danger of sacrificing yourself (or, if you were wearing white, perhaps your purity or innocence) to a person who is wrong for you? Are you in danger of becoming a martyr to an oppressive marriage? Heed the warning from your unconscious and try to resolve your worries before your wedding day actually dawns.

If marriage couldn't be farther from your conscious mind, yet you were surprised to find your-

into consideration, the significance of your wedding dream remains nebulous, it may be that the answer lies elsewhere, within yourself, especially if you did not recognize your dream bride or groom. Could your bride have been your anima (if you are a man), or your bridegroom your animus (if you are a woman)? Could your unconscious have been signaling the need to bring the masculine and feminine, or intellectual and intuitive, aspects of your personality into closer union? Does your male side secretly yearn to be tamed by your feminine qualities, for instance,

self happily playing a starring role in a dream wedding ceremony, there are a number of possible interpretations. If you were getting married to someone you know, it may be that you unconsciously harbor romantic feelings for him or her—feelings that your dream may have brought to

light. Alternatively, it may be that the purpose of your unconscious in sending you such a dream was to highlight another type of partnership that it may be time to formalize. If your dream portrayed you marrying a colleague and the two of you have been discussing leaving your company and setting up your own business together in waking life, for example, your unconscious may have been encouraging you to go ahead and "make it legal."

If, having taken all of the above interpretations

Opposite: You may have dreamed of agreeing to marry your boyfriend, but if the sight of a prenuptial agreement or wedding invitation chilled your dreaming self, are you sure that you are ready for marriage?
Above and right: Were you apprehensive or joyful in your dream wedding?

or does your female aspect long to be given a confidence boost through the presence of a manly champion by her side? Similarly, marrying a stranger in your dream may have denoted the desirability of uniting two individual, but potentially complementary, facets of your character (your artistry and practicality, for instance). Perhaps the resulting

partnership would empower you to take a new, dynamic direction in life (possibly a switch of career from banking to sculpting) and maybe even to produce progeny (such as a portfolio of sculptures).

If you dreamed that you witnessed someone else being married, your unconscious may also

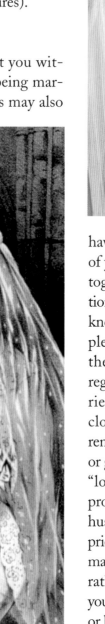

have been highlighting two parts of your personality being wedded together. An alternative explanation, however—particularly if you know one half of the happy couple in waking life and observed the wedding with a feeling of regret—is that you may be worried about somehow losing the close relationship that you currently enjoy with the dream bride or groom (just as parents may fear "losing" their daughter to their prospective son-in-law when her husband becomes her emotional priority). And if you were the best man or bridesmaid in your dream, rather than feeling delighted, did you feel jealous of the bridegroom or bride? If so, what did you envy? His or her "catch," or impending change in social status as a married person? A dream like this may simply reflect your attraction to the dream groom or bride (if

Opposite, top and left: Could the miniature bride and groom atop a dream wedding cake or a wedding from another time have represented the union of your feminine and masculine qualities? **Opposite, right:** If you dreamed of being jealous as you watched a bride and groom embrace, which of the two did you envy, and why? **Right:** A dream of your partner's unfaithfulness may have depicted your worst fears, prompting you to seek his reassurance in the waking world.

he or she is known to you in real life), or else your fear of remaining forever single, as in the old saying: "always a bridesmaid and never a bride."

Finally, if you have been married for more years than you care to remember, but dreamed of going through the marriage ceremony again with your husband or wife, your unconscious may have been reaffirming your feelings for him or her, which may remain as vibrant as they were on your wedding day. Alternatively, your dream may have been hinting that either you or your spouse—or both of you—are worried that the strength of your mutual love has waned. In this case, rather than literally renewing your vows (although that is certainly an option) in the real world, how about arranging a second honeymoon (which dreams of honeymooning also encourage), or at least booking a romantic dinner?

Unfaithfulness and Divorce

Did you wake up in a cold sweat, having endured a dream in which you caught your husband of ten years in bed with another woman (and when you awoke with the awful image still in your mind, maybe mystified your spouse by either clinging to him with relief or berating him for his dream infidelity)? An upsetting dream like this usually just reflects your feelings of insecurity about the constancy of your partner's love for you, although you may indeed be feeling threatened (albeit probably needlessly)—perhaps by a female colleague who's started working in his office, whose competence and humor he's been praising ever since she arrived. Alternatively, you may have unconsciously—or even consciously—detected signs that your husband is cheating on you in the real world, in which case your dreaming mind may have portrayed your worst-case scenario in an attempt to prepare you to confront, and deal with, the reality.

If, however, it was you who was cheating on your spouse in your dream, how were you feeling? Exhilarated or ashamed? If you relished your nocturnal fling, are satisfied with your marriage, but are nevertheless attracted to the person in your waking life who was cast in the role of your dream lover, your unconscious was probably fulfilling your secret desires in the safety of dreamland. If your marriage has actually hit a rocky patch, you have grown apart emotionally, or your sex life has become moribund, a dream like this may also have made your unconscious yearnings manifest, thereby underlining your dissatisfaction with the current state of your marital affairs. But if your dreaming infidelity left you feeling guilt-ridden and mortified and you have been tempted to have an affair in waking life, your unconscious was probably warning you of the emotional price that your unfaithfulness would exact from you. But what could such a dream have been signaling if you know that you have been utterly faithful to your wife or husband? In this case, ask yourself whether you really have been true to him in thought, word, and deed. Have you, for instance, snickered with friends about his plans to start following a weight-training regime? Have you cheated her out of an evening with her girlfriends by deliberately working late to avoid having to babysit? And aren't these both examples of small betrayals?

A dream in which you were distraught to hear your husband demanding a divorce may similarly have been concerned with anxiety about the robustness of your marriage, and only you will know whether your fears are justified or a product of your overactive imagination. Alternatively, it may be that the aim of your unconscious in traumatizing you with the prospect of divorce was to remind you how lucky you are in your husband, thereby warning you not to take him for granted. But maybe your dreaming self was surprised to feel relieved when your wife told you that your marriage was over and flounced out of your home for good, or perhaps you were star-

Below: By sending you divorce papers in your dream, your unconscious may have been urging you to cherish your spouse, or else drawing your conscious attention to your desire to be free of him or her.

tled to hear yourself asking your wife for a separation or divorce. What could such a dream have signified? Well, the answer may be that, although you are not yet consciously aware of it, you may indeed be longing to escape your marriage, which is admittedly a difficult issue to confront, but one that you should nevertheless mull over for both of your sakes.

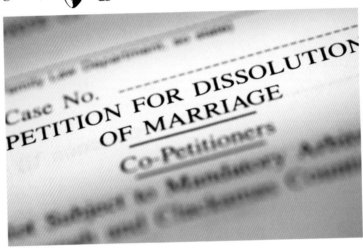

There may, however, be an entirely different interpretation for a divorce-related dream, one that does not concern your actual spouse. Could your unconscious have used your husband or wife as a symbol for something else to which you are "wedded," such as a job, ideal, or opinion, which, on waking reflection, may be causing you unhappiness? If so, could your dreaming mind have been signaling that it's time to leave your job, or to open your mind to other viewpoints, thereby injecting some thrilling independence, or a burst of fresh and stimulating ideas, into a life or mindset that has become stagnant?

☠ DEATH ☠

Although nature has primed us with the instinct to survive, each of us knows that we are inevitably doomed to die. Death is the greatest change that we face, and also the most mysterious, for while some of us have an idea of what will claim our lives, none of us know for certain what, if anything, awaits when we finally pass over to the "other side." And how will it feel to die? How will we cope if those we love the most predecease us? Such questions are so frightening, painful, and ultimately unanswerable, that it is small wonder that we push them to the back of our conscious minds while we get on with the business of living. We cannot banish them completely, however, and when the unconscious mind forces us to experience dreams of dying and death, it does so for a number of purposes.

When, for instance, we dream of the death of a loved one who is seriously ill or advanced in years, the unconscious may be rehearsing us for the actual event, thereby preparing and strengthening us. And when the dreaming mind summons up the dead, it may be trying either to comfort or enlighten us. Dreams of our own demise, of murder and killing, of execution, sacrifice, and martyrdom, and of funeral proceedings rarely refer to literal deaths, however. Instead, they are symbolic scenarios that may signal the end of one phase of life, point toward an external or internal conflict, or else mirror waking feelings of oppression or depression. So don't be alarmed by your death dream, for, as Jung put it, "When it is really a question of death, the dream speaks another language."

The Death of a Loved One

Did you wake awash with grief after a dream in which you sat by your elderly mother's bedside, holding her hand as you watched her breathe her last? And is your mother literally at death's door in real life? If so, your unconscious was reflecting the sadness that you are feeling at the prospect of her impending departure from your life, and trying to prepare you for the sense of loss that you will experience, the desolation of bereavement that you are dreading. By exposing you, in the dream, to the emotions that will overwhelm you, your shock may be lessened and your grief a little

Right: If you dreamed of the death of a child, is your son or daughter withdrawing from you emotionally, or becoming more independent?

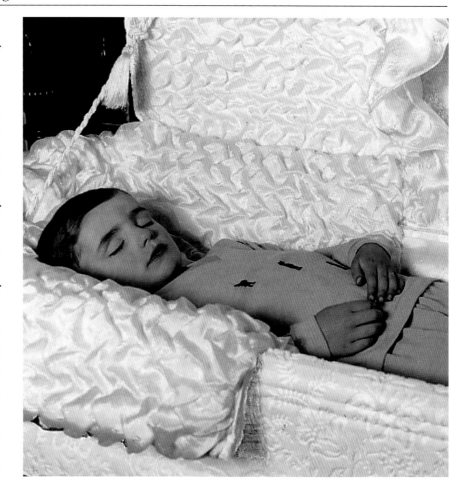

Below: If you dreamed of a family gathering to witness someone's final hours, you may be afraid of losing someone yourself. **Opposite:** If you dreamed that someone who has departed this life appeared to you in spirit form, did he or she impart a particular message to you?

less raw, and thus easier to bear, when your mother actually does die. If, however, you watched your mother die with a feeling of relief in your dream, it may be that you have already consciously come to terms with the inevitable and have accepted that death will release her from her suffering. Dreams like these may also be warning you to tell loved ones how much they mean to you before it's too late.

But what if you felt no emotion at all as you witnessed the deathbed of your much-loved sister, who, in the real world, is young, vigorous, and in the best of health? A dream like this is extremely unlikely to portend her actual death, unless your sister has a dangerous occupation, but even then, your feelings of neutrality about her passing point away from anxiety about actually being bereaved and toward another interpretation altogether. Could your dream sister have represented something in your life that is coming to an end, or perhaps should? Or an aspect of your personality that is about to be extinguished, or maybe should be? If, for instance, you associate your sister with your childhood, could her dream death have denoted either that you have left childhood behind and are now mature in every respect, or that it's time to grow up and behave like an adult?

An alternative explanation for a dream of anyone in your life dying is that you fear the death of your relationship, especially if you have argued with that person, or if he or she has withdrawn emotionally from you, in the waking world. If you felt bereft when you saw his or her life ebbing away in your dream, your unconscious may be warning you that this is exactly how you will feel unless you take steps to repair the rift or close the emotional distance between you. If, however, your feeling was of liberation rather than mourning, the dream is more likely to have indicated your unconscious desire to end the relationship altogether.

Visits From the Dead

Did your deceased husband, whom you've missed desperately since he died two years ago, appear to you in your dream? If so, you are no doubt treasuring the memory of having been reunited in dreamland, but did you awake with a renewed sense of loss? Or did you feel somehow comforted and reassured? Perhaps you felt a combination of both? When the unconscious sends someone who was once fundamental to your emotional well-being, but is now dead, to visit you in a dream, it is fulfilling—albeit only during your sleep—your heartfelt wish to be together again. If you woke feeling bereft, it is clear that you have not yet come to terms with your bereavement. But did the dream end with

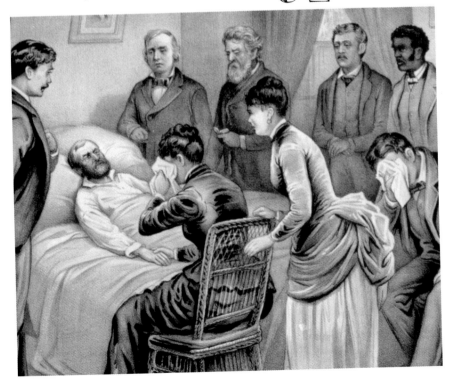

your husband fondly kissing you goodbye, turning and leaving you, and then turning again to give you a wave and a wink before walking toward a beautiful garden, and did you then wake up wreathed in smiles? A comforting dream like this may be a signal that accepting that your husband is in a better place (whether or not you believe in the afterlife) will empower you to let go of your crippling grief.

Perhaps your dead father came to you while you were sleeping and told you bluntly that he was disappointed with your cavalier behavior toward your older brother, from whom you repeatedly borrow money, but whom you always "forget" to repay. If his words rang uncomfortably true, his stern voice may actually have been that of your conscience, confronting you with your tendency to abuse your relationship with your brother and trying to jolt you into setting right your wrong. Alternatively, particularly if you are financially solvent and have no brother, ask yourself what your father represented to you, and which lessons he drummed into your younger self when he was alive. If he was financially frugal, accounted for every cent, and never splashed out on luxuries, could his appearance in your dream have been warning you that it would be unwise to take out that enormous auto loan that you're about to commit yourself to, because you'd struggle to keep up the payments? Or are you feeling guilty about your dissolute lifestyle because it flies in the face of the values and standards by which he lived? They may no longer be part of our lives in the real world, but deceased people continue to influence us in our individual inner worlds.

Dreams that re-create the cheerful occasions that you enjoyed with people who died many years ago, such as your grandparents, usually express nostalgia for those days, when life was simpler than it is now. But, if you are faced with a difficult problem that needs resolving in waking life, it may be that, by summoning your grandparents into your dreaming presence, your unconscious was trying to tell you that the solution lies in the past. If, for example, your grandparents made ends meet by renting out rooms when they fell upon hard times, and you have just lost your job in waking life, could your dream have been hinting that you could always follow their example?

Your Own Death

Unless you know that death is definitely drawing near—if you're in the final stages of an incurable disease, for instance—when your unconscious may be trying to help you to overcome your fear and prepare you for what is facing you, be assured that a dream of dying or of being dead is highly unlikely to presage your actual death. But what could such a dream mean? Considering the three following interpretations may enlighten you.

First, if you are preoccupied with a nagging concern about your health and were stricken by a fatal disease in your dream, your unconscious might have been amplifying your waking fears, in which case having a physical checkup may dispel your anxiety. But, if problem after insoluble problem seem to have been heaped upon your sagging shoulders in the real world, it may, secondly, be that by portraying your death, your unconscious was giving expression to your desperate desire to escape your difficulties in the most emphatic and effective way possible—that is, by being "dead to the world." The third possible explanation for a dream like this is that one phase of your life is either coming to an end, or perhaps should, thereby enabling you to start afresh. The natural world's cycle of birth, life, death, and rebirth has its parallel in our own lives, so that your dreaming mind may have used your "death" as a symbol for something that has run its natural course in your current existence. Could your unconscious have been telling you that it's time to retire after thirty years in your job? Or could your dream have referred to your divorce, which is about to be finalized in the real world? And if you came to life again in your dream, could you unconsciously have been anticipating your new, work-free or single existence?

Dreams of committing suicide can have similar explanations, although your unconscious may also have been warning that you have been exhibiting "suicidal"

Above left: Dreaming of being lifeless may reflect your longing to be "dead to the world." **Right:** Dreams of murder usually highlight a bitter waking conflict.

behavior in waking life—maybe by burning the candle at both ends and thereby endangering your health, or perhaps by taking too many financial risks.

Murder and Killing

Did you wake with a start from a dream in which you were arguing furiously with your mother in the kitchen, then picked up a knife, and stabbed her in the heat of the moment? And are you feeling angry with her during your waking hours, perhaps because she refuses to acknowledge your new partner's good points? If so, you probably had a safety-valve dream, in which you were able to give rein to your rage and frustration in the most dramatic of ways without causing your mother any actual harm. Whether you found your dream cathartic or grief-inducing, by highlighting your murderous feelings, your unconscious may have been warning that you are on an emotional "knife's edge." Perhaps you should consciously try to come to terms with your mother's obstinacy and find a constructive way of dealing with the situation, even if it means cutting the apron strings and choosing your partner over her.

Left and bottom left: If you killed an animal in your dream, what part of your personality are you trying to kill off? If it was a bull, your lustfulness? Or if it was a dog, your "bitchiness"?
Below: A dream noose may symbolize the choking constriction of your own guilt.

As well as emphasizing your anger with someone, dreams in which you killed another person may point toward an internal conflict, especially if you harbor no ill will toward your dream victim in the real world or, indeed, if he or she was a stranger, or if you slaughtered an animal. If you strangled an unknown man in your dream, did he provoke you into doing so? If so, how? The answer may tell you what it is about yourself that you are longing to "kill off." If, for example, you were laboring hard to build a house together in a race against the clock, but he suddenly dropped his tools, cracked open a beer, and sat laughing at you as you pleaded with him to start work again, so that you finally snapped and grabbed him by the throat, could he have represented your own *laissez-faire* attitude—your tendency to sabotage your career by idling away your working hours? Animals symbolize aspects of our instinctual nature, so if you casually killed a dog in your dream, ask yourself what the dog could represent within you. If your dreaming self snuffed out its life because you found its devotion stifling, for instance, do you long to extinguish your helpless, doglike attachment to your best friend, or else her oppressive and needy dedication to you?

But what might it have meant if someone was trying to murder you in your dream? By depicting you undergoing such a terrifying life-or-death crisis, your unconscious may have been alerting you to the real threat that someone poses to you—albeit probably to your emotional or professional welfare, rather than to your physical wellbeing. If, for instance, your junior colleague at work was your dream murderer, ask yourself if she may be a "character assassin" intent on thwarting your promotion hopes by poisoning your employer's mind against you. If your dream assailant is known to you in waking life—perhaps it was your partner—an alternative explanation is that something about your relationship is "killing you," perhaps because he is bleeding you dry financially or because her overdependence on you is deadening your individuality.

Finally, if you are unable to identify your dream killer or if the significance of your dream remains elusive, your unconscious may have been symbolically communicating your sense of being victimized in waking life, be it by a person (perhaps your boss), a group of people (maybe a clique of bullies at school), or a faceless entity (an overly bureaucratic organization, for example).

Execution, Sacrifice, and Martyrdom

Maybe you dreamed that you were standing on a platform, blindfolded and petrified, trembling in the awful knowledge that

you were about to be executed. If so, your terror is likely to have given way to a profound sense of relief when you awoke to the realization that you'd been dreaming. But why would your unconscious have inflicted such a harrowing experience on you while you slept the sleep of the innocent?

Well, the answer is probably that you do not think, on an unconscious level, that you are innocent at all, but that you are instead guilty of a crime that you feel deserves punishment or fear is about to be discovered (or both). Although your actual crime may well be something relatively innocuous, such as lying or deliberately slipping a candy bar into your pocket and leaving a store without paying for it, you cannot escape the condemnation of your conscience. You may be successfully suppressing your guilty feelings whenever you are awake, but when your unconscious, not your conscious mind, is in control, they will usually surface within your dreams. Such a dream may also be warning that, unless you put an end to your pilfering, the day will come when you are caught red-handed and will then face punishment in the real world, although not by death (the unconscious tends to conjure up the most drastic scenario possible in an attempt to shock you into returning to the moral straight and narrow). Also ask yourself if you feel that you are somehow "dead meat" or a "dead man walking," if you are waiting for the "ax to fall," or are in danger of "losing your head" in waking life.

If, however, you acted as the executioner in your dream, who were you about to put to death? Now ask yourself what "crime" he or she has committed in the real world that you feel deserves punishment. If it was your friend, do you believe her to be guilty of betrayal because she told your brother what you were planning to buy him for his birthday, even though you had sworn her to secrecy? Alternatively, and particularly if the condemned person was anonymous, is there an unpleasant task that you know you must "execute" during your waking hours, such as firing or disciplining someone who works for you?

Although the ritual sacrifice practiced by certain religions in times past (and, in the case of animals, also today) focuses on putting a living being to death, the sacrifice is enacted not because the victim is guilty of anything (unlike execution), but to appease vengeful deities and thus benefit the common good.

If you dreamed of someone being sacrificed (maybe even you), the message may, therefore, have been that the wellbeing of a community, be it a family or workforce, should take precedence over individual hopes and desires. So if, for instance, you were about to be sacrificed in your dream and you felt strangely sanguine about the prospect, it may be that you've come to terms with the need to prioritize your family's welfare and not to disrupt your children's schooling by regularly moving them from pillar to post—even if it means sacrificing your hopes for a military or diplomatic career.

If your impending martyrdom angered you, however, your dreaming mind was probably mirroring waking feelings of resentment. Who was wielding the sacrificial knife in your dream? If it was your partner, is she about to sacrifice your relationship on the altar of her career? If it was your friend, is he taking advantage of your kindly nature by always begging favors of you, but giving nothing in return? If it was your boss, are you being "crucified" by her constant demands? Alternatively, have you been made

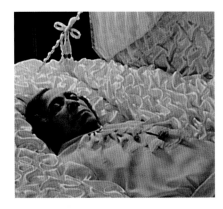

Opposite, far left: If you dreamed of acting as a hangman, whom would you like to "string up" in the real world? **Opposite, below left:** Dreams of martyrdom usually denote self-sacrifice. **Right:** Did seeing yourself in a dream coffin mirror your waking sense of isolation? **Below:** A dream of receiving honors and eulogies at your own funeral may have raised your self-esteem.

a scapegoat or forced to carry the can for something that you did during your waking hours, when those around you were equally guilty (such as being singled out for punishment because you joked with your friends in class)?

Funerals, Burials, Cremations, and Graveyards

Were you surprised to find yourself observing your own funeral service, gathering, or wake in your dream, but rather than feeling sad or regretful, was your overriding emotion curiosity about what would be said about the dear departed? Because ill is rarely spoken of the dead—and, indeed, their virtues are usually eulogized—it may be that you are feeling in need of a confidence boost in real life and you wish that your family and friends

would praise your positive qualities instead of constantly putting you down. By giving graphic expression to the petulant phrase, "You'll be sorry when I'm dead!" a dream of witnessing the grief and contrition of the assembled congregation is, therefore, often a form of self-validation, compensating for feelings of having been hurt or neglected by the people whose appreciation you long for. Who were the mourners in your dream, and were you gratified by what they said about you?

In the realm of the unconscious, funerals furthermore share the various interpretations associated with dreams of death and dying (see above), so it may be helpful to ask yourself if worries about your health are preying on your mind, if there's anything in your life or character that you long to "lay to rest," or whether the dream funeral (particularly if it wasn't yours) could have represented a relationship that you'd like to end. And if an undertaker loomed large in your dream, consider whether your unconscious may have been pointing toward a disagreeable task that you must soon "undertake" in waking life.

Did you find yourself lying in a coffin in your dream? If so, you probably felt constricted, claustrophobic, and panic-stricken. As well as being symbols of death, thereby denoting the end of a certain stage in life, dream coffins can represent feelings of isolation, stifling confinement, and hopelessness. By portraying you in a coffin, your unconscious may have been highlighting feelings of being alone or powerless to rise above the problems that have "boxed you in."

Or was it a burial that you witnessed in your dream? If so, whether you or someone else was being interred, your unconscious may similarly have been signaling that a life phase is about to be "dead and buried," or else that you wish that something problematic in your life could be. If, for example, you dreamed of attending the burial of your former spouse, and you never really got over your divorce, could your dream have been either expressing your desire to "bury" your continuing love for her (thereby

freeing you to forge a new romantic relationship), or telling you that you have indeed now succeeded in "burying" your feelings? Dream cremations send the same message, the symbols of fire and ashes furthermore hinting at imminent rebirth, just as the mythological phoenix, which burned itself to death when it reached the end of its life span, rose renewed from the ashes.

Although gravestones, graveyards, and cemeteries do, of course, have connotations of death, in the landscape of dreams they are more likely to act as signposts to the past. Did you dream of visiting your grandfather's grave? If so, could your dreaming mind have been trying to focus your conscious attention on a characteristic of his, or a piece of advice that he once gave you, that may be

relevant to your current situation? Alternatively, your dream may simply have been reflecting your nostalgia for those joyful childhood days when you could pay him a real-life visit. But, if you dreamed that you stood by the grave of someone who is still alive and mourned that person's departure from your life, your unconscious may have been warning that your relationship with him or her is in danger of being consigned to the grave and—unless you concentrate on keeping it alive—that you may soon experience the same sadness in the real world.

Above and right: Graveyards, and the gravestones of long-dead people, often signal that a possible solution to a real-life problem lies buried in the past.

AUTHORITY FIGURES

Most of us had no choice but to develop a healthy respect for authority in childhood, when our parents' word was law and we were reprimanded, or even punished, for disobeying that law. As we grew older, other authority figures joined our parents in instilling spiritual, intellectual, and social lessons and values in us, so that as adults, we have a clear idea of the behavior that our "elders and betters" expect from us—even if we don't agree with them. And if, as grownups, we deviate from this socially acceptable behavioral blueprint—which, after all, ensures that we all live together in relative harmony—then further authority figures, ranging from our professional superiors through the upholders of the law of the land to the enforcers of the rule of state, are standing ever ready to whip us back into line.

When authority figures appear in our dreams, they generally do so for one of three reasons. Firstly, as the voice of our conscience, rebuking us for a transgression of thought, word, or deed that goes against what we have been taught is right. Secondly, as advisors and guides, helping us to see the best course of action (for example, when we are faced with a critical decision). And thirdly, to warn that we may be abusing our own authority, which brings a duty to act kindly and fairly to those over whom we wield power. We may rebel against authority, but the appearance of its representatives in the dream world, be it as themselves or archetypal figures, commands our respect (whether grudging or unquestioning) and reminds us of the importance of behaving responsibly.

Father Figures

Although both of your parents may have assumed responsibility for teaching you what was acceptable behavior and what would not be tolerated when you were a child, your father may have been the ultimate arbiter in your household when it came to matters of discipline. And if your father appeared in your dream to castigate you for actually having called your office recently, pretending to be sick when, in fact, you just wanted to hang out with your friends that day, you may well have been uncomfortably reminded of the time when he punished you for playing hooky from school. If, however, your school record was unblemished by absence, or if your father did not feature in your childhood in the real world, your unconscious may have summoned up the father archetype to underline your immature attitude, prick your conscience, and thus try to

Above: The father archetype may act as a kindly protector or a brutal ogre when he appears in dreams. Was the example set by your dream father figure one to emulate or avoid?

encourage you to mend your idle ways. In both instances, the message being communicated is that you know, deep down, that you have fallen short of the standards expected of you (by yourself, as well as by others) and that you should try to behave better in the future.

Your older brother, uncle, or male boss may also assume the dream role of the archetypal father, a benevolent provider and protector who uses his authority to enforce social and traditional standards, as well as wisely guiding those under his care. If, for example, your kindly uncle paid you a visit in dreamland and imparted the perplexing message that you shouldn't keep company with bandits, your unconscious may have

assigned him the character of the father figure to alert you to the criminal behavior of a new circle of flashy friends that you've made in the real world. Have you been so seduced by their glamorous and dashing lifestyle that you've turned a blind eye to some of the sleazy activities that fund it?

But did you dream that you were reduced to tears of helpless frustration when your boss bawled you out in front of your coworkers, accused you of idiocy and incompetence, ignored all your protests, and then fired you on the spot? And is your boss an understanding man, and are you the most conscientious of workers, during your waking hours? What could the message from your unconscious have been then?

Remember that a father figure can also abuse his authority, maybe by beating his children black and blue, by constantly denigrating their best efforts, or by spending his wages on liquor while his family goes hungry. In archetypal terms, he is the ogre, the cruel and sadistic face of authority, who—unlike the ideal father—uses his power unjustly and simply ignores his victims' pleadings as he thrashes them into submission. By portraying your compassionate, fatherly boss as a brutal and pitiless ogre, your unconscious is unlikely to have shown him in his true light, but may instead have been pointing to your own tendency to treat your subordinates with unthinking viciousness or ruthlessness.

If, however, your boss really does rule your office with a rod of iron and treats you as his personal slave in waking life, and you dreamed that he heaped yet more indignities and humiliations upon you, your dream was obviously a literal reflection of your real-life situation. But why would your unconscious have re-exposed you to your daily feelings of unhappiness and frustration when you had taken refuge in the sanctuary of sleep? It may be that you are so preoccupied with fulfilling your boss's every demand during your waking hours that you haven't had the time—or the courage—to think about standing up for yourself. By shining a spotlight on your boss's tyrannical treatment and emphasizing how helpless and miserable it makes you feel, your unconscious was probably highlighting the urgent need for you to put a stop to your current situation. Not only is rebelling against parental authority a healthy part of growing up, maturing, and becoming an adult, questioning and challenging dictatorial behavior is vital if you are to retain your self-confidence and individuality.

Spiritual Authorities

Did you wake squirming with remorse from a dream in which the Pope granted you an audience, only to berate you for not having attended mass recently, and are you in fact a Roman Catholic, whether practicing or lapsed? If so, your unconscious may have been reflecting your suppressed feelings of guilt about not having been to church for a while, or about not having confessed to a transgression that your religion deems a sin, thereby receiving absolution. By invoking the aid of the highest living representative of your religion, whoever it is, and whatever that may be—or even the archetypal high priest, prophet, or supreme being— your unconscious mind may have been pointing out that heeding the creed in which you were instructed as a child, or adhering to its tenets, may bring you peace of mind. If, however, you received the pontiff's blessing in your dream, your unconscious is likely to have been indicating that you are on the right spiritual course.

Teachers and Professors

Were you dismayed to find yourself back in class in your dream, being shouted at again for your inability to do math by the same teacher who made your life hell during your schooldays? If so, you were, no doubt, relieved to find yourself back in the real world when you awoke. There was, however, almost certainly a reason why your unconscious transported you back to that particular time and place, one that may well point to a lesson that your former teacher tried to drum into you. Could it be that, by summoning the math tyrant into your dream, your unconscious was alerting you to the need to check your bank statement more carefully because it (but not your conscious mind) has noticed that the figures don't add up? Or could your nightmarish teacher have been urging you to enroll in night school to study for the math exam that you flunked at school because your inadequacy in this area is holding you back in your career? Alternatively, are you suffering from stress? Or could the teacher have represented an aspect of yourself? Have you been overly hard on your teenage son for constantly exceeding his allowance, for instance?

Opposite: If you dreamed that your boss, in reality a gentle mentor, mutated into a vicious slave-driver, was the reference to your own tyrannical tendencies? **Left:** If a spiritual authority appeared to you in a dream, your unconscious may have been urging you to obey the teachings of your faith. **Below:** Your dream of a moral lesson might indicate a guilty conscience.

Maybe you were mystified by a dream in which you found yourself at college, raptly listening to an unknown professor deliver a fascinating lecture on the topography of Australia, because you never went to college in the real world and you have little waking interest in geography. Could it be that, by conjuring up a professor to pique your curiosity in an academic subject, your unconscious may have been trying to draw your conscious attention to a mind that is crying out for stimulation and knowledge? Your dream may not have been referring to a thirst for geographical knowledge, but to a desire to expand your intellectual horizons.

Referees and Umpires

Did you dream that you were playing in the men's final against the reigning tennis champion on Wimbledon's Centre Court and you hit what you knew was the winning shot, only to have the umpire call it out? If so, your dreaming reaction was probably, "You cannot be serious!" But what could your dream have meant? Think back over recent events in your waking life. Umpires and referees are charged with impartiality, but has someone who has authority over you—perhaps your mother—made what you consider to be an unjustified decision and penalized you unfairly, maybe by ruling your sister the winner of your latest squabble, despite being unaware of the facts? Was your dreaming mind accusing your mother of misusing her authority?

Alternatively, if you dreamed that you were refereeing a game of hockey and were struggling to impose your will on the bad-tempered and defiant players, your unconscious may have been mir-

roring your waking circumstances. Are you currently trying to keep the peace between two warring groups (perhaps within your circle of family or friends) in real life, and are you constantly having to admonish them to adhere to the rules of "fair play"?

Heads of State

Be it a president or a monarch, the symbolic role of a head of state is to act as the "father" or "mother" of the nation, to govern or rule wisely and justly, and to protect the welfare of the country's citizens or subjects. The unconscious mind may, therefore, sometimes summon a head of state into our dreams to represent the father—or mother—archetype, be it to reprove or guide us or to alert us to dictatorial behavior (as described above).

But did you wake up smiling after a dream in which the president paid a surprise visit to your house, accepted your invitation to join your family and friends for a barbecue, and, when he left, praised your steak as being the best he'd ever tasted? If so, your unconscious may have been compensating for your disgruntlement

in waking life. Do you feel unappreciated and undervalued by those around you (perhaps, but not necessarily, because they make fun of your barbecuing skills)? And was your self-esteem boosted in dreamland by the admiration of the world's most renowned steak aficionado, not to mention the holder of the highest office in the United States?

Another possible explanation to consider when a president, prime minister, king, or queen graces your dream is that he or she may represent your actual parent or boss. If your female boss is the "queen bee" of your hivelike workplace, for instance, and the queen of England honored you with her presence in a dream in which she graciously told you to carry on the good work, your dreaming mind may have disguised your boss as a monarch in order either to compensate for her cold, queenly indifference to all your efforts during the day or, alternatively, to reinforce her recently voiced appreciation of your outstanding contribution to a project you have been working on.

The Face of the Law

Did you dream that you stood quaking before a stern-faced judge as he passed sentence upon you? Dreams of being tried and sentenced often express feelings of guilt about something you've done that you recognize, at some level, deserves punishment. The aim of the unconscious in portraying you in a judicial situation is usually to warn you against perpetuating your "crime," which, in the waking world, could be something as trivial as betraying a confidence. Alternatively, if you knew that you were innocent and were outraged to receive a "guilty" sentence in your dream, your unconscious may have been reflecting your waking sense of grievance at having been the victim of a "miscarriage of justice," perhaps because you were fined for a parking violation when, in fact, the meter was out of order. If someone you know was passing judgment on you in dreamland, have you offended against that person's moral values, which you respect, or did he or she judge you unfairly?

If, however, you played the part of a judge in your dream, who was on trial, and why? Now ask yourself if your verdict was just or whether your judgment may have been prejudiced. Try to draw a parallel with your waking life. Have you, for instance, justifiably (in your opinion) condemned your friend for having "murdered" your trust by lying to you, or are you biased against your "treacherous" colleague because he has recently switched his allegiance to a rival football team?

Did your dreaming vision home in on a jury? If so, were the jurors trying you or were you one of their number? Because it comprises twelve people, the inclusion of a jury in your dream suggests that you are either being subjected to a collective social judgment (maybe your family is united in its disapproval of your "alternative" lifestyle or that you have joined forces with others in judging someone else (perhaps even your-self). And if you were locked into a cell by a jailer in your dream, did you recognize him or her? If you did, is that person restricting your freedom of action in waking life? But if you were the prison officer, whom did you imprison in your dream? If it was someone you know—perhaps your girlfriend—could your dream have been warning that your overly possessive behavior is crippling her individuality? If the dream prisoner was just a stranger, however, could you be acting as your own jailer by caging yourself in with fears and inhibitions?

Uniformed Authorities

The collective authority of soldiers and policemen as upholders of the rule of state and law of the land is symbolized by the depersonalizing uniform that they

Opposite, top: Dream referees often denote the need to be impartial in waking life. **Opposite, below:** Could the regal figure who graced your dream have represented a queenly mother figure whose approval you long to receive? **Top right:** Dreaming of enduring a trial by jury may have mirrored your feeling that your behavior is being judged by others in the real world. **Right:** If a policeman cautioned you in your dream, are you feeling guilty about something you have done recently?

wear. Did you dream that you'd just been inducted into the army and were standing on the parade ground feeling quite out of place among the smartly uniformed soldiers lined up around you because you were out of formation and wearing civilian clothes? By depicting you in this scenario, your unconscious may have been underlining your uneasiness at having fallen "out of line" with those around you, perhaps with your colleagues because you haven't taken company policy seriously enough or are the only one to dress down rather than wearing a suit.

Although dreaming of being arrested by a team of uniformed policeman can, of course, hint at repressed feelings of guilt about having committed a social offence (which may have been something as innocuous as not having offered your seat to an elderly lady on the bus), such a dream may similarly indicate that you feel that you have somehow deviated from, or infringed, a social code. Did you feel contrite during your dream? If so, you probably long to regain the approval of those whose collective values the uniformed officers enforced in your dream, perhaps that of your organization's management if you have recently been cautioned about your lack of self-discipline and failure to contribute to a team project during your working hours. If, however, you resisted arrest, your unconscious may have been highlighting your lack of respect for the faceless agents of "Big Brother" and your desire to assert your individuality and nonconformist nature.

Professional Authorities

When representatives of professional authority appear in dreams, their significance (which is usually advisory) lies in their area of expertise. If your dream depicted a doctor taking your blood pressure, for instance, your unconscious may have been sending a

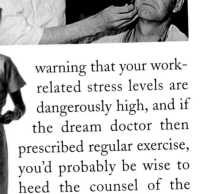

warning that your work-related stress levels are dangerously high, and if the dream doctor then prescribed regular exercise, you'd probably be wise to heed the counsel of the physician within.

Or did you dream that you were taking flying lessons from a pilot and, by following his instructions, gradually gained mastery of the aircraft? A dream like this may have been hinting that both rigorous mental control and the experienced guidance of your superiors or elders are needed if you are to steer a successful course through life. Indeed, if you can make a link with the profession that the dream authority figure embodied and the relevant area of your waking life, you may find that your unconscious has offered some illuminating advice.

Left and above left: Uniforms and badges of office symbolize the power of the state or law when they feature in dreams. **Above right and top:** If a health-care expert gave you advice in your dream, consider seeking a second opinion from a real-life medical professional.

THE BODY

If your dreaming mind shone a spotlight on part of your body, it is likely to have been highlighted for one of three reasons. The first is that it has been at the forefront of your waking mind, too. So, for example, if your dream homed in on the radically different hairstyle that your stylist gave you yesterday, your unconscious is merely mirroring reality.

The second is that you have unconsciously detected that all is not physically well: you may have dreamed of having a throbbing head, for instance, and then woke to find that you had indeed been stricken with a headache while you slept. If you are in the best of health, yet dreamed of being eaten up by cancer, however, be reassured that it is most improbable that an army of malignant cells has actually taken possession of your body. Although it is, of course, possible that your unconscious may have correctly diagnosed a serious disease like the cancer that blighted your dream, it is more likely to have used the cancer as a metaphor for an emotional, rather than a physical, problem.

This brings us to the third, and often most pertinent, explanation for a dream that features part of the body, and that is symbolism. Think of the body-related expressions that we use to describe feelings, such as "I lost my head," "I didn't have a leg to stand on," or "I couldn't stomach it." When we say these things, we don't mean that we have literally been beheaded, that our legs have been amputated, or that we have eaten something indigestible. But the unconscious often portrays exactly these images and scenarios in dreams to express the emotions that such phrases convey, namely loss of control, helplessness, or revulsion. So when trying to make sense of your dream, look especially for puns and then try to connect their meanings with your emotional response to your waking circumstances.

In Sickness and in Health

Unless you are actually in the grip of a disease or illness, a dream of being sick rarely refers to your physical health, but rather to your emotional wellbeing—although if you are profoundly worried by such a dream, particularly if it recurs, consulting your doctor may put your mind at rest. It may be, however, that by depicting you lying on your sickbed, your unconscious was warning that this is how you may end up if you continue to work 24/7 and don't take better care of your health.

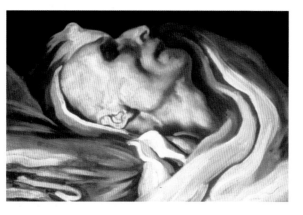

Most dreams of sickness usually refer to a psychological or emotional disturbance, and your unconscious will sometimes use the language of the medical textbooks to signal where the problem lies. So try to make a link between your dream ailment and your waking life. If your dreaming self had an asthma attack, for instance, what is causing you to "fight for breath" while you're awake? Your stifling marriage or your claustrophobic relationship with your friend? Or, if you dreamed of cancer, what is "eating away" at you during your waking hours? Could it be guilt about something you've done, or maybe the corrosive neediness of your partner? Perhaps you suffered from a dream bout of vomiting; if so, are you becoming increasingly "nauseated" by someone in the real world, or do you wish that you could purge yourself of some "sickening" problem? If you had a high temperature in

Left: A dream of being stricken with an illness is likely to have pointed toward an emotional problem rather than a physical malady.

your dream, are you in a "fever" of excitement or anxiety about an actual impending event? Could your dream numbness have been telling you that you have become emotionally unfeeling? And if you had leprosy in your dream, do you feel like a social outcast?

Dreams of physical impairment send similar messages. If someone was using crutches in your dream, was it you? If so, do you fear that you've become emotionally "crippled" and are you relying upon "crutches" such as alcohol or nicotine? But if a person known to you was limping along in dreamland, could your unconscious have been alerting you to his or her emotional incapacitation and need for support?

Bones and the Skeletal Body

Did you dream that you were looking at an X-ray of your arm, and are you indeed consciously concerned that you may have fractured it when you fell over recently? If so, your dream was likely to be mirroring your waking worries. But if you were examining a scan of your heart in your dream, and you know that your cardiovascular health is excellent, your unconscious may have been sending an entirely different message. If your waking preoccupation is with finding a solution to a problematic project at work, could it have been telling

you to look at the "heart of the matter" or, if you were poring over an X-ray, to get down to the "bare bones" of the issue? X-rays and scans reveal hidden truths, so if you were worried about someone, perhaps your friend, seeing an X-ray of your head or a scan of your brain, are you concerned that he will discover the truth about you, see you as you really are, or find out what you actually think of him?

Did you dream that you opened a closet in your parents' bedroom and got the shock of your life when the door swung open to reveal a grinning skeleton? If so, your unconscious may have been hinting that your family (perhaps including you) is concealing a "skeleton in the closet," not an actual cadaver, but maybe a family secret that is considered shameful, but would be healthier to bring out into the open.

Finally, skeletons, skulls, and

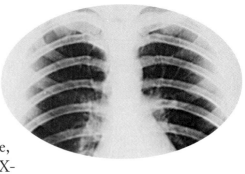

bones are all symbols of death, so if you were frightened by their appearance in your dream, this could point to your fear of dying, or of a loved one's demise. ☠

Blood and Guts

When people are mortally wounded and bleeding to death, horrified onlookers often speak of seeing the "life ebb out of them," and the symbolism of blood in dreamland is precisely that: the life force. Whether you dreamed of nicking your finger while chopping onions or that you were more seriously injured in a knife attack, your dream loss of blood may have denoted your loss of vitality in waking life—be it self-inflicted because you've been working so hard to provide for your family, or because a con-

Opposite, top: X-rays reveal hidden truths in both the real and dream worlds. **Opposite, center:** If someone used crutches in your dream, does he need emotional support in waking life? **Opposite, bottom:** A dream skeleton may symbolize a guilty secret or fear of death. **Right:** A drop of blood in dreamland could represent your recent loss of energy in waking life. **Below right:** Dream wrinkles imply worries about aging.

flict with someone is sapping your strength. If you dreamed that your partner stabbed you in the heart and you suffered a hemorrhage, for instance, could he be "bleeding you dry" in the real world through his incessant demands, so much so that he's "killing" your love for him? If you then received a life-saving blood transfusion in your dream, did you recognize the person who administered it? If you did, your unconscious may have been signaling that he or she has the potential to revitalize you. Alternatively, if you are a woman of childbearing age, a dream that features blood may sometimes herald the onset of menstruation, or else reflect pregnancy-related fears or hopes.

If your sleeping self experienced stomach or intestinal pain, the indigestion from which you may actually have been suffering, perhaps due to eating too late, may have intruded into your dream. If this is unlikely to have been the

case, however, could it be that you are finding it hard to "digest" something that you have learned in waking life, maybe something unpleasant that you have discovered about your friend, or else the overload of information that you are having to absorb in preparation for an exam? Or can't you "stomach" the idea of having to go along with the changes that are about to be enforced at work? Alternatively, could your stomach have been protesting in your dream because it was crying out for nourishment, either literally or because you are feeling starved of love in the real world? And if your intestines were the source of your discomfort, could your unconscious mind have been focusing your attention on them to ask if you have the "guts" to do something that you've been dreading, such as breaking up with your girlfriend?

The Skin
Were you deeply saddened—or even appalled—when you looked into a mirror in your dream and saw a wrinkled face gazing back at you? If so, such an image is likely to have expressed your fears, or regrets, about the inevitability of aging and the effect that it will have, or has already had, on your appearance.

Maybe you were perplexed to see a scar on your body in dreamland, even though you have no

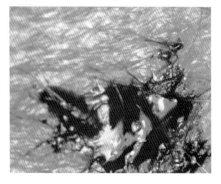

such blemish in the real world. What could that have meant? Because scars denote wounds that have healed, but are constant reminders of the original injury, could you have been "scarred for life" by an emotional hurt that someone once inflicted on you, one that you have got over, but whose memory never fades?

Perhaps you were having a conversation with a colleague in your dream when you suddenly noticed that he had a large mole on his face, one that isn't there in waking life. If so, consider the possibility that your unconscious has identified him as a "mole" and is trying to alert you to his double-dealing, perhaps by acting as a spy for a rival company. If it was you who had the mole in your dream, however, and it is also present in the real world, you may be advised to visit your doctor or dermatologist because your dream may have been warning that a melanoma is developing. Dream freckles often denote the freedom of an outdoor life, while pimples may refer to an adolescent attitude—so if you, or anyone you know, was freckled or pimply in your dream, can you draw a real-life parallel?

Finally, if your skin was itching unbearably in your dream, you broke out in a rash, or were plagued by sores, and you have discounted any physical cause for your nocturnal discomfort, ask yourself what could be acting as an irritant or allergen, or what you may be feeling "sore" about during your waking hours.

Heads and Faces

Because the head houses the brain, its symbolism is that of thinking and intelligence, of conscious reasoning and control. If you had a nightmare in which someone was threatening to cut off your head, who was that person? If it was your boss, is he putting you under so much pressure in the real world that you're on the verge of "losing your head" and doing something stupid? Or, if your friend dealt you a painful blow to the head in your dream, are you finding her reckless behavior a real "headache" in waking life? When interpreting any dream that focuses on a head, be it your own or someone else's, also consider whether your unconscious may have been referring to "getting ahead," or achieving progress (to the "head" of a family or work unit, for example), or simply to your or another person's intellect (or lack of it).

The face that we show to the world is a vital part of our persona, or the image that we present to others, and in the parallel world of dreams the unconscious sometimes passes comment on the current appearance of that "face."

So if, for example, you dreamed that your head had ballooned to double its size, could your unconscious have been signaling that you have become "big-headed," or that others perceive you as being "swollen up" with self-importance? Because faces also often betray emotions, if you saw yourself blushing in your dream, are you feeling "red-faced," that is, guilty or embarrassed about something that you regret having done during your waking hours? Or if your features were twisted into a hideous grimace in dreamland, are you currently in the grip of an "ugly" emotion, or do you worry that others may consider you repulsive, be it on account of your actual appearance or your obnoxious behavior in waking life? If your dreaming mind transformed your face into a vision of extraordinary beauty, is this how you would like others to see you? Do you long to be acclaimed for your lovely appearance or character? But if someone thrust his threatening face

into yours in your dream, it may be that your unconscious was warning that you will soon have to "face up" to something unpleasant, perhaps in connection with the person who confronted you in your dream. Did you dream that you glanced into a mirror and were shocked to see that you had no face at all? If so, do you feel that you have "lost face" recently, perhaps because someone humiliated you, or are you finding your life "featureless"?

Finally, if your dream focused on another person's face, it may have been highlighting your unconscious perception of him or her—but don't discount the possibility that the message projected by your unconscious onto his or her face may have referred to you, rather than to that individual.

Hair and Whiskers

Just as the biblical Samson lost his superhuman strength when shorn of his magnificent mane, the unconscious mind often uses hair to denote both intellectual and physical power and, in the case of

Opposite, top: A dream rash may have mirrored your own "allergic" reaction to an irritating someone, or something, during your waking hours. **Opposite, center:** If you dreamed that you had become a vision of loveliness, do you long for your inner beauty to be celebrated in real life? **Opposite, bottom:** A full head of hair signals virility in the language of dreams. **Below and right:** Eyes are instruments of vision and communication, both in reality and in dreamland, while mustaches convey male vigor.

men, virility. Because it is also crucial to our image, the unconscious may focus your dreaming attention on your hair to underline how attractive you are feeling, especially to members of the opposite sex. Hair being a reflection of general physical and emotional wellbeing, its portrayal in dreamland sends a more specific message.

Did you dream that you'd suddenly grown a luxuriant head of hair? If so, your unconscious may have been mirroring your waking satisfaction at looking good and feeling good, although it may alternatively have been compensating for your dissatisfaction with your waking appearance. But if you struggled to run a comb through your hopelessly tangled tresses in your dream, are you wrestling with "knotty" problems during your waking hours, or are you trying to extricate yourself from an emotional "entanglement"?

Maybe you were having a haircut in your dream. If so, were you instructing the barber or stylist and consciously controlling the reshaping of your image? If you were asking him to shave your head, for instance, it may be that you are itching to be free of worldly matters and yearn to lead a more ascetic life. But if you were being shorn against your will, especially if you are a male dreamer, the identity of the hairdresser is especially significant because your unconscious may have been hinting that that person is draining your strength, or

threatening your potency, in waking life. Whether you are male or female, if your hair is thinning in the real world, a dream of being bald points to a fear of failing strength, with particular emphasis on the loss of sexual virility (if you are a man) or attractiveness (if you are a woman), and may also denote worries about aging.

Although it can have symbolic significance, hair color in a dream frequently reflects your own personal preferences and dislikes, with one exception. Because white hair is universally associated with the wisdom and dignity of old age, if you dreamed of a person with silver hair, consider the possibility that your unconscious summoned an archetypal high priest or priestess to visit you as you slept, maybe in the guise of a grandparent. Did he or she give you a salient piece of advice? If so, it may have relevance to a real-life problem.

Your personal partiality, or aversion, to facial hair will often also have dictated your reaction to a bestubbled, mustachioed, or bearded man in dreamland. All types of facial hair have general connotations of "he-man" masculine vigor and strength. But if your normally clean-shaven friend, for example, suddenly sprouted impressive whiskers in your dream, could your unconscious have been warning that he is hiding his "chinlessness," or lack of courage or integrity, behind a strutting display of macho bravado?

The Eyes and Seeing

Did you find yourself gazing appreciatively into your friend's eyes in your dream? If so, your unconscious may have been mirroring waking feelings of seeing "eye to eye" with her, of being in complete agreement with each other. But if you found yourself facing your mother in dreamland, and if she told you to "Look me in the eye, and tell me it isn't true," but you were unable to meet her eye, you are probably feeling guilty about having done something which you know she'd disapprove of. Said to be the "windows to the

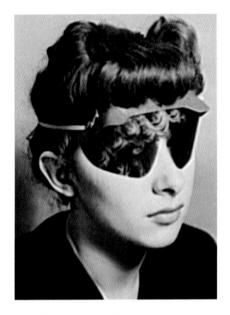

blind eye," to the truth about something. Perhaps there is an intrigue going on under your nose that you'd prefer to ignore, rather than confront? And if you found yourself wearing spectacles or contact lenses in your dream and they improved your vision, do you need to focus on an issue in order to see it more clearly? Alternatively, if you admired the *gravitas* that your dream glasses lent you, do you wish that others would respect your intelligence more?

The Nose and Smelling

What sort of nose poked itself into your dream? Was it probing and inquisitive? If so, whose was it, and could your unconscious have been signaling that he or she is "nosy" in waking life? Or did you watch with astonishment as the dream nose grew and grew? Could its owner, like Pinocchio, be telling lie after lie in the real world? If it was a Roman or aquiline nose, was your dreaming mind registering someone's leadership potential? Or perhaps you looked into the mirror and saw that your normally straight nose had been transformed into a broken one. Could the break have been inflicted, in dreamland, by someone with whom you are about to fall out in the real world?

If you had a blocked nose in your dream, you may have sim-

ply burrowed so deeply into your pillow that you were having difficulty breathing, although an alternative explanation is that something about your waking circumstances is "getting up your nose." But if your nose was assaulted by a repulsive smell in your dream, ask yourself what is rotten or corrupt in your life or, alternatively, if your unconscious may have been telling you that it had "smelled a rat," "sniffed out" trouble, or "scented danger."

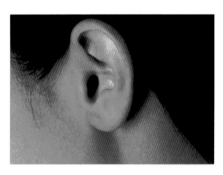

The Ears and Hearing

Did your dreaming vision home in on an ear, be it yours or someone else's? If so, could your unconscious have been alerting you to the need to keep your "ear to the ground," to stay informed about what is going on around you at work, for instance, or else to pay more attention to what people are telling you? Alternatively, maybe you have been "closing your ears" to an unpalatable truth, or perhaps someone is ignoring your opinions or turning a "deaf ear" to your entreaties for assistance in the waking world. Or could the appearance of ears in your dream have been an allusion to "wagging ears," that is, to the circulation of titillating gossip?

soul," eyes are, therefore, instruments of unconscious communication, as well as of vision.

Did the color of someone's eyes catch your own eye in your dream? If so, consider whether you regard him as a "blue-eyed boy" who can do no wrong, or her as a "green-eyed monster" possessed by jealousy, or whether you melt under the soft, brown-eyed gaze of a person to whom you are attracted in the waking world. But if your dreaming mind unaccountably inflicted a squint on you, could the message have been that you are looking at things in a skewed, or "cock-eyed," way?

Finally, if you dreamed that your eyes seemed to be glued shut, or, worse still, that you'd actually gone blind, your unconscious may have been alerting you to your tendency to "close your eyes," or "turn a

The Mouth, Tasting, and Teeth

Did you stand open-mouthed in your dream as you watched your girlfriend's lips working overtime while she berated you for your alleged unreliability? If so, your unconscious could have been reflecting your increasing intolerance of her constant nagging or stream-of-consciousness chatter. Because lips are also associated with female genitalia, your dream may alternatively have been signaling a quite different reaction to your girlfriend, one that only you can interpret. If you had any dream that highlighted a mouth, consider how it appeared: a smiling mouth clearly indicates pleasure, while a pursed or tight-lipped mouth signifies either disapproval or discretion. Now ask yourself which quality has relevance to your waking life. Or was someone, perhaps your teenaged daughter, paying "lip service" to your opinions in your dream by glibly agreeing with you, although her eyes told a different story?

Did you sit down to a lavish feast in your dream, take a bite of a succulent delicacy, but then find that it didn't register at all with your taste buds? If so, could you have lost your "appetite" for something that you once relished, and that gave you emotional nourishment, in your waking life? If, however, your feasting self seemed to be caught in a time loop in which you endlessly chewed your mouthful, could the message have been to "chew over" the facts before making an important decision? Apart from chewing, the function of teeth is to bite, so if someone you know bared their teeth menacingly at you in your dream, your unconscious may have been trying to draw your conscious attention to his or her hostility in the real world.

Most of us have the occasional anxiety dream about our teeth falling out, and sometimes the explanation has a direct connection with your real-life situation. You may have been grinding your teeth while you slept, for example. Or maybe you were actually suffering from toothache, or you are due to keep a dental appointment. But if you are at a critical stage of life, one that involves a significant change—perhaps you are on the verge of starting a new job or of being divorced—your dream may have been reflecting your emotional reaction to your impending change in circumstances. When we lose our milk teeth, we are starting to leave childhood behind; when our wisdom teeth surface, we are usually approaching adulthood; and when our teeth begin

Opposite, top: Could your dream spectacles have suggested that more focus is needed during your waking hours? **Opposite, center:** If an ear featured prominently in your dream, should you be keeping "an ear open" in real life? **Opposite, below:** Was a dream nose pointing out someone's inquisitiveness? **Below left:** In dreamland, a smiling mouth may have indicated that all is well in your waking world. **Bottom:** Dreaming of losing your teeth often reveals apprehension about entering a new phase in life.

to loosen in their sockets they usually do so because of our advanced age. Teeth are therefore associated with periods of momentous change in life, which is why the unconscious sometimes also depicts their loss in the dream world to mirror your waking sense of loss in the real world. Are you feeling regretful about what you are leaving behind and apprehensive about what your new job or life as a single person will bring, for example? Or are you worried about losing your youthful good looks, "losing your bite," or vigor, or of being unable to "bite back"? If your teeth were crumbling in your dream, are you being "ground down" in waking life?

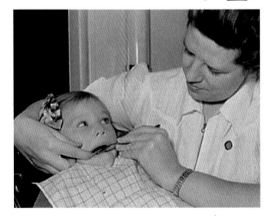

The Throat and Neck

Were you alarmed to find yourself choking in your dream? If you wrenched yourself out of your asphyxiating nightmare and sat bolt upright, you may have corrected the cause: your tongue's

temporary obstruction of your airway while you were lying on your back. It may alternatively be that your unconscious was portraying your waking sense of unhappiness, your feeling of being "choked up" with grief. But if someone was choking you, or you were throttling another person in your dream, your unconscious was almost certainly highlighting feelings of personal hostility.

You may have been aware of having an ache in your neck while you were dreaming, and then awoke to find that you had indeed developed a cricked neck, in which case your unconscious was merely incorporating your actual discomfort into your dream. But if all was well with your neck, ask yourself whether your unconscious could have graphically portrayed a pun and, if so, why. Are you being a "pain in the neck," or "getting it in the

neck" from someone in waking life? Are you "sticking your neck out" over something or taking a significant risk—indeed, even "risking your neck"? Or are you "up to your neck" in problems?

The Shoulders and Back

Did someone place a heavy load on your shoulders in your dream? If so, who? If it was your sister and she has asked you to take charge of her chaotic financial affairs in real life, could your unconscious have been mirroring your waking sense of having been burdened with "shouldering" the responsibility for her monetary problems? Did you stagger under the weight or struggle determinedly on? The dreaming mind sometimes uses the shoulders as a symbol of support, and another interpretation to consider is whether you, or another person in your life, need a "shoulder to lean on."

If you were stricken with a backache in your dream, it may be that it was real, but if this was not so, ask yourself whether your unconscious could have been focusing on your "backbone" for a specific reason. Are you, for instance, considering "backing down" over a contentious issue at

work, and could the message have been that you're about to behave "spinelessly"? Or is something going on "behind your back"? But if your father, for instance, turned around and walked resolutely away from your dreaming self and he's recently expressed disapproval of your lifestyle, do you fear that he's about to "turn his back on you" in the waking world?

The Chest and Heart

The chest (was someone's puffed out with exaggerated pride in your dream?) houses many of the internal organs—notably the heart, whose primary symbolism in both the dreaming and real worlds, is, of course, love. Did simply catching sight of someone you know cause your heart to jump in your chest in your dream, and, if so, why? Could your dreaming reaction have been prompted by feelings of love, or, alternatively, of shock or fear? Your dream may have been signaling how you really feel about that individual.

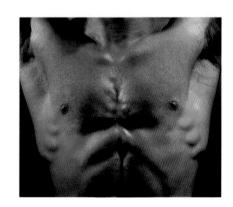

The heart's physiological function is to pump blood around the body, so if you felt it faltering in your dream, your unconscious may have detected that it isn't performing as well as it should. So, if your dream worries you, consult a doctor. Otherwise, could the message have been that your emotional strength is failing because your difficult partner is placing too many demands on it?

The Arms and Hands

In the secret life of dreams, arms generally denote strength, and hands and fingers dexterity, but it is important to consider how your unconscious depicted them when trying to interpret your dream, because they often convey more subtle inferences.

Did your boss welcome you into his house with "open arms" and then tell you that he considered you his "right-hand man," for instance? Did your mother lovingly wrap her arms around you and reassure you that everything would work out alright? Did you notice your friend's clenched fists in your dream, and have you actually argued, or could your unconscious have been alerting you to her "tight-fistedness?" Do you wish that your sister would "lend a hand"? Are you "armed" with enough information for your forthcoming exam? Could your dream of dropping a

hot plate have been warning that you'll get your "fingers burned" if you attempt to grasp the money-spinning opportunity that you've been offered on a plate in the real world, because it's "too hot to handle"? Is your relationship with your partner based on a healthy balance of "give and take"? Perhaps your fingers and thumbs turned green in your dream. If so, could your unconscious have been encouraging you to "turn your hand" to cultivating your garden? Similar expressions may also have relevance when considering the meaning of a dream that shone a spotlight on arms, hands, or fingers.

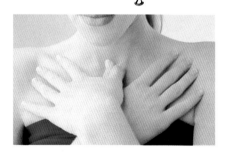

Breasts and Genitalia

If a pair of exposed breasts featured in your dream, your gender is likely to have determined your reaction to them, and hence their significance to you. If you are a woman who was enchanted by a dream tableau of a mother breast-feeding her baby, you are probably yearning for a child of your own. But if you are a man, it is more likely that you are crav-

ing mothering, to be taken into someone's bosom and given the emotional sustenance that comes with "mother's milk." But when a sleeping man is thrilled by a woman's baring of her breasts in dreamland, the unconscious is usually fulfilling his wishes.

Genitals are, of course, the instruments of sex, and your dreaming response to them is likely to have betrayed your real feelings about sexual intimacy, and perhaps also anxiety about your sexual performance, especially if you are a man. But were you astonished to see that you had developed the genitalia of the

Opposite, far left: If your neck troubled you in a dream scene, is someone being a "pain in the neck" while you're awake? **Opposite, center:** A dream that shone a spotlight on your back may have been urging you to develop some "backbone." **Opposite, bottom:** If your upper torso was highlighted in your dream, is there something you're longing to "get off your chest"? **Top left:** If your heart troubled your dreaming self, could it have reflected the "heartache," or "broken heart," that you're nursing? **Above left and top:** Dream breasts can signify erotic arousal or motherhood.

opposite sex in your dream? If your most fervent desire is a sex-change operation in the waking world, your unconscious was literally making your dream come true, albeit only in your sleep. But if the thought of undergoing gender reassignment appalls you, the meaning of your dream is almost certainly less sinister than you may fear. Our personalities all harbor characteristics of the opposite sex, and your dream may simply have been signaling the need to tune into your masculine or feminine side, particularly with regard to your sex life (do you secretly wish that you could be more assertive or submissive in bed?) And if you were confused to discover that you'd turned into a hermaphrodite (someone with the sexual organs of both sexes) in your dream, your unconscious may have been highlighting your waking confusion in the face of a decision whose pros and cons appear to be equally balanced (only you can know if your dream referred to sexual confusion).

If you are a man who dreamed that your normally loving partner suddenly bared her fangs and was about to bite off your penis, you suffered a classic male anxiety dream. But why would your unconscious have inflicted such a fearful image on you? Well, in symbolic terms, the penis represents masculine power, so it may be that you are feeling "emasculated" by your dominant partner's tendency to wear the trousers in

your relationship and that your dream reflects your feelings of "impotence" (which may also have a literal parallel) and loss of self-respect. But if you are a woman who castrated a man in the dream world, the meaning is reversed: you deeply resent that individual's power over you and long to render him impotent.

The Legs, Knees, and Feet

Unless they mirror an actual physical problem or waking concern, dreams of the legs, knees, and feet generally refer to issues

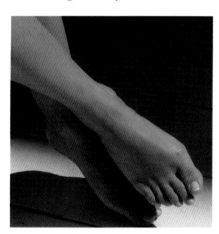

of progress or support (or the lack of either) in the real world. So if, for example, you were frustrated to find yourself hindered by a limp as you hurried to catch a dream train, could your unconscious have been saying that something is hampering your career progress during office hours? Or, even worse, if your dreaming self was appalled to discover that you had no legs at all, have you come to a standstill in waking life and do you feel powerless to move forward? Alternatively, perhaps you were

so frightened in your dream that your legs "turned to jelly" and you were unable to "stand up for yourself." If so, who, or what, caused you to feel such extreme fear?

Although knees are part of the legs, their symbolism usually refers to paying, or being shown, respect, or else to supplication. If you were gratified to see your colleague kneeling in front of you in your dream, and he was initially dismissive of an idea of yours that your boss later thought brilliant, could your unconscious have been rewarding you with his respect (especially if it has not been forthcoming in the real world)? But if you were kneeling in front of your wife in your dream and you are feeling guilty about your recent behavior toward her, was your unconscious urging you to plead for her forgiveness when you woke up? Proposals are also traditionally made on a bent knee, so if your dreaming mind depicted your boyfriend kneeling in front of you, are you actually hoping to become engaged? Alternatively, if you were kneeling before him in your dream, has his incorrigible philandering brought you "to your knees?"

Because bare feet come into direct contact with the earth, if you dreamed that you were walking barefoot in the park, could your unconscious have been highlighting the need to "ground" yourself better in waking life? Or maybe your dream was confirming that you are at last standing on "your own two feet" now that you've left school and started work in the waking world. Did you "put your best foot forward" as you stepped out jauntily along the dream highway, or did you "drag your feet," thereby signifying reluctance? Could your dreaming self's itchy feet have betrayed your unconscious desire to travel and see the world?

Bodily Functions and Cleanliness

When we urinate or defecate, we are ridding ourselves of bodily waste, and when the dreaming mind portrays us performing these functions, the reference is similar—albeit to emotional waste, such as unpleasant memories, or tough lessons you have digested that are now redundant (but are nevertheless burdening your mind). So if your dream depicted you rushing to the bathroom and emerging with relief, what would you benefit from flushing out of your system in the real world? The occasionally troubling memory of a vicious argument with a schoolmate, whom you haven't seen for years and are unlikely ever to meet again, perhaps? Or do you wish that you could "purge" yourself of the toxic jealousy that you know is poisoning your relationship with your girlfriend?

Did you have difficulty "letting go" in your dream, were you incontinent, or did all proceed satisfyingly smoothly? The answer will tell you whether you are emotionally "constipated," "blocked," or "anally retentive," emotionally out of control, or else functioning quite healthily. Perhaps you were desperate to find a toilet, but searched in vain, or maybe it was locked in your dream. In such instances, it may be that you still haven't found the catalyst for, or key to, emotional release. Alternatively, if you or your property were defiled by someone else's urine or feces, do you feel that you have been contemptuously taken advantage of, or "dumped on," by the culprit in waking life?

If your dreaming mind homed in on a scene in which you were frantically washing yourself, of what were you trying to cleanse yourself? Did you have someone's blood on your hands? If so, you may be feeling guilty about having metaphorically stabbed your coworker in the back in the real world, perhaps by having deliberately thwarted her hopes for a promotion, and you consequently have a stain on your conscience. Or maybe your friend refuses to listen to your advice and you wish that you could simply "wash your hands" of her. Alternatively, do you long to wash away the memory of an abusive relationship, thereby enabling you to resume your life refreshed and renewed?

Height and Visibility

Were you delighted to find that you'd turned into a giant in your dream? If so, and you've recently been promoted at work, your unconscious may have been mirroring your waking feelings of self-satisfaction by portraying you walking "ten feet tall." But if you were horrified to discover that you'd shrunk to miniature proportions, it may be that you are feeling insignificant and "looked down upon" by those in your waking life, or that you long to shrink away from a problematic situation. Dreams of being invisible send similar messages of either feeling overlooked by others or of wishing that you could leave your troubles behind by "disappearing."

Opposite and left: Dreams of well-tended feet and of shapely buttocks may be erotic, but they can also symbolize something in your waking life. **Above:** A dream of shooting upward in height may have reflected your perception of yourself as being a person of stature or greatness.

🌀 CLOTHING AND ADORNMENTS 🌀

Whether you select them carefully or simply throw on the first garments that come to hand in the morning, your clothes make a statement about the sort of person you are. And when people meet you for the first time, their initial impression will, no doubt, be based on what you are wearing. Perhaps they'll mentally brand you a fashion victim or a slob, a sober businessperson, or a bohemian, creative type. Similarly, you may be unconsciously intimidated by a person in uniform, and you may even cross the street to avoid someone whose ragged garments identify him or her as a down-and-out. Clothes therefore project an image, whether consciously manipulated or accidental, which is why they are such an important part of the persona, the façade that each of us presents to those around us.

As well as transmitting a visual signal that informs others about our personality, job, status, and values, our clothing also reflects our self-esteem, or lack of it—the nature of our self-image being betrayed by our choice of apparel. And when the unconscious assumes the function of a behind-the-scenes costume director in a dream movie production, its selection of garments will tell you much about how you perceive both yourself and the people in your life. This chapter explores the dream-world symbolism associated with various types of clothing and adornments; but for dreams of being inappropriately clothed or naked, consult the chapter on Anxiety and Frustration; for dreams of wedding-related clothing, refer to the Marriage chapter; and for dreams that focus on uniforms, refer to the text on Authority Figures.

Image Projection and Image Consciousness

Did you astonish yourself in a dream of shopping for clothes, when you excitedly picked out a garment that you'd never consider wearing in a million years in real life? If you normally dress conservatively, for instance, maybe your dream depicted you trying on a daring new style that your sensible, conscious mind (had it been in control at the time) would have branded outrageous, and certainly not for you. If so, your unconscious may have been indicating that you have become too set in your ways and outlook, so much so that others may regard you as being boring and predictable, and perhaps with good reason. Although you may balk at buying a similar outfit in the waking world, is it time to jazz up your image, to open your mind to alternative opinions, and maybe even to live a little dangerously? And if it is, would your adoption of a more fashionable image be prompted by your own yearning to break out of a rut or would it be more concerned with making the people in your life sit up and take notice of the surprising new you?

Conversely, if you dress ultracasually during your waking hours and you dreamed of wearing a business suit, could your unconscious have been hinting that you'd benefit from adopting, or projecting, a more businesslike or professional image? And if you were trying on someone else's clothes for size in a dream bedroom, was your dream highlighting your desire to be like that person? If so, ask yourself what you particularly envy or admire about him or her.

Maybe you were surprised by the color of the clothing that you, or another individual, wore in your dream. If so, does that particular hue have personal significance to you, so that you respond to it either positively or negatively? It may be, for example, that you love yellow because it conjures up a vision of sunshine, but that you have an aversion to green because it reminds you of the green uniform of your unhappy schooldays. Individual associations apart, bright, vibrant colors generally express cheerfulness or exuberance, while dark or drab shades usually convey sadness or depression. Pure white, furthermore, denotes innocence; and black, mourning. What was the emotion or quality that was being signaled by the color that caught your attention in your dream, and who was projecting it through his or her clothes?

Were you dressed in expensive designer clothes and did you relish the feeling of basking in others' admiration in your dream? If so, you may have enjoyed a wish-fulfillment fantasy, especially if you are very fashion-conscious, although your unconscious may also have been mirroring a more general desire to rise in status. But if you were clothed in shabby old garments in dreamland, and you felt miserable and self-conscious, it may be that this is precisely how you are feeling in the real world, and that your unconscious was telling you that you are perceived as such, too. And if you found yourself sewing a patch onto an article of clothing in your dream, was your unconscious speaking in puns? Is there some-thing in your life that needs "patching up"? Alternatively, if you were stitching a patch onto the sleeve of a dream shirt, could the message have been that, after many years of exposure, you are trying to hide something about yourself from others, such as the big, easily broken heart that you've tended to wear on your sleeve until now?

Fabrics and Fastenings

If you are a woman and dreamed that you felt all of your senses come alive as you ran your hands down the fabulous satin evening gown that you were wearing and cast appreciative glances at your reflection in the mirror, your unconscious was probably merely reflecting your desire to look equally stunning in waking life. (And if it was a wedding dress, it may be that your most fervent wish is to be married—or not, depending on whether you felt elated or suffocated by your dream gown.) Because such prized fabrics as silk, chiffon, and leather denote high quality (and the means to afford them), their inclusion in dreams may also reflect a dual longing to be perceived as a cut above the rest and to enjoy a luxurious lifestyle. In addition, because they titillate the senses of sight, touch, smell, and hearing by their shimmering or transparent appearance, their silky or

Opposite: If you dreamed that you were inappropriately dressed for an interview, should you project a more professional image? **Left:** A dream of wearing clothes that made you feel frumpy may have mirrored your poor self-image. **Below:** Did your dream reflect your desire to project a stunning image to others?

smooth feel, the unmistakable aroma of real leather, or the rustling that they make as the wearer moves, such materials may also have connotations of sensual—even sexual—arousal in dreamland.

Your unconscious may, by contrast, make use of manmade fabrics like nylon, polyester, or plastic in the dream world to point out that someone's appearance or persona (perhaps even yours) is artificial—or else that his or her (or your) means are limited. These fabrics can also feel itchy, so if you were maddened by the irritation that your manmade clothing inflicted on your tender skin in

your dream, can you draw a parallel with an unbearable irritant in your waking life? Or was your itchiness self-inflicted: is your conscience constantly being pricked by feelings of guilt, and did your unconscious emphasize your discomfort by forcing you to wear a "hair shirt" in your dream?

Whether or not you were wearing an instrument of torture, did you rip off the buttons of your blouse or shirt in your dream? If so, have you been too "buttoned up" in the waking world, to the extent that you're bursting to tear down your façade, relax your guard, and reveal the real you? A dream of letting out your belt a notch with a sigh of relief may, by contrast, have mirrored a release from a constricting pressure in waking life. But if you tightened your dream belt, your unconscious may have been alerting you to the metaphorical need to "tighten your belt," that is, to economize. And if your dream homed in on a zipper, you may also want to mull over the puns associated with zips. Do you long for more "zip," or thrills, in life? Should you "zip up your mouth" and keep your thoughts to yourself? Or, if your dream zipper would not budge, however frantically you tugged at it, are you feeling similarly "stuck" in the teeth of a dilemma or in a humdrum existence, and do you crave release?

Hats and Headgear

With the exception of such casual headgear as baseball caps, few of us wear hats on a day-to-day basis, although women sometimes get decked out with them for special occasions like weddings. Therefore, a dream hat may denote a laid-back attitude or a team allegiance on the one hand, or a festive mood on the other, and, if everyone had donned similar hats in dreamland, collective values. The wearing of hats of one kind or another was, however, almost socially compulsory in times past, so if you dreamed of a man who was wearing an old-fashioned hat, with whom do you associate it? A derby with old-time comedians Laurel and Hardy, for instance, or with a family photograph of your great-grandfather? A slouch hat with a gangster like Al Capone

or a debonair actor of the era of black-and-white movies? If you can identify the association, try to draw a parallel with the dream wearer and your waking life.

But if you dreamed that someone, maybe you, was wearing a skull cap, an item of apparel that remains a sign of religious observance (when worn for example, by Jewish males or by Roman Catholic dignitaries), what does it tell you about that individual, whether or not you know him to be pious? Indeed, as well as denoting authority (be it spiritual or otherwise), because hats are worn on the head, whose traditional symbolism is that of intelligence and higher consciousness, any dream hat may symbolize aspirations, whether they are being protected from an emotional rainstorm or attention is being focused upon them. Did you have a feather in your cap in your dream? If so, was it your "thinking cap," and are you feeling pleased with yourself for having solved a particularly difficult problem recently? If you were wearing a tall hat in your dream, but everyone around you was bareheaded, what could the aim of your unconscious have been in depicting you set apart from the crowd by your headgear? Do you think differently from those around you? Did you tip your hat to anyone, thereby paying a like-minded soul respect? Or was it knocked off by someone, perhaps because she accused you of having ideas above your station? And if your head was graced with a magnificent crown, have you been elevated in your own eyes by an outstanding personal achievement, one that you feel deserves the acclaim of others in waking life?

Shirts, Collars, and Neckties

If your dreaming vision zoomed in on a shirt, it may just have been an unconscious reminder that you need to iron your shirt when you awake, or even that you should buy a new one.

Otherwise, consider your dreaming mood in the light of the following puns. Were you clinging on to someone's shirttails, and are you overdependent on his help in the real world? If you rolled up your shirtsleeves, is a forthcoming task looming large in your conscious mind? Or are you in danger of "losing the shirt off your back" and going bankrupt?

If you were being choked by an unbearably tight collar or necktie in your dream, your unconscious may have been expressing waking feelings of restriction, maybe in relation to your job (particularly if a necktie was responsible, this being an item of apparel that is worn almost exclusively by professional men). Alternatively, the dream may have been literal, in that you may have developed a sore throat during the night, your discomfort simultaneously being incorporated into the dream scenario. And because neckties offer sober-suited men a way of expressing their personality (some analysts believe the tie can also be a phallic symbol), if a necktie drew your dreaming attention, who was the person wearing it and what did it look like? Was it flashy, conservative, colorful, or wacky, and what does its appearance say about its wearer—perhaps you?

Opposite page: In dreams, as in real life, headgear can signal a celebratory mood, draw attention to your achievements, or mark you out as being above the crowd. **Above left:** Neckties and bowties offer men a means of self-expression, be it in the real or dream world. **Top right and right:** A dream that featured swimwear may have been encouraging you to take a much-needed vacation.

Sleepwear, Swimwear, Lingerie, and Pants

If you dreamed that you were lounging around the house in broad daylight in a comfy nightgown or pajamas, your unconscious may merely have been encouraging you to relax and catch up on much-needed sleep. And if you were frolicking on a dream beach in a bikini or bathing suit, maybe you were enjoying a wish-fulfillment dream and it's high time that you took a vacation. Perhaps you enjoyed flaunting your body in sexy lingerie in the dream world, in front of a person to whom you're attracted to in the real world. Did your "come-hither" strategy work? If so, your unconscious is, again, likely to have been granting your wishes, albeit only during your sleep.

But if you were mortified when you looked down at your lingerie in your dream and saw with a start of horror that it was dirty, could you be harboring feelings of sexual guilt? Or did

you feel humiliated in your dream when someone—perhaps your wife—discovered you with your pants pooled around your ankles? Did your unconscious portray you like this to warn that you are in danger of being caught with your "pants down," perhaps because you've been having an affair? And if you are a man who dreamed that you were the object of a jeering crowd's derision because you were not wearing pants at all, did you feel ashamed or panic-stricken? A dream like this may have been expressing either fear that your true sexuality is about to be exposed or concerns about your sexual potency. But if you dreamed that your wife, who prefers to wear skirts in the real world, strode across the stage of your dream in pants, could your unconscious have been mirroring her tendency to "wear the pants" in your relationship?

Shoes and Socks

Did you dream that your shoes caused you agonizing pain because they pinched or rubbed? If you did, you may actually be suffering from a foot disorder whose symptoms intruded into your dream. Alternatively, because feet are a symbol of advancement, and shoes enable us to walk for long distances, is your freedom of movement being

restricted in the waking world? Have you been feeling the financial "pinch" recently? Maybe your dream pain was inflicted because you were wearing another person's shoes. If so, could your unconscious have been advising you not to judge her so quickly because if you were able to "walk a mile" in her shoes, you'd soon discover that she finds it harder to make progress than you?

If you dreamed that you laced up a new pair of hiking boots and then set off enthusiastically to explore new pastures, your boots were clearly made for walking, and your unconscious may have, therefore, been encouraging you to indulge your passion for travel and exploration. But if you were shocked to find your booted self trampling on your prostrate junior colleague in your dream, could it be that you are "walking all over" him during office hours? And if your dream shoes were down at heel, did they correspond with how you are feeling in the real world, that is, shabbily treated and downtrodden?

In the secret life of dreams, socks that are full of holes may similarly hint at feelings of demoralization, feelings that you may be managing to hide from others by concealing them with metaphorical shoes. But if you were perplexed by a

dream in which you waved a sock at someone, did you do so merrily or threateningly? Depending on your relationship with that person during your waking hours, could you have been inviting her to "sock it to me" or, in other words, to impress you? Or were you warning that you were about to "sock," or hit, him?

Coats and Coveralls

When we put on a coat, cloak, or overalls, we usually do so for a practical purpose, namely to protect ourselves from the cold or else from the dirt and debris of our working environment. So if you dreamed that you were wearing any of these garments, what sort of contamination are you trying to ward off in the waking world? An icy atmosphere at home, perhaps, or the fallout from a messy situation in the office?

Because these articles of clothing are also concealing, could a dream of wearing a camouflage jacket have been indicating that you're trying to hide the real you from others, and to protect yourself from potential exposure and attack by blending into your surroundings? What is it that you are trying to cover up from the scrutiny of those around you?

Handbags, Purses, and Wallets

The very thought of losing our handbag, purse, or wallet makes most of us shudder while we're awake, so if your unconscious inflicted such a disastrous dream scenario upon your sleeping self, you must have had a nightmare. Your dream could, of course, have been simply alerting you to the need to be less careless with your possessions or to be more security-conscious in waking life, but another interpretation may be pertinent, too. Handbags in particular are highly personal items, in which women carry everyday and emergency objects, not to mention address books and cell phones—keys to communication with the people in our lives. The loss of a dream purse, if you are a woman, or a brief case, if you are a man—and, more importantly, its contents—may thus reflect anxiety about a loss of identity, or of the various aspects of our character or life that together make us unique individuals. If, however, you were rooting around in another person's bag in your dream, you're probably curious to know more about them, to discover what makes them tick.

As symbols of femininity, handbags and purses may also symbolically refer to female sexual organs or the womb. So if you are a woman who dreamed that you snapped your handbag shut to stop your husband from taking coins from your wallet, could you be feeling angry with him for undermining something that you value in life (not necessarily money, but perhaps happiness), so much so that you're giving him the cold shoulder in bed? Or were you ashamed by your scuffed and shabby bag? If so, are you feeling sexually unattractive during your waking hours?

Umbrellas and Gloves

Umbrellas are protective accessories, so if a sudden downpour rained down upon your dreaming self and you were forced to take shelter under an umbrella, are you feeling under siege in the real world? Because rain shares water's symbolic association with the emotions, are you being battered by a storm of turbulent emotions, perhaps even your own?

Did you pull a pair of gloves on or off in your dream? If so, can you remember why? If you took off your right-hand glove in order to shake hands with someone, your dream gesture clearly reveals friendly feelings for that person. But if you did not greet his appearance in your dream with pleasure, were you "taking the gloves off," thereby showing your willingness to "fight dirty," whether or not the dream gloves were boxing gloves? If you put on a pair of gloves in your dream, could it have been because you are worried about "revealing your hand," be it your true motives or the metaphorical "ace" that you're hiding up your sleeve? Or is someone in your waking life behaving so unpredictably that you feel compelled to treat her with "kid gloves"? Alternatively, is there an unpleasant task that you'll soon have to undertake in the real world, one with which you do not wish to "dirty your hands"?

Masks and Costumes

Did you dream that you came face to face with someone in your dream, except it wasn't really face to face because he or she was wearing a mask? If so, did you try

Opposite center: If you flaunted your sexy lingerie in a dream, who were you hoping to seduce? **Opposite bottom and top:** Shoes can denote how you are progressing along life's path, so was your dream footwear individualistic or uniform? **Above:** A purse is a symbol of feminine identity. **Above right:** If you used an umbrella in your dream, are others' accusations raining on you in the real world?

to snatch off the mask to reveal the person's identity? A mask is the symbol of the persona, the face that we present to the world, so your dreaming reaction was probably sending a powerful message that you believe someone to be wearing a "false face." Who, in the real world, do you wish would either "abandon the act" or "unmask"? But if you were wearing the mask, what is it about your true nature that you're concealing from those around you? Although they also hint at flirtatious behavior, fans similarly hide the holder's face, as do veils (which furthermore have connotations with grief or mystery) and hoods (which have sinister associations with death), so if any of these accessories featured in your dream, try to make a link with your waking world.

Perhaps you attended a dreamed masquerade, where all of the guests, including you, were masked. If so, could your unconscious have been referring to a real-life situation that is also a "masquerade," a pretence in which you, and those around you, are colluding, such as pretending to admire your new boss when you actually loathe her? If you found yourself at a fancy-dress party in dreamland, what

sort of costume were you wearing? If you were dressed as Napoleon, for example, could your unconscious have picked this costume to highlight your desire to show off your leadership potential? Alternatively, if you are a woman who was outfitted as a man, or a man who was in drag, could your unconscious choice of outfit have been intended to draw attention to your masculine or feminine qualities?

Jewelry and Gems

Did you dream that you were thrilled when your boyfriend presented you with a sparkling engagement ring, and are you hoping that he'll propose to you in the real world? If so, your dream was mirroring your waking wishes. Whether you are single or married, a man or a woman, receiving a gift of jewelry denotes the love and appreciation of the giver, so that the purpose of your unconscious in presenting you with a glittering love token in your dream may similarly have been to fulfill your deepest desires. Was a brooch or badge pinned like a medal onto your breast? If so, how was it fashioned, and for what achievement or quality were you being honored?

Unless you dreamed of a specific piece of jewelry that you either covet or actually own (and if you lost it in your dream, your unconscious may have been sending you a literal warning that its clasp is loose), dream jewelry, gems, and precious metals rarely represent themselves. Instead, these items embody a precious abstract value or quality, such as the inner beauty, vivacity, or purity of the recipient, or the commitment, loyalty, love, or friendship of the giver. Rings, in particular, symbolize partnership, and bangles and bracelets also denote wholeness and eternity through their circular shape. But did you dream that a necklace, or a string of beads or pearls, that your partner had given you, suddenly broke while you were fingering it? If so, is there a weak link in your relationship, one that could cause your commitment to each other to disintegrate completely unless steps are taken to strengthen it? Earrings draw attention to the ears, so if the camera of your dream production zoomed in on an earring, could it be alerting you to the need to keep your ears open during your waking hours?

Although gemstones can have general symbolic significance (a diamond, for instance, denoting hardness or wealth), if you dreamed of a particular precious or semiprecious stone, its significance is likely to relate to your personal association with it, perhaps because it is your birthstone or it was your mother's favorite stone. But, because a precious stone can represent both the inner self and the "gem," or partner, in your life, if you admired its cut, could your unconscious have been highlighting the brilliance of your multifaceted personality? Or else, could your unconscious have been directing your conscious eye to the many sides of a relationship that, in your real life, seems one-dimensional? Did you take your husband's gift of a gold, diamond-set necklace to a jeweler to be cleaned, only to be shocked when you were told that it wasn't worth the effort because it was a fake? If so, your dreaming mind may have spoken reams about the true nature of your marriage: has your husband been stringing you along all the while? You may have thought that he had a "heart of gold," or that he was a "diamond," one in a million, but, on consideration, is he actually also a "fake"?

Cosmetics and Body Art

Were you carefully applying makeup in your dream? If so, what did you see when you looked appraisingly in the mirror to check the effect? If you are a woman and you were pleased with your appearance, your unconscious may have been signaling your conscious feelings of self-approval and confidence regarding your appearance. Alternatively, and especially if your self-image is poor, your dream may have been responding to your wish to present a more attractive face to others, be it literally or metaphorically. And because lips are symbolically associated with female genitalia, a dream of applying lipstick may furthermore have signaled a desire to attract the attention of a potential lover (who was your dream date?). But if you are a man who was applying cosmetics in dreamland, could the message have been to adopt a more feminine approach to a problem in your waking life, perhaps by being more empathetic?

Whether you are a man or a woman, did the dream scenario portray you anxiously trying to conceal blemishes or flaws on your face with base, foundation, or concealer? Were there pimples or dark circles under your eyes? And do you wish that you could hide your adolescent viewpoint or mental fatigue from those around you? Or were you trying to transform your appearance completely, much as an actor applies greasepaint or dons a mask, in order to present a totally different "face" to your "audience"?

Did you dream of having yourself tattooed? If you found yourself in a tattoo parlor in the dream world, what motif did you choose, and for which part of your body was it destined? If it was a butterfly to embellish your ankle, could your unconscious have been highlighting your chronic flightiness and inability to stay in one place for long, your desire to fly free, or your yearning for transformation? If you had your partner's name tattooed on your chest, could your dreaming mind have been underlining your enduring love for her? But if you watched as a skull-and-crossbones took inky shape on your arm, could your dream have been making a statement about your incorrigible tendency to cause mayhem in waking life? In both the dream and real worlds, tattoos denote permanence, while decals imply a current fad, so if you dreamed of either, heed the message of your unconscious.

Opposite, center left: Why did your unconscious select such a wacky alter ego if you wore a comedy mask? **Opposite, bottom:** If you adopted a Napoleonic persona, do you secretly wish that others would acknowledge your leadership qualities? **Opposite, center:** A dream ring may have symbolized love and commitment. **Left:** Body-piercing often highlights attention-seeking tendencies in the language of dreams. **Below:** Your choice of dream tattoo may have revealed your true colors.

THE HOME

It's not really surprising that so many of our dreams are played out against the backdrop of the home. After all, not only do we spend a considerable amount of time in our homes, they are places in which we have usually invested much of our money, energy, and hopes for the future. They are also personal havens to which we return from our forays into the unpredictable outside world, places in which we feel secure and where we can relax and be ourselves.

Dream homes can, however, represent far more than just accommodation. Jung famously termed the house the "mansion of the soul," and most analysts agree that houses frequently transcend their mundane function as places of residence in our dreams to become symbols of our holistic selves: body, mind, and spirit; physique, personality, and aspirations; past, present, and future. When interpreting a dream that featured a home or house, you'll therefore need to decide whether your dream was literal (if you were clearing out a dream attic, is this on your list of things to do?) or whether it relates to some aspect of yourself (could your dream be telling you to sort through, and maybe reassess, your spiritual values?). Taking note of the emotions that the house evoked in you, be they of pride, satisfaction, safety, confusion, foreboding, or fear, will help you to clarify the dream message.

Houses and Gardens

If the house that featured in your dream was your actual home, and some aspect of it was highlighted with which you are currently pre-occupied in waking life, your dream may simply have been reflecting your concern. If, for instance, you dreamed that you were decorating it and you've been meaning to do so, but keep putting the job off, your dream may be telling you that it's high time you picked up your paintbrush. If,

however, there's no clear connection between that aspect of your dream and your waking life, or if the dream house is unfamiliar to you, it may be that it relates to something about you yourself.

Was the residence that you dreamed about one that you once lived in, but that is no longer your home? If so, it may be referring you to some nuance of your past that has a bearing on your present situation. If you were happy there, dreaming of the home in which you grew up, for instance, may signal a yearning for the security or carefree times that you enjoyed in childhood, or may reflect feelings of nostalgia. If, however, you dreamed of a house that you associate with unhappy memories, it may be that you are repressing feelings about something that happened there that you need to face up to in order to

move on. And if you dream that you are packing up your possessions prior to moving house, it is likely that you are indeed ready to enter a new phase in your life. Maybe your dream home was a house that you've never seen before, or perhaps you were even engaged in constructing a new

Opposite and left: Houses represent you as a whole: your body, mind, and spirit. **Above:** If a house purchase is at the forefront of your mind, dreaming of buying a house either reflects your waking concerns or fulfills your wishes, albeit only in the dream world.

Above: An isolated, down-at-heel house mirrors both your current state of mind and appearance. **Right and opposite:** Be they ordered and tidy, or cheerfully colorful and somewhat out of control, dream gardens reflect your personal growth.

home. Such dreams similarly suggest that you are considering making a dramatic change to your life, even to the extent of rebuilding it completely.

What form did your dream house take? Was it a mansion, a cottage, a semidetached house, a condominium, or even a mobile home? The answer to this question will tell you both how you view yourself and how you relate to others. If you dreamed of owning a grand mansion or snug country cottage, you may simply have had a wish-fulfillment dream: perhaps you wish to climb to the top of the social tree or are looking forward to a happy retirement, in which case these houses represent your "dream home." Because these buildings are usually set apart from other proper-

ties, ownership may alternatively signify that you are a self-contained person, unlike the inhabitants of semidetached houses or apartments in condominiums, with whom some interaction with neighbors is inevitable. A mobile home or caravan, by contrast, implies a peripatetic, adventurous, or rootless personality.

Whatever the type of house, was the exterior immaculately presented and in a state of good repair, shabby and somewhat dingy-looking, or dilapidated and in urgent need of remedial attention? The appearance of the façade is related to your persona—how you present yourself to other people—and hence also to your feelings of self-respect. If the house was structurally sound and gleaming with a fresh coat of paint, for instance, it is likely that you also project an aura of stability, self-confidence, and pride in yourself, but if the dwelling looked uncared for and its wood- and paintwork were starting to flake away, you might be starting to let yourself go, while

if it looked a total wreck, it may be that you have become depressed and emotionally withdrawn and no longer care what others think of you. Another consideration to take into account is how easy or difficult it was to gain access to the house. Was it surrounded by a forbidding-looking fence or hedge? Physical obstacles like these can represent on the one hand the barriers that you may have thrown up to prevent people from getting too close to you, or, on the other, may suggest a need to become more self-contained and less open to others' demands. And if a fence was broken, ask yourself if you need to "mend fences" with someone you've quarreled with recently.

Did your dream house have a garden? If so, how did your garden

Structural Features

If your dream home represents yourself, what did your dream tell you about your foundations and structure? Were they sturdy and able to withstand all that the weather threw at it? If you dreamed that your house was built on subsiding land and seemed in danger of collapsing, ask yourself if the values and relationships that underpin your life are in danger of giving way. Was the roof intact, had it developed holes or, worse still, was it so rotten that it seemed on the verge of falling in? A sound roof suggests that you will be able to stand emotionally and spiritually firm when buffeted by the tempests that sometimes blow up in life; a leaky roof implies that you are increasingly being affected by the drip, drip, drip of some niggling emotional or aspirational irrita-

grow? Considering its features will tell you whether you are successfully cultivating the seeds of your potential or are instead allowing them to become choked by weeds, as well as indicating how you perceive peripheral aspects of your life. If your dream garden was a floral paradise, an exuberant riot of color, it indicates that your endeavors have caused your personality to flourish and blossom. But was the garden rather too tidy and somewhat sterile in appearance? If so, you may be taking an overly controlling, excessively organized approach to life, nipping something about your personality in the bud and thereby preventing it from flowering and achieving its full potential. An overgrown, weed-choked yard, by contrast, warns that you have so neglected your personal growth that you have ceded control. Is it time to take command, to clear away the weeds, cut back the overgrown shrubs, let in the sunlight, and start nurturing your talents?

As well as being dedicated to growth and cultivation, gardens are places of private recreation, contemplation, and relaxation. Were you alarmed to see a trespasser invading your personal sanctuary? If so, you may be unconsciously aware of a threat that someone poses to your emotional security by trying to get too close to you. Dreaming of your house being burgled sends a more powerful warning: is someone trying to violate your privacy by forcing his or her way through your personal defenses? Another interpretation may be that you fear being robbed of something that you value, not necessarily your own cherished possessions (though the dream could indeed be urging you to replace a broken lock or install a burglar alarm), but perhaps a new idea, your integrity, or your good looks. Pondering the burglar's identity, point of access, and target will help you to pinpoint the source of your fear.

warmth prevails, but because a chimney's second symbolic significance lies in its phallic shape, it may also suggest sexual heat, or possibly an absence thereof.

Did the walls of your dream house attact your attention? If so, how did they make you feel: were you securely enclosed or hemmed-in and claustrophobic?

Depending on the emotions that they aroused in you, your home's walls could signify either solid protection from the hostile forces without or unwelcome confinement. Whatever you decide that they represent, remember that they are walls that you yourself have constructed around you and that you have the power either to strengthen or demolish them. Take note of their color, too, because that may have an important bearing on the message of your dream.

Doors and Windows
Did you open a door in your dream home? If so, what lay behind it? Doors are transitional points that offer new openings and fresh opportunities: open a

Opposite, top: A dream burglar warns that someone is trying to breach your personal defenses. **Opposite, below:** In dreams, the roof represents your ability to withstand the storms of life. **Left:** A cozy hearth symbolizes emotional warmth. **Below:** Locks and keys signify secrets and solutions, respectively.

door and cross the threshold, and you have left an old place or situation and now face an entirely new scenario, sometimes inspiring and exciting, sometimes daunting and worrying, but always replete with possibilities. More specifically, a front door usually admits unfamiliar outside influences (and if your unconscious homed in on a doormat, are you allowing others to walk all over you?), while a back door sees more familiar traffic in the form of people with whom we have comfortable, informal relationships. If your dreaming mind portrayed you stepping through a door, it signals your willingness to embrace change—maybe even the unknown—while letting someone in through a door indicates that you are willing to interact with him or her. If you were faced with a bewildering array of doors, however, you could be feeling overwhelmed by a myriad of choices in life and unsure which opening is the right one for you.

Alternatively, did your dreaming self search des-

tion; and a dilapidated roof warns that the very structure of your life is on the point of collapsing on top of you.

Chimneys usually have one of two symbolic meanings in the dream world. The first relates to the hearth, the traditional heart of the home, around which family members gather to warm themselves and relax together at the end of the day. If your dream home had a smoking chimney, its smoke signal imparts a message that an atmosphere of emotional

perately, and fruitlessly, for a door through which to make your escape? If so, the lack of an exit point suggests that you feel trapped within a certain situation from which you feel that there is no way out, but because the unconscious mind sometimes uses the symbol of a door to represent the mouth, it may also be that you feel unable to express yourself or to speak out about something of concern.

If you were confronted by a locked door in your dream, what was your reaction? Were you furious or curious? If the former, your unconscious may have been signaling frustration that an opportunity seems to be closed to you. If the latter, it signifies that something is being withheld from you and that you are longing to make the breakthrough and to learn what lies within. Did the locked door

lead to a room? If so, consulting the associations given below for the various rooms in a house may point you toward the nature of the secret. If it was a cupboard door, it may contain something that your conscious mind has suppressed, a "skeleton in the closet" whose existence you are trying to deny or forget about, but that nevertheless haunts your unconscious.

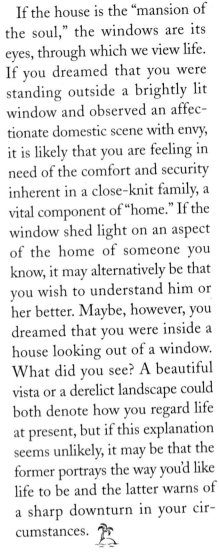

If the house is the "mansion of the soul," the windows are its eyes, through which we view life. If you dreamed that you were standing outside a brightly lit window and observed an affectionate domestic scene with envy, it is likely that you are feeling in need of the comfort and security inherent in a close-knit family, a vital component of "home." If the window shed light on an aspect of the home of someone you know, it may alternatively be that you wish to understand him or her better. Maybe, however, you dreamed that you were inside a house looking out of a window. What did you see? A beautiful vista or a derelict landscape could both denote how you regard life at present, but if this explanation seems unlikely, it may be that the former portrays the way you'd like life to be and the latter warns of a sharp downturn in your circumstances.

But what if your dream home had no windows at all? If this was the case, or if drapes obscured your view of the outside world, it is likely that you are taking a shuttered approach to life, preferring either to close out outside influences and live in your own world or to shut your eyes to a specific problem. Opening the drapes, however, will let in the light and open your eyes to a world of possibilities, while opening the window denotes a willingness to let some "fresh air" into a life that has, perhaps, become stale.

A Tour of the Dream Home

Perhaps you dreamed that you unlocked the front door and entered a house. Did you find yourself in a hallway? Like doors, hallways and corridors represent places of transition and choices to be made. Where did you decide to go? Down into the basement or cellar? If so, you probably descended the stairs with some trepidation, wondering uneasily what you would find there. In dreamland, these underground rooms symbolize the unconscious mind, where our "baser" instincts, energies, and urges are stored and where we conceal things that we would rather not put on display: possibly things about which we feel ashamed, yet cannot bring ourselves to let go of or throw away, but also items

that we don't need right now, but may come in useful in the future. But then wine is traditionally kept in cellars, and the contents of the unconscious can similarly harbor valuable treats that we bring out with a flourish for special occasions. Did you enter the cellar to seek out an issue that you either need to confront to find peace of mind, or else to bring to light, and make good use of, a bold quality that you've suppressed in waking life?

Maybe you ignored the stairs and decided to investigate the ground floor, the floor that symbolically denotes the conscious mind. If you went into the living room or dining room, how did it look? Homey and comfortable, elegant and imposing, cluttered and untidy, or dusty and shabby? These are the rooms in which we usually receive and entertain guests, and their decoration and condition in your dream will tell you how you regard, and socialize with, those whom you invite into your home, that is, the collective body of people with whom you have contact in your waking life. Are your social skills easy and welcoming, grandiose and a little intimidating, confused and flustered, or rusty and awkward?

Did you enter your dream home's kitchen? If so, was it warm

Opposite page: In dreams, windows reveal our view of life, or lack of it. A shuttered window suggests that you have chosen to close your eyes to the outside world, while a view from a dream window usually represents how you currently regard life. **This page:** Specific items of furniture and furnishings can symbolize aspects of your personality, such as your solid, no-frills, traditional nature or your zany streak and love of novelty. The purpose to which they are put may also be sending you a message: if you dream of a chair or sofa, do you need to take it easy? If you focused on a light or lamp, are you looking for illumination?

and welcoming, with a saucepan bubbling merrily on the stove, and, when you opened the cupboards, were they full to overflowing? Or was it a cold, sparsely furnished space, notable mainly for its austere atmosphere and lack of food? Kitchens are rooms in which we transform raw ingredients into hearty, delicious dishes with which to feed and satiate ourselves and others, thereby giving both physiological and emotional satisfaction. What did your dream kitchen tell you about how well you nourish yourself or, alternatively, are nourished? Is your emotional life replete, or is it starved of love and affection? Did the kitchen encourage you to linger by offering rich food for thought, or was it a barren room that depressed you because it offered no temptations or stimuli?

Below: Dreaming of climbing the stairs to the attic indicates the need to transcend everyday matters and to revisit your highest aspirations. **Bottom:** A dream fourposter bed signifies a yearning for old-fashioned romance. **Right:** Attics contain all kinds of "lost" treasures. Did your find remind you of something that you've long been meaning to do?

If you left the kitchen in search of a more welcoming room, maybe you climbed the stairs to the next story of the house. Ascending a flight of stairs denotes another transitional state, in this case, following your rising aspirations. The second floor of the dream house represents a higher level of consciousness beyond the day to day, and here we find bedrooms and bathrooms. Was your dream bedroom your ultimate personal refuge, a place where you felt safe and secure enough to surrender yourself to the oblivion of sleep? Or was it a bower of love? Your answers to these questions will usually reflect your current needs, be they for rest and recuperation or erotic stimulation and sexual satisfaction. Bathrooms, on the other hand, are rooms in which we clean our bodies and rid ourselves of waste matter. If you dreamed of washing your hands or taking a bath or shower, is there something that you're anxious to "wash your hands of," someone that you wish you could "wash out of your hair," or troubles that you long to send spiraling down the plughole? All of these actions imply the need to cleanse yourself of an issue that is tainting your conscience, while using the toilet implies a need to relieve, or even purge, yourself of problems or unwanted feelings or memories. We also tend to look at ourselves the most critically in the bathroom mirror. What did your reflection look like? Did you see a different person? Did your appearance please or worry you? The answers to all of these questions relate to your self-image.

Did you end the tour of your dream home in the attic? In actual life, this room is scarcely visited, but is nevertheless a repository for cherished items of sentimental value like journals, photograph albums, and clothes that we can't bring ourselves to throw away because they evoke such powerful memories. Despite the cobwebs that may festoon it because we pay it so little attention in our busy waking lives, the attic symbolizes rarefied consciousness and is a place of ideals and even spirituality. If you found yourself discovering a long-forgotten treasure in this room, does it remind you of an aspiration that you once cherished, but that has lain dormant because you've been too overwhelmed by the demands of working and family life to pursue it? Did you grab a broom and start to brush away the cobwebs, thereby making sweeping changes? (Indeed, if you wielded any household implement in your dream, it's helpful to consider its function and relate it to something that's been troubling you. If you dreamed that you were wielding a pair of scissors, for instance, is there a connection that you need to sever?)

Finally, if you were astonished when you stumbled across a "secret" room while touring a dream house that you thought you knew, be it in the basement or on one of the above-ground stories, you should consider whether it represents a quality that you never knew you possessed. Now that your unconscious has prompted you to discover it, will it provide you with inspiration, along with the wherewithal and self-confidence to take a new direction in your waking life?

FOOD AND DRINK

When we eat and drink in the real world, we are usually responding to the physical triggers of hunger and thirst that prompt us to provide our bodies with the nutrients needed for health and performance. Yet unless you went to bed hungry, or became increasingly dehydrated during the night, dreams that feature food and drink rarely refer to a physical requirement for nourishment, instead pointing to a need for emotional, intellectual, or spiritual sustenance, or else sensory, or sexual, gratification.

Dreams of being parched with thirst, drinking, or being drunk; cooking, comfort eating, or enjoying a meal; fasting, dieting, or gorging on food, therefore, all send powerful messages about your current state of mind. And if a specific food or beverage was highlighted by your unconscious, understanding its symbolic significance may be of further help when trying to decode your dream.

Thirst, Drinks, and Drinking

Did you dream that you were besieged by an overwhelming thirst for a long drink of cool, refreshing water as you were making your way through an arid, sun-scorched landscape? If so, it may, of course, have been that you had become hotter and hotter, and thirstier and thirstier, as you slept, and that your unconscious worked your physical discomfort into your dream. If you don't believe that this explanation applies, however, considering your dream in symbolic terms may enlighten you. In the language of the unconscious, water is often used as a metaphor for the emotions, so could it be that you are beginning to feel emotionally parched, perhaps because you have been single for so long in waking life? Are you "thirsting for" affection and longing to "drink in," and be emotionally revived by, someone's love? ∞

Maybe you dreamed that you made yourself a mug of warm milk and observed to your dreaming self that this reminded you of your childhood, when your mother used to give you a drink of milk at bedtime. If this is the case, and you are finding waking life particularly demanding, your dreaming mind may indeed have provided you with a sensation of warmth, comfort, and security, such as you enjoyed when you were small, in compensation for your currently stressful circumstances. Because we relied on our mothers for milk when we were babies, your dream may also have been referring to your need to be mothered and cherished by a maternal figure (if not your actual mother), a provider of the "milk of human kindness." And if you are a woman who was breast-feeding an infant in your dream, or who poured a glass of milk for a toddler, and you are not a parent in the real world, the implication may be that you're hoping

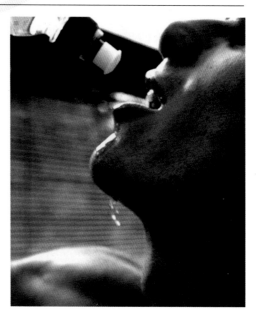

Above: A dream of being so parched that all you could think about was quelling your raging thirst usually has one of two interpretations. Either your body really was dramatically dehydrated or your dream was mirroring your emotional deprivation.

to become one soon. Whether you are a man or a woman, an alternative interpretation for a dream in which your unconscious shone a spotlight on milk is that it may have represented semen, and thus your desire for a sexual relationship.

Did you enjoy a cup of tea or coffee and a good gossip with your best buddy in dreamland? Although a dream of these beverages will probably have reflected your personal preferences, people generally drink tea when they feel in need of a break, and coffee when the brain needs a kick start, so that in dreams, tea may signal the need for relaxation, and coffee for stimulation. But, be it tea, coffee, or alcohol, dreaming of having a drink with friends may refer to a social life that has dwindled into nothing and could do with reviving. If you felt suffused with a sense of wellbeing as you shared a beer or a bottle of wine with someone during your dream, your unconscious may have been showing that you'd benefit from enjoying some stimulating conversation while you relax in the company of friends in the waking world. And if you

popped open a bottle of champagne in your dream, are you celebrating a real-life achievement, or are you hoping to?

If, however, you were dismayed to see your dreaming self intoxicated and lurching drunkenly all over the place, there are a number of possible explanations to consider. Firstly, if you tend to hit the bottle during your waking hours, could your unconscious have been mirroring reality by portraying you as a drunkard? Secondly, and especially if you rarely drink alcohol, if at all, are you in danger of losing emotional control in real life? Or, thirdly, are you actually feeling "drunk" with success? If so, could your unconscious have been warning that it's time to reign in your exuberant triumphalism because it's starting to annoy those around you? If it was your friend who was inebriated in your dream, any of these interpretations may also be pertinent, but if she drunkenly accused you of

undermining her confidence by constantly criticizing her, don't dismiss her dreamland message. There is some accuracy in the Latin phrase *in vino veritas* (wine reveals the truth), so consider whether your unconscious could have put these accusatory words into her mouth to alert you to an uncomfortable fact.

This page: A dream of sharing a beer, giggling over cocktails, or having a cup of tea with a friend may have been advising you to prioritize your social life. But if you watched your dreaming self becoming drunk, your unconscious may have been admonishing you. **Opposite:** Dreams of eating or cooking often indicate a need for emotional sustenance, intellectual stimulation, sexual gratification, or parenthood.

Hunger and Eating

Were you so ravenous in your dream that you went rushing urgently up and down the street looking for a fast-food restaurant, but in vain? If you later awoke feeling equally starving, your dream was almost certainly literal, but if you awoke only mildly looking forward to breakfast, the explanation for your enormous dream appetite may lie elsewhere. Deprivation sharpens the appetite, so ask yourself for what you are hungering, or of what you are currently starved, during your waking hours. Could it be the comfort of a fulfilling emotional or sexual relationship, or the satisfaction that comes from enjoying your job and doing it well? Or is it "food for thought," or intellectual stimulation, that is lacking from your life at the moment? Similarly, if you dreamed of comfort eating, the most likely

explanation is that you turned to eating in the dream world (as you may also be doing in the real world) in an attempt to fill a gaping emotional hole. What is currently missing from your waking situation that is so crucial to your emotional wellbeing? What really whets your appetite for life?

Did you dream of relishing a delicious meal with your family and friends? If so, and your dream mirrored reality, your unconscious was clearly emphasizing the emotional nourishment that you receive from your loved ones, as well as the stimulation that you derive from "feeding off" their ideas. If you were the dream cook yourself, it is likely that your family members rely on you to give them love, comfort, and support. So did you feel contented or resentful as you prepared the dream meal? And because a cook transforms raw, often indigestible, ingredients into a palatable dish, is there something that you're "cooking up" during your waking hours, perhaps a plan that's simmering in your mind that you hope will soon be ready to set before others? Similarly, if you were baking, what could you have been incubating in your

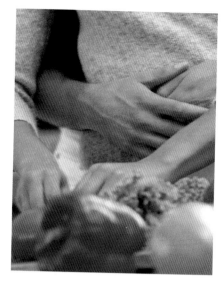

dream oven? An idea? Or, if you are a woman who is hoping to conceive, could your dream have expressed your urge to become pregnant, or to "have a bun in the oven"? But if someone else was bustling around the dream kitchen in an apron, you probably regard him or her as a source of emotional sustenance.

If you found yourself enjoying a dream date in an intimate corner of a restaurant, who was sitting across the table from you? If it was someone to whom you're attracted in real life, your unconscious was, no doubt, signaling your desire to have a closer relationship with him or her, be it a sexual one or an emotional or intellectual meeting of the minds. Further clues may lie within the dream scenario. Swallowing oysters, licking dripping butter off asparagus spears, or sucking the juice from a luscious fruit, for instance, all point toward sensual and erotic arousal; sharing a green salad or rice-based dish may denote a desire for a fresh, uncom-

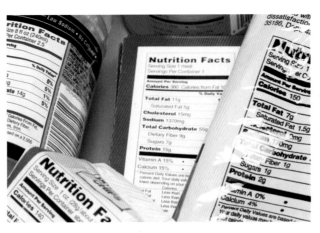

plicated, or "wholesome" relationship; while feeling your tongue tingle as you tasted a tart dish may signify a need for verbal or intellectual stimulation.

Weighty and Dietary Issues

Did you dream that you had ballooned into an obese person in your dream, and were you so shocked by your bloated appearance that you immediately resolved to go on a fast? Or maybe you were bingeing greedily on a mountain of food in your dream because you'd suddenly become a wraithlike figure who urgently needed to pile on the pounds. Either dream scenario may, of course, have mirrored waking reality (although, in reflection of your poor self-image, your unconscious probably exaggerated your actual fatness or thinness), but if you aren't consciously preoccupied with your weight or counting the calories, you were probably baffled by your dream.

If your dream focused on the need to diet in order to lose weight, do you feel weighed down by weighty problems that you long to shed in the waking world? Otherwise, could your dream have implied that you are

suffering the consequences of overindulging, not necessarily in food, but perhaps in a hobby with which you've become obsessed, so much so that your waking life has become unhealthily imbalanced? Alternatively, if you are studying for an exam in the real world, have you "taken in" so much information that your brain has become overloaded and feels as though it is ready to burst? If your dream was concerned with being too thin, however, have you been starved of vital nourish-

ment—be it emotional, sexual, spiritual, or intellectual—in the real world, and are you metaphorically wasting away as a result? Was someone turning a deaf ear to your pleas and withholding food from you in your dream

Top and left: If you were obsessed with counting calories or monitoring your weight in an anxiety-ridden dream scene, but have no such concerns in waking life, could the reference have been to ridding yourself of an overload of obligations? **Above:** A dream of preparing a meal for four and then greedily devouring it yourself may have implied that you are feeling starved of something that is vital to your sense of wellbeing in the real world.

Left and right: A dream of suffering from malnutrition may have referred to emotional starvation, but a dream of craving fish ("brain food") may have urged you to nurture your intellect. **Below:** Dream candy may have advocated rediscovering your childlike side. **Below left:** Bread is a symbol of survival, in both the real and dream worlds. **Below right:** If you are Christian, a dream of Easter eggs may have been holding out the hope of spiritual rebirth.

kitchen? If so, could that person be responsible for your emotional malnourishment, or was he or she trying to protect you from your self-destructive appetites? And if your dreaming self knew that a bout of food poisoning was responsible for your thinness, could whoever had cooked the tainted dream meal (do you know who it was?) be deliberately trying to poison your mind by feeding it toxic thoughts in the waking world? Or are you literally poisoning yourself, perhaps with your excessive nicotine, alcohol, sugar, or saturated-fat intake?

Food for Thought

Whatever it was that you were eating in a dream, your response to it is likely to have corresponded to your waking likes and dislikes, so that if you loathe cabbage, but your mother made you eat it as a child, you may associate it with punishment. Religious observances regarding food may also send powerful signals when they feature in dreams, so that, if you are Jewish or Hindu and were forced to eat pork or beef at a dream table, the message may have been that you are being metaphorically contaminated in waking life by intimate contact with something that you consider forbidden or impure. The following foods have universal symbolic significance, however, as do certain fruits and vegetables, for which refer to pages 223–29.

Bread has been a staple food for centuries in the West, which is why its primary symbolism is that of life and survival (and, if you are a Christian, your dream may have been referring to spiritual sustenance). When trying to interpret a dream in which bread appeared, also consider some of the expressions associated with it. If you were "breaking bread" with your troubled friend in your dream, are you "casting your bread upon the waters" in the real world—that is, selflessly helping her out, even though you know that she isn't in a position to return the favor? Did you dream of having a sandwich at work? If so, are you employed in a mere "bread-and-butter" job—one that pays the bills, but does nothing else for you? Or could your unconscious have been using slang? Did the "bread," or "dough," in your dream refer to money, and perhaps the butter with which it was spread to your ineffectiveness in negotiating a pay increase because you are "as soft as butter"?

The symbolism surrounding eggs is also ancient, and focuses on birth, be it literal or metaphorical, as well as on the potential for spiritual regeneration and growth (an association that is underlined by Easter eggs, which may have particular significance in dreams if

Below and bottom: The inclusion of a sugar-laden dish like a pie or cake in a dream scene may have reflected your waking sense of finding life sweet at present. **Below center:** Did your dream of tucking into a succulent roast turkey refer to your carnal appetites?

you are Christian). If you are a woman who is hoping to have a baby in waking life, a dream of an egg may, therefore, have reflected your desire to conceive. But if you were gathering eggs from a dream chicken coop, yet you decided to leave one behind on the spur of the moment, could your dream have been highlighting the potential "hatching" of an idea that is currently gestating in your mind? There are also certain egg-related verbal expressions that you should take into consideration. If you were busily transferring eggs from the hen house to a basket in your dream, are you actually contemplating putting "all of your eggs in one basket" by taking an all-or-nothing gamble in the real world? Or if, after your dream breakfast, you looked in the mirror and saw that you had egg all over your face, have you actually made yourself look stupid recently?

If you were eating meat in your dream, have you been "chewing over" a "meaty," or substantial, piece of information that's come to your waking attention? Or if you distractedly prepared a beef pot roast for supper, are you currently "in a stew," or troubled, because you have a "beef" with your husband's tendency to stay out until late at night? Alternatively, and especially if you craved the taste of meat, even though you knew that you were in a vegetarian household in your dream, could you be yearning to savor the "sins of the flesh," or to satisfy your sensory or sexual carnal cravings? And if you relished the exotic taste of your dream curry, do you long to "spice up" your waking life?

Salt is said to be the essence of life, so if you dreamed of sprinkling salt all over your food, what is essential to your life? And if you dreamed of grinding pepper over your meal, could your unconscious have been encouraging you to "pep up" your waking existence, or was it referring to your "pep-

pery," or uncompromisingly honest, tongue? If you drizzled oil over a dream salad, are you trying to smooth things over in the real world, or are you "pouring oil over troubled waters," perhaps because you're having to keep the peace between your wife and daughter? And if you then added vinegar to the dream dish, could your unconscious have been commenting that your waking role as a peacemaker is proving difficult because of your wife's "vinegary," or acerbic, views? If you devoured pickles—perhaps gherkins—in dreamland, are you currently in a mess, or "a pickle," in the real world? Or if you reached for a dream mustard jar, are you hoping to "cut the mustard," or to satisfy your own expectations at a forthcoming interview?

If you dreamed of savoring the sweet sensation of eating honey, sugary cookies, pies, cakes, or desserts in your dream, your unconscious may either have been expressing satisfaction with the sweetness of your actual circumstances at present, or else compensating you for their bitterness. Is your life currently as "easy as pie," or do you wish that it was? Are you longing for a "piece of the cake," or are you already enjoying it? But if you dreamed of eating gelatin or popcorn, is an element of childish fun and excitement lacking from your waking world?

ANIMALS

Whether reassuring or terrifying, dreams that feature animals can often be difficult to interpret, and you may have to use a process of elimination when trying to decipher the message sent by your unconscious. The first thing to consider is your emotional response to the dream animal in waking life. You may, for instance, either adore dogs and regard them as loyal companions because you have always had a pet dog, or else be afraid of them and view them as hostile attackers because you were bitten by one as a child. If, however, your feelings about the creature concerned are neutral, try to identify the quality with which you primarily associate it: perhaps a tiger with ferocity or a mouse with timidity. Because animals are said to represent our base instincts and urges, it may be that your unconscious used the tiger or mouse to highlight your own, or someone else's, innate fierceness or shyness. Thinking about that aspect of yourself, or of another person, within the context of the dream should then tell you whether it is striving to come to the fore, or has already done so, in waking life. But if you remain puzzled about what the creature could have represented, it may be that the animal's symbolism lies in an archetypal, traditional, mythological, or legendary association or that it embodied, or acted out, a pun.

Pets

Many of us willingly share our homes with animals, and when a past or present pet appears in a dream, your unconscious may simply be a reflection of your conscious feelings toward your creature companion, be they of affection, anxiety, or loss. If, however, you don't have a pet and don't want one in the real world, but dreamed of cooing over a cute kitten or puppy, it may be that your dream emphasized your desire for a human baby rather than a feline or canine one. Alternatively, and particularly if your dream pet was fully grown, your unconscious may have summoned it into your sleep to represent someone in your real life (perhaps you) who is feeling very vulnerable and who would appreciate some emotional "petting." Another possible interpretation to consider is whether the animal that featured in your dream depicted you, a facet of your character, or your reaction to your present circumstances. Are you so dependent on your girlfriend for scraps of affection that you feel more like her puppy than her boyfriend, for instance? Or if you looked through the bars of a cage and watched a hamster running fran-

tically around its wheel in your dream, are you feeling equally confined—as though you are pounding away at the treadmill of waking life, always striving to move forward, but not getting anywhere?

If a dog romped through your dream, was it friendly or aggressive, and what are your conscious feelings about dogs? If you like the canine species and the dream dog and you struck up an instant rapport, it may be that you are craving more fun and friendship in the

This page: If it featured a pet, your dream may have reflected your affection for your furry friend. But you may want to lavish love on a fellow creature, not necessarily an animal.

waking world. Since dogs are traditionally regarded as faithful companions and protectors who love their owners unconditionally, it may be that your unconscious was either highlighting these qualities within yourself or else underlining your desire to have an emotional shield from the upsets of the real world in the form of a person whose fidelity and devotion to you is beyond question. Dogs can, therefore, represent friends in the language of dreams. So if your unconscious depicted you walking a pack of

Maybe an enormous dog started barking as you approached it in your dream, the barking giving way to ominous growling and then to the baring of fangs. If dogs make you apprehensive, your unconscious was probably just reflecting your waking fear. But if this does not explain your dream, it may be that the dog represents a friend (maybe an out-and-out "bitch" who, until now, has been unusually nice to you) who is about to turn on you in the real world.

and whether its demeanor typifies a pun. If you dreamed of a dog whimpering pathetically in its kennel, for example, are you currently feeling like a "whipped dog," or as "sick as a dog," because you are now "in the doghouse" at home?

And if your dream pet dog bit you, could its behavior have mirrored that of your teenage son, who has metaphorically "bitten the hand that feeds" him by exhibiting surly ingratitude toward you recently?

While dogs are generally symbols of masculinity, cats usually represent femininity in the language of symbolism—that is, unless you are a man and your dream focused on a strutting tom, in which case it may have referring to your tendency, or desire, to "tomcat" around with women. Also perceived as enigmatic, independent creatures, with astonishing survival skills (the proverbial "nine lives"), dream felines can denote feminine mystery, wisdom, and intuition. But

dogs, each straining so hard at the leash that you were having difficulty keeping them under control, could your dream have been referring to a waking struggle with your buddies? Are you attempting to keep a check on their enthusiasm for a current fad, a passion that you do not share and that is threatening to run away with them? And if the pack did indeed break away in the dream park, are you afraid of losing your friends' loyalty?

Alternatively, could the barking of the dream dog have signaled a warning that the "animal" in you, perhaps your anger, is on the verge of breaking free, causing you to launch a vicious attack on the person who provoked your rage while you were awake? If so, is your "bark worse than your bite"? In any dream scene that involves a dog, also consider how it behaved

when interpreting your dream, your real-life reaction to cats is crucial. If you like them, and a member of the feline fraternity sauntered into your dream, it may have been a manifestation of one of the positive aspects of the female principle (the mother, princess, amazon, or high priestess), one that has pertinence

to your life as a woman. But, if you are male, it may have been your anima, similarly guiding your unconscious attention toward a facet of your feminine side. Could your dream have been telling you to rely on your instincts when dealing with a current problem? If you dislike cats, however, your dream feline may have represented a negative feminine archetype (the terrible mother, siren, huntress, or witch), an association that is underlined if you believe that cats are aloof, dangerously alluring, cruel, or evil creatures. Or is there a stealthy and deceitful woman in your life (maybe you yourself) who is behaving "cattily," or spitefully? Alternatively, did the cat's behavior in your dream remind you of a pun? Are you feeling smug in waking life, like the "cat that ate the canary," or were you even being

reminded that "curiosity killed the cat" and being warned not to probe too deeply into an intriguing mystery in the waking world?

Agricultural Animals

Because agricultural animals are neither pets nor wild creatures, their symbolism in dreams often refers to personal qualities that you have tamed to a certain extent, although there remains a danger that they will escape your conscious control and run amok. Taking the context of the dream into account is especially important when trying to analyze a dream that featured a working or farmyard animal, because it may mirror your feelings about the impositions under which you are laboring in waking life.

Ever since humankind first tamed the horse for use as a means of transport, it has been credited with a number of symbolic attributes, including nobility. Its primary significance in dreams, however, is unconscious energy and drive, which, if the dream horse acquiesces, is controlled by the rider (the conscious

Opposite page: Canines can be friends and protectors or aggressors. Was your dream dog underlining a waking prejudice? **Left:** A caged cat is a sad sight, and if you dreamed of a captive kitten, was the reference to your own crippled independence? **Below:** If you dreamed of a sheep, are you feeling "sheepish," or embarrassed, in real life? **Bottom:** Horses often symbolize unconscious drive in dreamland.

mind), but which may buck against the rider's restraint if the steed is headstrong. So if you were riding a powerful horse in your dream, did you relish the exhilarating feeling of being at one with your mount? If so, the implication was that your rational mind and your emotional needs are working in harmony. But if the horse skittered, reared, and tried its utmost to unseat you, your dream may have been warning that you are trying in vain to restrain an urge that will no longer be repressed, be it by you or by a person who dominates your waking hours. This urge may be emotional—are you unconsciously rebelling against "being taken for a ride" by your overly demanding boss?—or physical, and because

mounting and sitting astride a horse have obvious sexual connotations, the message may refer to your conscious suppression of your sex drive. Try to put yourself in the dream-world horse's position. Are your unconscious needs refusing to be bridled? Are they harnessed and under control? Are they being reined in or given restrained head? Are they trying to escape? Or was your "nightmare" even running riot? Remember the many puns associated with horses and horseback riding, too. Are you currently "riding high," or feeling assured, for instance? Or could your confidence be misplaced arrogance, so that you are actually on your "high horse" and "riding for a fall"? Have you been "riding roughshod" over someone's opinions in the real world, or were you just "horsing around"? And if your mount was newly shod with horseshoes (symbols of luck) in the dream, are you hoping that your waking hours might be touched with good fortune?

Although asses, or donkeys, and mules can also be ridden, humans mainly use them as pack animals, so if one of these beasts

of burden plodded through your dream, have you been feeling weighed down by others' demands and unappreciated in real life? How did the dream donkey react to carrying its weighty load? If it trudged along uncomplainingly, the message may have been that you will, or should, exercise similar patience and stamina in dealing with your workload. But if the dream mule came to an abrupt halt and then flatly refused to budge, would you benefit from following its mutinous example in the waking world, or is some other person being as "stubborn as a mule"? Again consider the puns: who is being "an ass," or foolish, in waking life? Is it you?

Many ancient peoples venerated cows (notably the ancient Egyptians) as well as bulls (the Minoans and ancient Romans, for instance), and cows are still regarded as sacred creatures in Hindu India. In symbolic terms, milk-producing cows represent the nurturing mother archetype, so if you are a woman who is yearning to start a family and dreamed of a cow contentedly feeding her calf, your unconscious may have been reflecting your waking wishes. But if you are already a parent of teenagers and

your dreaming vision homed in on the calf, could it have been a reference to your daughter's "calf love," or recent crush on someone? Alternatively, and whatever your sex, if you dreamed of a herd of cows placidly chewing their cud in a field, could your dream have been mirroring the bovine, or sluggish and complacent, attitude that you've adopted when you're awake? Has your tendency been to go along with the views of the "herd"? And if a cow threatened to attack you in dreamland, have you, or has a woman whom you dislike, been behaving nastily to others, or like "a cow," in the waking world? Oxen are castrated bulls, emasculated beasts who have to work hard for their keep, so if you dreamed of watching a pair of cattle pulling a plow, do you similarly feel that you are

Opposite, top: Are you controlling, or being driven by, your unconscious energy, or personal "horsepower"? **Opposite, center:** Was the mule that dug its heels into your dream mirroring your own stubbornness? **Opposite, below:** Could a dream cow have symbolized your maternal instincts? **Right:** Llamas and goats represent agility. **Below:** The appearance of a flock of sheep in dreamland may have symbolized your conformist tendencies.

"under a yoke" and being forced to toil ceaselessly on others' behalf when you're awake?

Unlike cows, bulls are emphatically not placid creatures, instead being decidedly temperamental and even dangerous when provoked with the proverbial red rag. And unlike oxen their fury is testosterone-fueled, which is why their symbolic associations center on masculine virility, might, and anger. If you are a man who dreamed of being a matador in a bullfight, your unconscious may have depicted your waking struggle with subduing the beast within, possibly your lust. If so, are you losing the fight, or would you secretly be happier if you did? And if you are a woman who was charged by a snorting bull in a terrifying dream scenario, can you

link it with a sexually aggressive man by whom you feel threatened in the real world? If, however, the dream bull was quietly minding its own business and you are interested in astrology, could it have represented someone you know who was born under the zodiacal sign of Taurus? Or if your waking preoccupation is with financial matters, could your unconscious have depicted a bull to stress your hunch that the stock market is going up, or to encourage you to buy some shares that you suspect you could later sell at a higher price?

If you dreamed of being surrounded by a flock of sheep in a dream pasture, the message from your unconscious may be that you are not being assertive enough at work. Perhaps you have been falling in line with your intimidated coworkers, who would rather toe the party line than rebel against company policy. If so, is it time to express your individuality, to break free of the flock mentality, and thus regain control of your life? Lambs are traditionally associated with gen-

tleness, innocence, and sacrifice. If you identified with a lamb in your dream, do you feel like "a lamb to the slaughter," that is, unable to resist the tendency of another person, or many people, to take advantage of your good nature, even though your acquiescence is now "killing" your emotional health? Of all of the members of the ovine family, the ram, or the male sheep, is the most wayward and self-confident, which is why its symbolic significance revolves around rampant masculine sexuality. Can you equate your dream ram with a man who is known to you in waking life or, if you are male, with your own sexual needs? Otherwise, could this thrusting creature have represented someone born under the zodiacal sign of Aries? "Separating the sheep from the goats"(did you dream of doing this?), goats are renowned for their individualism, their mischievousness, and also their lustfulness. So if a goat, or perhaps someone with a "goatee" beard, caused havoc in dreamland, who is causing similar mayhem in the

waking world, and is he "getting your goat," or annoying you, with his idiosyncratic or salacious behavior? Or is an aspect of yourself making a desperate bid for self-expression?

Whether you dreamed of a pig, hog, swine, or wild boar, what springs to mind when you first consciously focus on this creature? Greed and dirtiness? Or intelligence and friendliness? Pigs often provoke positive or negative reactions in people, but if you harbor no strong feelings about them and dreamed of a pig rolling uninhibitedly in the dirt, could your unconscious have been warning that you have been behaving like "a pig," that your manners are bad, your appearance is unkempt, and your behavior toward others has been uncaring? Have you been a "swine" to your wife? Or is your home a complete mess? Are you acting like a "male chauvinist pig" by patronizing the women in your life, or are you being "pig-headed," or stubborn,

in the real world? And if a boar blundered into your dream, are you being a "bore" and wearying people with the tedious details of your current obsession?

Wild Animals

Unless you found yourself in a dream zoo (when your unconscious may have been mirroring you and your coworkers' real-life situation in being under both the restriction and scrutiny of your company's management) and dreamed of encountering a wild animal, your dreaming self probably experienced a start of terror. What were the animal's intentions toward you in the dream scene? Did it confirm your worst fears and launch itself savagely upon you, or were you mightily relieved when it regarded you benignly? When a wild creature enters a dream, it usually symbolizes a deep-rooted instinct, which is the "beast" within you. Further, the more wild or dangerous the dream beast, the greater the danger that that basic, suppressed aspect of yourself will break loose from the control of your conscious mind, thereby forcing you to confront and deal with it

(perhaps using desperate measures). An animal attack in the dream world could, therefore, have indicated that you are in the grip of a ferocious rage that you fear unleashing in reality on account of the potentially disastrous consequences. In this case you should, perhaps, acknowledge and either express, or deal with, your anger in a controlled manner before it bursts forth during your waking hours. If the animal merely observed you, however, your unconscious was probably reminding you of its existence, the tacit warning being that you should not forget, or neglect, the personal quality that it represents.

Characterized as the "king of the beasts," the lion is said to be proud, noble, courageous, powerful, dangerous, and the embodiment of masculine strength. So if a lion suddenly turned tail and fled in your dream, could your unconscious have been signaling that your pride, courage, or strength is about to desert you in the face of your difficult waking

circumstances? Or if you are a married man with children and you watched a dream lion luxuriating in the midst of a group of lionesses and cubs, could your dream have been reflecting your pride and satisfaction at being the "king cat," or alpha male, in your household? As well as symbolizing the zodiacal sign of Leo, in many cultures the lion is furthermore equated with royalty and the sun, so try to identify its significance to you when interpreting your dream. The tiger shares many of the lion's symbolic associations (as do other big cats), but with the additional element of stealth. It also has a man-eating reputation, so if you are a woman who dreamed of witnessing a tigress prey on a helpless man, whether or not he is known to you in waking life, could your unconscious have been highlighting your own vampish tendencies as a sexually voracious huntress of men? Don't forget the puns associated with big cats either. If you dreamed of a watchful lynx, for example, could your unconscious have been alerting you to the need to be "lynx-eyed," that is, to show keenness of vision in the waking world (not necessarily literally, but maybe by sharpening your imagination)? If your dream featured a leopard, was your unconscious informing you that you will never succeed in "changing your spots," or disguising your true character? And if a cheetah streaked through your dream, was it telling you that you

are a "cheater" in the real world, or could it have been referring to the speed with which you're tackling your waking workload?

Elephants are usually regarded as wise and friendly giants, who are also credited with the ability never to forget, so if this creature lumbered into your dream, could your unconscious have been drawing

Opposite: Could a dream pig have denoted intelligence or slovenly habits? Did a giraffe's neck signify exposure or intrusion? Was a lion denoting bravery or self-importance? **Top:** Could a dream of zebras have referred to your black-and-white viewpoint? **Above:** Was your dream elephant urging you to retrieve a buried memory from your unconscious?

your conscious attention to any of these qualities within yourself? But if your dream elephant was an albino, could the reference have been to a "white elephant," that is, either a characteristic that you wish you didn't possess or an expensive venture on which you've embarked in the real world that you suspect, deep down, may ultimately prove fruitless? Or did a rogue elephant stampede through your dream? If so, could it have represented an antisocial quality within you that is threatening to wreak havoc in the waking world? Did you dream of a rhinoceros, and, if you did, could your unconscious have conjured it up to tell you that you need to stop being so sensitive to criticism and to develop a thick skin, or that you have become "hidebound," or resistant to new ideas? Or does the phallic symbolism of its horn have more pertinence to you? And if a camel swayed onto the dream stage, could its appearance have been a warning to start saving your resources in preparation for lean times, much as a camel stores fat, a source of sustenance, in its hump?

In times gone by, bears were imbued with powerful symbolism, their tendency to respond to any threat to their cubs with a fierce counterattack causing them to be especially equated with strength and the mother archetype. So if you dreamed of a bear and are actually a mother, could the creature have been referring to your powerful maternal instincts? Alternatively, because bears hibernate during the barren winter months, could it have mirrored your desire to beat an emotional retreat from other people in order to catch up on some much-needed rest and recuperation? Or did it signal the need to batten down the economic hatches in order to survive the tough financial period that you are currently enduring? If your dream bear was bad-tempered, are you behaving the same way in real life, or is there someone, or something, that you cannot "bear" in the real world? But if your waking hours are concerned with stocks and shares, could the appearance of the dream bear have denoted a falling bear market, or are you considering selling some shares with the intention of buying them back again more cheaply?

Many analysts regard animals' horns and antlers as phallic symbols, and few creatures are more magnificently endowed in this respect than stags, whose association with virility is further compounded by their habit of locking horns with rival males and by their rampant sexual behavior during the rutting season, even though they are otherwise solitary creatures. Pride, the masculine libido, and a tendency to confront competitors aggressively, but also to remain aloof from the herd, therefore cause stags to be symbolically associated with

young bachelors (also lending their name to prenuptial "stag nights," or bachelor parties). So if you are a man who dreamed of a stag, could it have symbolized your marital status, or your sexual behavior, or even your antagonistic relationship with male colleagues? Or if your conscious mind is focused on the stock market, are you hoping to make a swift profit by selling the shares that you have recently bought? But if you dreamed of a deer of nonspecific sex or age, could it have portrayed a gentle and timid "dear" in your waking life, perhaps even you?

The wolf shares some of the stag's symbolism in that it, too, can be a solitary figure, or "lone wolf" who lives apart from the pack, also being equated with masculine sexuality, albeit of a more predatory, deceptive, and stealthy nature. So if you are a woman who dreamed that you found yourself in Little Red Riding Hood's situation, could the dream wolf have denoted a male stalker in your waking life? But if you are a man who dreamed of a wolf, could it have been portraying your rather "wolfish" character? Whatever your gender, did you empathize with the dream wolf's solitary lifestyle? If so, do you wish that you could tread a similarly independent path in waking life? If you dreamed that you were pursued by a salivating wolf, but managed to rush home and set up a makeshift barricade, could your unconscious have been alerting you to the need to "keep the wolves from the door," or to take steps to protect yourself from the lean times that are looming in the real world?

If a chimpanzee was monkeying around in dreamland, were you irritated or amused by its antics? Monkeys are renowned for their mischievousness. But mischief can be motivated by malice or playfulness, so depend-

Opposite: A dream bear may represent a protective mother; stags can denote young, unmarried men; and chimpanzees represent mischief. **This page:** In dreams, ferrets, hares, and foxes symbolize persistence, speed, and slyness, respectively.

ing on how the monkey behaved in your dream, your unconscious may have been alerting you to your own, or maybe someone else's, tendency to revert to juvenile behavior in waking life, thereby spreading chaos, at worst, or mayhem, at best. Alternatively, and particularly if your dreaming self found its unruliness infuriating, could the monkey have been the trickster in disguise, an archetypal figure that your unconscious summoned to tell you not to take yourself so seriously? Because monkeys are, furthermore, skilled mimics, could the implication of your dream have been that you are "aping," or emulating, another person in the real world? But if a kangaroo bounced into your slumber, could its message have been that you're similarly hopping restlessly from person to person, or from project to project, during your waking hours?

Foxes have been associated with cunning for many centuries, and by numerous cultures. So if one slunk into your dream, could it have been alerting you to the need to "outfox," or outwit, a real-life adversary? Or could your unconscious have detected someone in your life being as "sly as a fox," a person who is "foxing" your waking mind with his wily tricks? Ask yourself who, or what, this devious trickster could represent (or was it the trickster archetype?), and then try to decipher the message from your unconscious. Alternatively, could the dream fox have represented a "foxy" woman of your acquaintance, or, if you are a female dreamer, your own sexual magnetism? Jackals are notorious for their habit of preying on the weak, their greed for carrion, and their cowardice in the presence of stronger creatures, so if one lurked in the shadows of your dream, do these qualities remind you of anyone? Does someone you know—and it may even be you—have a tendency to con emotionally vulnerable people and to beat a hasty retreat when an authority figure enters the scene?

In the symbolic lexicon of many cultures, the prodigiously fecund rabbit denotes fertility, this creature also being said to possess the characteristics of gentleness, sensitivity, and nervousness. So if a rabbit is featured in your dream, are you longing to be the parent of many children? Or should you perhaps be more kind and understanding in your dealings with others? Or have your waking circumstances caused you to feel transfixed with fear and indecision, like a shy rabbit caught in bright headlights? Ancient Europeans attributed sacred qualities to the hare, but the modern mind primarily associates this animal with speed, so if a hare raced across the terrain of your dream, could its appearance have denoted your urge to streak ahead in life? Alternatively, if you saw a pair of dream hares boxing each other, as they often do in the spring, could your un-

conscious have been commenting that you (maybe along with another person) are behaving like a "mad March hare," or that your attitude toward a real-life situation is "harebrained," or foolish?

Many animals have contributed to the English language through the behavior that they exhibit. If your dream vision was of a badger that emerged from its sett, for instance, and you're annoyed with your colleague for not having returned a book that you lent her in the waking world, could your unconscious have been prompting you to "badger," or pester, her until she remembers? But if you watched a mole surfacing from a molehill, could it have been referring to the "underground" activities, perhaps double-dealing or spying, in which someone (maybe you) is covertly engaged in real life? Otherwise, could the message have been that you are making a "mountain out of a molehill" by worrying obsessively about an issue that is not actually very important? And if you admired a beaver tenaciously building a dam as you slept, could your unconscious have been advising you to take an equally patient and hardworking approach to your work, or to "beaver away" at shoring up your relationship with your partner? But if your dream featured

a ferret, do you need to "ferret" out a piece of information in order to discover the truth about an issue that's been confusing your waking hours?

Perhaps you had a dream of a dark, worrisome scenario that included a mean, scuttling rat. If so, could the reference have been to a human "rat" in your life—maybe a colleague who's been "ratting," or informing your boss about your habit of arriving late to work? Alternatively, could your unconscious have "smelled a rat," and was it trying to tell you that your friend has been behaving suspiciously? If a tiny mouse scurried into your dream, however, was the reference to your timid nature, or do you feel that someone in the real world is playing a game of "cat and mouse" with

you, or toying cruelly with your feelings? Squirrels hoard nuts to ensure that they survive the winter, so if you watched this bright-eyed, bushy-tailed creature busily gathering nuts in your dream, the message may have been to energetically "squirrel away" as much money as you can before your financial situation worsens in the real world. Because the appearance of hedgehogs and porcupines is defined by their protective spines, if either of these creatures made an entrance into your dream, have you had to deal with a defensive and bad-tempered person during your waking hours, or is it you who is behaving in a "prickly" manner? Finally, if you dreamed that a bat flitted noiselessly across a twilit dream sky and you are afraid of these creatures, your dream may have expressed your intuitive feeling that you are actually about to be the victim of an attack from a sinister source. Otherwise, could your unconscious have been indicating that you are becoming "as blind as a bat" and that you should have your eyes tested by a real-life optometrist, or else that your recent waking behavior has been "batty" or "bats," that is, eccentric or even crazy?

Above: Did a dream bat fill you with fear and trepidation, or simply seem eccentric? **Left:** If you are terrified of mice, your dream may have reflected your phobia.

BIRDS

The physical characteristic that both defines and sets birds apart from the animal kingdom is their wings, the means by which most members of this class of creatures are able to escape the limitations of being earth-bound by flying wherever their fancy takes them. Their mastery of the element of air—itself associated with aspirations, ideals, and spirituality—has caused them to become symbols of high-flying ambition, the soaring quest for enlightenment, and hence transcendence. Because they are, furthermore, able to observe the world below from a high vantage point, their "bird's-eye view" is equated with wide-ranging vision, or the ability to take an overview of a situation. When they appear in dreams, birds can therefore represent freedom, transformation, and the higher self, or objectivity and far-sightedness. In many cultures, birds are also traditionally considered messengers from the divine realms and sometimes even the souls, or spirits, of people, be they living or dead.

If your dreaming eye alit upon a bird on the wing, it is important to ask yourself whether you are yearning to take similar flight from your waking circumstances, leaving them far behind as you explore pastures new, "as free as a bird." Alternatively, was your unconscious referring to a "flight of fancy," a brilliant concept that's formed in your mind, which, if made manifest in the real world, would enable you to escape the psychological restrictions and monotony that are blighting your everyday existence? If so, are they spiritual, intellectual, or creative heights that you are longing to attain? Or could your dream bird have been advising you to look at the wider picture, rather than magnifying the importance of small details, when trying to resolve a problem that is troubling your conscious mind? Finally, because the unconscious sometimes summons birds into dreams to reflect the dreamer's waking behavior and emotional state, also consider the symbolism inherent in the following avian dream scenarios, along with that associated with specific types of bird.

Avian Scenarios

When speaking the language of dreams, your unconscious may depict a flock of birds to represent you and those around you. So, if you dreamed of watching a flight of migrating birds pass overhead and you and your family are considering emigrating to another country in the real world, did the sight make you feel exhil-arated or regretful? If, however, your dreaming self observed a flock of pigeons huddled together on a roof, could your unconscious have been commenting on your preference for surrounding yourself with like-minded people in waking life, much as "birds of a feather flock together"? But is your allegiance to "the flock" stifling your individuality?

Did you encounter a caged, dejected-looking bird in dreamland, and, if you did, did you feel sorry for it? If so, your unconscious may have been drawing a parallel between the bird's captivity and your own sense of

Above: The dreaming mind may depict you and the people in your social circle in the guise of a flock of birds.

feather traditionally denotes cowardice, for example, while the feathers on ceremonial Native American headdresses represent heroic achievements, a connotation that is echoed by the expression "having a feather in your cap." But maybe the feather hinted at the fallout from a disagreement that you've recently had with a friend in waking life, one that "ruffled your feathers," or made you so angry that you launched into a vicious attack, thereby causing the "feathers to fly." Alternatively, by sending you the dream feather, could your unconscious have been signaling that you are taking a "featherbrained," or frivolous, attitude to an aspect of your waking life?

imprisonment (whether emotional, intellectual, or physical) during your waking hours. How is your freedom being restricted? By your overly possessive partner, your humdrum job, or your lack of an automobile? Or are you so caged in by your own inhibitions that you no longer feel able to express your true personality? And if you opened the door of the cage and joyfully observed the dream bird hopping tentatively out and then soaring away to freedom, the message was almost

certainly that you should take steps to release yourself from the confinement of your waking hours. Dreaming of a bird with a broken wing may also mirror feelings of helplessness and despair at being prevented from flying high, or free, in the real world. But if the bird's wings were clipped, your unconscious may have been hinting that someone in your life is deliberately limiting your independence and crippling your ability to escape his or her clutches.

Perhaps you dreamed that you were sitting in your garden, enjoying the sunshine, when a feather drifted onto your lap. Could it have been a message "from above," and, if so, what was its meaning? Your interpretation will, of course, be influenced by your personal reaction to feathers (to which you may be allergic, for example, in which case they may symbolize irritants), but there are some common associations with feathers. A white

Because birds line their nests with down, and humans stuff pillows and comforters with them, feathers are also associated with warmth and coziness, which you may be in serious emotional need of. (If, however, your dream highlighted a feather-filled mattress, ask yourself if your unconscious was referring to your company's policy of "featherbedding," or artificial job creation, in the waking world.) Unless you suspect that it

Opposite, top: Caged birds can be a dream metaphor for a restricted lifestyle. **Opposite, top center:** A dream nest often symbolizes the home. **Opposite, right:** A dream of birds in flight can indicate a desire to rise above mundane problems. **Opposite bottom:** A dream bird may embody your longing to travel far and wide. **Below:** Did a clutch of dream eggs express your wish to have a large family? **Center right:** A dream dove may advocate acting as a peacemaker. **Right:** The gimlet gaze of a dream bird of prey may denote penetrating insight.

was commenting on your hairstyle, or someone else's, a bird's nest usually symbolizes the home. If you are single in real life, dreaming of seeing a pair of "love birds" build a "love nest" probably reflected your desire to set up home with a partner. But if you watched a bird lining its nest with feathers in your dream, could its busy activity have signified your desire to "feather your nest," or to accumulate material possessions or money?

If your dreaming vision homed in on a solitary egg in a nest, it may have represented your "nest egg," or the funds that you've been saving, or should save, for your retirement. Otherwise, eggs often represent the gestation of

something with great potential (and the hatching of a chick, its emergence), so that an egg in a dream nest could indicate the dawning of a new, exciting idea in your mind, or else your wish to have a child or children. If the dream nest contained smashed eggs, however, your unconscious may have been reflecting your sadness that your hopes, whatever they were, have been dashed in the real world. Did your dream focus on the attempts of a baby bird to leave the safety of its nest for the first time, and are you the parent of a young adult or a teenager who has just graduated from school? Your unconscious may have been depicting your child's emotional preparations for leaving home, or else your own preparations for your child to leave home. Similarly, if an empty nest captured your dreaming attention, could it have mirrored your real-life melancholy and loneliness now that your own brood has "flown the coop"?

The Feathered Family

Certain birds will, no doubt, have personal significance to you, perhaps because you live in a city and regard the pigeons that infest it as pests or vermin, or because the sight of the U.S. emblem, the bald eagle, fills you with patriotic pride. If you dreamed of a specific type of bird, but don't consciously associate the bird with

anything, however, considering its general symbolism may help to explain why your unconscious summoned it into your dream.

The Old Testament records that, after the biblical floodwaters had subsided, Noah sent a dove from the Ark to search for dry land, which it found, subsequently returning to Noah bearing an olive branch in its beak. Both the dove and the olive branch have consequently become worldwide symbols of hope and peace. So, if a dove flew across your dream scene, could it have been urging you to make the peace, perhaps between feuding members of your family, or could it have been holding out the hope that the strife that characterizes your waking life will soon give way to harmony? The dove is, furthermore, a symbol of the Holy Spirit in Christian belief, so if this association resonates with you, could your unconscious have been pointing toward your desire for

Left: A dream that focused on the spectacular plumage of a crowned crane may have been highlighting your intellect. **Center left:** Did your dream turkey refer to Thanksgiving? **Below:** Was a dream egret advising you to descend from the realm of your high-flying ideals to "fish out" an unconscious intuition? **Opposite, right:** If a red-winged blackbird alit in your dream, was it referring to your territorial instincts? **Opposite, far right:** A dream flamingo's pink feathers may have hinted at romance. **Opposite, below left:** Could your dream owl have represented a wise mentor? **Opposite, below right:** Black-hued birds often symbolize death and mourning.

spiritual fulfillment? If, however, a pair of turtledoves billed and cooed contentedly at each other in your dream, and you are single, it may be that you are longing to find a gentle, loving person with whom to settle down and enjoy a blissfully happy marriage.

If doves denote peace-loving tendencies, hawks—in reality, keen-eyed birds of prey—symbolize aggressive intentions (hence the origin of the phrase "doves and hawks," referring to pacifists and warmongers, respectively). So, if a hawk hovered overhead in a dream scene, could it have represented you, or were you the hapless victim that it held in its sights? If the former scenario is the case, on whom are you about to pounce in the real world? But if your dream followed the latter scenario, could

someone be getting ready to mount a deadly attack on you? Alternatively, could your unconscious have been urging you to watch a person "like a hawk," or intently, in waking life? The "king of the birds," the eagle has been credited with mythical status by many cultures, and the eagle is primarily equated with the sun and solar divinities, with national and imperial might, and with domination and victory. Take these associations into account when trying to interpret any dream through which an eagle soared. Can you link it with a country, a person (perhaps yourself), or a quality that has pertinence to your waking life, or could your dream have been advising you to be "eagle-eyed," or to sharpen your vision, in pursuit of a lofty ambition?

Did an owl startle you by swooping noiselessly past your dreaming self? Or did you find yourself aware of a pair of

"owlish," or solemn, eyes regarding you unblinkingly in your dream? Because it is a nocturnal hunter that glides almost silently through the night sky, some early peoples branded the owl a bird of evil intent and associated it with death and witchcraft. And if you, too, consider the owl a "night hag," your dream might have reflected your waking fear of being the target of sinister forces. The owl is more usually regarded as a symbol of wisdom, however, probably on account of its large, piercing eyes and penetrating night vision. So, if this association better strikes a chord with

you, could your unconscious have sent you a dream owl to mirror your wish to be guided through a murky real-life situation by a "wise old owl" or mentor? Or could the "wise old owl" have been a dream-world manifestation of the archetypal wise old man (high priest) or woman (priestess)? If so, did he or she direct you toward, and perhaps illuminate, a dark corner of your unconscious mind? Or could the "night owl" merely have been commenting on your tendency to burn the midnight oil?

In symbolic terms, the ostrich is the antithesis of the enlightening owl because of the old belief that an ostrich will try to shut out any unpleasantness to which it is exposed by burying its head in the sand. So if an ostrich featured in your dream, could your unconscious have been drawing a parallel with your own tendency to close your eyes to uncomfortable facts or predicaments in waking life? Because ostriches are also flightless birds, could the message have been that your own stupidity or self-restricted vision is preventing you from achieving your ambitions? Peacocks are renowned for their magnificent tail-feather displays and vanity, so if a peacock strutted onto the dream stage, and you are a man, maybe it reflected your desire to impress those around you with a flamboyant new image. Or could the implication have been that you're feeling as "proud as a peacock" in the waking world, but perhaps that others perceive you as putting your conceit and boastfulness on display?

Both storks and pelicans are traditionally associated with off-spring—storks because they were once said to "deliver" newborns to their parents, and pelicans because they were thought to peck open their own breasts to enable them to nourish their young with their lifeblood. If you are a woman who is hoping to conceive in the waking world and a stork appeared to your slumbering self, you have probably experienced a wish-fulfillment dream. But if you are already a parent who is struggling to make ends meet during your waking hours, a dream pelican may have denoted the selfless sacrifices that you are making to feed and care for your children.

Vultures, ravens, and crows all feed on carrion, which is why their leading symbolic associa-

tion is with death. So, if you were uncomfortably aware of being eyed greedily by a group of vultures in dreamland, do you feel that you have suffered a fatal blow in the real world (maybe because your business is on the verge of bankruptcy) and that the "vultures" are circling, waiting impatiently to feast on the remains? Alternatively, could your unconscious have chosen this bird to appear in your dream to draw your conscious attention to the need to "pick over the bones" of your failed relationship, or perhaps to "pick someone's brains," and thus gain valuable insight? But if a crow was cawing raucously in your dream, are you annoying others with your tendency to "crow," or brag about yourself, in waking life?

The funereal hue of their plumage is another reason why crows and ravens are linked with death, and why blackbirds also share this significance, albeit to a lesser extent. Blackbirds are better known for their territorial

ent from the rest of the family. Magpies and jackdaws are the thieves of the avian world, so if your unconscious summoned either of these birds into your dream, could the warning have been that another person's beady eye is focused on something that you value (not necessary a material possession, but perhaps the love of your partner) and that he or she is waiting for a real-life chance to steal it from you?

If the enchanting song of a lark, nightingale, canary, or other type of songbird reverberated through your dream, it may be that you are hoping to hear some sweet news that will gladden your ear in the real world. If you dreamed of a lark, also consider whether your unconscious was referring to your wish to "lark around," or enjoy some fun and frolics, during your waking hours, or else to the advisability of getting up "with the lark," or very early. But if the warbling of a canary drew your dreaming attention, could your unconscious have been reflecting your habit of "singing like a canary," or telling your mother what your brother's been up to in the real world, even though he's sworn you to secrecy? Mynahs, budgerigars, and other "talking" birds, but especially parrots, have a talent for

instincts, however. So, if you dreamed that you watched a male blackbird chase off another male, an intruder into its patch, and you are a male dreamer, could this scenario have mirrored a waking

Above: If a parrot chattered inanely in dreamland, did it mirror your tendency to "parrot" others' opinions unthinkingly? **Above right:** Could a magpie have landed in your dream to alert you to an opportunistic thief? **Right:** If a canary graced your dream, have you recently won a prize or achieved something significant?

dread that your position as a husband and father is under threat from another man? A similar interpretation may be relevant if you dreamed of a cuckoo (if you are a man, perhaps you fear being cuckolded). Because cuckoos lay their eggs in other birds' nests, the reference may have been to someone, perhaps you, metaphorically being a "cuckoo in the nest," or markedly differ-

mimicry, so if you dreamed of hearing one of these feathered creatures speaking "human," its message may have had relevance to your waking situation. But because the meaning of the words that they repeat is beyond these birds' comprehension, it is more likely that your unconscious was commenting on your own "bird-brained," or unthinking, propensity to "parrot" others' opinions without really understanding them.

When trying to interpret avian dreams, it is always helpful to mull over the meanings of the various expressions to which birds have given their names. If you dreamed of an albatross, for instance, could it have represented an "albatross around your neck," or a tremendous burden that you feel forever doomed to bear, such as those exorbitant alimony payments to your ex-wife? Or, if a duck waddled into your dream, was your unconscious telling you that you're trying to "duck" a difficult issue during your waking hours? Or are you so impervious to your husband's criticisms that they are sliding off you like "water off a duck's back"? Or, alternatively, have you taken to your new hobby enthusiastically, like a "duck to water"? If a swan glided elegantly into your dream, do you wish that you could idly "swan

around" in your waking world, or do you envy this bird's swan-necked beauty and grace? Geese are popularly characterized as being silly. So, if a goose made a guest appearance in dreamland, was your unconscious warning you against becoming a "goose," or behaving unwisely—maybe because you're considering making a quick buck by selling a potentially lucrative investment, thereby "killing the goose that lays the golden egg"?

If a chicken featured in your dream, was it a rooster or a hen? The rooster, or cock, "rules the roost" and keeps his hens firmly in line, so if a cock strutted self-importantly into your dream, it may have reflected either your domestic arrangements or else your "cockiness," or arrogant self-assurance. Cocks are also associated with lust, conceit, and boastfulness, but also consider whether its dream crowing was reminding you to get up at "cock crow," or dawn, tomorrow. Hens are said to embody the maternal instinct, so if you dreamed of a hen sitting drowsily on a clutch of eggs, could it have mirrored

Left: A dream of clucking chickens may suggest either maternal instincts or cowardice.
Below left: If you dreamed of a swan, did you envy its elegance and indolent lifestyle?
Bottom: A swaggering dream cockerel may have referred to your own habit of strutting conceitedly through life.

your own motherliness (or your yearning for children), or else your wish to be cosseted by a "mother-hen" figure in waking life? Alternatively, could your unconscious have been advising you against "counting your chickens before they are hatched," that is, not to become carried away by your ambitions for a plan that you're "hatching" because it may never come to fruition in the real world? "Chicken" is a word that is used to denote cowardice, so if your dream concerned a chicken of indeterminate sex, your unconscious may have been highlighting your own, or another person's, spinelessness in a real-life situation. But if your dream depicted a group of chickens settling down for the night, consider the implication that your "chickens have come home to roost," or that something you've done in the waking world is about to rebound on you, with potentially disastrous repercussions.

FISH, REPTILES, AND AMPHIBIANS

Because their element is water, itself a powerful symbol of the unconscious mind, fish, aquatic mammals, crustaceans, mollusks, and other creatures of the deep generally denote deep unconscious instincts and emotions whenever they swim or sidle to the surface of our dreams. Pinpointing the nature of the behavior, or pun, portrayed by that creature should enable you to identify which feeling or emotion is pertinent to your current situation.

There are a number of possible explanations for a dream through which a snake slithered, because it may have represented danger, powers of healing and transcendence, dormant energy and potential, or the stirring of male sexuality. A dream that focused on a snake can therefore be difficult to interpret, although your unconscious reaction to this reptile will give you a vital clue to its significance. Similarly, when other reptiles or amphibians appear in dreams, menace or transcendence are usually indicated, and it's also important to consider whether your unconscious was using wordplay to transmit its message.

Fish and Other Creatures of the Deep

In symbolic terms, large bodies of water, such as oceans and seas, and also lakes and rivers, are equated with the unconscious, and because fish inhabit these watery depths, they are said to represent aspects of the instinctive mind, such as basic emotions, intuitions, or creative inspiration. Did you dream of seeing a flash of silver as a flying fish leaped out of the ocean before swiftly returning beneath the waves? You may have witnessed the brief emergence of an intuition: an elusive, unconscious feeling relating to your waking circumstances or personality that you have not yet consciously grasped. Did you dream of visiting a dream aquarium? If so, your dream may have been hinting that different facets of your unconscious personality are being prevented from expressing themselves freely, while a dream that featured a goldfish bowl may have been similarly commenting on your emotional restriction, perhaps because you find the close scrutiny of others inhibiting in the waking world.

If, however, you dreamed that you were fishing, it may be that your dream was mirroring your unconscious efforts to "fish out," or extract, a deeply submerged insight that would throw light on a problem with which your waking mind is wrestling. Try to work out what you were "fishing for" during your dream scene. Compliments, perhaps? The truth underlying a "fishy," or suspicious, situation in the real world? Or, if your dreaming self cast a line into the water, are you "angling for" love, thereby hoping to "bait" and then "hook" a potential partner during your waking hours? Did you catch the dream fish? If so, and you are facing a real-life dilemma, you may soon find that the fish works its creative magic and that the answer suddenly pops into your conscious mind. Alternatively, if your catch gasped for breath as it flopped around on the ground, could it have portrayed your sense of being "a fish out of water" during daylight

Above: Sharks nearly always warn that a predatory person is circling you.

Right: Like stars, starfish can represent your destiny in life, of which you may already be unconsciously aware. **Below center:** Dreaming of a goldfish bowl may have mirrored your uneasy sense of being under observation during your waking hours. **Bottom:** If a fish swam through your dream, it may have represented an intuitive feeling that is about to surface in your conscious mind.

hours, perhaps because you've just started a new job and you do not yet feel "in your element"? And if it wriggled frantically as you tried to pick it up, thereby successfully eluding your hands, could your dream have been drawing your conscious attention to a "slippery fish," or an evasive person (perhaps you, yourself), who is part of your waking world? But if the fish eventually gave up the struggle and you were struck by how cold it felt when you finally got hold of it, could your unconscious have been referring to a "cold fish," or a dispassionate or unemotional person in your life, maybe even you?

Fish have an array of further symbolic significance that may have relevance to your dream, and hence to its meaning. The fish is one of the oldest symbols of Christianity, for example, and the New

Testament called Christ a "fisher of men," so if you are a lapsed Christian, it may be that a dream of a fish, fishing, or eating fish was reflecting your unconscious craving for spiritual sustenance. Additionally, the elongated shape of many fish gives them phallic connotations, while, because the females spawn a multitude of eggs, fish are also symbols of boundless fertility. (This is why dreaming of an eel probing for tidbits among a riverbed's stones may denote male sexuality, while a dream of a female fish laying a mass of eggs may denote feminine fertility.) If a fish swam through the waters of your dream, could it alternatively have been offering an oblique reminder not to forget the birthday of someone who was born under the zodiacal sign of Pisces?

When it comes to specific types of fish, certain cultural associations may imbue them with meaning for you. If you are familiar with Celtic lore, for instance, you may equate the salmon featured in your dream with wisdom; or if you are of Japanese extraction, you may associate a dream carp with endurance, courage, love, or good luck. If you are aware of the salmon's

epic migratory journey to its spawning grounds, you may otherwise associate this fish with single-minded perseverance. Or could the dream carp have been pointing toward your tendency to "carp at," or nag, your friend? The shark has the universal significance of the deadly predator so if you dreamed of splashing around happily in the water, but were then terrified to see a telltale fin looming before you, your unconscious may have been alerting you to a dangerous presence in the waking world—maybe a "loan shark," someone who's recently offered to lend you money at an exorbitant rate of interest.

Although they are mammals, not fish, dolphins are also marine creatures, and ones that have overpoweringly positive associations in both the real and dream worlds. Celebrated for their intelligence and friendliness, dolphins are reputed to steer to safety sailors whose ships are in trouble, and were once believed to guide the spirits of the dead to the afterlife, which is why the dolphin is a symbol of Christ. So if you dreamed of sailing through clear waters accompanied by an apparently laughing dolphin, you probably felt uplifted, but only you will be able to ascertain whether it held out the reassuring hope of spiritual salvation, or simply of fun and friendship. The whale symbolizes the womb (probably on account of its enormous belly), and thus also the mother archetype, so if a whale hove majestically into view in a dream ocean, ask yourself why your unconscious could have conjured up its appearance. Are your adult circumstances so trying that you're longing to return to the warmth and protection of the womb, for instance? Or did the whale represent a terrible-mother figure who might be threatening metaphorically to devour you in the real world (don't forget that the biblical Jonah was swallowed by a whale)? Or do you merely wish that you could have a "whale of a time," that is, enjoy some thrills and exhilaration, during your waking hours?

Crustaceans and Mollusks

Because crabs and other crustaceans mainly inhabit the sea, they, like fish, can be associated with primal facets of the unconscious personality. Their armor-plated bodies additionally imply the wish, or need, to ward off outside influences, while their pincerlike claws can mount a painful counterattack if these creatures are menaced. So, if you found yourself confronting a crab on a dream shore, could it have embodied the "crabby," or bad-tempered, side of your nature that resists the attempts of others to penetrate the tough outer shell that you've developed to protect your softer emotional core? (And if your sleeping self observed any crustacean or mollusk without its shell, its defenselessness may have mirrored your own sense of emotional vulnerability.) Did the dream crab scuttle sideways as you approached and, if it did, did it mirror your own, or another's, tendency to take evasive action when anyone threatens to get too emotionally close to you in the waking world? Alternatively, can you equate the crab of your dream with someone who was born under the zodiacal sign of Cancer?

Did you dream that you were wandering along a beach when a shell caught your eye, and are you a man? Because shelled mollusks such as cowries and scallops can resemble female genitalia, it may be that your unconscious was commenting on the current state of your sex life. But if your dreaming self came across an oyster shell, was it closed or open? If it was clamped firmly shut, your unconscious may have been hinting that it contained a pearl, perhaps a "pearl" of wisdom, or else a female "pearl," maybe your ideal partner. Oysters are also traditionally said to be aphrodisiacs, so could the message otherwise have been that it's high time you pepped up your love life? But if the shell was empty, could your unconscious have been reflecting your sadness that life's opportunities seem to have passed you by, and your belief that the world is no longer your "oyster"?

Both freshwater and land-based snails will withdraw into their shells when menaced or sleeping, so if you saw this happening in a dream, do you wish that you could similarly retreat into your "shell" during your waking hours? If so, why? Snails are also said to

Opposite, top: Whales can symbolize the mother archetype. **Opposite, center:** Could the slow progress of a dream snail have reflected that your career is advancing only at a "snail's pace"? **Opposite, bottom:** Did a dream crab highlight your own "crabbiness"? **Right:** An octopus may have reflected your multitasking approach to your waking life. **Below:** Snakes are ancient symbols of healing.

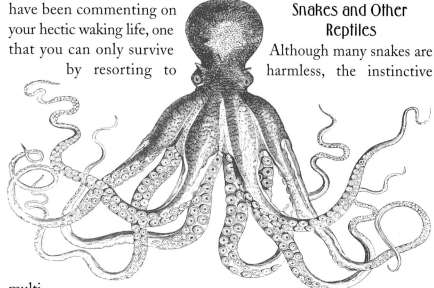

carry their homes on their backs, and they certainly move at a slow pace, so if you watched a snail laboriously inch its way across the dream stage, could your unconscious have been lamenting the length of time that it will take to repay your mortgage?

Although they lack a shell, octopuses are distinguished by their independently operating tentacles, so if your dreaming attention was seized by one of these marine mollusks, could your unconscious

have been commenting on your hectic waking life, one that you can only survive by resorting to multi-

tasking? But if you dreamed that you were scuba diving and startled a squid, who responded by squirting a cloud of blinding black ink in your face, can you equate its defensive behavior with your partner's habit of obscuring the issue rather than confronting your emotional differences?

Snakes and Other Reptiles

Although many snakes are harmless, the instinctive responses that they tend to arouse in people are those of fear and loathing, a near-universal reaction bequeathed to us by evolution. Indeed, if you have had a frightening encounter with a snake in the real world, you may even have developed a phobia about these reptiles, so that if your dreaming mind focused on a snake, your dream was, no doubt, a nightmare. If, however, you admire snakes, perhaps even keeping them as pets, a dream that featured a serpent is unlikely to have been sinister. A creature that we therefore regard ambivalently, the snake is also an ancient archetypal symbol that similarly has both negative and positive connotations, being on the one hand deemed an evil predator and, on the other, an agent of healing and transcendence.

Because it is a slithering, cold-blooded, well-camouflaged creature of both land and sea that either injects its prey with venom or crushes its victim to death before devouring it, dreaming of

facing a serpent that is poised to strike, or of becoming immobilized by its constricting coils, may have been warning of the danger posed by an emotionally ice-cold, venomous, or suffocating person in your waking life. Could the message have been that you are nursing a "viper" in your bosom, someone who appears friendly enough, but who may be about to launch a malicious and wounding attack on you? Or was your dream referring to a "snake in the grass," a deceitful person who may soon ambush you with his or her treachery? If you are a Christian, your attitude toward snakes may also be colored by the serpent's tempting of Eve in the Garden of Eden, as well as its association with Satan. In this case, your dream snake may have represented someone who is trying to persuade you to deviate from the moral straight and narrow in the real world.

The snake's positive associations with healing predate its negative Christian significance, however. A snake was depicted coiled around the staff of Asclepius, the Greek god of medicine, a symbol today used to represent the medical profession. And the caduceus, the staff of the Greek messenger god Hermes (or the Roman Mercury), bore two entwined snakes, representing the harmonization of two conflicting forces. If a snake or two appeared to your sleeping self, your unconscious may, therefore, have been indicating that a process of physical or emotional healing has begun. But if you watched a snake slough off its old skin in your dream, it may have been pointing toward your desire either to be spiritually or emotionally reborn or to cast off, or transcend, life's encumbrances and to begin afresh. Furthermore a symbol of latent instincts, energy, and dynamic potential, according to Indian mystical belief, the kundalini snake sleeps at the base of the human spine until aroused by the unblocking of the positive and/or negative energy channels within the body, causing it to make its way up through the chakras (energy centers) until it reaches the crown of the head, where enlightenment is attained. So, if you dreamed that you found yourself in an

Eastern-style bazaar, watching entranced as a serpent slowly uncoiled itself and then rose and swayed to a snake-charmer's tune, could the snake have represented your spiritual or intellectual awakening or illumination? It was Freud who first attributed phallic symbolism to the long and muscular snake, so if a serpent slithered stealthily toward you in a dream jungle, also consider whether it could have denoted your repressed sexual urges (if you are male) or your sexual fears (if you are female).

Left: If you dreamed of a snake's fangs dripping venom, could the reference have been to a malicious person's poisonous words in the real world? **Below:** By summoning a lizard into your dream, was your unconscious commenting on a lounge lizard, or social climber, in your waking life? **Opposite, top:** A dream crocodile may have been warning that your friend is actually crying insincere "crocodile tears." **Opposite, center:** Turtles and tortoises sometimes have cosmic significance in dreamland. **Opposite, bottom:** Frogs denote fertility or transformation in the lexicon of dreams.

Many lizards, such as slow worms, resemble snakes, which is why they share the serpent's general symbolic associations, something that you should take into account when trying to interpret a dream that included one of these reptiles. But if you observed a chameleon's skin slowly changing color until it blended in with the rock onto which it had crept, ask yourself if your unconscious may have been signaling the advisability of camouflaging your true feelings, or whether it was highlighting your fickleness, in waking life.

If you dreamed that you were about to seat yourself on a log when it suddenly turned into a fearsome crocodile or alligator, your dream was almost certainly warning that you are under threat by someone dangerous in the real world. But whom could your unconscious have identified as harboring vicious intentions toward you? Because these creatures are masters of disguise who are said to shed "crocodile tears," or to weep insincerely over their victims in order to attract further prey, it is probably a person who usually presents a deceptively sympathetic face during your waking hours, but is, in fact, just biding his or her time until the time to attack arrives.

The turtle's age-old symbolism relates to wisdom (due to its longevity and wizened face, a significance shared by the land-based tortoise), to fertility (it is a prolific egg-layer), and particularly to the cosmos (which many early cultures thought that it embodied, others believing that it supported the world on its shell). So, if you dreamed of watching a turtle lying helplessly on its back, frantically waving its legs in an attempt to right itself, could your dream have mirrored your waking sense that your real-life circumstances been turned upside down recently?

Amphibians

Although toads and frogs are both amphibians that lay their eggs in the water, being otherwise land-based creatures, that's where their similarity ends (in symbolic terms, at least). Its hideous appearance, notably its warty skin and squat body, along with its habit of secreting poison to protect itself from predators, has caused the much-maligned toad to be characterized as a malevolent creature. So, if you dreamed of coming face to face with a toad, can you associate it with someone whom you believe to be a metaphorical "toad," or a loathsome and malicious person, in the real world?

If a frog hopped into your dream, the message is likely to have been far more positive, however—namely, a message of transformation. This association is derived from the frog's life cycle, in that it starts life as an egg, develops into a tadpole, and changes finally into a frog. This process of transformation is echoed by the fairy tale of the frog prince, whose human good looks were eventually restored by a princess's kiss. Frogs are also symbols of fertility (due to the masses of eggs that they produce), so if you dreamed of gathering frog spawn, could your dream have been mirroring your desire to transform your waking life by having children?

🕷 INSECTS 🕷

Most of us dislike insects, with the possible exception of the iridescent butterfly and the pretty, aphid-eating ladybug. Whether they are still at the larval stage or have reached their final incarnation, many members of the insect family irritate us by munching their way through our gardens or crops, demolishing our clothes or woodwork, feeding off our very bodies, inflicting painful stings, or spreading disease. In short, insects are pests in the real world, and this is generally exactly their significance in the dream world, too.

Some insects do, however, have their uses: honey-producing bees, for example, which, like ants, organize themselves into industrious colonies, the better to work for the common good. Although still capable of annoying us, social insects can, therefore, set a helpful example when they appear in our dreams. Be they spiders or scorpions, arachnids rarely send a positive message, however, warning as they do of predatory or poisonous influences in our lives.

Caterpillars, Butterflies, and Moths

Did you watch a caterpillar creeping slowly along a twig in your dream? If so, and you are a keen gardener, your unconscious may simply have been confirming your waking annoyance with its real-world counterparts' voracious appetite for your cherished plants. If your conscious response to these butterfly larvae is neutral, however, it is possible that your dream was hinting that you are about to undergo a wonderful transformation in your waking life, much as a caterpillar emerges as new from its shroudlike chrysalis after having metamorphosed into a glorious butterfly.

While the caterpillar is a symbol of latent potential and transition, the butterfly itself represents that potential made gloriously manifest. Did you dream of admiring a butterfly that briefly paused on a flower, and are you still (unhappily) at school? If so, your unconscious may have been holding out the hope that you, too, will undergo a magnificent transformation, perhaps physical or maybe emotional, once you have gained the freedom of adulthood. But if you are already grown up and you felt frustrated when a dream butterfly constantly dodged your attempts to appreciate the markings on its wings, the reference may have been to your own restlessness. Are you a "social butterfly" who flits fickly from person to person in the real world, thereby avoiding others' efforts to forge a close relationship with you?

If you have recently been bereaved, you may have felt comforted when a butterfly fluttered through your dream. Because the soul of someone who has died is traditionally said to take the form of a butterfly, your unconscious may have been signaling that your loved one's spirit has been liber-

Opposite page: Was a butterfly drawing attention to your potential or flightiness? **Right and below:** Both real and dream bugs have destructive appetites. **Below center:** The scarab beetle was a sacred symbol of regeneration in ancient Egypt. **Bottom:** Dream ladybugs can denote childhood.

ated from the pain and suffering of this world and is now able to fly joyously. Remember, too, that a butterfly may represent your own soul or psyche in the dream world, so that if you envied a dream butterfly's freedom of movement and you are currently feeling overburdened during your waking hours, your unconscious mind may have sent you a wish-fulfillment dream.

Although moths are members of the same order of insects as butterflies, we rarely celebrate their beauty, instead lamenting the damage that they do to our clothes, which rapidly become "moth-eaten" when these insects covertly set up home in them. So, if you dreamed that you were saddened to discover that your favorite garment had been subjected to a moth attack and was full of holes, ask yourself what that item of clothing represents to you (a coat may symbolize protection, for example) and why your unconscious was hinting that this aspect of your life is being eaten away. Moths are also (suicidally) attracted to naked

flames. So, if you watched as a moth flew directly toward a burning candle, could your dream have been warning that your own helpless fascination with someone in the waking world is potentially dangerous, and that you'd be "playing with fire" if you tried to get closer to him or her?

Bugs and Beetles

We rarely greet the sight of even a solitary bug or beetle with delight in the real world, instead either giving it a wide berth, sweeping it aside, or squashing it dead. Our reaction is partly because (the ladybug apart) we find insects' appearance repellent, and partly because they may be harbingers of an invasion, and consequently also of disease and destruction. And when faced with an infestation of bugs, especially verminous cockroaches, extermination is usually the only option. Small as they are, not only can bugs spread disease, but termites and woodworm (the larvae of the deathwatch and furniture beetles) can undermine the very foundation of our homes, while crop-feeding pests

like the Colorado beetle present a real threat to agriculture.

All in all, we generally consciously abhor bugs. And when the unconscious mind sends them "beetling" into our dreams, it may be reflecting the petty irritations that are besetting our waking hours (who is "bugging you" in the real world?) at best, and, at worst, alerting us to a minor threat that may escalate into disastrous proportions if ignored. So, if you noticed that the floorboards in your dream home bore the telltale signs of woodworm infestation, could your unconscious have been warning that, unless

you take pre-emptive steps, something, or someone, troublesome may soon crawl out of the "woodwork," ultimately causing your personal world to collapse around your ears? And if you were disgusted to see hundreds of roaches scuttling around the kitchen in your dream, could your unconscious have been pointing toward an actual hygiene or health problem? Or was it referring to the lowlife company that you are keeping during your waking hours? But if your dream focused on a field of insect-ravaged crops, could the implication have been that those around you in real life are so greedy for your time and attention that they are fatally sapping your emotional strength?

Locusts, Grasshoppers, and Crickets

Maybe your sleeping self was appalled to witness a swarm of locusts descend upon a field full of maize and then proceed to strip it bare. If so, your dream may have been mirroring the horde of ugly problems with which you are being plagued during your waking hours, and which you dread may have disastrous consequences.

If you dreamed of a grasshopper or cricket, however, the message is likely to have been far less menacing. Because we associate the "singing" of these insects with the warm and lazy days of summer, if your dream occurred during the depths of a cold and difficult winter, your unconscious may have been sending you a simple wish fulfillment. Grasshoppers hop from blade to blade at random, so also consider whether your unconscious could have been commenting on your "grasshopper mind," or inability to focus on anything for long before turning your attention to something more diverting. And if you are familiar with the old story of Pinocchio and Jiminy Cricket, and a cricket chirped away in your dream, ask yourself if your dream was telling you to pay more heed to your conscience.

Flies and Bloodsuckers

If the buzzing of a fly reverberated around your dream, it is possible that a real fly was trapped in your bedroom and that your

Above: Could a plague of insatiable dream locusts have represented the problems that are ravaging your waking world? **Center and left:** The dragonfly's flight path is erratic, so if this insect flitted through your dream, could it have referred to your own inconsistency?

account of their tendency to spread disease), or both? If the former, could your unconscious have been mirroring your irritation with a persistently pesky person, perhaps a talkative colleague whom you're itching to "swat," or slap down, because he or she is the "fly in the ointment" who is ruining an otherwise enjoyable office atmosphere? If the latter, could your dream flies (or their larvae, maggots) have been reflecting your health worries? But if you dreamed of observing a fly that had settled on a wall, do you wish that you could be a "fly on the wall" and thus discover the intimate details of your friends' lives? Or if, in a dream scene, everyone was frantically swatting away flies apart from your brother, who remained miraculously free of their attentions, could your unconscious have been commenting on his smartness by depicting "no flies on him"? There are three issues to consider if you dreamed of a bloodsucking insect like a gnat, mosquito, flea, or louse. Firstly, was your unconscious drawing a parallel with a person whose emo-

Left: A swarm of dream insects can denote a mass of real-life difficulties. **Bottom:** Did someone who bothers your waking self continue to torture you in dreamland, albeit disguised a fly? **Below:** In dreams, bloodsucking insects can symbolize human parasites in your waking world.

tional or monetary neediness is "sucking you dry" and draining your energy and your financial resources in the waking world? Alternatively, because the real-life bites of these insects cause intolerable itchiness, and sometimes full-blown allergic

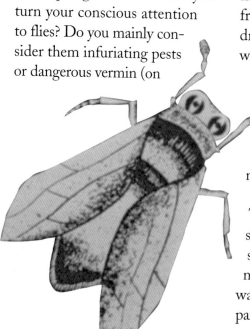

unconscious incorporated the annoying noise that it was making into your dream. Otherwise, what springs to mind when you turn your conscious attention to flies? Do you mainly consider them infuriating pests or dangerous vermin (on

reactions, are someone's behavioral tics and quirks irritating you beyond endurance during your waking hours, so much so that you've become "allergic" to him or her? Otherwise, was your unconscious resorting to wordplay? Or are you feeling "lousy," or bad, because you've recently behaved meanly, or like a "louse," to your partner"?

Ants and Honeybees

You may not like ants in the real world, but you probably grudgingly admire their industriousness, exemplary organizational skills, and highly regimented teamwork. Honeybees similarly live in colonies that we celebrate for their inhabitants' discipline, hard work, and self-sacrifice when working for a common cause. So, if your dreaming self observed a line of ants laboriously maneuvering a morsel of food toward their anthill, or some busy bees returning to their hive, your unconscious may have been advising you to follow their example and to work in diligent and productive harmony with your family, coworkers, or friends (and maybe with the other members of your quilting "bee").

Alternatively, consider the expressions that ants and bees have contributed to the English language. If you dreamed of leaping around maniacally as you tried to brush off an army of ants that was marching up your leg, are you feeling "antsy," or do you have "ants in your pants"? (In other words, are you fidgety and restless during your waking hours?) Or perhaps you dreamed that you were tend-

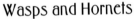

This page: A dream of social insects like honeybees and ants may have been advising you to be equally industrious in a waking working environment.

ing a beehive when you realized that a bee had crept under your protective headgear. If so, could it have represented the "bee in your bonnet," or the obsession that's preoccupying your waking thoughts? And could the dream beehive have denoted the "hive of activity" that is currently your workplace?

Wasps and Hornets

Members of the wasp family contribute little to humans apart from their stings. So, if you warily eyed a wasp in the dream world, could your unconscious have been alerting you to someone in your waking life, perhaps a "waspish," or bad-tempered character, from whom you should expect to receive a "stinging" rebuke? Or maybe you dreamed that you prodded a large, strange-looking protrusion on a tree and were then forced to flee from the swarm of enraged hornets that emerged from it. If so, could the message have been that you'll provoke a furious, real-life backlash from those around you if you "stir up the hornets' nest," or upset the status quo, maybe at work?

And if you were stung in your dream—by any insect—was your unconscious trying to "sting" you into action, perhaps by "stinging" your conscience? Have you been

emotionally "stung," or hurt, by someone's criticism? Or was your dream referring to a "sting," or swindle, that someone is perpetrating in waking life?

Above and right: Spiders were regarded with awe by many ancient cultures on account of their ability to spin intricate webs, which were compared to the web of life. Although once venerated as cosmic creators and the architects of fate, spiders are today usually considered scary creatures, a human phobia immortalized by the nursery-rhyme character Little Miss Muffet (right).

Spiders and Scorpions

Unless you are aware of the spider's ancient symbolic links with the cosmos and fate, a dream in which you were exposed to a spider is more likely to have been reflecting either your actual arachnophobia, or your waking helplessness when in the presence of a predatory, dominating person in your life (probably a woman, and perhaps a representative of the terrible-mother archetype). Indeed, if you are a married man, your unconscious

may have been drawing a parallel between the black widow spider (who consumes her mate after he has served his purpose) and your wife (who, perhaps, having taken you for every penny you've got, is now becoming increasingly aggressive and confrontational).

Similarly, because spiders weave sticky webs in which to entrap any hapless fly that alights upon them, if you watched a spider lurking at the corner of a dream web, it may be that your unconscious was alerting you to a trap that someone in your life has set for you (or maybe one into which you've already fallen), or to a "web of deceit" that has been spun in the real world. Alternatively,

could an intricate dream web have symbolized the complexities and entanglements of your waking circumstances? Or was it a reference to the World Wide Web? If so, and you knew that it was the work of a money spider, could your unconscious have been mirroring your conscious belief that participating in an Internet venture might prove lucrative? If, however, your dreaming self walked into a room that was obscured by cobwebs, ask yourself how that particular room pertains to you. If it was a living room, for example, could your unconscious have been signaling that you've led a hermit-like existence for far too long, and that it's time to blow away the cobwebs and enjoy an active social life again?

You probably froze if you found yourself confronted by a scorpion in the dream terrain, instinctively recognizing that your life was endangered by the venomous sting in its tail. If you found yourself in this dream scenario, your unconscious may have been warning that a relationship in the waking world that was once hostile, but now seems harmonious, may hold a metaphorical "sting in the tail," so that it will end catastrophically for you. Or was your dream pointing toward a human "scorpion" at work, of whose hatred and jealousy your conscious mind remains blissfully unaware, which is why your unconscious was alerting you to the treacherous intentions it has detected? Alternatively, and especially if you observed a dream scorpion without experiencing a fearful reaction, consider whether your dream could simply have been referring to someone born under the zodiacal sign of Scorpio.

Top: Unhappily married men's dreams may be darkened by their aggressive wives in the form of black widows, or predatory female spiders. **Above and right:** The scorpion hides a poisonous sting in its tail, so if you dreamed of this arachnid, could it have represented a very real threat to your happiness, of which you are not consciously aware?

TREES

Humans have venerated trees for millennia, not only in gratitude for the timber or fruit that they yield, but also for the profound symbolic qualities with which they have been imbued. In the Judeo–Christian Old Testament, for example, we learn of the trees of Knowledge and Life that grow in the Garden of Eden, as well as of the Jesse Tree, Christ's genealogical line of descent, while we are told in the New Testament that Christ was crucified upon a tree. These biblical trees have their counterparts in other cultures' faith and myths, with cosmic trees that unite, protect, and sustain the underworld, earthly world, and divine world also abounding, perhaps the best known being the Norse Yggdrasil, a mighty ash.

The tree is thus an archetypal symbol that can represent knowledge, life, the human family, cosmic unity, and more, but in dreams it generally denotes you: your past, present, and future, and your physical, emotional, and spiritual growth. (And in Islamic belief, a tree symbolizes a person who has grown to spiritual maturity.) Because each element in the tree's structure also relates to you, and consequently to your life—what has been, the here and now, and what may come—the condition of a dream tree's roots, trunk, branches, and leaves all send important messages, as does the tree's situation, be it solitary or alongside others. And if you dreamed of a particular type of tree, understanding its symbolism may add further nuances to the meaning of your dream, and therefore also to your self-knowledge.

The Anatomy of the Tree

According to Jung, the tree is "a symbol of the self…depicted in the process of growth." If this interpretation rings true, recalling how a dream tree looked will tell you more about yourself and your personal growth. (If, however, you felt no personal connection with the dream tree, or its characteristics seemed more suited to an older or younger person, don't discount the possibility that it represented someone important in your life rather than you.)

Roots represent both your unconscious mind and your family, childhood, and geographical "roots," so if your dream tree's roots appeared strong, the implication is that the past influences

Left: The Tree of Life that grows in the Garden of Eden is said to bear twelve fruits.

that have shaped your personality are stable, supportive, and sustaining, so that you are well rooted in the past. If the tree was a youthful one that exhibited signs of a recent spurt of growth in dreamland, and you are a young adult who has recently set up home with your partner in the real world, the message may have been that, having "put down roots" and started to establish yourself in your new life, you are now set to flourish.

The dream tree's trunk, which links the roots and the branches, denotes your conscious mind and also your individuality, while its bark symbolizes the protective face, or persona, that you present to others. If the tree's trunk was straight as a die in your dream, it is therefore likely that your conscious approach to life is straightforward and rational, but if the bark was peeling away in places, are you feeling vulnerable because you suspect that others can see through your "façade?" Tree sap can be equated with blood, so if insects were feeding so voraciously on the trunk that your dream tree had started to ooze sap, is your own vitality being "sapped" by countless petty irritations in the waking world?

Were the tree's branches strong and widespread, with lots of offshoots, in your dream? If so, they may on the one hand have marked the various directions that you have taken in life by "branching out," be it as part of your career development or by broadening your personal interests, or, on the other, have represented the proliferating branches of your family tree through the arrival of children in the real world. Be they those of leaves or flowers, buds can also symbolize children, or else the dawning of new ideas within your conscious mind, which, as they develop, may flourish and eventually bear fruit, much as spring blossom holds out the hope of a crop of fruit in the fall. But if new leaves signify the development of fresh interests, whether personal or professional, withered foliage hints

Top left: A dream tree's roots can symbolize your own "roots." **Top right:** Branches are said to mirror a dreamer's personal growth and development. **Left:** A vertical tree trunk can denote an upright person in the language of dreams. **Above left:** Dream leaves can be equated with flourishing interests. **Above:** Bark represents the dreamer's persona, or protective façade.

Left: Dream evergreens hint at enduring youthfulness. Right: A devastated dream forest may mirror a ravaged real-life community. Below center: The various species that grow in a dream forest can represent the different people in your waking world. Bottom left: In dreams, acorns sometimes symbolize unborn children. Bottom right: A deciduous dream tree's seasonal appearance can refer to the dreamer's age.

that these enthusiasms may be waning, and fallen leaves suggest that they are now things of the past. (This interpretation applies to deciduous trees only, however, and because evergreen trees retain their leaves throughout the year, in dreamland they generally denote an "evergreen," or enduringly healthful and vigorous, approach to waking life.)

Indeed, were you conscious of the seasonal appearance of the tree that featured in your dream? Because the stages of human life are mirrored by the effects of the passing seasons on a deciduous tree, if your dream tree was covered in the tiny leaf buds or blossoms of spring, the association is with the vigor, fertility, and potential of youth; if its verdant foliage signaled summer, the reference is to being in the prime of life; if its autumnal leaves were starting to

drop, the link is with middle age; and if the tree looked skeletal in the winter gloom, old age is signified. Arboreal seeds like acorns

and nuts can similarly denote an unborn baby (or the germ of a new idea), while seedlings and saplings can be equated with children and young people, flourishing and established trees denote maturity, and ancient trees represent old age. But if you came across a dead tree in the landscape of your dream, it may symbolize someone whose death you are grieving. When considering such a dream, it may console you to remember that although all living things must inevitably die, they live on in their offspring, thus perpetuating the eternal cycle of life.

Did your dreaming self notice whether the tree had a crown, or a well-defined apex? If it did, it may have denoted your own efforts to "reach for the sun" and attain spiritual or intellectual enlightenment, a meaning that is underlined if you dreamed of scrambling up the tree and striving hard to reach for the top. Alternatively, could the reference have been to your ambition to reach the "top of the tree" in your professional life?

Woods and Forests

Did you dream of wandering through a sun-dappled forest, admiring the different species of trees that coexisted alongside one another? Just as the unconscious sometimes uses the symbol of a single tree to represent you, and your progress in life, so it may conjure up a group of trees in a dream scene to represent a community of which you are a part in the real world, be it at school or work, or in your domestic or personal domain. The sunshine, your ease of movement, and enjoyment of being in your dream forest may together have signaled your contentment within a real-life communal environment in which the individuals who surround you are all in harmony with each other. If, however, you ventured a little farther into the dream forest and were saddened to see that a number of trees had been felled and that those that were left were now growing some distance apart, the implication may have been that certain people's association with your social group has come to an abrupt end, perhaps due to a bitter falling out, with the result that there is now an emotional distance between the rest of you in waking life.

Perhaps you found yourself in the heart of a dark, sinister forest, whose densely crowded trees blocked out the daylight to such a degree that you couldn't see a way out. Maybe you then became increasingly panic-stricken as you pushed your way frantically through the unyielding branches and brambles, which responded by scratching and poking you with their sharp twigs and thorns. If you suffered a dream like this, did your sleeping reaction mirror how you are feeling during your working hours, namely overshadowed by your seniors, the victim of your colleague's wounding barbs, and altogether hopelessly trapped? Did you eventually emerge from the forest into the sunlight in your dream? If so, your

Top left: If you felt uneasy in a dream forest, are your waking circumstances filling you with similar apprehension? **Above and left:** If you came across a tree that had been chopped down in a woodland dream, it may have represented someone who has been "cut down," or has died, in the prime of life. But if you were confronted by a dream clearing created by a mass felling, could it have reflected your own suddenly depopulated community? **Opposite:** Forests can hint at a peaceful and harmonious waking environment.

unconscious might have been heartening you by holding out the hope that there is light at the end of the tunnel if only you pluck up the courage to take the necessary steps to end your waking nightmare (and your dream may even have indicated which path would lead you to freedom).

Forests are also symbolically associated with the unconscious, however, so if you felt at peace in a dream forest, your dream could have been a reflection of your need to escape the demands of the outside world by retreating into your own inner environment for some much-needed self-contemplation and emotional recuperation. And if you were curious about what you would come across as you wandered through a forest in your dream, the message may have been that you are looking for an answer to a real-life problem that may lie within your unconscious mind. If you stumbled across a hideous sight in the dark depths of a dream forest, could it have represented the memory of something awful that you've done, or experienced, in the waking world, a memory that you've consciously suppressed, but cannot banish from your unconscious mind?

The Dream Arboretum

If your dreaming vision homed in on a specific type of tree, was this one that you recognized? Perhaps it was the magnolia that graced your garden when you were small, so that your unconscious may have been responding to your nostalgia for your childhood. A dream featuring a Christmas tree festooned with

glittering baubles and tinsel may similarly have evoked comforting memories of heart-warming times spent with your family and friends, happy days that may seem far removed from your lonely life in the waking world. But if the dream tree reminded you of nothing in particular, it may be that you are unconsciously aware of its traditional, mythical, or religious symbolic significance, and that this may have pertinence to your situation

in the real world. Although a dream holly tree over which ivy clambered may have reminded you of the winter festive season, for example, holly was sacred to the Roman god Saturn (Romans

Top left: In the parallel universe of dreams, woods and forests can symbolize either the people who surround you during your waking hours or your unconscious mind. **Above:** The moss-covered trunks of fallen trees may represent long-dead family members. **Left:** If a dream tree seemed to be striving to reach the heavens, it may have reflected your own quest to attain spiritual enlightenment.

decorating their homes with it in his honor during Saturnalia, a December festival that predated Christmas), also being said to represent Christ's crown of thorns, while the evergreen ivy is an ancient symbol of immortality. Do any of these associations have significance to you? If so, can you link the message of your dream with your waking circumstances?

If your dream featured a palm tree silhouetted against a sunny sky, it may simply have been a manifestation of your longing to take a vacation in exotic climes. Otherwise, consider the palm tree's ancient connotations. A symbol of victory in Roman times, it has numerous symbolic significances in Judaism (among others, representing the righteous person) and Christianity (when this recalls Christ's entry into Jerusalem, medieval

pilgrimages to the Holy Land, and resurrection). Or was your unconscious referring to the palm of your hand, which you should perhaps extend to someone with whom you've been feuding during your waking hours as a sign of peace and reconciliation? If your dreaming mind was drawn to an olive tree, your unconscious may similarly have been advising you to make the peace, or to hold out a metaphorical "olive branch," in the waking world. The olive's association with peace is derived from the Old Testament, which recounts that the dove returned to Noah's Ark bearing a branch from a tree that grew on the Mount of Olives, but because it bears olives, a source of valuable oil, it also denotes fertility and wealth. If you are Jewish, a dream olive tree may therefore have signified Jerusalem to you, or else your fervent desire for a prosperous, child-blessed future. But if your dream tree was a cedar, could it have been a cedar of Lebanon, and, if so, what significance does the Lebanon hold for you? Or if you dreamed of a maple tree, whose foliage is an emblem of Canada, could it

have represented a Canadian in your waking life?

Victors have been crowned with laurel leaves since the days of ancient Rome, so if a laurel, or bay, tree was the focus of your dream, could it have been reflecting your longing to be fêted for your professional achievements in the real world? Or was your unconscious warning you to keep someone "at bay"? The

Top left: Olive trees symbolize peace and prosperity. **Center left:** If you are a Christian, a thorny bough, prickly bush, or holly tree in your dream may have implied Christ's crown of thorns. **Above:** A dream palm tree may have suggested a vacation or victory. **Above left:** A dream that featured a maple leaf may have referred to a Canadian of your acquaintance. **Left:** The appearance of a Christmas tree may have temporarily immersed your dreaming self in an atmosphere of comfort and cheer.

laurel is an evergreen, and as the shedding of evergreen leaves is imperceptible to the human eye, early peoples deemed such trees symbols of immortality. So, if you dreamed of visiting a graveyard in which a loved one's grave was sheltered by a yew, your unconscious may have been highlighting its dual symbolism in both Celtic and Christian belief, namely of mourning, but also of eternal life. The cypress is similarly a funereal tree (because it was once thought to

prevent corpses from decaying), but, like many evergreens—or, indeed, any tall, thin tree—may also be a phallic symbol, as may pinecones, which, being the fruits of evergreen trees, may denote feminine fertility, too. If you dreamed of a cypress tree, are any of these associations relevant to your waking world, or was your unconscious making an oblique reference to Cyprus? Or if the sight of a pine tree gave you melancholic feelings in dreamland, are you "pining" for someone, or something, during your waking hours?

The ash, beech, birch, rowan, and hawthorn were all regarded as sacred by early European peoples, but it is the oak whose profound symbolism resonates the most strongly down the millennia. Dedicated to such gods of thunder and lightning as the ancient Greek Zeus, the Roman Jupiter, the Norse Thor, and the Teutonic Donar, the Druids designated the oak the embodiment of such masculine qualities as strength, solidity, and steadfastness, characteristics with which it continues to be linked to this day. So if your dreaming vision fell upon a venerable oak, was your unconscious advising you to stand firm against the barrage of slings and arrows to which

Left and bottom left: The mighty oak tree symbolizes masculine strength, and its acorns extraordinary potential. **Below center:** Depending on the context of your dream, a pinecone may have signaled either masculine virility or feminine fecundity. **Bottom center:** A mistletoe-festooned dream scene may signify your attraction to someone in the waking world.

you're being subjected in waking life? But, while the mistletoe that often grows on oak trees represented the feminine principle in Druidic belief, you may associate it primarily with Christmas and the tradition of embracing beneath it. So, if your dreaming attention was focused on a mistletoe sprig, is there anyone whom you're yearning to kiss in the real world?

Many other types of trees have been credited with specific powers and sacred connotations over many centuries, so if you believe that your unconscious was trying to transmit an important message by bringing your sleeping self face to face with a mulberry tree, for instance, but you have no idea why, it may be worth taking your ethnic background into account and then researching its traditional meaning. If you are of Chinese descent, for example, does the Chinese belief that the mulberry symbolizes industry have relevance to your waking life?

FLOWERS

The loveliness of their velvety or waxy petals, their jewel-bright or pastel colors, and their often exquisite fragrance have caused flowers to be regarded as the ultimate symbols of beauty, which is why we give them to people whom we love or admire. Because it is so fleeting, it is a beauty tinged with melancholy, however, for the moment when a once tightly furled bud fulfills its promise by bursting into glorious bloom also spells its doom. Flowers can thus represent the ephemerality of human life, yet because their death brings seeds into existence, and thus the next generation of flowers, they are also a symbol of hope for the future. As in the real world, so in the world of dreams: when the unconscious presents our sleeping selves with flowers, its purpose may be to raise our self-esteem, to denote the blossoming of potential, to reflect how we are feeling about ourselves and our relationships, or to console us by planting the seeds of optimism in our conscious minds.

When interpreting any dream that featured a flower, also remember that a bloom is a plant's reproductive structure, the carpel that it contains being the female reproductive organ, and the stamen, the male. If your dreaming mind zoomed in on a flower so that you had a detailed view of its internal components, the reference may, therefore, have been sexual. And if the flower that bloomed in your dream was one that you recognized, its personal or universal symbolic meaning may have further relevance to your waking life.

Buds and Blooms

Perhaps you dreamed that you ventured outside on a cold spring morning and were enchanted to notice that the bush growing beside your door bore the first tiny bud of the new season. If the dream occurred during the gloomy winter months, your unconscious may simply have been mirroring your longing for the arrival of the warmer days of spring. Alternatively, could it have highlighted the bud to draw attention to a budding relationship, your own latent potential, perhaps as an artist, or else to your young 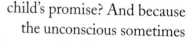 child's promise? And because the unconscious sometimes uses buds to represent children, and seeds to symbolize unborn babies, if you are actually childless, a dream like this may have been highlighting your yearning to become a parent in the real world. If your dreaming eyes focused on a seed or bud, otherwise consider the possibility that the seed signified the potential germination of an idea, or the bud the early growth of your brainchild. But if you dreamed that you pinched out the bud, perhaps to encourage lateral growth, could the message have been that you should

Above and left: Dream buds usually denote the potential of a child, concept, or talent, and blossoms, the fulfillment.

Right: If the stamens were evident, or the blooms were particularly deep and receptive, your dream flowers may have had a sexual connotation. **Center right:** If your dreaming attention was arrested by the sight of a flower in full bloom, did it reflect your own sense of having reached a high point in life? **Bottom:** The seed-stuffed head of a dream sunflower may have suggested that your mind is bursting with ideas, some of which may take root in the real world.

nip your nascent concept in the bud, or put a halt to it before it develops any further, to encourage the development of other, more fruitful, avenues in the waking world?

A dream bud may therefore represent the conception of a new life or idea, which, once made manifest, grows steadily larger until it reaches maturity, when it bursts into glorious bloom. So if you dreamed of regarding a plump, vigorous-looking bud with pleasure, could it have represented your daughter, who has just come of age, or else your brainchild, which seems to have developed a life of its own since you launched it into the real world? A flower may also represent you, however, so if you have reached the stage when all of the disparate elements of your waking life seem to have come together, so that you feel exhilarated and fulfilled, a dream in which you reveled in the beauty of a magnificent bloom may have been reflecting your sense of being in your prime, of

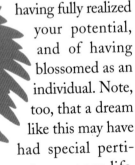

having fully realized your potential, and of having blossomed as an individual. Note, too, that a dream like this may have had special pertinence to your sex life, particularly if the flower's stamen (a phallic symbol) was prominent and you are a male dreamer, or if you watched a honey bee being enveloped in the folds of the bloom's lush petals and you are a female dreamer. But if you consciously feel that the "flower" of your youth has faded and your dream featured a blowsy bloom that had started to drop its petals, it may similarly have echoed your regret at having entered middle age.

Floral Scenarios

It is important to take the context into account when interpreting any dream in which flowers played a part. We generally give people flowers to congratulate them on a special occasion or achievement, or else as a gesture of love, friendship, appreciation, or condolence. If, for example, your partner presented your dreaming self with a bouquet of luscious blooms, did your dream reflect his or her loving behavior in waking life, or was your unconscious compensating you for your disappointment at never receiving a similar love token in the real world? If, however, you were the giver of flowers, who was the dream recipient? If it was someone whom you regard as being nothing more than an acquaintance during your waking hours, your dream may have been hinting that you harbor latent feelings of friendship for that person, or perhaps even that love is blossoming. Or was your unconscious implying that he or she is in need of a tangible ego-boost, or else your thanks or sympathy?

Maybe you were taken aback when your sister handed you a bunch of wilted blooms in a dream scene. If you are confused about the message inherent in your dream, think about the nature of your recent dealings with your sister, because it may be that your unconscious has detected a cooling in the warmth of her feelings for you and was warning that your relationship is weakening. And if you were pricked by a hidden thorn as you accepted a spray of roses from a colleague who was congratulating you on a promotion in the dream world, it is possible that she is concealing real feelings of resentment toward you in office life, hostile feelings that

Above: Flowers are symbols of feminine beauty, in both the real and dream worlds. **Left:** If you were thrilled to be presented with a bouquet in your dream, your unconscious may have been rewarding you with a well-deserved compliment, one that someone has neglected to give you in real life. **Below:** A dream of an inviting, flower-filled garden scene may have been encouraging your waking self to relax.

your unconscious is trying to bring to your conscious attention. Similarly, if you dreamed of giving a wreath composed entirely of dead flowers to the teacher who made your life a misery at school, your dream is likely to have highlighted your extreme dislike for him, although you probably don't actually wish him dead in the real world.

Perhaps you dreamed that you lounged lazily in a garden, imbued with a deep sense of peace and wellbeing as you surveyed the flower-filled borders. If so, your unconscious may on the one hand have been mirroring your waking sense of satisfaction with your current circumstances, or, on the other, have been urging you to take time out from your frantic working schedule to relax and enjoy the simple pleasures of life. Was your dream garden a riot of wildflowers (indicating a relaxed and creative approach to life), or were the blooms carefully regimented (suggesting a controlling and blinkered attitude)? Did you dream that you were relaxing in your garden when you suddenly realized that the flowers were drooping and that the earth beneath them was parched, causing you to rush to find water to revive the blooms? Because water symbolizes unconscious emotions, and earth, stability, perhaps a dream like this was implying that you are neglecting those around you and that the various personal relationships that underpin your waking life—symbolized by the wilting flowers—are by now in urgent need of reinvigorating and nurturing if they are to survive.

If you dreamed that you were arranging flowers in a vase, did you do so artlessly or take extreme care to place each bloom just so? The former approach suggests a *laissez-faire* approach to your relationship with others, while the latter signifies controlling tendencies. If the dream flowers were artificial, however, is it possible that those whom you think of as friends are actually showing you a false face, or persona? And if they were dried blooms, are your memories of past relationships more important to you than your interaction with the people who are currently part of your waking life?

When trying to interpret a dream that included flowers, remember, too, that the color of the flowers is significant, red, for instance, often hinting at love or vitality and white at innocence or mourning.

Opposite: A dream of wildflower vista may have implied that your creative talents will flourish if given free rein in a relaxed, natural environment. **Above right:** The positioning of the flowers in a dream floral arrangement can mirror how we unconsciously relate to others. **Right:** The colors of flowers may add an extra nuance to dreams. Pink blooms may denote wellbeing or romance, for example.

A Bouquet of Symbolism

If a particular type of flower was highlighted in the dream world, did it awaken a personal response in your dreaming mind? It may be, for example, that you have had an aversion to lilies ever since you saw them bedecking your grandmother's coffin at her funeral. Or maybe lilies hold a special place in your heart because you carried them in your wedding bouquet. But if the flower that featured in your dream evoked no strong personal associations, it is possible that your unconscious raided the lexicon of universal symbolism in an attempt to transmit its message to your conscious mind.

If you dreamed of a lily, but don't associate it with a funeral (when it may denote mourning and the afterlife) or a wedding (when innocence and hope are signified), are you a Christian? If so, the lily may have reminded you of the New Testament story of the Annunciation, when the Archangel Gabriel appeared to the Virgin Mary to inform her of her impending motherhood. If you are hoping to conceive, could this have been a wish-fulfillment dream, or was your unconscious advising you to follow Mary's example and be more compassionate to others during your waking hours? The white rose is also a symbol of Mary's virginity, as are rosebuds, but because the red rose was sacred to Aphrodite and Venus, the Greek and Roman goddesses of love, a dream in which a red rose featured is more likely to point toward a man's sensual, red-blooded love for a woman.

This page: If you dreamed of roses, lilies, or tulips, you may be unconsciously aware of their symbolic meaning. Roses (top) generally symbolize love and feminine beauty, white ones often signifying virginity, and red ones, sexuality. Lilies (center left) represent purity, but are also considered flowers of mourning. More prosaically, because the tulip (left) is its national flower, these blooms can represent The Netherlands.

Right: It is said that if you blow away all of a dandelion's seeds in one puff, your wish will come true. If you did this in dreamland, what was your unconscious wish? **Below right:** The chrysanthemum (at left) denotes longevity in Chinese and Japanese belief. **Bottom right:** Dream sunflowers may promise sunny times in the real world. **Below:** The lotus is an Eastern cosmic symbol.

If the rose reigns supreme in the garden of Western symbolism, its counterpart in the East is the lotus, whose seemingly miraculous ability to flower within murky waters has caused it to be venerated as a cosmic symbol that unites the underworld, earthly world, and spiritual realm, furthermore representing death, rebirth, and enlightenment. Sacred in ancient Egyptian belief, Taoism, and Hinduism, and honored as a heavenly flower in Islam, Buddha is sometimes termed the "Jewel in the Lotus," this flower also being equated with the yogic chakras, or energy centers, within the human body.

While the lotus stands for summer in traditional Chinese belief, the chrysanthemum symbolizes fall, as well as the virtue of scholarly retirement, so if you are of Chinese descent and dreamed of a chrysanthemum, your unconscious may have been urging you to study harder for the summer exams that you may be facing in the real world. Alternatively, because the chrysanthemum appears on Japan's national flag in stylized form, does Japan hold any significance for you? And if you admired the magnificent, seed-packed head of a sunflower—the floral embodiment of the summer sun—could it have portrayed your cherished hopes for the summer of your life?

Golden-eyed daisies (which also imply childhood innocence) and marguerites are both further solar symbols that may signal sunny optimism when they feature in dreams, unlike the poppy, a narcotic-yielding flower whose symbolic association with oblivion, and hence death, dates back to ancient Greece, when it was dedicated to Hypnos (the god of sleep) and Morpheus (the deity of dreams).

The poppy has become inextricably linked with death, but also with remembrance and rebirth, ever since blood-red poppies sprang up over World War I's fields of carnage, so if a poppy swayed gently in the breeze of your dream, could it have denoted your emotional numbness, or your poignant memories of a loved one who has departed this world?

If you are intrigued by the possibility that the inclusion of a specific flower in your dream may have been sending you a message, it's worth researching its medicinal and secular associations, as well as its spiritual and historical links. A final tip is to take the name of the dream flower into consideration. If your

dream homed in on a forget-me-not, could it have been reminding you that your mother's expecting you to pay her a real-life visit? Or, if you dreamed of a bleeding heart in full bloom, are you, or is someone close to you, heading for a broken heart?

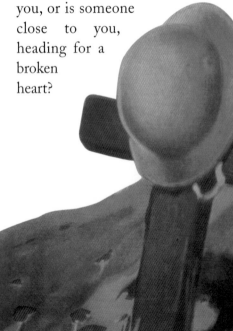

Top center: Dream daisies conjure up a vision of innocence and childlike fun. **Top right:** Did a dream cactus remind you of a "prickly" person in your waking world? **Above:** Foxgloves yield digitalin, a drug that is used to treat heart problems, so if you dreamed of this flower, was it referring to your broken heart or reminding you to see a doctor? **Above right:** The thistle is Scotland's national flower. **Right:** Poppies denote oblivion and death, but also commemoration.

🍎 FRUITS AND VEGETABLES 🍎

In the real world, fruits and vegetables provide us with a vital source of food, but, while their significance in the land of dreams is also linked with nurture, the reference is usually to feeding the emotions rather than to nourishing the body. Ripe fruits may also represent the fruits of your labor or loins in the language of dreams, and thus a sweet reward for the hope, time, and effort that you've invested in their cultivation.

In ancient times, fruits were considered symbols of both feminine fertility and immortality (on account of the seeds that they contain), an association that is echoed by the rounded shape of such fruits as apples and melons, which suggest the child-bearing womb, as well as breasts. And as a result of the influence of Freudian theory, certain fruits, notably the banana, along with cylindrically formed vegetables like cucumbers and carrots, are today considered phallic symbols, while a parallel is often drawn between nuts and the testes. So if any of these fruits or vegetables are featured in your dream, consider their possible meaning in relation to your sex life.

Although herbs are also edible plants, their age-old use as natural remedies has imbued them with healing symbolism, so if you dreamed of gathering mint and your waking hours are plagued by digestive problems, perhaps your unconscious was suggesting a treatment that may actually prove effective.

Fruits and Nuts

Maybe your dream found you up a ladder in an orchard, plucking apple after rosy apple from a tree. If so, your dream may have been confirming your sense of satisfaction with your waking life, perhaps because, after years of hard graft, your business is finally profitable or because your children have grown up and are doing well for themselves. In other words, thanks to your careful nurturing, the seeds that you once planted—whether they represent the offspring of your mind or your body—have thrived, flowered, matured, and borne fruit, so that you are now being rewarded with the sweet taste of success.

Left: Fruits offer the sweet taste of success when they appear in dreams. This apple tree, for example, implies that the fruits of your labor are now ripe for the plucking.

Right: If you believe that your dream bananas were phallic symbols, were they transmitting a message about your sex life? **Below center:** In dreams, rounded apples and oranges sometimes represent breasts. **Bottom:** Did the peaches in your dream confirm your waking belief that your circumstances are "peachy" at present? **Bottom right:** The pineapple is an ancient symbol of fertility.

Similarly, if you dreamed of feeding and watering a vigorous young fruit tree, your unconscious may have been highlighting your conscious efforts to nurture and cultivate either the promising plan that has recently sprung up in your mind, or else your young son, for whom you cherish the highest of hopes. But, if we metaphorically reap what we sow, or receive the rewards that we deserve, if your dream crop was stunted or blighted, your unconscious may have been reflecting your real sense of disappointment that the fruits of your labor have been spoiled, be it by a pernicious external influence or because you neglected them at a crucial stage of their development. So, if you had a dream like this, could your unconscious have been warning you to take steps to safeguard your family or business before any incipient damage becomes irreversible?

Fruits have connotations other than just reward in the language of dreams, however, and when interpreting any dream that highlighted a fruit, it is important to take its shape, texture,

and freshness into account, because your unconscious may have selected it to reflect your sexuality. The banana is closely associated with masculine virility on account of its phallic shape, so if you are a man who dreamed of this fruit, was it a green banana, indicating youth and sexual immaturity; a ripe, yellow banana, signaling a man at his sexual peak; or a brownish, shrunken banana, suggesting an older man who has passed his sexual prime? Curvaceous fruits like apples, pears, and melons have long been compared with female breasts, so if you are a man who took a lingering bite out of a yielding, juicy pear in an exquisite dream moment, could your dream have been mirroring your desire to become intimate with a certain woman in waking life? But if you are a woman who dreamed of looking sadly at a shriveled pear that you held in your hand, could your unconscious have been echoing your regret for your lost youth?

If you dreamed of a particular type of fruit, especially if it represented an exotic departure from the fruits that you usually enjoy, it may be that you are unconsciously aware of its cultural significance, and that this pertains to your waking world. The poets of Arabia

famously compared the peach's dimpled appearance to a pair of young, pert buttocks, for instance, so if you dreamed of admiring a velvety peach, could it have represented your own derriere, or that belonging to someone to whom you're attracted in real life? Otherwise, are you pleased that your life currently seems "peachy," or in excellent order, or was your unconscious commenting on your feelings for your new girlfriend, whom you consider to be wonderful, or a "peach"? In Chinese and Japanese traditions, the peach is furthermore a symbol of immortality, so that a dream peach may have hinted at your sense of invincibility, or your

Above: Dreaming of a fruit bowl overflowing with the bounty of nature may have reflected your own sense of being amply blessed at this stage in your life. **Top right:** If you are a Buddhist, a dream fig may have recalled the sacred bodhi tree under whose shelter Buddha gained enlightenment. **Above right:** A choice of dream cherries may have referred to real-life "cherry-picking." **Right:** Could a dream of lemons have highlighted your current sour state of mind?

satisfaction that you will live on in your children after your death.

Numerous cultures have associated rounded, seed-packed fruits with the fruitfulness of the womb, so if you are a woman who is hoping to conceive in real life, it could be that dreaming of eating a pomegranate, for example, affirmed your waking wishes. The fig is also a symbol of fecundity, but if you dreamed that you refused a fig that a friend offered you in your dream, and you have fallen out with her during your waking hours, could you have been unconsciously expressing your feeling of not "giving a fig," or caring about, your friendship any more? Indeed, remember the many slang expressions to which fruits have lent their names. If you dreamed of savoring a date, for instance, could it have represented a dream date on which you're hoping to be asked? Or if

you plucked a cherry from a dream tree, could your action have referred to your tendency to "cherry-pick" the best players for your work or sports team, or was the cherry a reference to someone's virginity? And could your dream plum have symbolized the "plum," or highly paid, job for which you've recently applied?

Not all fruits have entirely positive connotations. In Judeo–Christian belief, for example, the apple denotes temptation and sin, as exemplified by Adam and Eve's expulsion from the Garden of Eden after the serpent had tempted Eve to taste the apple growing on the Tree of Knowledge, while many classical myths tell of the "apple of discord." So if you're married, but were tempted to take a bite from an apple that was being proffered by an attractive stranger in a dream scene, could the apple have represented "forbidden fruit," or the attractions of a marriage-disrupting affair? And in contrast to the orange, which resembles the sun and may recall sunny times in dreams, the lemon can be mouth-puckeringly sour, so if you dreamed of sucking a lemon, was it mirroring your acerbic behavior or acid tongue in waking life?

Below: Tomatoes were once thought to be aphrodisiacs, so if you ate a tomato in dreamland, should you be pepping up your love life? **Right:** Because we are said to reap what we sow, an abundant dream crop may have been holding out the hope that your hard work will be rewarded by an abundant harvest that will safeguard your future.

They may be less juicy than fruits, but nuts are also part of nature's bounty and therefore share fruits' overall symbolism of fertility, prosperity, and well-being. And because their edible kernels are encased in hard shells, they may furthermore denote hidden wisdom. Did you dream of having to exert almost superhuman force before cracking open a nut? If so, your unconscious may have been referring to a "tough nut," or someone who presents a hard face to the world at large, but whom you suspect is far sweeter inside, or else to a difficult problem with which you're wrestling in the waking world, which is proving "a tough nut to crack," although you hope that you will be well rewarded when you finally do so. There may also be a sexual subtext when your dreaming vision homes in on a particular type of nut. Because the almond's shape resembles female genitalia, and because it is a symbol of the Virgin Mary in Christian belief, a dream almond may have denoted a girl's virginal state, for instance. Remember, too, the meanings associated with the slang word "nuts," so that if you dreamed of a bowl filled with nuts, could your unconscious have been making an oblique reference to testicles, or was it reflecting the current craziness of your waking circumstances?

Cereals, Vegetables, and Herbs

Cereal crops like maize, wheat, and rice—staple foods the world over—have a shared, and universal, significance when they appear in dreams, one that amplifies the message denoted by harvesting dream fruit. If the crop appeared healthy and abundant, your dreaming mind was, no doubt, reflecting your optimism that you will reap a rich harvest, or rewards, for the emotional effort that you have invested in your waking ventures, but if it was blighted and sparse, you are probably unconsciously aware that there are hard, unproductive times to come.

Like fruits, vegetables provide nutrients and nourishment, but unlike luscious fruits, we rarely regard them as sweet treats, which is why they signal only basic emotional sustenance in dreams. And because we often insultingly refer to people who are dull, lazy, sluggish, or even clinically comatose, as "vegeta-

Left: In dreams, vegetables can signify a mind that is "vegetating." **Below left:** A dream mushroom can signal that something is "mushrooming," or growing rapidly, in the waking world. **Below and opposite, bottom left:** If you dreamed of digging up vegetables, can you equate them with personal qualities that you want to unearth in yourself? **Opposite, right:** Was a dream of garlic advising you to add more flavor to a bland lifestyle? **Opposite, far right:** If potatoes are a staple of your waking diet, was a dream potato telling you to seek vital emotional sustenance? **Opposite, bottom right:** Could your unconscious have summoned mint into your sleep to urge you to take this remedy for your digestive problems or halitosis?

If your dream highlighted a cucumber, was your unconscious advising you to be "as cool as a cucumber," or to remain calm and self-possessed, during the interview that you're scheduled to undergo tomorrow? Or if the

bles," "cabbages," or "couch potatoes," it's important not to dismiss this possible meaning when interpreting any dream that highlighted vegetables because your unconscious may have been alerting you to your tendency to "vegetate," or slip passively into an idle, monotonous, and unstimulating existence. Remember that your personal preferences may also influence a dream in which you were confronted by a plate of vegetables, so that if you detest peas, for example, but were forced to eat them as a child, you may still associate them with punishment. But if, having taken all of these considerations into account,

you remain flummoxed by your vegetable dream, it may be that your unconscious was drawing from a wider source of symbolism than your own limited experience in order to send its message.

If you dreamed of a long, rigid vegetable—perhaps a cucumber, or else a carrot or leek—could your unconscious have summoned a phallic symbol into your dream, and, if so, why? Whatever your sex, maybe it referred to your sexual appetite, or, if you are a woman, to intimacy issues. But also consider the expressions associated with such vegetables.

dream vegetable was a carrot and you're having problems controlling your wayward teenage son in the real world, could your dream have been advocating dangling a "carrot," or reward for good behavior, under his nose? The leek is the emblem of Wales, so could a dream leek have been referring to a Welsh person in your life, or was your unconscious warning that someone is "leaking" confidential information during office hours by passing it on to a rival company? Similarly, if you dreamed of taking a bite from a baked potato that had just come out of the oven and burning your mouth, did it parallel the "hot potato," or awkward situation, with which you're having to deal in the real world? And if you found yourself shelling peas in your dream, which individuals in your waking life (and do not discount yourself) are like "peas in a pod," that is, virtually indistinguishable because they look and behave so similarly? Could a dream in which time seemed to have been speeded up and you watched mushrooms multiply at an astonishingly fast rate have indicated that your family business is "mushrooming," or growing at such a rapid pace, that you're having difficulty keeping up with demand?

Onions are notorious for their power to stimulate tears when cut, so if you dreamed of weeping copiously while laboring over a chopping board, did your dream onions provide a much-needed catalyst for emotional release, enabling you to shed the tears of sadness or frustration that you are holding back during your waking hours? But if you dreamed of peeling a clove of garlic, also a member of the *Allium* family, do you regard it as a flavor-enhancer (do you crave more sensory stimulation in waking life?), as a shield against vampires (is someone draining your vitality in the real world?), or as a powerful antioxidant and friend to your cardiovascular system (are you worried about your health)?

Indeed, garlic's medicinal properties have earned it the respect of herbal practitioners over the course of many centuries, and if your dream drew your attention to any type of herb, consider the possibility that your unconscious has detected

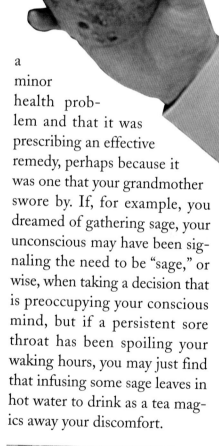

a minor health problem and that it was prescribing an effective remedy, perhaps because it was one that your grandmother swore by. If, for example, you dreamed of gathering sage, your unconscious may have been signaling the need to be "sage," or wise, when taking a decision that is preoccupying your conscious mind, but if a persistent sore throat has been spoiling your waking hours, you may just find that infusing some sage leaves in hot water to drink as a tea magics away your discomfort.

FIRE

In times past, the human body was said to contain the four elements (fire, earth, air, and water) in fluid form. The predominant element, or "humor," was thought to influence the character, so that fire bestowed a choleric, or bad-tempered, nature. Similarly, in astrological belief, a person born under a zodiacal fire sign (Aries, Leo, or Sagittarius) is said to possess the masculine qualities of aggression and vigor. These traditional beliefs contribute one strand of meaning to a dream in which a fire roared, when its flames may have denoted your own fiery, or passionate, temperament or volatile energy.

The second potential significance of fire in dreams lies in its power to transform and purify everything that its all-consuming flames encounter. This interpretation may apply if your dreaming self felt strangely uplifted and relieved as you watched your possessions being destroyed in a raging inferno. Indeed, your dreaming reaction to the fire, along with its context, will give you vital clues as to your dream's meaning.

A controlled fire, such as one that burns merrily in the fireplace of a family home, creates a warm and cozy atmosphere, so that a third possible interpretation of a fire-featuring dream points toward domestic contentment, or else the need for it. Alternatively, because a candle's flame illuminates its surroundings, if your dreaming eyes focused on a flame, intellectual or spiritual enlightenment may have been signified.

Finally, fire dreams may be anxiety dreams. It is possible that your unconscious has detected an actual fire hazard, so if your dream was particularly disturbing, or recurring, it would be wise to check electrical fittings, smoke alarms, and areas of your home that contain potentially flammable clutter. Alternatively, your fears may stem from your own careless attitude to fire hazards or the presence in your waking life of an enemy whose anger has recently been inflamed.

Kindling, Fanning, and Stoking the Flames

If you dreamed of lighting a fire, what sort of fire was it, and was anyone else present? Because the kindling of a flame can indicate that a vital form of energy has been summoned into being, if it was a fire in a hearth, your dream may have reflected the emotional energy inherent in close relationships with loved ones, a sustaining warmth in which you are

either currently cocooned or yearn to enjoy. If you dreamed of lighting a stove or barbecue in preparation for cooking a meal for friends and family, however, the reference may have been to your willingness to devote your energy to providing those around you with emotional nourishment. But if you lit a candle at the center of a table set for two in a romantic dream setting, who was your dinner date? The message imparted by your dreaming action may have hinted that a flame of passion for that person has recently been ignited within you. Had the dream candle thrown new light on your feelings for him or her when you awoke? Conversely, if you blew out the candle in your dream, could the message have been that your former lover is now an "old flame"? If you dreamed of curling up with your girlfriend in front of a log cabin's roaring fire, the dream flames may have reflected the sexual "heat" that characterizes the relationship between the two of you.

We often harness the power of fire to help us to create objects and products, so if you dreamed that you were working at a forge or furnace, could the implication have been that, having developed a "burning interest" in a certain creative or intellectual concept in waking life, you are now pouring all of your energy into making it a reality, or that you should do so? We also use fire to destroy our unwanted items, however, so if you dreamed of building a bonfire in your yard, what were you about to consign to the flames? Was it fallen leaves or other garden detritus? If so, could your unconscious have been signaling that it's high time you cleared your mind of the clutter of the past (when your dream may alternatively have portrayed you destroying old papers or photographs), leaving you feeling mentally and emotionally reinvigorated? Or if your dreaming self was about to incinerate a pile of old clothes that had seen better days, could your dream have been attempting to encourage you to transform your image?

Opposite, center: Dream flames may mirror a fiery temperament. **Opposite, bottom left:** If you lit a match in a dream scene, has a spark of passion been kindled in your heart recently? **Opposite, bottom right:** Blowing out a dream candle may denote the snuffing out of a burning interest. **Left:** Dream candles can symbolize intellectual illumination or romantic feelings. **Bottom:** If you harnessed the power of fire in a dream, was your unconscious telling you to "fire up" your creative energies?

Whatever your purpose in lighting your dream fire, did it burn vigorously or did you have to fan it, stoke it, and feed it more fuel in order to keep it alight? If so, your unconscious may have been warning that the love, passion, creativity, or desire for transformation that your dream flame symbolized is flickering, waning in strength, and in danger of dying unless you take steps to revitalize it. So if, for example, boredom is creeping into your relationship with your partner, do you need to "fan the flames" of your ardor before it peters out and dies? Or if the demands of

your working life have forced you to neglect your real passion, perhaps a hobby, could your dream have been urging you to inject more time and energy into reviving it because it has the power to transform your life? When interpreting any dream in which you lit a flame or fire, it's important to remember that it may have denoted the kindling of a positive energy or enthusiasm within yourself, which is why both the dream fire's subsequent vigor and your control of it are significant. So, did you actively encourage it to burn brightly or did you dampen down its flames?

Fireworks and Explosions

Perhaps you dreamed that you stood enthralled and elated as you watched fireworks exploding overhead, brilliantly illuminating the dark night sky. And are you celebrating a stellar achievement in the real world, such as a promotion at work? If so, it may be that the dream fireworks were highlighting your intense, albeit fleeting, feelings of ecstasy at your waking triumph. Because fireworks are often used to symbolize sexual climax in the language of the movies, don't disregard their erotic connotation when trying to interpret your dream (particularly if the fireworks were rockets, which your unconscious may have selected for their phallic symbolism), or forget that we sometimes speak of "fireworks" to denote explosions fueled by incandescent rage.

Indeed, any dream explosion may have reflected your own "short fuse," quick temper, or feelings of pent-up fury or frustration, which are building up to such an extent that they may soon detonate in your waking world, or perhaps already have. Did your sleeping self "get a bang," or thrill, out of the dream explosion, or is there something in your life to which you wish you could put an emphatic end, thereby "going out with a bang"? If so, was it you who lit the fuse and detonated the explosive in your dream, and what did the explosion destroy? Can you make a link with what is infuriating you in the real world?

Blazing Infernos

Did you wake in a fever of terror from a dream in which you watched helplessly as a raging inferno threatened to consume everything that you hold dear in waking life: your home, your possessions, and possibly even your loved ones? If your dreaming self was exposed to such a nightmare scenario, consider the possibility that you may have unconsciously noticed a fire hazard in your home, heed the message of your dream, and carry out some safety checks as soon as you can. Yet rather than having been a literal warning, a dream like this is more likely to have highlighted your emotional state, or a situation in the real world

Opposite: In the language of dreams, fireworks can signify celebrations, climaxes, or explosions of anger. **This page:** A dream in which a fire raged out of control was almost certainly a warning. Was the message that your vehicle, home, or workplace is really about to go up in smoke, or that your rage may soon ignite your waking world?

personally? Would they be catastrophic? Would expressing your fury result in you being "fired" from your job, a relationship "going up in smoke," and all that you have consciously worked for being reduced to cinders? Or would you actually feel liberated by giving free-reign to your all-consuming anger, and, having metaphorically discharged your "firepower," then "burned your bridges," and put the past behind you, would you welcome the chance to start afresh? Your dreaming response to the devastation wreaked by the inferno should tell you whether the destructive energy emitted by the blaze has a positive or negative parallel in the real world. Remember, too, that total destruction cannot be bad if, like the mythical phoenix, you arise renewed from the ashes.

that has become so overheated that it is threatening to ignite and then burn out of control, with devastating consequences.

Maybe the dream blaze mirrored your own burning anger in the waking world, an interpretation that may be particularly pertinent if you dreamed of your home catching fire, it being said that houses represent ourselves (and if you dreamed that the fire started in a particular room, refer to the chapter that discusses the home, pages 162–70, for the room's symbolic significance). If you think that this may be the case, ask yourself who, or what, has provoked you to fly into such a towering rage (family arguments, perhaps?), and whether the full force of your anger is about to burst loose from your conscious control in the real world. And if it were to do so, what would the consequences be for you

Did you become transfixed with horror as you were watching the flames leap and crackle in your dream, or did you frantically try to fight them back? If you assumed a firefighter's role in a fiery dream scene, the implication is that you are battling to keep your passions (not necessarily angry ones) under control in the wak-

Opposite, top: Did a dream inferno fill you with terror or a strange sense of release? **Opposite, bottom:** If you raised the alarm in your dream, who started the fire or where did it break out? Your unconscious may have been telling you to tread cautiously around the dream arsonist or to carry out some safety checks during your waking hours. **Left:** Bringing a dream fire under control suggests that you are managing to dampen down your fiery emotions. **Below left and below:** If smoke permeated your dream, take it as a warning signal.

ing world, and may very well be successful. Did you dream that you inadvertently caused the fire in your dream, maybe because you were so thrilled by the sparks that were generated when you threw wood onto the hearth that you got carried away and forgot about the hazard that you were creating? If so, the reference could have been to your burgeoning lust for someone in your waking world, a person with whom it would be dangerous to have a sexual liaison, perhaps because one of you is married. Could your unconscious have been warning that you are "playing with fire" and in danger of having your "fingers burned"—or, indeed, far worse—unless you dampen down

your feelings for that individual? And if you found yourself on fire in dreamland, struggling unsuccessfully to smother the flames that had taken hold of you, it is likely that your passion is devouring you. But if, in your dream, you then poured bucket after bucket of water over the flames and managed to contain them, your unconscious could have been suggesting that you are actually reasserting control over the fire that was raging within you. If, however, your lasting memory of your dream is of having been unable to escape the all-consuming flames, you probably feel hopelessly trapped by your blazing desire.

Smoke, Embers, and Ashes

Although they imply fire, and thus all of its symbolic meanings, smoke, embers, and ashes have specific connotations of their own when they appear in dreams. If clouds of black, choking smoke obscured your dreaming vision, but there was no sign of a fire, for example, ask yourself what your unconscious was suggesting that you are unable to recognize. It is said that there is "no smoke without fire," so could the suggestion have been that you are unable to pinpoint the cause of your waking feelings of claustrophobia and uneasiness? What is making you fume in the real world? Could it

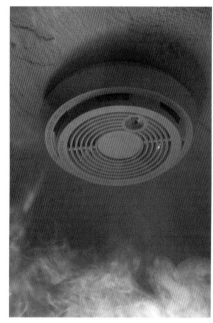

flare up at any moment if provoked during your waking hours? Or did the embers represent your love for your former husband, a fondness that you never quite managed to extinguish? And if you dreamed of rooting around in the ashes of a long-dead fire, searching for the remains of the wedding ring that you'd consigned to the flames as a symbol of your divorce, could you

that your marital relationship is now dead and buried? Finally, also consider the possibility that your unconscious was warning that you face a real risk of "burnout" if you continue to concentrate your waking energies exclusively on your career.

be a stifling relationship or your own simmering anger? Or was your unconscious sending you a "smoke signal" to tell you that there's something that you need to "smoke out," perhaps the secret that your teenage daughter's hinted at keeping, but is refusing to divulge, during your waking hours?

If you observed the glowing embers of a dying fire in your dream, they may have suggested that a passion that once burned brightly in your heart is waning, or else that it could be reignited if fed the right fuel. Could a dream like this have referred to your smoldering anger, which you have managed to calm, but that may

have been metaphorically "raking over the ashes," or remembering how happy you were as a newly-wed, even though you are certain

Top left: If the shrill sound of a smoke alarm deafened your dreaming self, could it have been triggered by the fire that is burning within you? **Left:** Dreaming of a dying fire implies that the warmth that once pervaded your domestic life is cooling, while an ash-heaped fireplace suggests that the affection in which you once basked has died. **Below:** A dream obscured by a cloud of dense, asphyxiating smoke can mirror a sense of being suffocated by someone's seething anger in the real world.

EARTH

Like its fellow elements, earth has ancient associations with the human body and personality. The governor of one of the four "humors" that were once thought to flow within the body, an imbalance weighted in earth's favor was traditionally said to impart a melancholy, or gloomy personality. Furthermore, according to Western astrological belief, people born under the zodiacal earth signs of Taurus, Virgo, and Capricorn are believed to be characterized by their patience and emotional solidity, or "earthiness." Because your unconscious mind may have tapped into these age-old principles, always take them into consideration when trying to make sense of a dream that highlighted the earth.

If you are a gardener, you will know that cultivating the earth can reap astounding rewards in the form of flourishing flowers and fruits, which is why the earth is associated with the bountiful fertility of "Mother Earth," also the giver of sustenance, stability, and security. But because the cycle of earthly life ends in death, when earth is featured in a dream, it may instead denote the culmination of a phase of your life. A dream of digging, feeding, or watering the earth may therefore have portrayed your wish to bring a new existence into being, while one of being underground may have implied a desire to undergo a profound transformation, the death of your old self enabling you to be reborn as a new individual.

While a dream of standing on solid ground may have mirrored your own "groundedness" in the real world, one in which the ground gave way under your feet probably reflected your unconscious insecurity and uneasy sense of having to dodge the pitfalls that strew your passage through the waking world. And if you suffered the nightmare of being buried alive, do you feel that the demands of others are suffocating your individuality and freedom of action? But, if you managed to discover a subterranean means of escape from your living tomb, did you stumble across anything significant as you made your way to the surface? If so, your dream may have provided you with the key to transforming your current circumstances, thereby allowing you to live your waking life in the sunshine, not the darkness.

Cultivating the Soil

Plant a seed, and, if the conditions are right, the earth will encourage its germination, as well as providing the nourishment that it needs for growth and solid foundations in which to root itself. So if your dream depicted you sowing a seed in the dark, rich earth, try to make the link between the dream scene and your waking world. Could the seed have represented the baby that you and your partner are hoping to conceive in real life, and the soil, the physical and emo-

Left: Be it in the real or dream world, seedlings will only thrive if rooted in stable, sustaining foundations. **Above:** The sowing of dream seeds may refer to the planting of a concept in fertile ground, or a receptive mind, much as Liberty was once envisaged scattering the seeds of victory over the earth.

Left: A dream of healthy crops can suggest that your waking ventures—or children— are flourishing. **Below left:** Could a grassy lawn have referred to your "turf," or the place where you are grounded? **Below:** Arid earth implies exhausted energy reserves.

Did you dream that you seized a shovel and started digging a hole in the earth, not for the purpose of planting anything, but because you hoped to uncover something? If so, did your shovel reveal what you were looking for? A dream like this may have a number of meanings. You may, for example, be carrying out a research project during your waking hours, but need to "unearth" a vital piece of evidence before you can complete it, in which case your dream discovery may have symbolized that crucial missing link. Otherwise, could your unconscious have been alerting you to the need to "get to the bottom of," or learn the truth about, your friend's behavior, which has been suspiciously out of character recently? Or, if you are consciously preoccupied with finding out more about your family history, was your dream mirroring your quest to discover more

tional nurturing that it would receive, enabling it to grow and thrive in a loving and supportive family environment? Or could your dream instead have referred to an intellectual or creative seed that has recently been planted, or taken root, in your fertile imagination, one that has the potential to blossom and bear fruit if cultivated and cher- ished? If, however, you dreamed of scratching around in a patch of parched, bar- ren-looking earth, the implication may have been that you have become so drained by the demands of your waking life that your emotional and physical reserves have now become dangerously depleted.

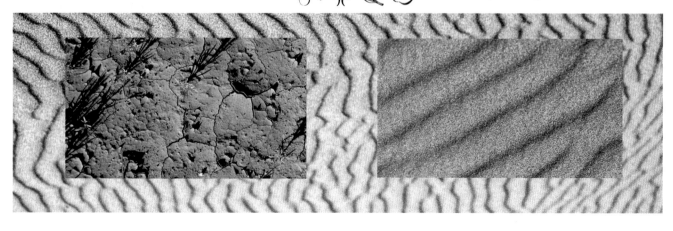

about your "roots," much as an archeologist digs downward, through the layers of the past? But if you dreamed of burying something in the earth, what are you trying to "bury," cover up, or hide from others in the real world? A shameful secret, perhaps, the very thought of which makes you feel "soiled," or dirty?

When trying to decode your dream, also consider the expressions associated with digging. Were you "digging in" in dreamland, or preparing to protect yourself from a verbal attack (perhaps "a dig," or hurtful comment) that you anticipate being launched on you in the waking world? Or did your dream reflect your

"entrenched," or firmly established, opinions? Alternatively, was your unconscious advising you to adopt a more "down-to-earth" approach to your daily life by being more realistic, sensible, or practical?

That Sinking Feeling

Maybe you dreamed that you were struggling to keep your balance as you slipped and squelched your way across a waterlogged field before finally falling over and ending up covered in mud. If so, do you feel that your reputation has been besmirched during your waking hours, and that you have lost the respect of others as a result? Has your "name been dragged through the mud," perhaps because you've been accused of behaving badly toward someone, or have you been the victim of "mud-slinging," or slander, in your waking world? Alternatively, have you been

involved recently in a situation, or with a person, that has made you feel somehow grubby, sullied, or guilty?

But rather than sliding on the surface of the mud, did you dream that you became stuck in it, and that it then sucked you ever downward, despite your frantic efforts to free yourself? A dream like this may have depicted your waking sense of being caught fast in a situation that is threatening to consume your individuality or

Above left: A dream of a person or animal digging in an apparently tranquil landscape may highlight your fear of unpalatable hidden truths being exposed, disrupting your waking world. **Below left and below:** A dream of being covered in mud usually has negative connotations, that is, unless you observed a pig rolling ecstatically in the mire. Could your unconscious have been urging you to take a "down-to-earth" approach in the real world?

you been turning a blind eye to his mother's hostility to you, and does she have the power to wreck your relationship?

Did you lose your balance and fall into the huge hole that gaped beneath your feet in your dream? If you did, could your unconscious have been sending an urgent signal that you are on the verge of "putting your foot in it," or making a catastrophic blunder, in real life? And if your dreaming self scrabbled frenziedly, but in vain, to clamber out of the abyss, did your dream parallel your hopeless sense of being "in a hole," or a desperate situation,

Left and opposite, bottom: In dreams, plunging clefts in the earth may warn of dangerous hazards that are waiting to trap and swallow you up in the real world. **Opposite, top, and below:** The entrance to a dream cave may have been inviting you to return to the metaphorical womb, while a dream of someone digging a grave may have reflected your desire to undergo a symbolic death and be reborn as a new person.

energy, and your powerlessness to break free of its clutches. Ask yourself what this dream scene could have represented in the real world. Could the clinging mud have symbolized an archetypal terrible-mother figure in your life, someone who is dominating or suffocating you, undermining your sense of self, and feeding off your energy? Could it have referred to your constricting, soul-destroying marriage, which is swallowing up your hope and love of life? Or was your unconscious signaling that you have become a prisoner of your own blinkered vision or inhibitions, so that you have become a "stick-in-the-mud"?

Perhaps you dreamed that you were strolling through the green and pleasant countryside when the earth suddenly opened up in front of you and you found yourself teetering on the brink of a yawning chasm. If so, your dream was probably warning of a hidden "pitfall" that you are about to encounter in the waking world, a potentially significant problem, or even a trap that someone has laid for you, that you have unconsciously recognized, although your conscious mind has disregarded the threat. You may, for instance, believe that your relationship with your new boyfriend is going swimmingly, but have

in real life—for example, are you deeply in debt? Another possible interpretation for dreams like these may be your insecurity, the root of which may be your constant anxiety about making the wrong decision, or of being "wrong-footed," during your waking hours.

Being Buried Alive

Having plummeted into a hole in your dream, did your efforts to climb out again dislodge the earth above you, prompting it to collapse around your head and pinning you to the ground? As you lay in the oppressive darkness, fighting to breathe and des-

perately trying to claw your way out, your anxiety dream must have mutated into a nightmare. But why did your sleeping self dream up this horrific scenario? The most probable explanation for the nightmare of being buried alive is that you have allowed the demands, obligations, and worries of daily life to get so on top of you that you have become paralyzed with depression and feel that you are at the bottom of a "black hole" from which you can see no way out. If your dream mirrored

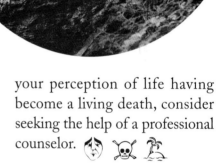

your perception of life having become a living death, consider seeking the help of a professional counselor.

A more specific threat may have been highlighted if your dreaming self was certain that someone (maybe a rival at work in waking life) deliberately buried you alive, however. Indeed, by depicting you in such a nightmarish position, your unconscious was almost certainly trying to force you to consciously recognize that person's overwhelming hostility toward you, and his or her desire to see your hopes and ambitions "dead and buried."

Going Underground

Perhaps your dream hole was of your own making, however, and you observed yourself tunneling energetically into the depths of the earth in your dream. If so, what was the purpose of your

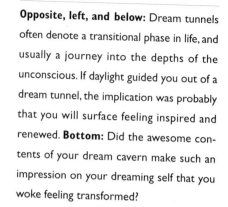

Opposite, left, and below: Dream tunnels often denote a transitional phase in life, and usually a journey into the depths of the unconscious. If daylight guided you out of a dream tunnel, the implication was probably that you will surface feeling inspired and renewed. **Bottom:** Did the awesome contents of your dream cavern make such an impression on your dreaming self that you woke feeling transformed?

excavation? If you are a male dreamer, you may be interested to know that many dream analysts equate holes with the vagina, so that your dream may have been imbued with sexual innuendo. And whatever your sex, because the vagina leads to the womb, it may be that your waking experiences are currently so unpleasant that you long to shut out the wounding influences of the outside world by retreating into the sanctuary of a warm, protective cocoon. Similarly, would you welcome the opportunity to "hole up," or withdraw, take cover, or hide, from others for a while in the waking world in order to regain your strength or retreat to lick your wounds? Alternatively, was your dream shining a spotlight on your "underground" tastes, that is, your secret, subversive, or experimental leanings, to which you are unable to give expression in real life?

There is another explanation for a dream of burrowing underground, or of entering a subterranean tunnel, however. The tunnel is a symbol of transition, while the bowels of the earth may signify the deepest levels of your unconscious, so that a dream of journeying underground may have denoted your search for the key to your potential transformation, a key that lies buried deep within you, but may be difficult to find. Having passed through the tunnel, did you find yourself in an underground cavern in your dream, and, if so, who, or what, did you encounter there? At the end of the dream scene, did you then see the "light at the end of the tunnel" and make your way to the surface full of hope for a better future? And do you now feel ready to wave goodbye to the old you, and are you looking forward to beginning a new phase of life?

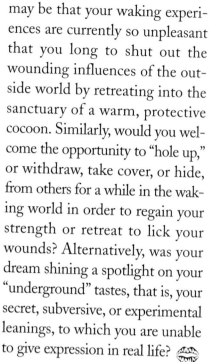

AIR

We may not be able to see it, but air is crucial to our survival, which is why it can be a symbol of life and wellbeing. A dream of fighting for air may therefore have reflected the psychologically suffocating circumstances of your waking life. Because the sky, which is composed of air, is said to provide access to the heavenly realms, this element represents spiritual aspirations, too, and through its association with "higher things," also intellectual aims or career ambitions. Dreaming of soaring through the air may consequently have mirrored your own quest for spiritual or intellectual inspiration or achievement.

If you felt thrillingly weightless and free during your dream flight, your unconscious may otherwise have been referring to your sense of liberation and adventurousness, or else to your desire to rise far above the mundane restrictions and concerns of your waking life. A dream of flying a kite, or of letting a balloon drift upward, sends a similar message, but if you dreamed of falling through the air attached to a parachute, the implication was more likely to have been your need to escape a difficult situation in the waking world, maybe by "coming back down to earth." If, however, you dreamed that you were floating in the gondola of a hot-air balloon and admired the view, your unconscious may have been advising you to look at the wider picture when trying to resolve a problem that is dogging your waking hours.

Further considerations to take into account when trying to decipher the message of a dream in which the air seemed significant are this element's traditional associations. According to the theory of the elemental "humors" that were once thought to course through the human body, for example, air's influence bestows an optimistic and confident outlook. In addition, if you were born under one of the zodiacal air signs (Gemini, Libra, or Aquarius), astrologers regard you as having intellectual and spiritual aspirations.

The Breath of Life

Did you wake up with a gasp of relief after having endured a dream in which the stifling, airless atmosphere made every breath seem like a battle for survival? If so, it may have been that your bedsheets were obstructing your nose or mouth, that you had developed a blocked nose, or that you suffered the onset of a real respiratory problem, such as sleep apnea (a temporary inability to breathe), while you were sleeping. If none of these physical causes are likely to have accounted for your dream, however, could your unconscious have inflicted the symptoms of suffocation on your sleeping self to force you to recognize how you are feeling when you're awake? Perhaps you are in a relationship with a partner who

hates letting you out of her sight, and feel that your lack of freedom to do as you will, and to come and go as you please, is stifling your individuality. Or do you despairingly feel that the demands of your dead-end job are killing your intel-

lectual curiosity or creativity? Are you searching for "inspiration" in the waking world? Alternatively, could your unconscious have been reflecting your mounting excitement at the prospect of a real-life party to which you've been invited by implying that you are "breathless" with anticipation? Whatever you decide caused you to fight for air in your dream, be it a negative or positive influence, your unconscious was probably warning you to broaden your horizons, free your mind, and let some metaphorical "fresh air" into a waking life that has become unhealthily one-dimensional.

Perhaps you dreamed of walking through an alpine landscape, appreciatively taking great gulps of air

Opposite and below left: If you struggled to breathe in the smog- or smoke-choked atmosphere of a polluted dream environment, could your bedclothes have been smothering you, or are you finding your real-life circumstances equally claustrophobic? **Above and below:** A dream of feeling thrillingly energized after inhaling either fresh mountain air or pure oxygen may have reflected your sense of being inspired and stimulated in waking life.

that seemed as pure and invigorating as bottled oxygen. If you savored a dream like this, have you recently managed to break the bonds that tied you to a deadening relationship or job? If so, your dream was probably unconsciously expressing your joy at your release and your feeling of "airiness," or jauntiness, as you relish the intoxicating sense of freedom that now pervades your waking hours. Otherwise, could your dream have been advising you to "clear the air," or resolve a tense situation, in the real world?

Flying High

Did you tear yourself regretfully from a glorious dream in which you'd discovered that you were able to fly and you soared and swooped through the air, laughing with delight? You must have found your dream experience exhilarating, but what, if anything, could it have signified? This question has preoccupied dream analysts for decades. Some believe that dreams of flying (with or without wings, but not in an aircraft) recall the memories that we have collectively inherited from

our prehistoric, birdlike ancestors, while others are convinced that they are a form of astral projection, or out-of-body experience, when the dreamer's spirit actually leaves the body and travels through space. Another school of thought suggests that the act of breathing, when the chest falls up and down as it inhales and exhales air, triggers such dreams, while Freudian theory holds that they express the urge to enjoy unlimited sexual freedom and to indulge in erotic experimentation. Although you may find any of these hypotheses persuasive, there may be yet another explanation for your flying dream: do you feel as free as a bird, or do you yearn to?

Above: In the parallel universe of dreams, we are able to transcend our earthly limits and soar as high, and as far, as we please. **Left:** A dream of flying through the air may have mirrored your waking exhilaration or encouraged you to fulfill your intellectual potential.

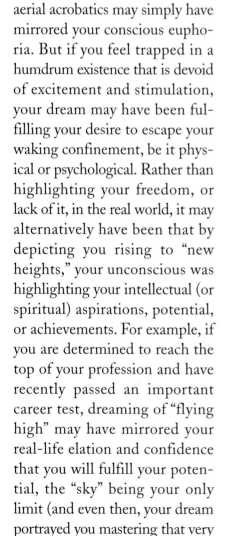

If you currently feel as though you are "walking on air," or heady and elated, perhaps because you have fallen in love, because your career prospects have received a wonderful boost, or because you

have discovered a spiritual side to your nature, a dream in which you performed aerial acrobatics may simply have mirrored your conscious euphoria. But if you feel trapped in a humdrum existence that is devoid of excitement and stimulation, your dream may have been fulfilling your desire to escape your waking confinement, be it physical or psychological. Rather than highlighting your freedom, or lack of it, in the real world, it may alternatively have been that by depicting you rising to "new heights," your unconscious was highlighting your intellectual (or spiritual) aspirations, potential, or achievements. For example, if you are determined to reach the top of your profession and have recently passed an important career test, dreaming of "flying high" may have mirrored your real-life elation and confidence that you will fulfill your potential, the "sky" being your only limit (and even then, your dream portrayed you mastering that very

limit). If, however, your interest in pursuing an academic career is being held

back by a practical need to earn money, even if it means working in a mind-numbingly boring job, a dream of flying may have denoted your longing to "take

flight" from, or flee, your current occupation and to be free to follow your dream to improve your mind or circumstances.

Because taking an airplane allows us to travel to exotic places in the waking world, your flying

Above: A dream of flying may have been urging you to become more adventurous. **Below:** Your unconscious may have been advocating adopting a wider outlook by giving you an aerial view of a dream landscape.

Right: If you dreamed of ejecting from an airplane, activating your parachute, and descending safely to earth, could your unconscious have been advising you to bail out of a overly ambitious scheme in the real world? **Below:** If mist obscured your dreaming view from on high, could the implication have been that you are unable to see your waking situation clearly? **Opposite:** A dream of hot-air balloons may have been encouraging you to rise above your mundane problems.

dream may also have pointed toward a wish to enjoy a more adventurous or active life and to have the freedom to go wherever your fancy takes you. Do you wish that you could "broaden your horizons," be it by seeing more of the world, living life to the fullest—even if it means taking a few risks—or else by widening your waking interests? And if your dreaming self saw an object "on the horizon," could your unconscious have been using this pun to hearten you and inspire optimism by implying that the achievement of your ambition, whatever that may be, is indeed in sight, and that you will "rise to the occasion," when the opportunity finally arrives?

Means of Ascent and Descent

You may have dreamed of powering your own flight, but in the real world our only way of flying is to board an aircraft. Hitching a ride in a hot-air balloon can, however, enable us to rise upward through the air and gain appreciable heights. If this scenario featured in your dream, your unconscious may have been sending you any of the positive messages attached to a dream of flying (outlined above). Do you long to be able to "rise above," or to have the power to overcome, or at least ignore, the problems that plague your waking hours, for instance? Although they can float, drift, or remain static at great heights, hot-air balloons are directionless and cannot therefore be said to fly, yet their lack of motion gives them the advantage of enabling their passengers to appreciate the vista laid out beneath them. So if you dreamed of leaning over the edge of a gondola and of observing the miniature landscape below with detached interest, could your unconscious have been advising you to take an overview of your waking situation rather than letting your vision become bogged down in its petty details?

But if your vantage point bored you after you'd been floating in the air for a while in dreamland, could your dream situation have paralleled your dissatisfaction with "floating" pointlessly through your waking life, perhaps because you feel somehow detached from the reality of your circumstances or lack a sense of commitment to anything? An awareness of drifting through the air in your dream may have signaled a similar lack of direction in waking life, but if you felt increasingly alarmed as you were carried inexorably toward dark storm clouds, could the message have been that you are drifting into a dangerous situation during your waking hours and are about to be buffeted by forces beyond your control? Or were you terrified because you thought that you were in danger of plummeting to the ground in your dream? If so, your unconscious may again have reflected your fear of losing control over your waking life, and perhaps also of failure. Were you relieved when the hot-air balloon gradually descended before landing with a bump on solid ground? In this case, could your unconscious have been encouraging you to "come down to earth," or to stop daydreaming and return to reality? A dream of parachuting to safety from an alarming height

Left: Were your dream balloons alerting you to your childishness or expressing your desire to drift through life for a while? **Below right:** Kites can represent controlled ambitions in the lexicon of dreams.

may similarly have denoted the urgent need to lower your aspirations dramatically, thereby escaping from a potentially perilous situation in the waking world that once seemed dizzily intoxicating, but over which you ultimately have no control.

If you dreamed of clutching a balloon in your hand, suddenly letting it go, watching it drift lazily skyward, and then wondering where it would end up, your unconscious may also have been commenting on your lack of direction, or focus in the real world. Your dream may have suggested that you seem to have no goals or ambitions—a message that may have been underlined if you associate balloons with childhood, when your unconscious may have been implying that your conscious mindset is immature. However, it may simply have been highlighting your desire to coast lazily through life for a while, particularly if your real-life circumstances are dominated by others' dictates and deadlines. Because we have some measure of control over these playthings, a

dream of flying a kite may have been signaling that even though your feet remain firmly on the ground, or rooted in reality, you're starting to give controlled reign to your ambitions, in the process directing them higher and higher. But what could it have meant if the kite disappeared from view and the line that connected you to it suddenly snapped? Well, the inference was probably that you have been overly ambitious and have become so carried away with your stellar hopes for your "vision" that it has become detached from reality and consequently stands no chance of success.

WATER

There are two straightforward explanations for a dream that incorporated water: that you developed a raging thirst or that your bladder became full to bursting while you were sleeping. If you didn't wake desperate for a glass of water or to rush to the bathroom, however, a dream of being in any watery situation may have puzzled you, in which case this chapter may bring enlightenment.

In symbolic terms, water's primary association is with the unconscious mind, a significance that stems from our first nine months, when, as unconscious, unborn babies, we were cushioned in the warm fluid of the amniotic sac. This is also one of the reasons why we speak of the "waters of life," water being an element without which no creature can exist (and that makes up 60 to 70 percent of the human body). In addition, in both the dream and real worlds, water has the power to cleanse and purify (the spirit, as well as the body, which is why Christians are baptised with water), as well as to relax and reinvigorate. A dream in which you plunged into a pool of cool, refreshing water may therefore have a number of interpretations, ranging from a desire to plumb the depths of your unconscious, a longing to wash away the "sins" of your past and be spiritually reborn, through a profound need to unwind, to a yearning for emotional or sexual stimulation. Water can be portrayed in many forms and contexts in dreams, each scenario representing a subtle variation on these broad themes and usually reflecting your current emotional state.

You may also find water's traditional associations relevant when considering your dream. As one of the elemental "humors" that were once believed to flow within the human body, water was thought to bestow phlegmatic, or calm and unexcitable, characteristics, while as the governing element of Cancer, Scorpio, and Pisces, it is said to endow people born under these zodiacal signs with the feminine qualities of gentleness and changeability.

Not all water-related dreams have positive connotations, however, as you may have experienced if you dreamed of being deluged by water or in danger of drowning. You may have feared for your life, yet your dream was unlikely to have warned of physical danger, instead reflecting your sense of being emotionally overwhelmed during your waking hours.

Seas and Oceans

The largest, deepest, and most changeable of all bodies of water, seas and oceans harbor marine life and are believed to have been human beings' ultimate place of origin, too. As such, they can represent both life (and their saltwater its essence) and the mother archetype. Yet when it comes to interpreting dreams focused on seas and oceans, perhaps their most pertinent symbolic association is with the unconscious mind, and with the ebb and flow of feelings that can sometimes build up into a tidal wave of emotional upheaval. Did you dream of floating serenely in a sailboat? If so, the implication was almost certainly that your life is untroubled by worries. Perhaps you dreamed that you then cast a line from the deck and waited for a fish to take

Above: Dream seas and oceans represent the unconscious emotions, instincts, or urges that are influencing your conscious reaction to your waking circumstances.

the bait; if so, are you mulling over an important dilemma during your waking hours? It may just be that your dream depicted you "fishing around" in the depths of your unconscious for a solution (and when you awoke, had the answer indeed surfaced in your conscious mind?)

If, however, you had a nightmare in which you were clinging to a life raft in the midst of a turbulent ocean, the heaving waves seemingly doing their utmost to loosen your grip, are you waking emotions equally tumultuous at the moment? Maybe, for example, you are seriously considering leaving your partner, and weighing up the pros and cons of such a drastic, life-changing decision is making you feel "all at sea," or in a state of fearful confusion. Or perhaps your relationship with your dominant mother has come to resemble a state of warfare in the waking

world, and you are terrified that she will win the battle of wills and drag you under. And if this dream scene wasn't horrendous enough, if your dreaming self was then petrified when a hideous sea monster surfaced from the unfathomable depths and threatened to devour you, could it have symbolized an unconscious fear, or even an aspect of yourself, that your conscious mind has suppressed as being too appalling to contemplate?

Rivers and Streams

Rivers and streams differ from oceans and seas because their water is fresh rather than salty, bounded by banks, and flows in a definite direction. In the language of dreams, rivers (and to a lesser extent, streams) therefore usually represent your feelings as you navigate your way through life, and specifically your current emotions.

Did you dream of a meandering river or one whose course was direct? The first scenario may have denoted the many emotional twists and turns to which you are being subjected in the real world, and the second, a straightforward emotional passage through waking life.

If the water in the dream river seemed static, your unconscious may have been commenting on your lack of drive or direction,

Above: If you dreamed of a still, moonlit river, do you feel that you have come to a temporary standstill in life, perhaps because you are absorbed in self-contemplation? **Left:** Waves rushing back and forth on a dream shore can symbolize the ebb and flow of emotions. **Below:** A dream that focused on a fast-flowing river may have paralleled your tendency to power your way through life. **Opposite, above:** If you dreamed of throwing a stone into the water, did the ripples that formed mirror your sense of going around in circles in the real world? **Opposite, below:** A dream lagoon can be a metaphor for the womb.

while if it was flowing rapidly, dynamism may have been indicated. But if the waters were rising rapidly, so much so that they were on the verge of breaking the banks of the river, are you feeling swamped by emotion during your waking hours, and are your feelings preventing you from moving decisively forward in the real world? And if the word "brook" suggested itself to your unconscious mind as you stood beside a stream in your dream, could it have been signaling the need to "brook," or put up with, your current waking circumstances?

Perhaps you dreamed of standing on a bridge spanning a river and observing the patterns that the water made as it flowed beneath you. The unconscious often uses bridges as symbols of transition, so could the meaning of your dream have been that you are at a turning point in waking life and that the events of the past are now "water under the bridge"?

Still Bodies of Water

Unlike those of seas, oceans, and rivers, the waters of lakes, lagoons, ponds, and pools are generally still, so if you dreamed of any of these tranquil bodies of water, could your unconscious have been reflecting your

own calm emotional approach to waking life? But if you were struck by the mysterious appearance of a dream lake or lagoon, was your dream reminding you that "still waters run deep," thereby referring to your own "hidden depths"? Alternatively, could your dream have been telling your conscious self that although you seem unruffled to others, deep down you are in emotional turmoil? Some dream analysts believe that lakes symbolize the womb. Could your dream of a lake or lagoon have denoted your longing either to take refuge from the difficulties of the waking world by retreating to a safe haven, or else your desire to be "reborn" as a better person? Or, if you are a woman, are you longing to conceive a baby? And because lagoons often offer beautiful, sheltered spots in which to bathe, if you are a man, was your dream lagoon a metaphor for a certain woman with whom you'd love to become intimate in the real world?

Did you dream of taking a walk through a forest and coming across a pond bustling with waterfowl, fish, and other types of wildlife? If so, it is possible that your dream pond reflected your unconscious personality, facets of which were represented by the various creatures so obviously at home in it. If, however, your dream pond was devoid of activity and its water was stagnant,

your unconscious may have been mirroring your waking sense of having become mentally stale and sluggish, perhaps because your emotional life is currently so unstimulating. If you dreamed of gazing into the limpid waters of a pool, did you see anything moving around beneath the surface? If so, it may have symbolized the stirring of an unconscious instinct, so if you watched a fish swimming to the surface of the crystal-clear water, could it have represented an intuition that has yet to crystallize in your conscious mind, but that may soon manifest itself?

Certain types of pool are anything but still, however, and if you became dizzy as you watched the swirling waters of a whirlpool, eddy, or maelstrom in dreamland, can you make a connection with the emotional turbulence or confusion that you are experiencing in waking life?

Springs and Wells

Both springs and wells have strong symbolic links with birth because their water originates deep in the earth, a source of terrestrial life and thus also a symbol of the womb. So if you are a woman who dreamed of discovering the source of a stream, your unconscious may have portrayed your longing to become a mother. Otherwise, and whatever your sex, a dream that featured a spring may have been highlighting your untapped creative potential, which may be about to bubble forth into the waking world. Because another word for a spring is a "font" (or "fount"), and because we often describe learned or intelligent people as being "fonts of knowledge," your dream spring may alternatively have been drawing your conscious attention to your innate wisdom, and perhaps the advisability of exercising it.

Did you dream of throwing a coin into a well and making a wish? If so, can you remember what you wished for? It may have been that your dream wish mirrored a waking longing, but if you were surprised by your

dreaming self's request, don't dismiss it, because your unconscious may have pinpointed something that could bring you happiness if your wish really were to come true. Wishing wells have been credited with wish-fulfillment powers since Romano–Celtic times, when wells and sacred pools were believed to provide a direct link to the otherworld, and specifically to the particular goddess associated with each one. Throwing offerings, including coins, into such sacred wells would, it was thought, please the goddess and persuade her to exercise her mystical powers, particularly to bestow fertility upon, or heal, the supplicant. So if you dreamed of drawing water from a well, it may be that you wish to conceive a child (if you are a woman), or else that you are in need of physical or psychological healing. Your dream well may alternatively have symbolized the depths of your unconscious mind or emotions, and hence your inner wisdom. Because wells supply drinking water, the implication of your dream may have been that your waking life has become emotionally arid and that you are thirsting to experience a revitalizing flood of feeling.

Opposite: In dreamland, springs (center and bottom) can represent a source of creativity, while wells (top) hint at either emotional revival or the granting of wishes. **Above and right:** If you were confronted by an effervescent waterfall in dreamland, did its tumbling, foaming waters mirror your own bubbly and ebullient mood at present? **Bottom:** Dreaming of a dam that is functioning properly suggests that you have found a healthy outlet for the emotions that have been building up within you.

Waterfalls and Fountains

Waterfalls, or rapids, and fountains are celebrated for the energy of their gushing, shooting, and tumbling waters, so if you had a dream of laughing with carefree exhilaration as you observed the awesome phenomenon that is Niagara Falls, for instance, your unconscious may have been mirroring your waking sense of euphoria. But why are you feeling so exuberant? Is it because your creative powers have suddenly burst into sparkling life in the waking world? Some dream analysts believe that jets or torrents of water symbolize ejaculation, so if you are a man, is your love life the source of your current ecstasy? Remember, too, that "fountain" is an alternative word for "font" and "fount" (see above), so that if you were captivated by a fountain's dancing waters in your dream, could it have been advising you to bring your unconscious knowledge or wisdom into play in a real-life situation?

Canals, Reservoirs, Dams, and Floods

Canals, reservoirs, and dams are all manmade structures designed to regulate the flow of water, which is why their appearance in dreamland often hints at how successfully your rational, conscious mind is controlling your unconscious emotions. Did you dream of walking alongside a canal? If so, and depending on whether you felt soothed or frustrated by the monotony of your route, your unconscious may have used this visual metaphor to signal either that you are containing your emotions effectively or that you are being too emotionally restrained during your waking hours. If you are a pregnant woman, also consider whether your dream canal could have symbolized the birth canal, or vagina, and thus whether your dream may have been reflecting your conscious anticipation of giving birth.

Below: If you dreamed of wading through flooded streets, your unconscious may have been warning that you are in danger of being deluged by emotions, be it your own or someone else's. **Bottom:** Dream icebergs often denote frozen emotions. **Opposite, top:** A dream of skating on thin ice may have graphically expressed your sense of needing to exercise caution in a potentially treacherous situation in the waking world. **Opposite, bottom:** If you dreamed of a swimming pool, is a real-life vacation long overdue?

Because water is collected and stored in reservoirs for communal use, if one of these bodies of water is featured in your dream, could it have denoted your own emotional reserves? The water level is particularly significant in a dream like this, so if you dreamed that the reservoir was in danger of drying up, are the incessant demands of others threatening to drain you emotionally dry in the waking world? If the reservoir's water level was high, however, it is likely that your emotional resources are equally abundant.

In the real world, dams are constructed to restrict the flow of water, be it to create a reservoir or to prevent flooding. In the dream world, dams generally signify the restrictive control of the conscious mind over unconscious instincts, so if you paid a visit to a dam in your dream, did it look structurally sound? If it did, the suggestion was probably that you are exerting a healthy amount of rational control over your emotions and that your conscious and unconscious minds are consequently in balance. But if you were alarmed to see that the dam had developed an ominous-looking crack, you may have suppressed your unconscious urges to such an extent that they will no longer be denied expression in the waking world. Indeed, the cracked dam of your dream may have been warning that it may not be long before you "crack" under the pressure of your own rigorous self-control, and that once it has found an outlet, your unconscious will unleash the full force of its destructive power by overwhelming you with violent emotions. So if you are feeling close to the edge during your waking hours, try to find a way of releasing your pent-up feelings gradually, and in a controlled manner, before the worst happens.

Ice and Icebergs

If floods represent the destructive potential of surging, chaotic, and ultimately overwhelming urges and feelings, ice can denote the exact opposite in the language of dreams, namely a mind that has become emotionally frozen.

Did you find yourself trudging through a silent, frozen landscape in your dream, and, if so, do you feel emotionally numb in the waking world, perhaps due to the shock of a recent bereavement? Alternatively, is your marriage going through a difficult patch, and do you feel that your partner has "frozen you out," perhaps because he or she has become emotionally cold or sexually frigid? If you noticed that the ice was melting in the terrain of your dream, however, your unconscious may have been trying to hearten you by suggesting that you are slowly returning to emotional life, or that your spouse's iciness is starting to thaw, and that the chilly atmosphere in your household is becoming warmer as a result.

Did you dream of trying to steer a boat around a huge iceberg that was obstructing your passage in a nocturnal polar scene? Although it may again have represented a significant person in your life who is behav-

ing icily toward you, if you can identify no such person, the dream iceberg may otherwise have denoted a significant problem that is blocking your progress in the real world. Could it have symbolized a difficult issue that you put "on ice," or pushed to the back of your conscious thoughts, a while ago, but that now looms so large in your unconscious mind that you have no option but to try to resolve it? And if you dreamed of gingerly picking your way across a frozen lake, terrified that the pressure of your feet would cause the ice to crack, could the message have been that you feel that you are walking on "thin ice," or that someone is making you feel so vulnerable in waking life that you are treading carefully in your dealings with him or her?

Diving, Floating, Swimming, and Drowning

Unless you were splashing around in a swimming pool, when your unconscious may have been highlighting your need to take time out of your busy waking schedule to relax and have fun, dreams of diving, floating, and swimming usually hint at your current emotional state, or the advisability of tapping into the resources stored by your unconscious mind. Did you dream of diving into the sea? If so, and you are mulling over a decision during your waking hours, your dream may have portrayed your dreaming self penetrating the depths of your unconscious in search of insight. While you were underwater, did the scene then shift to depict you interacting with your friends and family, all of you fully clothed and breathing, talking, and moving as if you were on dry land? A surreal dream scenario like this may have been suggesting that you've been too busy with other things to take the time to connect with your loved ones on an emotional level. Would you reap the emotional benefits of slowing down and devoting more quality time to them in the real world?

Perhaps you dreamed that you were floating blissfully in the sea, not thinking of anything at all as you relished the sensation of the warm water caressing and supporting your apparently weightless body. If you enjoyed a dream like this and your waking hours are fraught with anxiety, your uncon-

This page: Were you plumbing the depths of your unconscious or drowning in a sea of emotions during your dream?

scious may have been trying to comfort you by returning you to the security of the metaphorical womb. Similarly, your dream may have reflected your longing to be able to coast, or to float effortlessly, through life, letting all of the worries of the waking world wash over you without your emotional wellbeing being troubled. But if your dream of floating was accompanied by a sense of uneasiness, your unconscious may have been mirroring your conscious worry that you lack the direction and power with which to influence the course of your life, and your feeling that you are "treading water" as time moves inexorably on.

Did you have a satisfying dream in which you were swimming smoothly and swiftly through calm waters? When we are swimming, our progress is powered by our own physical efforts, so if you were pleased with your swimming technique in the dream sea, you probably feel that your waking life is going equally "swimmingly," or successfully, and that you are "in your element," or performing happily and effectively (and making significant advances, too), be it at school, work, or in the home. A dream like this also hints that your conscious and unconscious minds are working together in productive harmony. However, if you dreamed of struggling against a strong current, it may be that your conscious mind is battling to withstand a powerful unconscious urge or, alternatively, the force of "current" opinion in the waking world. Take your sleeping self's reaction to the dream scene into account when considering whether it would be better to "go with the flow," or to take the path of least resistance and go along with your unconscious instinct or the consensus of opinion, or else to continue to "swim against the tide." Maybe you then found yourself out of your depth in the dream ocean, in which case your unconscious may have been mirroring your waking sense of being out of your emotional "depth" whenever you're with your girlfriend, whose unpredictability may be so confusing or threatening that you fear that you have lost the power to exert any influence over your relationship with her.

It was already going badly, but perhaps your dream then took a turn for the worse and you found yourself desperately trying to keep your head above the water as the tumultuous waves tossed you around like a doll. Unless you actually have a water phobia or have suffered a similar experience in real life, when your unconscious may have been either graphically expressing your anxiety or forcing you to relive your memories, this nightmare is likely to have signaled emotional, not physical, danger ahead. Whatever the cause in the real world, its effect has almost certainly been to unleash a storm of unconscious emotions, powerful urges, and basic instincts. In short, is your current situation so desperate that you are heading for a nervous breakdown? If, however, you managed to strike out for the shore in your dream, the suggestion may have been that you'll survive the emotional inundation and reassert conscious control. But if you were profoundly relieved when a lifeboat hove into view, who was at the helm? It may be that you unconsciously believe that he or she has the power to throw you an emotional lifeline in the real world, thereby rescuing you from the inner turmoil that is threatening to engulf you. ✺

THE WEATHER AND NATURAL PHENOMENA

Whether the action was suffused with sunshine, shrouded in fog, saturated with rain, or buffeted by high winds, if the weather formed a significant backdrop to your dream, it is likely to have mirrored your current emotions in waking life. Although your unconscious may have translated your present sunny, gloomy, or stormy mood into the sunshine, murk, or tempestuous conditions that permeated your dream, there is another possible interpretation to take into account. The weather is notorious for its changeability, and your unconscious may have been forecasting your own imminent change of mood in the real world. So if you are feeling cheerful during your waking hours, but dreamed of being drenched by a downpour, for instance, your dream may have been warning that you may soon be exposed to a deluge of dispiriting emotions.

Mood messages like these are underlined if you felt unnaturally hot or cold while you were dreaming, or if the dream weather conflicted with the dream season. A dream in which you felt chilled to the bone could have recalled the icy emotional atmosphere that pervades your waking days, or may shortly do so, for example. (But it is always possible that you threw off the bedclothes while you were sleeping, causing your body temperature to drop and your real-life chilliness to be incorporated into your dream.) Similarly, if you dreamed of stripping off your clothes and sunbathing in a garden whose lack of foliage and frosty ground suggested wintertime, your unconscious may have been signaling that although your waking life seems cold and cheerless at the moment, it may not be long before you again feel imbued with warmth and happiness.

Dreams of natural disasters like volcanic eruptions, earthquakes, and avalanches denote emotions that are both so powerful and uncontrolled that they may have catastrophic consequences when unleashed in the waking world. Yet while such dreams may have been alerting you to an impending emotional calamity, they also hold out the hope of a fresh start once the worst is over.

Sunshine and Clouds

Perhaps your dream portrayed you and your partner lazing on a sun-drenched beach as you soaked up the solar rays. A dream scenario like this may have reflected your radiant joy in life at present, perhaps because your relationship with your partner couldn't be warmer, you are feeling positive and energetic, you are financially solvent, and there seem to be no clouds, or potential upsets, on the horizon. If your waking circumstances are far from ideal, however, your unconscious may have sent you this dream to allow you to escape your conscious worries and to encourage you to keep your spirits up by implying that brighter times await you.

Above: Gathering clouds may mirror real-life feelings of increasing gloom when they darken a dream sky. **Left:** A sunlit dream scene may have highlighted a sunny waking mood.

But did your sunlit dream idyll then take an unexpected turn for the worse? Perhaps you suddenly realized that you were suffering from excruciating sunburn in dreamland, or maybe a bank of black clouds arrived to block out the sun. Both of these scenarios hint that although you consider waking life wonderful at the moment, you are unconsciously aware that your happiness and confidence in the future may be spoiled by a looming problem. If you were sunburned in the dream scene, it may be that you have overexposed yourself to a "hot," or dangerous, situation or person in the real world, and that you're in danger of being "burned," or cheated. But if dark clouds scudded rapidly across the blue sky, casting a gloomy atmosphere over your dream, your unconscious may have been warning that you may soon be living "under a cloud" in real life, maybe because someone is about to point the finger of suspicion at you.

In the language of dreams, black, lowering clouds can signal the onset of a threatening episode or the dreamer's dark and pessimistic outlook—or both—while gray clouds usually denote despondence, and white clouds indicate contentment. If the clouds shifted slightly in the dream scene, allowing a shaft of sunlight to penetrate their dense cover, however, your unconscious may have been graphically depicting the ray of hope that may soon break through your depression and lighten your waking hours.

Fog and Mist

Did you dream of groping your way blindly down your street, unable to discern any of its familiar landmarks or features because it was so heavily blanketed in fog? If so, your dream is likely to have mirrored your current sense of being confused, lost, and unable to make progress in waking life because your view of the path ahead is so hazy. Dreams that are shrouded in mist or fog indicate that your conscious mind, or vision, is lacking in clarity, signaling in particular that you are unable to see an important situation, problem, or person, clearly, or for what it, he, or she really is. Both atmospheric conditions occur when water vapor condenses and is suspended in the air, and because water can symbolize the emotions, is it a myriad of feelings that is clouding your rational view, thereby making you

Above: If a bank of gray clouds blocked out the sunlight in a dismal dream scenario, do you feel as though your life is equally devoid of cheer?
Right: A dream rainstorm may have been warning that you are about to be battered by a deluge of raw emotions in waking life.

feel uncertain about how best to proceed? Did the fog then lift in your dream, so that everything became plain to you? If so, your unconscious may have been hinting that the fog of confusion will similarly clear from your waking mind, revealing previously hidden truths and thus also an obvious course of action.

Rain and Hail

Did you dream of sitting outside, enjoying the sunshine of a warm summer's day, when the heavens suddenly opened and you were drenched by a torrential downpour? If so, your reaction to being caught in the rainstorm may provide the key to deciphering your dream. How did you feel as you

Breezes and Winds

sat soaked and dripping in the dream scene? Shocked and miserable, or strangely exhilarated? If the former, it is possible that an outpouring of emotions—either your own or someone else's—is about to rain down upon your head, leaving you reeling from the onslaught and feeling wretched. Alternatively, could the dream downpour have symbolized the tears that you have shed, or wish that you could because they would provide some emotional release, during your waking hours? But if you felt uplifted by the dream deluge, could it be that your waking life has become emotionally arid—perhaps because you are currently single and your work dominates your thoughts—and that you long for the moment when your ability to experience love and passion is refreshed and revived, maybe by a romantic episode, so that you feel really alive again? Or do you wish that your waking problems, or else the baggage of the past, could be washed away, leaving you feeling emotionally cleansed and looking forward to a sparkling new future?

Although rain can have positive connotations in dreams, hail—frozen rain—usually sends a negative message, namely that you may be about to become the victim of a "hail" of bitter, stinging abuse.

Did you dream of leaving a stuffy building, stepping outside, and immediately feeling refreshed by the invigorating caress of a stiff breeze? Because breezes arise from the gentle movement of the air, they share this element's symbolic associations with the life force, the spirit,

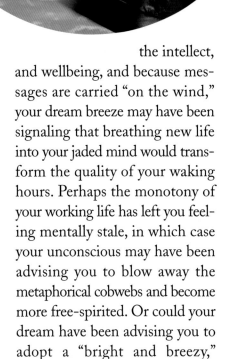

the intellect, and wellbeing, and because messages are carried "on the wind," your dream breeze may have been signaling that breathing new life into your jaded mind would transform the quality of your waking hours. Perhaps the monotony of your working life has left you feeling mentally stale, in which case your unconscious may have been advising you to blow away the metaphorical cobwebs and become more free-spirited. Or could your dream have been advising you to adopt a "bright and breezy," approach to waking life?

Any dream in which you were buffeted by strong winds may have mirrored your feeling of vulnerability through your exposure to powerful external forces in the real world, which is why it is important to take your dream mood into account when deciding whether your dream had positive or negative connotations. Remember, too, that your dream wind may have represented a "wind of change," so that if you were desperately attempting to stand your ground against a wind that was threatening to propel you rapidly forward in a dream scene, are you trying to resist the pressure that others are putting on you to switch direction, or objectives, in the real world? If you then lost your struggle against the wind in dreamland, could the implication have been that you have ceded control over your waking life and are being forced to go along with other people's wishes? But, if you reveled in the sensation of being carried along by the gusts of a dream wind, do you long for an element of unpredictability to blow into your waking world, or do you wish that you could relinquish your decision-making responsibilities and just "blow in the wind," or go with the flow, instead?

Above: If you felt invigorated by a stiff breeze in dreamland, was your unconscious trying to tell you that your life, or conscious mind, has become stale and needs enlivening with a "breath of fresh air," or a refreshing and stimulating change?

Gales and hurricanes spell danger in both the real and dream worlds, so if your dreaming self was assaulted by the full force of a howling windstorm, your unconscious may have been sending you an early-warning signal that it has detected a build-up of violent emotions, perhaps within your own mind, but more probably in someone else's. Are you about to become the target of another person's raging fury, did your dream mirror the powerful emotional conflict that you are yourself experiencing during your waking hours, or is a certain situation on the verge of blowing up into a crisis? A dream in which you felt increasingly terrified as you watched a tornado approach may similarly have reflected your sense of being powerless to withstand a tempest of violent and chaotic emotions, but a dream whirlwind sends a slightly different message. Are you spending your waking hours in such a "whirlwind" of activity that you're feeling confused and out of control, or was the reference to a "whirlwind romance" that may utterly change the course of your life?

Storms, Thunder, and Lightning

Whether they are depicted as taking place at sea or on land, dream storms usually symbolize overwhelmingly turbulent emotions, but because all storms blow over, their appearance in dreamland also implies that a threatening emotional crisis will eventually abate and calm will be restored. Also consider the possibility that your dream storm represented a "brainstorm," or the unleashing of your unconscious powers of creativity, an interpretation that may be particularly apt if bolts of lightning sizzled through your dream. Could the flashes of lightning that illuminated the dark dream sky have represented flashes of insight or inspiration generated by your "brainstorm"? And did you awake from your dream feeling enlightened regarding a problem that has been baffling your waking mind, or else enthused by a new idea?

Lightning can denote mental or spiritual illumination or revelation in the lexicon of dreams (as well as in Buddhist belief), but it is also a dangerous force of concentrated electrical energy that can destroy whatever it strikes, which is why ancient peoples regarded it as a manifestation of the awesome wrath of such sky gods as the Greco–Roman Zeus and Jupiter and the Norse–Germanic Thor and Donar. So if your dream portrayed you cowering on the ground as a firestorm of thunderbolts exploded above your defenseless head, could your unconscious have conjured up this image to underline your waking fear that, having angered an authority figure (perhaps your school principal or boss) in the real world, you are about to be punished for your transgression? And if your dream scene was played out against a soundtrack of rumbling, cracking thunder, could these terror-inducing noises have represented the thunderous voice of that authority figure railing at your quaking self?

Rainbows

Once the dream storm had finally died down, and you had recovered your equilibrium, were you enchanted to see a rainbow arching delicately over the battered earth? If so, the message being transmitted by your unconscious was almost certainly one of hope for the future, and not just because the shimmering spectrum of a rainbow's colors is such an uplifting sight. Indeed, the

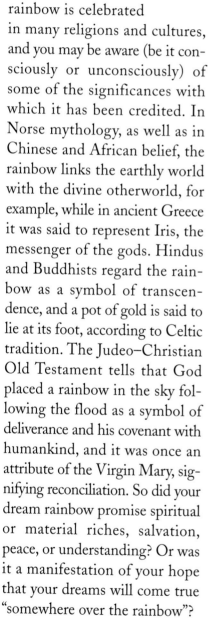

rainbow is celebrated in many religions and cultures, and you may be aware (be it consciously or unconsciously) of some of the significances with which it has been credited. In Norse mythology, as well as in Chinese and African belief, the rainbow links the earthly world with the divine otherworld, for example, while in ancient Greece it was said to represent Iris, the messenger of the gods. Hindus and Buddhists regard the rainbow as a symbol of transcendence, and a pot of gold is said to lie at its foot, according to Celtic tradition. The Judeo–Christian Old Testament tells that God placed a rainbow in the sky following the flood as a symbol of deliverance and his covenant with humankind, and it was once an attribute of the Virgin Mary, signifying reconciliation. So did your dream rainbow promise spiritual or material riches, salvation, peace, or understanding? Or was it a manifestation of your hope that your dreams will come true "somewhere over the rainbow"?

Frost and Snow

Perhaps you dreamed that you were wandering through a freezing landscape and becoming colder and colder and more and more desperate to return to the warmth of your house. Because frost is formed when water in the atmosphere is deposited as ice crystals on the ground, and water is symbolically linked with the emotions, a dream that focuses on frost implies icy feelings. Can you draw a parallel with waking life? Are you emotionally frozen, or is someone in your life currently behaving "frostily," or "icily," toward you? (Because your

Opposite, top: In dreams, lightning can symbolize a flash of inspiration or an authority figure's extreme displeasure. **Opposite, bottom:** Your unconscious may have placed a rainbow in a dream sky to lift your spirits and encourage you to regard your future optimistically. **Left and below:** Dream snowfalls suggest that the emotions to which you are currently being exposed in waking life are icy in the extreme.

dreaming self knew that a warm reception awaited you at home, it is unlikely that you are being "frozen out," or emotionally excluded, by your partner or family, so is a friend, or your boss, treating you coldly during your waking hours?)

A snow-blanketed dreamscape sends a similar, but more extreme, message. If you dreamed of being stranded all alone in a snowy setting, could your dream have been reflecting your own emotional coldness and isolation, or else the glacial atmosphere that pervades your interaction with others, or with a significant person, in your waking world? It may be, for instance, that your real-life divorce caused you so much pain that you have shut down your capacity to feel love or affection as a self-protective strategy with which to ward off yet another hurt. Or maybe your family is united in its disapproval of your lifestyle, or your partner is showing unmistakeable signs of emotional or sexual coldness whenever you are together. If, however, the snow was thawing in your dream, you may unconsciously have sensed that the icy mood that currently characterizes your waking hours is slowly warming and melting, and that your emotional life may consequently soon return to normal. When pondering a dream like this, also consider whether the reference could have been to being "snowed under," or overwhelmed, by work.

The Temperature

If you dreamed of sweating in the sweltering heat or of being chilled to the core, did you feel equally hot or cold when you awoke? If so, your unconscious no doubt simply incorporated your actual body temperature into your dream. But if this explanation doesn't apply, the answer may lie in your intense unconscious reaction to your present circumstances, or else to your frame of mind. So if you were aware of suddenly burning with heat when someone entered a dream scene, is he or she making your life "hot," or particularly unpleasant, in the waking world? Or do you consider that person to be "hot," or sexy, and consequently desire, or have the "hots" for, him or her? Feeling unnaturally hot in dreamland can also either warn of being in peril (are you in a real-life "hot seat" or "hot spot"?) or bring burning passions, such as lust or rage, to the fore. If you felt as though you were burning up with heat in your dream, your unconscious was therefore almost certainly advising you to remove yourself from a source of potential danger, or else to cool your ardor or anger, before you suffer the destructive consequences in the real world. And if the sticky, humid atmosphere made breathing difficult in dreamland, an additional nuance may have been that you find your waking situation oppressive and stifling.

If you were aware of feeling pleasantly warm—the ideal in terms of body temperature—while you were dreaming, the implication was probably that you are content in waking life, but if your dreaming self shivered with cold, your dream state may have reflected your current emotional reaction to your waking world. Is someone, or more than one person, behaving with cold indifference toward you, or offering you "cold comfort," or is the chilly atmosphere emanating from you? Alternatively, do you feel emotionally paralyzed, will you soon have to act in "cold blood," or ruthlessly, or is it fear that is making your "blood run cold" in the real world?

Volcanic Eruptions, Earthquakes, and Avalanches

Did you dream of visiting a famous volcano—perhaps Washington's Mount Saint Helens, or Sicily's Mount Etna—and then having to turn and flee for your life as it suddenly erupted into fiery life, spewing molten lava in your path? If so, have you been struggling to suppress your mounting fury during your waking hours, and could your unconscious have conjured up this dramatic image to warn that you won't be able to contain your anger for much longer before similarly "blowing your lid"? Alternatively, maybe your dream highlighted your partner or parent's volatile temper, and your fear of being exposed to the full force of his or her rage when it explodes into your waking world.

Opposite, top: If you dreamed of a glacier, can you equate it with someone's glacial, or cold and hostile, attitude toward you in the real world, or else your own sense of chilly isolation? **Opposite, below:** A dream of burning up with heat in a desert dreamscape may have referred to your overheated emotional reaction to a real-life person or situation. **Above and bottom:** When volcanoes erupt in dreamland, they may be warning that a torrent of fiery emotions is about to burst forth into your waking life. Remember, however, that although this would undoubtedly be a devastating experience, it may ultimately prove cathartic.

Perhaps you dreamed that you were quietly working at your desk when you heard an ominous rumble, your surroundings started shaking and shifting, and then there was an almighty crash as the ceiling and walls collapsed around your head. You must have woken with a profound sense of relief when you realized that the earthquake had been confined to dreamland, but don't dismiss your dream too quickly, because it may

warning that the foundations of your waking life are in danger of being swept away. And because avalanches dislodge masses of ice and snow, your dream may have expressed your fear of bearing the brunt of someone's devastating emotional coldness (perhaps your wife's) and the destruction of your relationship in the real world. Otherwise, could your dream avalanche merely have mirrored your feeling of being overwhelmed by the "avalanche" of work that your boss has just dumped on you during office hours?

Finally, when trying to interpret any dream that involved a natural disaster, remember that if you live in an area that is prone to them, your dream may merely have been reflecting your anxiety about being caught up in such a real-life catastrophe.

have been trying to prepare you for an impending seismic shift in your waking life. Because the earth symbolically denotes the solidity and stability that underpins your personality, dream earthquakes and landslides both signal that your emotional foundations are in danger of being shaken to the core, bringing the structure of your waking world tumbling around your ears and ultimately changing everything. Can you make a link between your dream and an area of your life that may soon undergo an equally tumultuous upheaval? Have you (consciously or unconsciously) detected signs that you may lose your job,

for instance, or that your husband is about to leave you? Both events would, of course, be emotionally traumatic, as well as having a devastating impact on the fabric of your life, but remember that rubble is cleared away and buildings are reconstructed following an earthquake in the real world, so that if the worst happened and you found yourself jobless or spouseless, you, too, would rebuild your life, perhaps even emerging a stronger person as a result.

If you dreamed that you were engulfed in an avalanche, your unconscious may also have been

Above: If you dreamed that an avalanche brought your progress to an abrupt halt, did it mirror your despairing waking sense of being "snowed under" by work? **Below:** Dream earthquakes warn that your waking world may soon be shaken to its very foundations, but also imply that you will be able to build on the ruins of your previous existence.

TIME AND THE SEASONS

Most of us regulate our daily lives by the clock, and although each minute that passes both ages us and brings death closer, few of us dwell on this uncomfortable truth as we wait impatiently for the clock's hands to signal our release from a trying day at work or school. We know, of course, that our time on Earth is limited, yet it is precisely the awful prospect of dying that causes us to dissociate the ticking of the clock with our dwindling lifespan. Yet while the conscious mind prefers to restrict our recognition of the passing of time to personal landmarks like birthdays and anniversaries, the unconscious is constantly marking time in the background. And because we increasingly understand in adulthood that every minute is precious, our dreams may sometimes urge our conscious selves to make the most of the time that remains to us. This is one of the reasons why clocks, watches, calendars, and diaries are occasionally highlighted in dreamland, although a more mundane explanation for such dreams is that the unconscious is simply prompting us to remember an important appointment or date, or else not to sleep too late the following morning.

The passage of the day and night, and the seasonal cycle of spring, summer, fall, and winter, all have their parallels with the stages of human existence, and may have particular pertinence to your life when incorporated into a dream. Rather than basing you in the here and now, however, some dreams may take you back to an episode or place that featured in your past, or else may visualize a future scenario. But why? If you dreamed of a past occurrence or environment, the answer may be either nostalgia, a reminder of a lesson that you learned then, or an attempt to force you to resolve a deep-rooted emotional problem dating from those days. But if your dreaming self was catapulted into the future, your dream may have been fulfilling your waking wishes or warning you of the course that your life may take unless you take corrective steps.

Watches and Clocks

Did you dream that you were packing to go on vacation, knew that you had to be at the airport in two hours, kept glancing at your watch to check the time, and became increasingly panic-stricken as you realized that the minutes were speeding past so quickly that you were doomed to miss your flight? A dream like this denotes anxiety, perhaps because you are actually due to set off on vacation tomorrow and are worried about completing your chores in time. If there is no obvious link between your dream and the near future, however, your unconscious may have inflicted this angst-inducing experience on your dreaming self to draw your conscious attention to your lack of preparation for an important, potentially life-changing, opportunity that is about to present itself in the real world. Have you done enough work to pass an exam that is looming, for instance, or do you feel that you are losing your focus and control of your waking hours? Alternatively, could your dream have reflected your frustration at a past failure to capitalize on a lucky break that you now know would have transformed your waking world for the better?

Left: If you dreamed of a stopwatch, did it emphasize your waking sense of working "against the clock," or of feeling pressured?

If you dreamed that the hands of a watch or clock moved unnaturally slow, take three possible interpretations into account when trying to make sense of your dream. Firstly, if the dream watch was the one that you wear every day, or the dream clock was a timepiece on whose punctuality you rely in the real world, could you have unconsciously noticed that it really does need new batteries, winding up, or repairing? Secondly, could this dream image have reflected your sense that time is dragging, maybe because your waking hours are so boring or because you're eagerly anticipating the arrival of an important day? Or, thirdly, could your unconscious have used the dream watch or clock to symbolize your heart, or "ticker,"

Top: If you dreamed of a malfunctioning timepiece, could you be coming to an emotional standstill? Above and right: If your dreaming vision focused on a timer or clock, was it reminding you to make the most of your time?

thereby highlighting a cardiac problem (of which you may already be aware)?

According to superstition, a clock that suddenly stops denotes someone's death (due to the symbolic link between ticking timepieces and the beating heart), but don't be alarmed if you dreamed of this happening, because your dream almost certainly had an entirely different meaning. In the vocabulary of dreams, clocks and watches often mirror your current emotional state (again as a result of their association with the heart, which is in turn a symbol of the emotions), so that a stopped clock may have mirrored your emotional paralysis and your consequent sense of time standing still in the real world.

It is always important to take the context and your dreaming reaction into account when trying to decipher a dream that focused on a timepiece, and to remember that it may have been measuring the passing of your lifetime. The ticking of a watch or clock in dreamland may have been a general reminder that the seconds, minutes, hours, days, weeks, months, and years of your waking life are ticking away, for example, and that there are still many things that

you'd like to accomplish before your time on Earth runs out. And if you are a female dreamer who intends to start a family in the future, could the ticking timepiece in your dream have represented your biological clock?

Calendars, Diaries, and Red-letter Days

Did a certain date loom large in your dream, perhaps because it was circled on a calendar hanging on a wall, or your dreaming self penciled an appointment for that day into your diary? If so, was it a date in the near future, and do you indeed have something out of the ordinary planned for that day in the waking world? If this is the case, your dream was almost certainly reflecting your conscious anticipation. But if you didn't associate the date with a future event when you awoke, it's worth checking your real-life diary because your unconscious may have been reminding you of a commitment that has slipped your conscious mind, one that you may need to prepare for between now and then. Instead of clocks or watches, the unconscious sometimes conjures a calendar or diary into a dream scene to alert you to the passage of time, so also consider the possibility that your dream was warning you

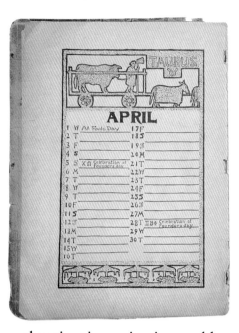

Left: Dreaming of an old calendar may have expressed your nostalgia for those long-gone days. **Below:** If you dreamed of a silver wedding anniversary or another significant date, you may be either dreading or eager to celebrate a personal milestone.

that time is moving inexorably on—or even running out—thereby urging you to focus on achieving your personal goals before it is too late. This message may have been underlined if you dreamed of someone (perhaps a person who has authority over you in the waking world, whom your unconscious cast in the implied role of Father Time) tearing out the pages of an old calendar or diary, the inference being that because you cannot relive the days of your past, it's important to make the most of those that remain to you.

If the date that was highlighted in your dream was a red-letter day, or an important occasion, was it your birthday, an anniversary, or a seasonal holiday? If so, do you consciously look forward to this annual celebration with excitement, or do you dread its arrival? The answer to this question, along with

your mood in the dream, has a significant bearing on the message from your unconscious. If your dream was concerned with your birthday, for instance, do you enjoy being the center of attention on this day of the year? If so, and your birthday isn't impending in the real world, could your dream have expressed your desire to be toasted, fussed over, and generally made to feel special during your waking hours, maybe because you feel that those around you take you for granted and never acknowledge your exceptional qualities? But if being the birthday girl or boy makes you feel uncomfortable in the real world, is it because you dislike being singled out for attention, and could your dream therefore have reflected your discomfort at having being placed in the lime-

light recently, perhaps because you suspect that those around you are making more of a waking achievement than you feel is deserved? Or is the prospect of your next birthday giving you cause for dismay because it represents a milestone in your life (are you about to turn forty?) and is thus a depressing reminder that your days are numbered?

Because anniversaries are usually less loaded with personal significance and intimations of mortality, they are often more straightforward celebratory occasions than birthdays. If you dreamed of commemorating an attainment like this, did your dream reflect your pride and pleasure in an actual anniversary that you are about to celebrate? Alternatively, was your unconscious metaphorically patting you on the back for having stayed with your partner or employer for so many years in the real world, perhaps in compensation for others' indifference to your staying power?

Seasonal holidays like Thanksgiving, Christmas, New Year, Easter, and Independence Day can communicate a variety of messages when they occur in dreams, and it is vital to take your personal

associations with that particular day into account when trying to decode your dream. Do you adore getting together with your family and friends on such occasions in the waking world because the collective mood is invariably happy and festive, or do you know from bitter experience that vicious arguments are inevitable? If you dreamed of spending a cozy Christmas with loved ones, could your dream have given expression to your yearning to be cocooned in an atmosphere of emotional solidarity and warmth in the real world? But if your dreaming self welcomed your guests into your festively decorated home with a sense of trepidation, have you unconsciously sensed the tension that is mounting among your nearest and dearest, and do you fear that the day (not necessarily Christmas) will soon come when all hell will break loose? If you are

a Christian, however, could a Christmas dream have had religious connotations, perhaps signaling your longing to be spiritually reborn, for instance?

Day and Night, Light and Darkness

Did you dream that you knew that you had to pick up your daughter from school in the afternoon, and were doing chores around the house when you were hit by the appalling realization that it was evening and you'd forgotten to go? Although any dream in which the time of day seemed important could have been underlining the real-life importance of being punctual (of which you were probably already consciously aware), an alternative explanation for a dream like this is that your unconscious was delivering a progress report on the course of your life so far. The

Above: In the language of dreams, darkness can symbolize ignorance, while lights denote mental illumination. **Below left:** A nighttime dream backdrop can be a metaphor for old age. **Bottom left:** If you relish exchanging gifts in waking life and dreamed of doing just that in dreamland, you may have enjoyed a wish-fulfillment dream. **Below:** The sun suggests waking optimism and clarity of vision.

twenty-four-hour cycle of day and night has a symbolic parallel with the cycle of both physical and intellectual life, so that dawn signifies birth and new beginnings; the morning, childhood, youth, and potential; midday, middle age and maturity; the afternoon, late middle age and relaxation; and the evening, old age and failing powers, with the dead of night denoting death. So could your dream of failing to retrieve your daughter from school on

time (particularly if you don't actually have a school-age daughter) have been observing that you are now in the "evening" of your life, but have neglected a certain aim that you'd always intended to have achieved by your sixties? If so, was your dream urging you to set your conscious mind on doing just that before it's too late? Or could your dream daughter have represented your "brainchild," in which case could the message have been that you have left a pet project on the back burner for too long, so that its potential for realization is fading, but not yet hopeless?

When interpreting any dream that was played out against a particular time of day or night, take your dreaming mood into account, as well as your circadian, or biological, response to that time in the real world. It may be, for instance, that you struggle to think clearly in the mornings and function best late at night, in which case your "night-owl" reaction to a dream set in the morning may be far more negative than that of an "early-bird" dreamer. You may similarly associate daytime with the tyranny of work, and nighttime with freedom and relaxation, so that your dream may have mirrored your

---

Right: Your unconscious may have been reflecting your mixed feelings at the prospect of entering middle age by setting your dream in a fall landscape that you admired for its beauty, but that also made you feel melancholy.

conscious feelings about these periods. That having been said, dreams whose action takes place in the bright light of day often impart feelings of optimism and cheerfulness, also implying that you consciously recognize the issues that you're facing during your waking hours. Conversely, dreams that are set in the dark of night are frequently imbued with a gloomy, sinister, or fearful atmosphere, furthermore suggesting that your unconscious

emotions are in the ascendant and that your conscious mind remains unenlightened, or "in the dark," about certain aspects of your waking life.

The Seasons

Just as the sequence of day and night is symbolically linked with the human lifespan, so the seasonal cycle can also parallel the course of human existence, so that each season represents a staging post along life's path. In

dreams, spring may therefore imply birth and childhood; summer, the prime of adulthood; fall, the maturity of middle age; and winter, physical degeneration and ultimately death. The seasons can alternatively signal your frame of mind when they form a backdrop to dreams, so that spring communicates a feeling of hopefulness and of beginning afresh; summer signals a sense of confidence and of being at the height of your physical and creative powers; fall signifies fruition and the reaping of rewards for past efforts; and winter suggests retreat and decline. So if you dreamed of harvesting the last of your garden's crop of berries with a feeling of pleasure because you were looking forward to eating them, but also of melancholy because there would be no more that year, could your unconscious have been reflecting your mixed feelings about being in the "autumn" of your years? Or was your dream referring to a vision that you have worked hard to fulfill in the waking world (perhaps to bring up a brood of children), one that you

are delighted to have achieved, although now that your work is done, you are feeling a bitter-sweet sense of loss (possibly because your children have left home).

The Past and the Future

Are you in your middle or later years, but became a teenager again in a dream scene that was filled with fun and laughter and peopled with friends from your schooldays, all dressed in the styles that characterized that early period of your life? If so, you probably woke with a smile on your face, but perhaps felt a tinge of regret for your lost youth, and maybe also your lost friends. A dream like this could have

This page: Spring symbolizes babies, children, and beginnings; a wintry dream scene may have been a reference to growing old; and a dream of the past may simply have reflected your nostalgia for happier times.

three possible interpretations, depending on your real-life circumstances. Firstly, by immersing you in an atmosphere of youthful merriment, was your dream compensating for your waking sense of having become old and careworn? Secondly, could your dream have been urging you to try to recapture the high spirits of your youth and adopt a more humorous, carefree approach to waking life? Or, thirdly, did your dream reflect your conscious nostalgia for those years? If so, you may have been wondering what became of your friends, in which case your dream may have been prompting you to try to make contact with them by hinting that you would enjoy an equally riotous reunion.

Left: A few days before he was assassinated, Abraham Lincoln is said to have had a premonitory dream in which he witnessed his death. Such dreams are very unusual, however.
Bottom: If you dreamed of a clairvoyant, are you eager to know the eventual outcome of a situation that's bothering you in the real world?

Another reason why you may have had a dream that focused on your past is that your unconscious was trying to remind you of a valuable life lesson that you absorbed at that time, one that your older self seems to have forgotten recently. If your teenage waywardness got you into all kinds of trouble in the real world, could your dream have been alerting you to your increasing tendency to behave willfully during your waking hours, and have been reminding you of the negative consequences of such rebellious behavior?

But maybe you woke in a cold sweat after a dream in which you were transported to a dark episode of your past, whose memory you have tried to suppress when awake because it causes you so much pain. Rather than trying to torture you by forcing you to relive the source of your anguish in your dream, the purpose of your unconscious was probably to oblige you to recall the details of the unhappy event and then rationally to examine and resolve your emotional reaction. Indeed, you may just find that facing your demons in the cold light of day causes them to disappear.

A dream of the future usually falls into one of three categories: wish fulfillment, premonition, or precognition. If you are cherishing a romantic obsession with a certain person in the real world, and your dream depicted you exchanging wedding vows with him or her, for instance, you were, no doubt, thrilled by the realization of your waking wishes in this wish-fulfillment dream.

You will certainly not have been so ecstatic if your unconscious sent you a premonitory nightmare, however, because these dreams are usually suffused with a sense of foreboding, and with good reason. You may, for example, have dreamed of cruising along the highway in your automobile—as you do every day in the real world— when the brakes suddenly failed and your vehicle started to career out of control, at which point you may have woken with your heart pounding. Although you may have expe-

rienced an anxiety dream (which has nothing to do with your actual automobile and may instead have mirrored your fear of losing control of your waking life), it is possible that your unconscious may have been signaling that you are due to take your automobile to a mechanic—before the worst happens and your dream comes true in real life.

If premonitory dreams arise from an intuitive recognition of a potential outcome, precognitive (clairvoyant or prophetic) dreams really do predict a future event, and sometimes even death and disaster. These dreams are extremely rare, however, and unless you know that you possess highly-developed psychic or telepathic powers, any dream that you had that mirrored an event that later occurred in the waking world is more likely to have been prompted by a premonition, or else was just a coincidence.

☆ ASTRAL BODIES ☆

Whether you dreamed of flying too close to the sun, taking a moonwalk, or simply lying on your back and marveling at the sight of twinkling stars punctuating the velvety-black sky, your dream is likely to have had questing overtones. If space is the final frontier that humankind has yet fully to explore and understand, the astral bodies that inhabit it collectively represent the ultimate in mystery, challenge, and potential achievement, be it in the dream or real world. This general symbolism is underlined by the expression "to reach for the stars," or to strive to attain the most stellar of ambitions, and if your dream focused on a particular star or planet, the purpose of your unconscious may have been to highlight the nature of your aspirations, be they intellectual, emotional, physical, or material.

Not only are the sun, moon, and each of the planets traditionally believed to exert a particular influence over the human psyche, but also over each person's destiny, which, along with the future of the cosmos, is said to be "written in the stars." If things go persistently bad for you in the waking world, you may be said to have been "born under an unlucky star" or to be "star-crossed," for instance, while if success seems to smile on you, others may talk of "your star being in the ascendant," or hint that you have your "lucky stars" to thank for your good fortune. Indeed, according to Western astrology, the zodiacal sign under which you were born, and therefore the position of the stars and planets in relation to your newborn self, is said to determine both your character and the course of your life. Whether you consciously accept or refute the principles of astrology (and even diehard skeptics occasionally sneak a look at their daily horoscopes in newspapers), your unconscious may have tapped into these ancient and enduring traditions while you were sleeping, which is why it is always worth considering them when trying to interpret your dream.

The Sun and Moon

Because dreams often convey the most bizarre images, you may have had a dream of flying through space, your destination the sun or moon. Or maybe your dream was more mundane and portrayed you luxuriating in the warming rays of the sun or contemplating the silvery orb of the full moon as it hung suspended in the dark sky.

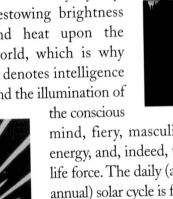

Whatever the context, both the sun and moon can imbue dreams with deep symbolic significance. The sun dominates the sky by day, bestowing brightness and heat upon the world, which is why it denotes intelligence and the illumination of the conscious mind, fiery, masculine energy, and, indeed, the life force. The daily (and annual) solar cycle is furthermore paralleled by the stages of human life, with dawn signifying rebirth (and enlighten-

ment, as signified by the expression "it dawned on me"); the rising sun, increasing vitality; the midday sun, the height of physical and intellectual energy; the setting sun, the waning of these powers; and the disappearance of the sun from the sky, death.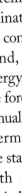

As the ruler of the night sky, the moon—a source of only gentle illumination and no heat—represents the mysterious, intuitive wisdom of the unconscious, which is sometimes perceived as presenting such a threat to the rational mind that we speak of people in thrall to their unconscious urges as being "moonstruck" or "lunatics." The moon additionally symbolizes feminine powers of fertility (partly because its waxing form recalls pregnancy and partly because it influences the menstrual cycle, as well as the ebb and flow of the tides), and thus also the life force. Like the solar cycle, the monthly lunar cycle mirrors the course of human existence, the waxing, crescent moon suggesting gestation (be it of a fetus or an unconscious idea); the full moon, maturity; the

waning, crescent moon, decline; the "black," or invisible, moon, death; and the new moon, rebirth.

You may find it useful to consider your dream of the sun or moon in light of these associations. Could your dream journey to the sun have portrayed your search for intellectual enlightenment, or your trip to the moon your pursuit of inner wisdom? Alternatively, could the dream sun have symbolized your desire for your waking life to be infused with optimism, a sense of wellbeing, and dynamic energy? Or did your dream moon signify your longing to experience the full flowering of your emotions or imagination, or, if you are a female dreamer, to conceive a baby? But if you were badly scorched as you drew closer to the sun in your dream, could your unconscious have been warning that you are in danger of intellectual "burnout"? And if you failed to reach your lunar destination, could the message have been that you are "reaching for the moon," or attempting the impossible?

Did you dream that you were transfixed by the sight of a solar eclipse, and that the dream day became darker and colder as the sun appeared to be gradually eaten up by the moon? Although eclipses of both the sun and moon inspire awe—and relief when the natural order is restored—in the real world, they sometimes send a warning when they occur in dreams. If you watched a solar eclipse in dreamland, the message may have been that the rational powers of your conscious mind are on the verge of being overwhelmed by the chaotic forces of your unconscious, or *vice versa* if you witnessed a lunar eclipse. Alternatively, and especially if you are a man, could the dwindling sun have mirrored your own sense of being overshadowed by your wife, or, if you are a woman who dreamed of a lunar eclipse, could it have denoted your husband's dominance of your relationship? Who is eclipsing your personality, or throwing it into the shade, thereby preventing it from shining brightly in the waking world?

Opposite: The rising sun (left) can represent either intellectual renewal or illumination in the language of dreams, while the setting sun (right) suggests dwindling mental powers. **Left:** A dream of a moon goddess bearing mistletoe (whose berries recall the full moon) and a sickle (a symbol of the crescent moon) may have hinted at harvesting the fruits of your life's labors. **Top:** A dream of a waxing moon may have referred to a growing baby or "brainchild," while a waning moon may have signified a life force that is weakening.

Stars and Comets

Perhaps you dreamed of walking home late at night when a solitary, twinkling star caught your dreaming eye, causing you to stop and regard it with silent wonder. It must have been a magical sight, but why would your unconscious have summoned a star into your dream? Because they light up the nocturnal sky, stars are said to be the "eyes of the night," so that one explanation for your dream could be that an insight has formed within your unconscious mind that may have relevance to a waking problem. Many cultures believe that human spirits manifest themselves as stars, so could your dream star alternatively have represented the ethereal soul of a loved one who has departed this Earth, or could it have been a portent of the birth of a baby in the real world, just as the Star of Bethlehem foretold Christ's birth, according to Christian tradition? Otherwise, consider whether your dream star could have symbolized your own "star," or exceptional qualities, your personal destiny or "lucky star," or else your most cherished ambition,

whose achievement may prove difficult and elusive, but that you nevertheless believe to be within your reach.

Did you see a shooting star, meteor, or comet flash across the night sky in a dream scene? If so, are you superstitious, and did your dreaming self shiver at the sight? If you subscribe to the traditional belief that shooting stars are a sign of impending catastrophe (partly because they can cause devastation when they collide with the Earth and partly because meteors are sometimes termed "falling stars," thereby implying a

doomed personal destiny), your unconscious may have been warning that your waking life is about to take a turn for the worse. But if you felt uplifted when you glimpsed your dream comet, could it have mirrored your own "meteoric," or rapid, rise in fortune in the real world (the suggestion being, however, that you may not be able to sustain your success), or else a brilliant idea that suddenly illuminated your thoughts before fading equally rapidly away?

Left and bottom: Nebulas are the birthplace of stars, so if you dreamed of observing one through a telescope, was the message that "a star is born"? Are you celebrating a birth or a significant career breakthrough in the real world? **Below left:** When comets streak through the dream sky, they may denote an elusive flash of insight, mirror a short-lived, stellar success, or warn of impending misfortune.

The Planets and Zodiacal Constellations

The planets and zodiacal constellations have inspired mythological tales the world over, along with the belief that their positions and movements influence human behavior and the course of worldly life. If your mindset is steeped in modern science, you probably consider the precepts of astrology—be it Western or Eastern—laughable; even so, if you know your sign of the zodiac, you have an unconscious awareness of this age-old tradition. This is why you should never dismiss a dream that touched upon the planets or zodiacal constellations out of hand because it may just have been that your dreaming mind was using the language of astrology to transmit a vital message. Each of the planets is named after a Roman deity, and is consequently said to share the traits ascribed to its namesake, so that if you are an astrological ignoramus, but were

taught Greco–Roman mythology at school, you may furthermore be aware of the planet's symbolic significance. Whether you dreamed of training a telescope on the morning or evening star (actually the planet Venus), heard a snatch of Gustav Holst's orchestral suite *The Planets* in dreamland, or were visited by a mercurial, martial, jovial, or saturnine figure, any dream that drew a particular planet (or Roman god) to your conscious attention may therefore have had pertinence to your waking life.

In Western astrology, every planet is thought to impart its unique characteristics to people born under the zodiacal signs that it governs, so if you dreamed of the planet in isolation, or else of one of its signs (whether or not it was your own star sign), your unconscious may have been signaling that your chances of

achieving your aims in waking life will be improved if you consciously work on developing these qualities within yourself. An alternative explanation for a dream that focused on a planet (or its namesake deity) is that it represents someone in your life who is bringing his or her influence to bear on you in the real world, with either positive or negative results.

A summary of each planet's attributions follows to help you to make sense of any dream in which it is featured. *Mercury* (the messenger god) represents communicational skills and a quick intellect, but is also a trickster figure. *Venus* (the goddess of sensual love) bestows feminine sexuality and an appreciation of esthetic beauty, but can embody the archetypal siren or huntress. *Mars* (the god of war) is the epitome of masculine virility, courage, and aggressive tendencies and is equated with the warrior or hero archetype. *Jupiter* (the father of the gods) is the ultimate authority figure, and, as such, the archetypal father, also signifying positive energy. *Saturn* (the god of agriculture and time) represents the wisdom that comes with maturity, but exudes gloom and pessimism, too. *Uranus* (an early Roman sky deity) emanates transcendent qualities, but also unpredictability. *Neptune* (the god of the sea) shares the symbolism of water, namely the latent powers of the

unconscious, including its emotional highs and lows. Finally, *Pluto* (the underworld deity) confers the potential for profound transformation through spiritual, intellectual, or emotional death and rebirth.

Left: If you are middle-aged and dreamed of the planet Saturn, was your unconscious reflecting the sense of melancholy that the passing of the years has evoked in you? **Below, top:** A dream of Neptune's trident (the symbol of this planet) may have been advising you to "spear" an unconscious insight. **Below, center:** The archer is the symbol of Sagittarius. Was your dream drawing your conscious attention to someone born under this sign? **Bottom:** Always consider their astrological associations when planets illuminate your dream.

If you dreamed of any of the zodiacal constellations or signs, your unconscious may similarly have conjured it into your dream to encourage you to cultivate its characteristics, or else to emphasize another person's behavioral tendencies and how they are impinging on your waking life. It's important to remember that the signs of the Western zodiac may manifest themselves in dreams in the form of their particular attribute (Aries, for instance, assuming the form of

a rampant ram), as may the twelve signs of the Chinese zodiac—the rat, ox, tiger, rabbit, dragon, snake, horse, goat, monkey, rooster, dog, and pig—in which case consulting the relevant chapters in this book may provide further enlightenment.

Understanding the qualities that each of the signs of the zodiac possesses (which are strongly influenced by its ruling planet and element) may prove illuminating when interpreting a zodiacal dream. *Aries* (the ram) is headstrong, selfish, and aggressive, but also decisive, courageous,

and passionate; a masculine sign ruled by Mars, its element is fire. *Taurus* (the bull) is grounded, practical, and sensual, yet stubborn, possessive, and temperamental, too; a feminine sign ruled by Venus, its element is earth. *Gemini* (the twins) can be restless and indecisive, yet possesses a versatile, mercurial mind; a masculine sign ruled by Mercury, its element is air. *Cancer* (the crab) is sensitive, intuitive, caring, and protective, but may tend to be emotionally clingy or withdrawn; a feminine sign ruled by the moon, its element is water. *Leo* (the lion) can be dominating, vain, and self-indulgent, as well as generous, exuberant, courageous, and creative; a masculine sign ruled by the sun, its element is fire. *Virgo* (the virgin) is conscientious, practical, and analytical, but may also be critical, unimaginative, and narrowminded; a feminine sign ruled by Mercury, its element is earth. *Libra* (the scales) can be romantic, emotionally well balanced, and display a strong sense of justice, but if the scales tip in the other direction, it may otherwise be spiteful, indecisive, and flighty; a masculine sign ruled by Venus, its element is air. *Scorpio* (the scorpion) is intellectually focused and emotionally

intense, but may furthermore be jealous and vindictive; a feminine sign ruled by Pluto (and traditionally Mars), its element is water. *Sagittarius* (the archer or centaur) may be restless, impulsive, and impatient, yet is also characterized by its energy, optimism, and versatility; a masculine sign ruled by Jupiter, its element is fire. *Capricorn* (the goat or goat-fish) is ambitious, reliable, and practical, but may be pessimistic and emotionally withholding; a feminine sign ruled by Saturn, its element is earth. *Aquarius* (the water-carrier) is a free, original spirit, who may

sometimes appear aloof, unpredictable, and impulsive; a masculine sign ruled by Uranus (and traditionally Saturn), its element is air. *Pisces* (the fish or fishes) is dreamy, sensitive, and creative, yet may also be an unstable, unrealistic character; a feminine sign ruled by Neptune (and traditionally Jupiter), its element is water.

Above: A dream of the Earth may have implied that you should be more realistic, or "come down to earth," or else have mirrored your sense of your current situation being wonderful, or "out of this world." **Center:** In the visual lexicon of dreams, the symbol of the planet Mars can also represent masculinity. Was your dream urging you to become more aggressive or assertive in the waking world? **Right:** Venus was the Roman goddess of erotic love, so if your dream self was dazzled by a vision of this sensuous deity, was she encouraging you to revitalize your sex life?

LANDSCAPES

If you are a lifelong city dweller, you may be wondering why your dream depicted you in alien territory, maybe huffing and puffing your way up a hillside, with no sign of civilization in sight. Perhaps the easiest way of decoding a dream scene like this is to imagine that it took place in a movie, not in dreamland, and that you were the director responsible for staging it. What were you trying to convey to your audience by depicting your leading actor laboring to reach the top of a hill? An uphill struggle to achieve a difficult aim, perhaps? If so, does this interpretation apply to an aspect of your waking life? Are you working at full throttle to win a promotion, but finding it tough to make headway, for instance? Do the pieces of your dream puzzle now slot into place?

Dreams in which the landscape forms a significant backdrop to the action usually mirror your emotional reaction to your real-life circumstances, be they pleasant or trying. This chapter gives you pointers toward understanding these dreams, but remember that it is also important to consider any personal associations that a dream landscape evokes. A sunny image of lazing on golden sands may have conjured up a vision of heaven for many people, for example, but if your skin is sensitive to the sun and you consider a beach vacation mind-numbingly boring, this dream environment may have epitomized your idea of hell.

Islands, Beaches, and Deserts

Did you dream that you were living in a makeshift hut, beneath palm trees on a desert island, and that you seemed to be the island's only inhabitant? If so, were you reveling in your solitude and natural surroundings, or were you desperately hoping to be rescued and anxiously scanning the horizon for a passing ship? If you regarded your island home as a blissful haven of peace and privacy, it may be that your unconscious transported your dreaming self to this secluded paradise to compensate for the frenetic pace of your people-packed waking life. Do you consciously wish that you could get away from it all to spend some time relaxing alone, and did your dream temporarily fulfill your wishes? However, if you hated being marooned on the remote island and you felt that your isolation was akin to solitary confinement, did your dream reflect your waking sense of loneliness and emotional separation

Above: In dreams, beaches and shorelines can represent a transitional point between the unpredictable ebb and flow of unconscious emotions, intuitions, and urges and the stability of a conscious mind that is grounded in reality.

from those who surround you in real life? Because islands are set in the waters of the ocean or sea, and water's primary symbolic association is with the unconscious mind, a positive dream of this nature may have been underlining your yearning for a period of emotional retreat, self-contemplation, and self-sufficiency. A negative dream, on the other hand, may have expressed your distress at having found yourself stranded in a sea of emotions (either your own or someone else's). The dream may also have signaled that you will only be able to escape your isolation by leaving the security of dry land (a symbol of personal stability), "taking the plunge," and immersing yourself in the very unconscious feelings and urges that caused you to become emotionally cut off in the first place. 🌱 〰️

Did you wake with regret from a dream in which you lay dozing on the soft, white sands of an idyllic beach, caressed by the warm rays of the tropical sun? If so, your dream may have been expressing your longing to escape your waking worries—and perhaps also the winter weather—by jetting off to enjoy a carefree vacation in just such an exotic paradise.

If you dreamed of hauling yourself out of the sea onto a beach, however, how did you feel after your swim in dreamland? Refreshed and renewed, or exhausted and thankful to have found your footing? Beaches are

places where the water (or, in symbolic terms, the unconscious) meets the earth (denoting the practical, conscious mind), so that leaving one for the other may have denoted your emergence from the changeable realm of the

emotions and your return to the security of the rational world. Such a dream may, therefore, have signaled the end of a period of emotional introspection or turbulence in your waking life. Depending on your feeling in the dream scene, the dream was probably reflecting either your sense of having been emotionally regenerated or else of having been emotionally battered, and your consequent relief at having regained some mental stability. And if you watched the sea wash away your footprints from the sand, could this image have reflected your desire to erase the mistakes and problems of the past

that burden your conscious mind, thereby enabling you to make a fresh start in life? Or if you dreamed of strolling along the dream beach, and of being in danger of losing your footing as the sand started shifting alarmingly under your weight, could it have mirrored your worry that the solid foundations that underpin your waking life are starting to give way? 🌱 〰️ ☂️

Sand is often the only notable feature of deserts—arid, infertile, and desolate environments within which few creatures can flourish. So if you dreamed that you were crawling over the baking sands of an apparently endless desert, the fierce sun beating down relentlessly upon your dehydrated body, could your unconscious have been observing that your long-standing emotional isolation from others in the real world has left you feeling parched of love and affection? Could this dream also have been implying that you are longing to be revived by a long drink of refreshing water, a symbolic agent of emotional revitalization? Or do you feel that your friends have "deserted" you, leaving you feeling shunned, lonely, and lost? Did a lush green oasis then rise up into view in the desert of your dream? Or did someone give you the long, cool drink of water you'd been longing for? If so, your unconscious may have been holding out the hope

that your period of emotional drought is drawing to a close, perhaps thanks to the person who offered you that precious drink of water. Is he or she someone whom you are in contact with during your waking hours?

Remember, too, that any dream that focused on sand may have been highlighting the sands of time (an association that is derived from the practice of filling hourglasses with sand), which may be running out for you in the waking world.

Jungles and Rainforests

Perhaps you dreamed of trying to hack your way out of the dense, menacing foliage of a jungle or rainforest, dodging venomous snakes and insects as you became increasingly exhausted and frustrated by your failure to clear a path to freedom. If you awoke sweating from a stifling, threatening dream like this, did you then have to prepare yourself to face yet another fraught day in the "concrete jungle," or your workplace in the city? Could your dream have mirrored your waking sense of being hopelessly trapped within an oppressive office environment, which you perceive as being a career hothouse filled with ruthless rivals, all doing their utmost to thwart your chances of success? If you can draw a parallel between your real-life working circumstances and your dream (which may be plaguing you night after night), maybe a change of job would help you to sleep easier.

Hills and Mountains, Cliffs and Precipices

Unless you consciously regard them as places of natural beauty,

Opposite, above: If you dreamed of being stranded in a desert, do you currently feel that your waking life could be compared to an emotional wilderness or cultural wasteland? **Opposite, below:** Sand can signify relaxation, instability, or the passing of time in the secret life of dreams. **Left:** Dream jungles often refer to an intensely competitive waking working environment, where ruthlessness, ambition, scheming, and backstabbing are vital prerequisites in the daily battle for survival. **Below:** Mountains and peaks symbolize the daunting challenges that we face in our journey through life, as well as the pinnacles of our ambitions.

relaxation, or adventure, the appearance of hills, mountains, cliffs, and other towering natural structures in dreamland usually denotes either ambitious goals—be they professional, social, or spiritual—whose achievement will prove difficult and daunting, or else the immovable problems that you will have to overcome in waking life. And the higher the mount, the more challenging the task ahead of you. The unconscious also sometimes uses crags to symbolize the course of your

life, the first half of which you may spend striving to rise to prominence. And although you may, indeed, reach the apex of your ambition in the peak of your years, there is nowhere else to go from there but downhill. So if you dreamed of standing at the foot of a mountain, shading your eyes as you gazed up at the summit, could your dream have referred to your fledgling career, and have you set your sights on reaching the top of your profession? Could the dream mountain have represented the "mountain" of work that you will have to surmount before success is yours? If you then started ascending your dream mountain and you found the going tough, your laborious climb may have reflected the toil required of you if you are to make any real-life progress. Maybe your dreaming self slithered and slid down the incline before abandoning the struggle and turning for home. If so, are you seriously considering giving up on your aspirations in exchange for an easier life? But if you found scaling the peak surprisingly effortless, are you finding it equally easy to climb the career ladder, and are you doing so sure-footedly and with confidence?

Regardless of whether your dream depicted you making the ascent, did you find yourself standing on the pinnacle of a mountain or cliff, basking in a euphoric sense of achievement? If so, have you conquered the obstacles that were standing in your way in the waking world, and do you now feel that you have reached a high point in your career? And as you looked down upon the dream scene, did you marvel at how small and insignificant the obstacles that you encountered on your route now seemed from your lofty vantage point? Or were you suddenly gripped by a fear of falling? In this case, your dreaming reaction to having attained your highest aspirations may have been reflecting your waking fear of losing the position, the kudos, or the financial rewards that you have worked so hard to win for yourself.

Did you dream of descending a mountain, and did you trek down purposefully and with a sense of relief that the end was in sight? If so, your dream may have mirrored your conscious pleasure at coming "back down to earth," or returning to the undemanding reality of everyday life, now that you have proved your mettle by rising to meet the career challenges that confronted you. If you plodded slowly downward with a sense of reluctance, however, did your dreaming reaction reflect your regret at being forced to abandon your professional status and standing, perhaps because you are about to retire from the world of work and you suspect that this will herald a physical and intellectual decline? But if you suddenly slipped and found yourself tumbling down a steep slope in your dream, do you fear that you are losing control of your working life and that your career is rapidly heading downhill and may even end up being a catastrophic failure? 🎭 🌱

Valleys, Chasms, and Caves

Although they are all depressions in the earth, there is usually an immense physical difference between valleys and chasms, abysses, canyons, gorges, and ravines. Valleys are typically long, wide dips in the landmass that provide protection from the elements, so if your unconscious depicted your dreaming self walking in a valley or dell, the implication may have been that you feel grounded and secure in waking life, albeit that your horizons may be somewhat limited. A sense of security is emphatically not offered by chasms and their ilk, however, whose deep, precipitous sides threaten to entrap and swallow up those unfortunate enough to fall into them.

If you dreamed that an abyss suddenly opened up in front of you, transforming a previously pleasant dream scenario into a terrifying one, could your unconscious have therefore been

transmitting an urgent warning that your position in the waking world is not as stable as you think, and that you may soon be facing an unsuspected pitfall of massive proportions? Perhaps you dreamed of teetering on the brink of the

Opposite, top: If you felt dwarfed by a sheer cliff face in dreamland, do you feel equally overwhelmed by an obstacle in real life? **Opposite, below:** A dream of standing on a lofty peak may have mirrored your waking feeling of being "on top of the world." **Below:** Both water and caverns can symbolize the unconscious mind when they are featured in dreams. **Bottom:** A dream canyon may warn that a disastrous pitfall or a bout of depression is threatening to engulf the dreamer.

ravine, petrified that you would lose your footing, when you saw your partner standing on the other side. If so, could the dream ravine have represented a rift in your real-life relationship, one that has widened so dramatically that it now seems unbridgeable? But if the camera of your dream production then shifted to capture an image of you lying inert at the bottom of the abyss, was your unconscious portraying the deep depression into which you have fallen during your waking hours, an emotional black hole out of which you feel powerless to pull yourself? Because the earth is the symbolic attribute of the archetypal mother, and dangerous, devouring chasms represent the nurturing mother turned ravening ogress, consider, too, whether your hopeless predicament is the work of a terrible-mother figure in your life, a woman who is intent on undermining you, dominating you, dragging you under, and ultimately engulfing you in her malevolent embrace. 🎭 🌱

Caves are also the province of the archetypal mother, or Mother Earth, and may therefore represent the womb in the language of dreams. So if you watched your dreaming self trudging through a cold, wet, inhospitable landscape, stumble upon the entrance to an underground cave, and then creep into its dark, welcoming warmth with a profound sense of relief, did your dream depict you making a symbolic return to the womb? Are your waking circumstances so unremittingly miserable that you are longing to escape your problems and to beat an emotional retreat to the comfort, shelter, security, and oblivion of an all-embracing cocoon, a place where no one can get at you? If you are a male dreamer, an alternative explanation is that your dream expressed your yearning to be steeped in the sexual fulfillment inherent in a heterosexual relationship. And whatever your sex, another interpretation of a dream in which you entered a cave arises from the symbolic association between the unconscious mind and the subterranean earth. When you stepped into the dream cave, or the realm of your unconscious, were you searching for an elusive insight, intuition, or memory that would help you to solve a conundrum that is currently flummoxing your rational, conscious mind?

Stones and Rocks

If a stone or a rock featured prominently in your dream, taking both the context in which it was set and your dreaming emotions into account is vital when trying to understand the message being transmitted by your unconscious. Maybe you were crunching your way along a stony dreamscape when your dreaming vision homed in on a pebble whose shape or color was so arresting that you stopped, picked it up, turned it this way and that as you admired it, and then slipped it into your pocket to keep as a talisman. If so, what attracted you to the pebble, or what caused you to identify with it? The reason for this question is that many analysts believe that when a specific stone is highlighted in a dream, it is because it represents the self—that core, unique, unchanging part of your personality that can be equated with your heart or soul and is therefore charged with mystical personal significance. What was it about you that your dream pebble represented? If, however, you picked up a random pebble and flung it at someone (did you recognize your target?) on a dream beach, could your missile have symbolized your "heart of stone," or emotional coldness, the hard feelings that you are harboring toward a certain someone, or your attempts to keep others at an emotional distance during your waking hours?

A nightmare in which you were pursued by a terrifying aggressor, but managed to elude him, her, or it by hiding behind a huge rock, similarly implies a very different meaning from a dream in which you found your progress impeded by a massive boulder sitting squarely in your path. Could the rock that proved your salvation have represented a steady, dependable person in your waking life, whom you regard as being both a source of emotional strength and a staunch protector? But if your passage through dreamland was halted by an immovable rock, could your unconscious have been making a link with a formidable obstacle that is facing you in the real world? If so, did your dream show you how to find a way around it, or did you give up and retrace your steps?

Meadows and Parks

Did you dream of strolling through a sunlit green meadow dotted with jewel-bright wildflowers, thinking of nothing in particular as you drank in the simple beauty of your surroundings? A dream like this may either have been mirroring your current sense of sweet satisfaction, perhaps because every aspect of your waking life seems to be flourishing, or else your longing to enjoy this idyllic state of affairs, in which case your dream may have temporarily fulfilled your wishes. A dream of ambling through a park may also have suggested that you are feeling either relaxed and at ease with your waking world at present, or else that you wish to be. Because parks are subject to rules and regulations and have to be shared with others, your dream may additionally have been implying that you are happy to follow society's rules, or it may mean that you tolerate the different personalities on the periphery of your personal life, with whom you come into contact in the real world.

Opposite, top: A dream of finding yourself trapped at the foot of a canyon may have reflected your despair at having hit "rock bottom" in real life. **Opposite, bottom:** Dream rocks and bricks can refer to the people who support and sustain us in the waking world—in other words, to human "rocks." **Top left:** If you managed to surmount a rock that was impeding your progress in dreamland, could the message have been that you will eventually overcome a problem that has brought you to a temporary standstill in waking life? **Above and below:** In dreams, fields of wildflowers and grassy meadows can denote waking feelings of contentment, ease, and freedom.

CITYSCAPES AND BUILDINGS

Just as a house can represent you—your mind, body, and spirit, or your conscious and unconscious thoughts, your physical health and appearance, and your highest aspirations and potential—so other types of buildings can symbolize specific aspects of your personality (or else the personality of someone close to you) when they are the focus of your dreams. When trying to make sense of your dream, remember that the environment, atmosphere, and your sleeping reaction to the building that was highlighted in the dream scene all contribute vital clues to its meaning. That having been said, the primary message that your unconscious mind was almost certainly trying to convey by including that particular structure in your dream lies in the purpose for which it is used in the waking world.

Castles and fortresses denote protection and self-defense, for example, while religious buildings represent inner peace or spiritual hopes and endeavors. Although soaring constructions can be phallic symbols, their uses are often very different: towers elevate, isolate, or imprison; lighthouses are beacons of hope and salvation to sailors; while skyscrapers may house homes or workplaces. Stores provide us with the necessities and luxuries of life—albeit for a price—but also offer retail therapy (shopping for emotional comfort), while places of entertainment, such as movie theaters, offer us mental stimulation, laughter, and a chance to escape our waking worries for a while. Libraries and museums supply us with information and thus feed our minds and broaden our knowledge; courts are places of social judgment, and prisons incarcerate transgressors against the legal code; hospitals are centers of healing, while hotels provide a home away from home. If you dreamed of any of these buildings, but remain mystified by its relevance to you and your waking life, this chapter may enlighten you, but for domestic buildings, consult the chapter on the home, and for schools or workplaces, fast-forward to the next chapter.

Cityscapes

Did you dream that you were wandering around a city, either one with which you are familiar in the waking world or one that exists only in dreamland? If so, did you enjoy strolling along its friendly and bustling streets, or did its unwelcoming atmosphere make you feel threatened or out of place? According to Jungian interpretation, population centers like cities (as well as towns and villages) represent the community in which you live, how you perceive yourself as fitting into it, and how well you are getting along with others. So if your dreaming self relished the hustle and bustle of city life and

interacted easily with the people whom you encountered in the dream scene, it is likely that you feel secure in your place within your real-life community and that you relate healthily to those around you. But if every passerby in the dream city exuded a sense of menace, if the buildings that lined the sidewalks seemed to be closing in on you, or if you became hopelessly lost as you wandered the streets, the implication may have been that you are intimidated by others, trapped by your oppressive waking situation, and consequently fear that you are losing your sense of security, identity, and direction. And if you dreamed of finding yourself walking the silent streets of a deserted or ruined city, did this abandoned cityscape mirror how you are feeling during your waking hours—namely desolate, lonely, and forsaken, with your family, social, and professional relationships in ruins?

Castles, Fortresses, and Strongholds

Dreams don't follow the waking world's rules, and often place certain buildings in inappropriate surroundings. Maybe your dream depicted you in a downtown setting, hurriedly entering a medieval castle, raising the drawbridge, lowering the portcullis, and then leaning back against a solid stone wall with a sigh of relief. But why would your unconscious have shown you barricading yourself into a dream fortress, desperate to hold the outside world at bay? Could it be that you have a real fear of being overwhelmed and defeated by a band of hostile aggressors, perhaps a group of schoolmates or colleagues who are ganging up against you in the real world? Or are you feeling so emotionally vulnerable that you are

Opposite: Dream cityscapes often reflect how you are feeling in relation to the community of which you are a part in the waking world. Was the implication that you are an accepted, fully integrated member or an excluded, isolated outsider? **Left:** If you dreamed of walking through a devastated city, do you feel that the social structure that once underpinned your waking life is now shattered and ruined? **Below:** Castles and portcullises keep out hostile intruders, so if you dreamed of barricading yourself into a stronghold, who do you feel the need to keep at bay during your waking hours?

throwing up formidable emotional defenses to prevent anyone from breaching your façade (or persona), and thus getting close to the real you? Alternatively, did your dream highlight your self-imposed isolation from others, and the sense of security that you derive from being emotionally self-reliant?

If your stronghold then came under siege in your dream, could you identify the faces of the besiegers? If so, are these the people who have launched verbal attacks on you during your waking hours, or are they the friends and loved ones from whom you have deliberately withdrawn emotionally? Did your defenses hold firm in the dream scenario (suggesting that you are successfully fending off others' attempts to wound or get through to your emotions), or were they penetrated by the besiegers (implying that your emotional barricades will soon crumble)? If you are a man who dreamed of laying siege to a castle, you may be interested to know that Freudian theory holds that such a dream expresses your desire to make a sexual conquest of a woman who has resisted your advances in the waking world. But if you are a woman who dreamed of leaning over the battlements of a citadel and pouring boiling oil over a man who was storming the ramparts, could your unconscious have been portraying your active defense against that person's persistent sexual advances in real life?

Towers, Lighthouses, and Skyscrapers

Maybe your dream depicted you standing at the top of a tower, gazing down at the teeming city streets below. How did you feel as you observed the people going about their day-to-day business in this dream scene? Relieved to be far removed from other people and their irritating tendency to demand your time and attention? Or wistful because you felt imprisoned and would have loved to leave your lofty jail to mingle with the crowd? Because they are tall structures that soar upward, toward the sky, dream towers may denote "towering" spiritual or intellectual aspirations. Yet towers are also isolating structures, and your dream may therefore have been commenting on your arrogance, intellectual aloofness, and unwillingness to abandon your "ivory tower" in order to descend to others' level. Alternatively, was the reference pointing toward your loneliness and your sense of having become a prisoner of your intelligence or the rarified beliefs that prevent you from interacting normally with the "man on the street"?

A dream tower can also represent a "tower of strength," or a person upon whom others rely for protection, support, and comfort, a symbolic association that may be especially pertinent if you dreamed of a lighthouse. Did you dream that you were sailing in a pleasure craft when a storm suddenly closed in, tossing your vessel so violently this way and that that you feared for your life, but that your hopes were then lifted when you caught sight of the steady flashing of a powerful onshore beacon? Consider the combination of symbols within a dream like this: the turbulent waters may have signifed the tumultuous emotions of the unconscious; the dry land, the stability of the rational mind; the light of the beacon, illumination and hope; and the lighthouse itself, an upright source of salvation. Could the message have been that you are currently being buffeted by a storm of dark, chaotic emotions, but that you have unconsciously identified a steady, sensible, dependable person in your waking life as being a beacon of hope (and your potential rescuer)?

Opposite, left: In both the real and dream worlds, skyscrapers proclaim their inhabitants' financial clout and elevated social and professional status. So if you dreamed of any of these ostentatious structures, was your unconscious highlighting your waking ambitions? **Opposite, right:** If you dreamed of fixing your eyes on the constant flashing of a lighthouse's beacon, was your unconscious holding out the hope that you will be able to navigate your way safely through a storm of dark, turbulent emotions, perhaps thanks to a steadfast friend's support? **Below:** The soaring spires of a dream church may have been drawing your conscious attention to your religious aspirations or yearning to attain spiritual heights.

Freudian dream interpreters equate towering structures with phallic symbols (and thus also macho tendencies), on account of their elongated and thrusting shape—a symbolic link that may be particularly apt if you dreamed of a skyscraper, often a vulgar statement of corporate or personal might, wealth, and prestige. So if you dreamed that you were living in a lavishly decorated penthouse apartment, hundreds of feet above the city, or that your handsomely furnished office occupied the top floor of a towering, multistory building, could your dream have depicted the zenith of your social or professional ambitions? Do you long to rise to stellar heights, to be richly rewarded for the single-minded aggression and ruthlessness that raised you far above the crowd, and consequently to show off your power and position for all to see, admire, and envy?

Religious Buildings

If skyscrapers are sometimes cast as temples of mammon, or embodiments of the "greed-is-good" creed in dreamland, temples, synagogues, churches, mosques, and other religious buildings highlight the dreamer's spiritual, idealistic, or peace-loving needs, tendencies, or potential. This interpretation usually holds true—whether or not you rigidly observe the tenets of your faith in waking life, if you dreamed of a mosque when you are actually a Christian or of a church if you are Jewish (that is, as long as you are tolerant of other religions), and even if you have no spiritual beliefs at all. Indeed, unless you are consciously preoccupied with an issue of faith during your waking hours, have recently attended a religious ceremony or ritual, or are due to (when your dream was probably simply mirroring your waking thoughts, memories, or anticipation), a dream that featured a religious structure is likely to have been sending an uplifting non-denominational message.

Did you dream that you were being harried and hassled on the city streets, that you saw a church, entered it on the spur of the moment, sank into an empty pew, and were then enveloped in a blissful feeling of utter calm? If so, is your waking world so crammed with obligations to your family, friends, and colleagues that there's no time or opportunity to withdraw into your inner world for some much-needed reflection, meditation, and contemplation? Was your dream urging you to beat a temporary real-life retreat from the demands of others, to find sanctuary in an inner haven? Might it be time to ponder what

is really important to you in life, to resolve to achieve it, and thus to find some inner peace? Have you been so busy earning a living and running your home that you've ignored the part of you that

is crying out for spiritual fulfillment? Or are you feeling guilty about having disregarded the altruistic, humanitarian ideals in which you once believed so passionately? Do you long for spiritual guidance in dealing with a waking problem, or for the comfort and support of living your life by a set of clear-cut, morally unimpeachable, and spiritually enriching rules? Or, if you entered a temple in your dream and were immediately infused with a sense of wellbeing, was your unconscious signaling that you would enjoy health, as well as happiness, if you treated your body as a "temple" and prioritized your physical, emotional, and spiritual welfare?

Stores and Places of Entertainment

Stores are buildings of interaction, be it a straightforward exchange of money for goods or the communication between salesperson and customer. As such, they point toward our basic requirements, the items that we consider objects of desire, and how well we go about obtaining these things. If you had a mundane dream in which you stocked up on provisions at a supermarket and paid for them uneventfully at the checkout, just as you do in everyday life, your unconscious may merely have been processing the memory of the shopping trip that you made that

day, or else reminding you that this chore is on your "to do" list for tomorrow. Otherwise, could your dream have been indicating that you are successfully taking care of your fundamental need for emotional sustenance? If, however, you are a female dreamer who found yourself in an agony of indecision in a dream shopping mall because you knew that you were down to your last few dollars and you couldn't decide whether to spend them on a book or on a hair-care product, could the implication have been that you are currently feeling torn between your yearning to turn inward to concentrate on furthering your self-knowledge and your desire to project a more attractive outward image? If you are a man, maybe you dreamed that your girlfriend had been transformed into a snooty store assistant who refused to sell you the set of designer satin sheets on which you'd set your heart—that is, unless you paid above the price tag. Could the suggestion have been that she is extracting too high an emotional price from you for the privilege of enjoying her sexual favors in the real world? Stores are buildings that, on the one hand, offer a multitude of delightful opportunities, or, on

Opposite: If you dreamed of being inside a church, your unconscious may have been encouraging you to rediscover your spiritual side. **Above:** A dream of slot machines may signal that the odds are stacked against you in a real-life gamble.

the other, threaten potential exclusion and humiliation, and the dream theme should tell you whether you are feeling empowered or denied in the waking world.

If your idea of heaven is going on an extravagant shopping spree in real life, or watching a funny movie, an intellectually challenging play, or attending a thrilling sporting event, a dream of having a fantastic time doing just that is likely to have temporarily fulfilled your conscious desire to escape the worries or tedium of your waking hours in the most satisfying or stimulating of ways. Buildings that are dedicated to entertainment, such as movie or stage theaters and sporting arenas, are also places of illusion and transience, however, in which factual and fictitious, triumphal and tragic events are fleetingly performed to divert, inform, or warn. So if your dream did not fall into the wish-fulfillment category, could it have portrayed you in the theater of the unconscious, watching your deepest intuitions

or fears being played out? Did your conscious mind grasp the message being transmitted by your unconscious production?

Libraries and Museums

Did your dream place you in a library, where you scanned shelf after shelf of volumes looking for a specific book? If so, can you remember the title of the book for which you were searching, or can you at least recall its subject matter? Because libraries contain an accumulation of human knowledge and ideas in the form of books, newspapers, and periodicals, their inclusion in dreams suggests the pursuit of knowledge, be it to broaden intellectual horizons or to solve a waking problem. If you dreamed of pulling a philosophy book from the shelf, for instance, it may be that you unconsciously

hunger for a deeper intellectual understanding of weighty existential issues. But if the book was a beginner's guide to plumbing, your unconscious may have been urging you to fix the dripping faucet in your real-life bathroom.

Like libraries, museums foster knowledge by giving people the opportunity to study objects from the past that are of historic, artistic, or scientific interest. When trying to decode the meaning of a dream that was set in a museum, any exhibit that caught your dreaming attention is of the utmost significance because it may have been pointing to something in your own past that has an important bearing on your present waking situation. Maybe your dreaming self was entranced by a primitive pot that reminded you

somehow of your own childish dabblings in the craft of pottery. If so, could your dream have been trying to inspire you to return to the potter's wheel, because expressing your latent creativity would give your waking hours a satisfying new dimension? Alternatively, if you were astonished to see the outfit that you actually wore yesterday enshrined in a display cabinet in the dream museum, could your unconscious have been telling you that it is a "museum piece," or that it is so out of style as to be historic, and that it's high time you caught up with current fashions and updated your real-life wardrobe?

Courthouses and Prisons

Unless you are actually a lawyer, judge, engaged in jury service, or work in a courthouse, the appear-

ance of a judicial building in dreamland often highlights either your feeling of being on trial during your waking hours or else a nagging sense of guilt about having broken a moral or social code. Were you filled with dread or stricken with remorse as you hurried past a forbidding courthouse in an anxiety-inducing dream scenario? If so, are you worried that your superiors at your new workplace will soon judge your waking efforts, find you lacking, and consequently let you go? Or have you consciously been suppressing the shameful memory of having swiped a few dollars from your father's billfold when he wasn't looking, a theft for which you know, deep down, that you deserve to be punished, even if your father never notices your "crime"?

Were you in the middle of a deeply unsettling dream in which you were being bundled into a prison, when you suddenly awoke, the sickening clang of the prison gates as they swung shut behind you still ringing in your ears? Whether you were at liberty when you caught sight of a penitentiary looming ominously ahead of you, were in the process of being jailed, or were languishing in a prison cell, any dream that confronted you with a place of imprisonment

Opposite, top: A dream shopping spree is often simple wish fulfillment. **Opposite, bottom:** A museum exhibit that captured your dreaming attention could have had relevance to your past. **Above:** If your dreaming vision focused on a courthouse, do you feel that you are being judged during your waking hours, or are you haunted by a wrongdoing for which you believe you deserve punishment?

was probably drawing a parallel with your waking sense of confinement or anticipated loss of liberty. So if you had a dream like this, ask yourself who (and perhaps your dream identified him or her by casting someone in your circle as your jailer), or what, is restricting your emotional, intellectual, or physical freedom. Are you a newlywed, for example, who is feeling suffocated during your waking hours by your demanding spouse or by the stifling conventions of married life? Do you feel trapped in a dead-end job that offers no mental stimulation? Are you a fun-loving teenager who has just been grounded by your parents? Or has your own shyness or timidity locked you into a prison of your own making in the waking world?

Hospitals and Hotels

Unless you work in a hospital in waking life, you are probably grateful that you don't have to set foot in a healthcare center because to do so implies illness or injury, either because you yourself require medical treatment or because someone you care about is undergoing a health-related crisis. If you dreamed of being a patient in a hospital, was it a frightening experience? If so, are you actually worried about your health? Maybe you are pushing your fears to the back of your waking mind because you're scared that they will be confirmed by a doctor's examination. It is unlikely that

you will be able to suppress your fears completely unless you confront them, however, and perhaps your unconscious conjured up this dream scene to force you to be brave and have a medical checkup, if only to set your mind at rest. But if you thoroughly enjoyed being fussed over by a

team of kind nurses in your dream, the suggestion may have been that you long to be pampered, cherished, have your every need taken care of, to be made to feel important, and to be relieved of the burden of your responsibilities in the real world. Either way, a dream that focused on a hospital and its staff suggests that you are in need of some physical or emotional attention or tender loving care.

Below: The dreaming mind often summons up hotels to reflect our reaction to a period of transition in waking life.

Did you dream of checking into a hotel? If so, were you charmed by its opulence and looking forward to enjoying its amenities, or did your heart sink at the prospect of staying there because it was dirty and shabbily furnished? If you are due to take a real-life vacation, your dream was probably reflecting either your excitement at the thought of temporarily exchanging your own home for a more luxurious one, or else your dark suspicion that you'll end up spending your nights in a dump. But if you are not consciously anticipating making a journey into the unknown, could the implication of your dream have been that you have entered a transitional stage in life, and that the dream hotel (which is, after all, a home away from home and may, therefore, like any dream home, be a symbol of yourself) mirrored how you are currently feeling about your change of circumstances? Maybe you have recently landed the job of your dreams and are basking in your promotion. Or perhaps you are about to be divorced and you feel depressed about your future prospects. Hotels are also impersonal places run by others, so do you yearn for some welcome anonymity and lack of responsibility, or, alternatively, do you dread losing your identity and self-sufficiency?

SCHOOLS AND THE WORKPLACE

If you are a student and your dream was set in the familiar surroundings of your real-life school, or if you have a job and your dream was played out in your actual workplace, it is likely that your unconscious mind was reflecting your conscious preoccupation with the issues that you face every day. But if it has been several years since you set foot in the classroom or workplace that formed the backdrop to your dream—or perhaps the location was even invented by your dreaming mind—it may be that your unconscious was pointing toward a past lesson or event associated with the dream scenario that has relevance to your current situation in the real world. An alternative explanation for a positive dream of an old school or workplace is that you are feeling nostalgic about a period of your life when you were unburdened by the responsibilities of adulthood, or when numerous opportunities beckoned. But if you hated school or your job and your dream reminded you why you found it so loathsome, it may be that you haven't resolved your feelings about that life experience and are therefore unable to put it behind you and move on. Whether you dreamed of a school or workplace, the reference may otherwise have been to your waking feelings of anxiety about how you are perceived or about how well you are performing. The dream could also have been pointing toward your sense of restriction, and your consequent inability to spend your waking hours doing as you please.

Remember, too, that because schools are places of education (as are some workplaces), your dream may have been encouraging you to feed your intellect, learn a new skill, or express an innate talent. Many workplaces inflict boring and repetitive tasks upon us, however, which we endure in order to earn money to fund the things that are really important to us in life. Wages, salaries, and pensions are furthermore tangible reflections of our worth or value in the job market and, as such, they may highlight our self-esteem, or lack of it, when they assume significance in dreamland. Finally, social interaction—with authority figures, seniors, peers, and juniors—is an essential aspect of both schools and places of work, so that your dream may have been drawing a parallel with how well you are relating to those who surround you during your waking hours.

Schools, Classrooms, and Teachers

Did you dream that you had become a child again—one who felt lost, lonely, and bewildered because your dream portrayed you on your first day at school? If so, have you recently started a new job or moved to a different area? The unconscious often draws on past experiences to reflect how we are currently feeling, and your reaction

Left: Your real-life sense of insecurity could have prompted your unconscious to return your sleeping self to your angst-ridden, childhood classroom.

to your dramatic change of real-life circumstances may have mirrored a childhood trauma of finding yourself in a new environment, among strangers, unsure of how to behave, and worried about what's expected of you and how others regard you. Dreams like these sometimes also occur when a childhood insecurity about being judged as inadequate by your peers, along with a related fear of being unpopular, or even shunned, are aroused in the waking world. Similarly, a dream of taking an exam, or of suddenly being singled out and put on the spot by a teacher, usually highlights a waking anxiety about failing a testing challenge that you are facing in real life.

Perhaps your dream transported you back to the very classroom in which your younger self spent so many hours, surrounded you with friends from that era, and positioned your former teacher in front of you. If you enjoyed this time in your life—be it because you had enormous fun with your schoolmates, because you found your lessons interesting, or because you really liked your teacher—your unconscious may have been giving expression to your nostalgia for those days. But if you were horrified to find yourself reliving this scenario in dreamland, maybe because your fellow students picked on you or your teacher constantly humiliated you, your dream was probably highlighting the grudges that you continue to nurse against those who inflicted such emotional pain on your younger, more vulnerable self. Could your unconscious have been encouraging you to reassess your schooldays from a rational, adult perspective and to come to terms with what happened then—thereby both banishing the ghosts of the classroom that are still haunting you and pacifying the hurting, howling child within? (This may be a particularly pertinent message if your dream was triggered by your dismay at finding yourself in a similar set of circumstances in the real world.) Another message that may have been signaled by a negative dream about being back in school—but less so if the institution was a college or university, where students are allowed more intellectual and personal freedom—is that you are feeling suffocated by the social, emotional, or moral rules, regulations, and restrictions that are chaining you to your real-life office or home and preventing you from living waking life as you would wish.

Our parents apart, teachers are usually the first authority figures to wield power over us, their use or misuse of their authority typically engendering either respect and obedience or resentment and rebellion. Because we were subject to their control at a deeply impressionable age, the stamp of their authority often remains imprinted on our minds, emerging in dreams whenever we

Top left: A dream of being a school-age child once more may have expressed your sense of nostalgia for your schooldays, particularly if, looking back, you now believe that they were the happiest days of your life. **Left and above:** Certain teachers continue to haunt our unconscious memories, and therefore also our dreams (left). And if a teacher who terrorized your younger self picked on you again in dreamland, causing you to become so tense that you snapped your pencil in half, you are probably still furious about how he or she treated you.

encounter a similar mentor or monster in waking life. So, if your dreaming self came face to face with a teacher who once dominated your days, could your unconscious have summoned him or her into your sleep to represent your boss, or even you, if you are in charge of others in the workplace? If you dreamed of a teacher whom you feared and hated when you were at school because he or she was an overbearing, sadistic bully, is your current boss cast in the same mold, and is he or she making your waking life a living nightmare by persecuting and belittling you? Or are you abusing your power over others in the same cruel way that your teacher once did?

But maybe you looked up to a particular teacher at school because he or she treated you kindly and patiently, seemed to care about you as an individual, and was a font of knowledge and wisdom. If that teacher paid you a visit in your dream, could the message from your unconscious have been either that you regard an older person in your waking world in the same light, or that you should emulate the example set by your teacher in your daily dealings with younger people? 🎭 🛡️

Lessons and Learning

The role of teachers is, of course, to educate their students in their own particular area of expertise, so if you dreamed of being instructed by a schoolteacher, college lecturer, or university tutor, your dream may not have been concerned with personalities or behavior, but with learning. When interpreting any dream in which a lesson that was being

Below left: If your dream focused on school-books, your unconscious may have been encouraging you to seek out a specific source of knowledge during your waking hours. **Bottom:** A dream of carrying out a laboratory experiment may have been advising you to take a more experimental approach to solving a real-life problem. **Below:** If a globe seemed significant in your dream, was the reference to globetrotting or brushing up your geography?

imparted seemed more significant than your fellow students or whoever it was who was teaching you, consider the lesson in the context of your past, present, and future. If, for example, you dreamed of being taught the rules of English grammar, do you vaguely recollect learning them as a child, have they since drifted out of your memory, and have you realized—consciously or unconsciously—that when you write business letters they are littered with errors? Could your dream have been advising you to return to the metaphorical classroom of your past, in order to relearn those important rules during your waking hours and consequently to create a better impression when communicating with others in writing (and thus improve your career prospects)? But if you dreamed of listening raptly to a teacher giving a history lesson, is this actually a subject in which you take a keen amateur interest, and have you long been frustrated by the lack of intellectual stimulation in your

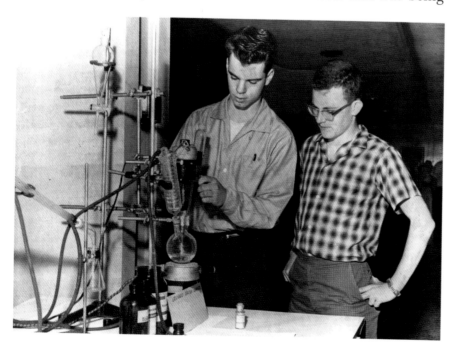

job? If so, could your dream have been encouraging you to pursue your interest, if not by literally returning to school, then at least by reading more history books in your free time, to compensate for the intellectual stagnation of your working hours? A dream like this may have been making an oblique reference to your unrealized potential, to your latent intellectual talents and abilities. The more advanced the educational establishment, tutor, or lesson in the dream, the greater the implication that you would find fulfillment and success if you devoted your conscious attention to nurturing your natural inclination and aptitude.

As well as highlighting a subject that could transform your life for the better if you focused on it in the real world, be it by improving

your English or by feeding your intellectual hunger with historical facts, a dream in which you opened a textbook (which symbolizes a source of authoritative information, know-how, and wisdom) or attended a lecture on a particular field of study may have been alerting you to the need to address a problematic aspect of your waking life that is somehow related to that subject. If you dreamed of puzzling over a textbook on calculus, for instance, rather than reflecting your affinity for math, could your dream have been advising you to calculate or analyze your income and your spending in order to better control your financial affairs in the real world? Or if you dreamed of listening uncomprehendingly to a lecture being delivered in a foreign language, could the message have been that your mindset has become too narrow and that you'd benefit from opening your mind to "alien" influences and trying to understand others' points of view, instead of rejecting them outright as being incomprehensible?

Workplaces and Employment

There are many similarities between schools and workplaces. Both types of establishment are centers of intellectual and physical industry, anxiety, and ambition, for instance, and are places where people interact (be it pleasurably or problematically, and usually within a well-defined social hierarchy). This is why schools

and workplaces are often interchangeable dream metaphors that the unconscious may use indiscriminately (unlike the conscious mind, which tends to make a clear distinction between the two) to act as a frame for its message.

A real-life boss may be cast as a dream schoolteacher, or a company chief executive officer as a principal, for example; colleagues may appear in the guise of schoolmates or rivals; while schoolwork may denote office tasks (or vice versa if you are actually still at school). So if your dream placed you in a workplace setting, remember to take the various interpretations linked with school scenarios into account when trying to decode your dream.

Left: Be they teachers or bosses, authority figures sometimes behave inappropriately, such real-life abuses of power often being highlighted in dreams. **Above:** If your waking life is dominated by deadlines, the pressure that you are under to work at top speed may have been spelled out in dreamland. **Top:** A dream of being riveted by an academic paper may have reflected your hunger for a greater degree of intellectual stimulation in the waking world.

Did your dream faithfully re-create the actual workplace where you spend your waking hours? If so, your unconscious could have been mirroring your waking preoccupation with your job, especially if you are finding it stressful. It may also have been drawing an issue to your conscious attention, of which you may not be fully aware, such as a colleague's efforts to sabotage your progress along your career path. If, however, you are currently unemployed in the real world, or if you dreamed of laboring in a factory when your workplace is, in fact, an office, your unconscious may have temporarily assigned you your dream job to highlight your attitude toward your daily activities and the effect that they are having on you. So if you dreamed of standing at an assembly line, punching hole after hole into an endless procession of identical metal plates, could the inference have been that you are finding your days boring, repetitive, and intellectually unstimulating? Or do you feel that others are treating you as though you were a mindless automaton by making relentless demands of you without ever considering your feelings? Do you feel undervalued as an individual or do you fear that your sense of personal identity and self-worth is being slowly, but surely, eroded by the people or tasks that control your waking

hours? If so, do you feel this way because you have become a real-life wage slave or because your family and friends are taking you for granted and abusing your innate helpfulness or generous nature? If you rather enjoyed your night shift in the factory of your dream, however, could the message have been that you would welcome surrendering your decision-making responsibilities in the real world? And if you dreamed that you enthusiastically constructed an artifact in a workshop setting, could your uncon-

Below: If you dreamed of clearing your "in" tray in dreamland, was your unconscious setting your idle or disorganized waking self an example to emulate? **Bottom:** A dream of owning a profitable business, when you are actually a wage slave, may have hinted that your dream could come true if you take a risk in the waking world.

scious have been encouraging you to give practical expression to your creative urges?

Perhaps you dreamed that you were standing in front of a filing cabinet in a busy office, deeply absorbed in filing away a sheaf of papers that you were holding in your hand. A dream like this may similarly have been commenting on the mentally unstimulating nature of your waking days, but may alternatively have depicted you unconsciously categorizing and stowing away memories that are no longer relevant to your daily life (perhaps of an event or a relationship that has recently ended), but that you may wish to retrieve and refer to at some point in the future. Otherwise, could your unconscious have been telling you to restore some order to a waking life that is littered with so many chores, obligations, and activities that it is on the verge of becoming chaotic?

In dreams, computers can be equated with the brain or mind, and machines with the body or driving energy, so that a dream that featured any of these sophisticated tools may have been commenting on your mental or physical performance or health (any of which may be working smoothly, subject to glitches, or about to break down completely in waking life). And if you found yourself in a dream warehouse engaged in a stocktaking exercise, could your unconscious have been advising you to "take stock" of, or appraise, your present circumstances because your emotional or physical reserves may be running dangerously low?

Pay and Pensions

Did you dream of being paid—be it a wage, salary, bonus check, or cash handout—and are you routinely reimbursed for your work or services in this way in waking life? If so, and you are worried about your financial situation, or if you know that you and your household could not cope without your earnings, your unconscious may have been underlining your conscious concerns and the importance that you credit to being paid in waking life. If you are not struggling financially in the real world, but dreamed that you were outraged because you were paid a derisory sum (did you recognize your paymaster?), when your dreaming self knew that you deserved far more, your unconscious may have been sending an entirely different message, how-

ever. In the language of dreams, money often symbolizes something of worth, so was your dream confirming your niggling suspicion that you, or your services, are being undervalued (but not necessarily at work) in the waking world? Do you feel that someone is cheating you out of your rightful reward? But if your dreaming self accepted your paltry pay without a murmur of dissent, has your self-esteem plummeted so low in real life that you cannot muster the will to insist on being treated fairly and with respect? Has your sense of self-worth hit rock bottom? If you dreamed of receiving a million-dollar paycheck, however, your dream was probably simply fulfilling your waking

wishes, either never to have to worry about money again, to attain the pinnacle of your ambitions, or else to be recognized as someone of great personal worth and importance (although the reference may not have been to your financial standing).

Pensions are generally synonymous with old age when they are highlighted in dreamland, so if you dreamed of setting up a pension or retirement fund, was your unconscious urging you to do exactly that

during your waking hours, to ensure that you spend your real-life retirement comfortably, and not in poverty? But if you received your first pension payout in your dream, how did you feel? Relieved because the ties that shackled you to your workplace

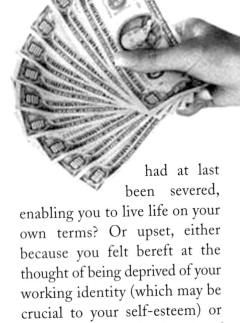

had at last been severed, enabling you to live life on your own terms? Or upset, either because you felt bereft at the thought of being deprived of your working identity (which may be crucial to your self-esteem) or because you hated the thought of becoming, or being regarded as, a "senior citizen"? The answer will tell you whether you are working to live or living to work in the real world, also providing an insight about how you feel about aging.

This page: Whether you were paid by check (above left) or with a wad of cash (above) for your labor in dreamland, your unconscious was probably reflecting the importance that you attach to being a breadwinner in the real world. If you dreamed that your employer unfairly withheld your wages or salary (left), however, it may be that you are feeling similarly cheated or undervalued during your waking hours.

⬡ COLORS AND SHAPES ⬡

If you were to look up from this book, gaze around, and count the number of different colors, and then the various shapes, that surround you, you'd probably be surprised by the total, as well as by your usual lack of awareness of this rich backdrop to your waking world. Although the conscious mind has become desensitized to the myriad hues and geometrical forms that the eyes take in at a glance, the unconscious is less blind to their presence and may consequently re-create them in dreamland. Our dreams may teem with different colors and shapes, only for the conscious mind to forget them instantly on waking, which is one of the reasons why many people believe that they dream in black and white (and perhaps some actually do). If you tend to notice and appreciate colors and shapes during your waking hours, you may be equally aware of them in your dreams. Yet because most of us regard dream colors and shapes as being incidental to the far more interesting action of the dramatic "dreamplay," we tend not remember them when we awake. We may, however, recall a sunny or gloomy dream atmosphere, thereby implying a level of color awareness—and, indeed, color is a crucial transmitter of mood and ambience in both the real and dream worlds.

If you awoke from a dream with the memory of a certain color or shape imprinted on your conscious mind, it is likely to have been sending an important message (why else would it have stuck in a waking mind that is otherwise generally dismissive of these details?) This message may have been connected to your personal association with that shade or form, or it may have had archetypal significance, as is explained in this chapter.

The Connotations of Color

Did your dream take place in the sunshine of a bright day or in the murkiness of a dark night? If it did, your memory of the dream's events is probably tinged with either a golden glow of optimism or a shadowy mood of pessimism, a feeling that may also pervade your waking hours. A dream that was unremittingly gray, for instance, may have been referring to the dullness of your waking existence. Background colors—or a lack of them—can thus play an important, though subtle, part in creating a dream's general ambience and influencing your sleeping reaction to whatever then occurred in the dream scene. And if you have a favorite color—maybe because you associate it with the football team that you support—or if you consciously dislike a certain shade—perhaps because the walls of your classroom, a place that you associate with childhood misery, were painted in it—its appearance in dreamland may have reinforced your positive or negative response to the dream situation. 🏠 🕐

Above: If you are a fan of the Boston Red Sox in the real world, the team's red socks may have imbued you with a fondness for that color. You should be aware of this positive association when interpreting any dream that featured this shade. **Left:** A drab dream scene may simply have mirrored your unexciting waking life.

This page: In the lexicon of dreams, red can denote ardor, which red roses popularly symbolize (below); vital energy, as is suggested by a pair of bright-red shoes (right); or a potentially dangerous situation, such as that signaled by a "stop" sign (bottom). If you dreamed of cutting a red ribbon (below right), however, was the reference to your desire to free yourself from the "red tape," or a frustrating bureaucratic obstruction, that is blighting your waking hours?

But maybe you are trying to make sense of a dream whose colors have faded from your memory—that is, apart from the crimson dress that your female boss, who unfailingly wears a dark suit during office hours, was clothed in while the two of you were arguing. Why would your unconscious have garbed her in such an incongruous, attention-grabbing color? The answer may well lie in bright red's archetypal meaning, which you may unconsciously, if not consciously, recognize. Ever since humankind discovered fire, its flaming hue has been universally associated with heat and danger. Your boss's dream dress may have been a reflection of the heated relationship (perhaps characterized by mutually angry or passionate feelings) that exists between you in the waking world, or else it may have been signaling your unconscious recognition of the real danger that she presents

to your career hopes. Indeed, any color that was highlighted in a dream in this way may have been sending a revealing message from the personal or collective unconscious, and your task is to try to make a link between that color's significance to you, the context in which it appeared, and your real-life circumstances. And although the personal associations that a particular color evoke may be unique to you, remember that the seven colors of the spectrum, or rainbow, as well as brown, black, white, gray, and silver, all have ancient and profound symbolic connotations (as are outlined below).

Red and Pink

Through its association with fire, red can either warn of a potentially dangerous person or situation in the waking world (as is reflected by the red "stop" signs of many countries' traffic-control systems) or emphasize overheated emotions, such as passionate love (symbolized by the red rose), lust, or fury (as is conveyed by the expression "seeing red"). Because red is the color of blood, it also denotes physical strength, vital energy, and thus the life force, which, depending on the nature of the dream theme, may have been depicted either surging strongly or ebbing away. The appearance of the color red in a dream may even have suggested the spilling of blood or a

mortal wound (a message that is encapsulated in the red poppy, millions of which sprang up over World War I's fields of carnage, causing it to become a British symbol of remembrance of the soldiers who perished in that conflict). An imminent conflict in the real world may also have been signaled by a dream in which red featured strongly, and your dream may have indicated the person who is likely to provoke it (maybe it was you who waved the proverbial red rag at a metaphorical bull, or a quick-tempered person). Alternatively, being in a room with red walls may have made you feel cozy and safe in dreamland, in which case could your snug haven have represented the womb?

Other considerations to take into account when trying to interpret a dream that focused on the color red include whether the reference could have been to being "in the red" (in debt), to a person who holds communist or socialist political beliefs (a "Red"), or to a "scarlet" (or sexually promiscuous) woman.

Pink is traditionally a color associated with young girls, romantic love, and also wellbeing (it being said that we are "in the pink" when we are feeling at our best). So if you dreamed of this shade, do any of these significances dovetail with an aspect of yourself or your waking world?

Yellow, Orange, and Gold

Yellow, orange, and golden hues are associated with the sun, and because the sun usually makes us feel happy and relaxed when we bask in its warmth and light, these colors generally impart a contented, sunny mood whenever they brighten a dream scene. A powerful source of energy, the sun furthermore symbolizes intelligence and intellectual enlightenment, so that if anyone in your social circle (or perhaps you yourself) was wearing yellow in your dream, it may alternatively have been drawing attention to his or her highly self-disciplined, intellectual, extroverted, or energetic character. Could the manifestation of this color in your dream otherwise have been advising you to adopt any, or all, of these qualities during your waking hours? If the yellow that attracted your dreaming attention appeared sickly in hue, however, it may have been warning that you (or else the person who was linked with that color in the dream) are jaundiced—either literally or metaphorically, by displaying signs of prejudice, jealousy, bitterness, or crankiness. Also consider whether a negative dream in which yellow was a significant feature could have been warning that someone (again, maybe you) is exhibiting "yellow," or cowardly, tendencies.

As well as sharing yellow's positive connotations, because it is synonymous with the precious metal that we prize so highly in real life, gold is a shade that we associate with wealth and success (and note that the reference may have been to material, emotional, or spiritual riches if gold gleamed in your dream). Orange, too, is a positive color that points toward a cheerful, friendly nature. So if an orange object—or else the fruit—caught your dreaming eye, could it have reflected your own upbeat and optimistic approach to the waking world, or could it otherwise have been advising you to transform your life for the better by being more positive, sociable, and outgoing?

Blue and Green

If you are wondering why something blue caught your eye in dreamland, was it bright or dark blue, and how did you feel as your dream unfolded? The reasoning behind this question is that the quality of the blue, and the events of your dream, may have mirrored how you are currently feeling in the real world. Clear blue skies generally infuse us with a sense of wellbeing during our waking hours, and the appearance of a sky-blue (or pale-blue) shade may similarly have denoted your waking satisfaction because all appears well with your personal world. And because the sky is symbolically linked with both the intellectual and heavenly realms, your dream may have been mirroring your sense of possessing clarity of intellectual vision or of being spiritually at ease. If this is not actually the case, however, could your unconscious have been trying to hearten you by suggesting that the inner serenity, or intellectual farsightedness, that you crave is within your reach? Alternatively, could the reference have been to your desire to take off "into the blue," or into the unknown, or to enjoy a more adventurous, unpredictable waking existence?

Top left: If you are a woman who dreamed of draping a pink feather boa around your shoulders, do you long to rediscover your romantic, girlish side? **Above left:** Your unconscious may have been emphasizing someone's sunny nature if he or she was clad in a T-shirt bearing a "smiley" in dreamland. **Above:** In dreams, a golden egg can symbolize something that has the potential to be wildly successful. **Above right:** A baby-blue dream hue may have denoted a baby boy.

Pale blue is traditionally the color in which baby boys are clothed, so if you are about to become a parent in the real world, could the appearance of this color in your dream have referred to your wish to be blessed with a baby son? Dreaming of a dark shade of blue, the color of the deep, blue sea, the province of the emotions, may, on the other hand, have reflected your waking "blues," or the unhappiness and depression that are tainting your waking hours.

Green is the color displayed by healthy vegetation and foliage, and it may, therefore, denote vigorous natural growth in the language of dreams, or else the mental relaxation that we derive from being surrounded by nature (something from which you may benefit in real life). Furthermore, environmentalists are described as "greens," while gifted gardeners are said to have "green thumbs," so if you dreamed of luxuriating among verdant surroundings, could your unconscious have been advising you to adopt a more environmentally friendly lifestyle, or to give rein to your horticultural tal-

ents? Consider, too, the other associations that are often made with this color: could your unconscious have been telling you that your approach to a waking issue is naïve, immature, or "green," for example? Or else that your cynical, jaded mind could do with an injection of freshness, vitality, and hope? Or was it observing that you have become a victim of the "green-eyed monster," namely jealousy, and that this is a destructive influence on your waking life? Alternatively, was it giving you the "green light," thereby signaling that the time is right to "Go!" or to set your plans for a business or family venture in motion?

Violet, Indigo, and Purple

Because they tinge the sky with their inky shades just before dawn breaks or night falls—transitional times that were once thought to be imbued with mysterious and otherworldly powers—violet, indigo, and, indeed, any shade of purple, are traditionally regarded as mystical colors that possess profoundly spiritual or religious qualities. Whenever they grace a dream, they are consequently believed to hint at spiritual inspiration, altruism, and compassion, or deep, intuitive wisdom, also holding out the promise of inner peace. A color worn by Roman

Catholic cardinals, and therefore a symbol of religious authority, purple was also once donned by royals and nobles to set them apart from common people. So if anyone you know was clothed in purple garments in your dream, could your unconscious have been reflecting your respect for the spiritual, regal, or gallant personal qualities that mark out him or her as being special, or else your irritation with what you regard as that person's self-important posturing? Alternatively, and particularly if he or she behaved in a timid fashion, could your dream have identified that individual as being a "shrinking violet," or a shy or modest soul?

Top left: If a brooding, deep-blue sky darkened a dream scene, it may have mirrored your gloomy, or "blue," waking mood. **Above:** Did your unconscious give you the "green light" in dreamland, that is, did it tell you to go ahead and set your plans in motion in the real world? **Left:** The color green's leading symbolic association is with plants and the natural world. **Below:** Precious stones can represent the true self, and the color purple, spirituality. If your dreaming gaze rested on an amethyst-hued quartz, was your unconscious urging you to focus on nurturing the mystical powers that lie within you?

Below right: If you are a female dreamer who was thrilled to be wearing a show-stopping black dress at a spectacular dream party, did your dream temporarily fulfill your conscious desire to be a sought-after sophisticate?

Bottom right: White symbolizes innocence, a quality that Roman Catholic girls are meant to embody by wearing white dresses on the occasion of their first communion.

Brown, Black, White, Gray, and Silver

Most of us probably associate the color brown most strongly with the earth, and this is indeed its leading symbolic significance in the lexicon of dreams. If you dreamed of walking on a brown carpet, for instance, you may be unconsciously longing to adopt a more down-to-earth lifestyle, perhaps by swapping your hectic urban environment for a simpler countryside setting and getting back to basics. Earthiness can also be a characteristic, so if your dream portrayed you coming face-to-face with someone you know who was wearing a brown outfit, could the reference have been to that individual's dependability or sensible, practical approach in waking life? The warmer the tone of the brown that was spotlighted in your dream, the more likely it is that the reference was to nature, be it to the natural world or to a natural, unaffected personality. A dark, drab brown that made your dreaming self feel downcast may have mirrored your own sense of melancholy, however, maybe because you are feeling oppressed by the joyless round of apparently endless duties and obligations that currently characterizes your waking existence.

If your predominant recollection of your dream was of blackness, your mood may be equally "black"—negative, angry, malevolent, depressed, or hopeless—and devoid of brightness or cheer in the real world. In Western tradition, black is furthermore a symbol of mourning, so if you dreamed of being clad from head to toe in this somber hue, could your funereal garb have been emphasizing your sense of loss, maybe because you have actually been bereaved? Or are you grieving for a phase, or aspect, of your life that has recently come to an emphatic end? It is always vital to take the context of your dream into account, as well as your dreaming mood, and if you dreamed of wearing a little black dress or tuxedo and moving confidently through a throng of admiring people at an elegant cocktail party, your unconscious probably clothed you in black for an entirely different reason. Did your dream reflect your conscious desire to rise in status and mix with the cream of society, that is, was it a wish-fulfillment fantasy? Or was it advocating cultivating a more sophisticated persona during your waking hours? According to traditional symbolism, black denotes wickedness, and if you believe in this popular superstition and found yourself in a nightmarish dream scenario in which you were menaced by a person dressed in this color, could your dream have depicted the embodiment of your darkest fears? Do you—either consciously or unconsciously—worry that someone (did you recognize the threatening dream figure?) harbors evil intentions toward you and consequently represents a sinister threat to your real-life health and happiness?

White is black's polar opposite, in terms of both its color and accepted symbolism, signaling as it does purity, goodness, and hope—qualities that Western brides hope to project by wearing white on their wedding day (and, in a more literal sense, white can signify a woman's virginity). Despite its impracticality, many parents similarly dress their babies in white—the traditional color of baptismal robes—as a sign of their innocence. If the color white featured in your dream in connection with an adult whom you know, it may therefore have reflected your faith in that person's innate goodness, and maybe you also regard him or her as a potential savior from everything that is less than pure within yourself. In addition, while black, or darkness, obscures our surroundings, white, or brightness, illuminates everything that it touches, which is why it can furthermore denote transparency and truth. If you dreamed of being bathed in a dazzling white light, your unconscious may therefore have been heralding a sudden, enlightening burst of self-knowledge that will wipe the metaphorical slate clean of the stains of your past transgressions, enabling you to make a fresh start in the real world. If you felt distressed when you found yourself trapped within an all-white dream scene, however, could the suggestion have been that you are tired of your virtuous, colorless waking life and that you long for more excitement, even if it carries the risk of occasionally "seeing red" or "feeling blue"?

Because gray lies somewhere between white and black, it may indicate ambiguity or neutrality when incorporated into a dream, sometimes alternatively referring to a character or life that lacks vibrancy, passion, and color. But if the gray that caught your dreaming attention had an iridescent shimmer, or was, in fact, silver, your unconscious may have been highlighting any of the subtle, feminine characteristics associated with the moon, such as instinctive wisdom, or the valuable metal that is the counterpart to gold.

The Symbolism of Shapes

You may not think that shapes feature in your dreams, but if you dreamed of paying a shopkeeper a coin, you were handling a circle, and if you ate a dream croissant, you devoured a crescent. Be they dots, spirals, circles, crescents, stars, triangles, squares, or crosses, shapes are an integral—if mundane—part of our everyday world, and also of the dream world, although when they are highlighted in our sleep, their significance is often far more profound. Indeed, of all of the archetypal symbols, shapes number among the most basic, ancient, and powerful. They are even said (especially by Jungians) to reflect the very structure of our minds.

Left: If a snow-white cherub hovered above you in a transcendental dream scene, was its appearance linked with your unconscious desire for spiritual purification? **Below:** If the iron-gray hue of a horseshoe (a symbol of good luck) captured your dreaming attention, it may have been warning that you will require unwavering determination, or an "iron will," if you are to make a success of a waking venture. **Bottom:** Shapes often manifest themselves as the most banal of objects in dreamland. The symbolism of the oval-shaped egg is linked to that of the dot and circle, both of which can signify a potentially promising starting point.

You probably already know that your absent-minded doodles can reveal reams of information about you. So, too, can the shapes that your unconscious mind describes in dreamland. Indeed, ever since our earliest ancestors first recognized that the sun is circular, that the moon often manifests itself as a crescent, that the horizon looks like a horizontal line, that a tree trunk grows in a vertical line, or that a mound of earth is triangular, the human mind has been conditioned to express abstract concepts as shapes and to read more into these geometrical forms than first meets the eye. So if you awoke preoccupied with a shape that figured in your dream, it may have been sending a message that has great relevance to your waking life.

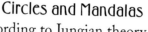

Dots and Spirals

Maybe your dream depicted you writing a letter and taking extra care to dot the "i"s as your pen moved across the paper. A dream like this may have been urging you to pay meticulous attention to detail in your daily activities. But if you dreamed of ending your letter with a period, or full stop, the reference may instead have been to bringing something to a close in the real world, perhaps your relationship with the person to whom your letter was addressed. A dot—a mark from which all other shapes flow—can also share the symbolism of the egg or seed (when it represents embryonic potential, or a starting point), in which case a dream that focused on a dot may have been highlighting something that is beginning, rather than ending, in your life.

In the real world, spirals can be seen as circulating centers of energy—such as the swirling whirlpool, whose momentum sucks water inward, or the spinning Catherine wheel, a rotating firework that flings its fiery sparks outward—and when the unconscious re-creates spirals in dreamland, it may do so to mirror the effect that your own energy—be it emotional, intellectual, or physical—is having on your waking life. Water is a symbol of the unconscious, so if you dreamed of a whirlpool, could it have

symbolized your emotional turmoil or waking sense of "going around in circles," that is, of getting nowhere, despite the conscious effort that you are devoting to trying to solve a real-life problem? Or could the Catherine wheel have represented your smoldering anger, complete with the flashes of rage that singe

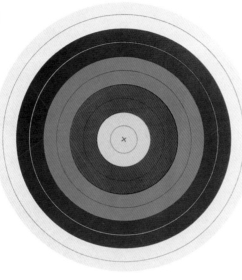

anyone unfortunate enough to come into your orbit during your bad-tempered waking hours? Inert, stylized spirals, like those that appear on seashells, or the winding paths of labyrinths or mazes, suggest a concentration of energy that may direct the seeker inward, toward a central source, which may be interpreted as a place of mystical spiritual or emotional understanding. So if you dreamed of a spiral, was it urging you to direct your dynamic, creative energies outward, toward the real world, or inward, thereby perhaps gaining a deeper level of self-knowledge?

Circles and Mandalas

According to Jungian theory, the circle represents the ideal self, within whom the psyche's various, opposing components have attained a perfect balance. It is a concept inherent in the Eastern yin-yang symbol, in which the white, active, masculine, yang principle is united in symmetrical equality with the black yin force of passiveness and femininity (each, furthermore, containing the seed, or potential, of the other).

Although circles may manifest themselves in the most banal of ways in dreamland, it's therefore always worth considering whether their appearance was telling you to work on harmonizing the disparate elements of your inner self in order to achieve true contentment and serenity. Did you dream of dropping a plate, thereby causing a large segment to break away, and of then spending time gluing the fragment in place again? It may be that your dream was graphically portraying a "breakaway" aspect of your character—perhaps your rebelliousness—that it would be better to integrate into your overall personality than to allow to run riot in the waking world.

Top: The yin-yang symbol represents the perfect balance of two opposing energies, an ideal that your dream may have been encouraging you to strive to achieve. **Center:** If you dreamed of a target enclosed within a circle, was your unconscious telling you to aim for psychic wholeness? **Left:** Could a dream "slinky" have symbolized your latent energies?

If your dreaming eye focused on the Eastern religious symbol known as a mandala (the Sanskrit for "circle"), the holistic message may have been even more emphatic. A mandala is a circular diagram or pattern that contains concentric geometric forms and images and is often very elaborate. In Hindu and Buddhist belief, the mandala's circumference represents the universe, its center signifies spiritual perfection, and, if there is a square within the circle, this symbolizes the earth. Eastern religions regard the mandala—a metaphorical fusion of matter and cosmic energy—as sacred, as well as a powerful meditational aid to the achievement of spiritual enlightenment. In Jungian psychology, contemplating a mandala (which Jung likened to a map of the human mind) is similarly believed to offer a means of healing a fractured psyche and thus attaining individuation, total self-understanding, or the seamless melding of the individual consciousness and the collective unconscious to create a whole personality, soul, or spirit. You may not have recognized the symbol as being a mandala, but if you dreamed of standing in an art gallery gazing at an abstract painting whose subject was a circle, or of creating a circle with a pair of compasses and then ruling geometrical shapes within it, it may indeed have been a mandala.

As well as holding out the hope of unity, wholeness, and perfection, circles have further profound symbolic associations. Because they have no beginning or end, they may represent eternity, or the constantly turning wheel of life that encompasses the cycle of the seasons and birth, life, death, and rebirth, a meaning that may have been implied by the circular face of a dream clock. Because they enclose, circles may additionally denote security and protection, and particularly the sanctuary offered by the womb, but also the void, or infinite emptiness. And because the sun is circular, this shape may furthermore signal masculine, active, solar energy—and sometimes the life force itself—or else spiritual enlightenment. Yet circles have feminine connotations of fertility, too, due to their resemblance to eggs. With so many interpretations to take into account, you may find it difficult to decide what a dream circle may have been implying, but considering the context of your dream alongside your waking circumstances may help to clarify the nature of its message.

Crescents and Stars

If the circle can represent the sun, or one of its many symbolic meanings, the crescent often symbolizes the waxing and waning moon and its inherently feminine, intuitive, unconscious energies and powerful influence over female fertility. Indeed, maybe you dreamed of seeing a crescent moon gently lighting up a dark night sky. If so, and it appeared as a "C" shape, it may have signified that something in your life, maybe an innate attraction, is waning or disappearing; but if it was a reversed "C," waxing and growth may have been implied, and perhaps even the conception of a baby in the real world. If you are a Christian, you may alternatively have identified the dream crescent as being an emblem of the Virgin Mary, or if you are a Muslim, as being a symbol of Islam (particularly if a star twinkled within its embracing arms), in which case your dream may have been focusing on your faith.

Stars are often considered to denote either the enlightenment of the unconscious mind or personal destiny when they illuminate a nocturnal dream sky. But if you dreamed of a star that was graphically portrayed, and especially if you noticed that it had five or six points, a dream pentagram or hexagram may have been sending a different message. Because it has five points, and five is said to be the number of humankind, the pentagram is the symbol of cosmic man, whose body is the mirror image of the universe. In magical tradition, it is a sign of protection, and when depicted pointing upward, it is believed to represent goodness, but when shown pointing downward, it is said to signify evil. Do any of these significances have relevance to your waking world? Do you feel that you might need protection from a malevolent force, for example? The six points of the hexagram represent the union of fire (whose symbol is the upward-pointing triangle) and water (represented by the downward-pointing triangle), and hence the reconciliation of polar opposites, such as masculinity and femininity, or activity and passivity, into a harmonious whole. Sometimes called the Seal of Solomon (a

defensive symbol in Kabbalistic and magical belief), and sometimes the Creator's Star (because its six points can be equated with the six days in which God created the world, according to Judeo-Christian tradition), the hexagram is perhaps better known as the Star of David (or the Magen David, the "Shield of David"), the national emblem of the state of Israel. So if you dreamed of a hexagram, can you make a connection with any of these associations and your situation in the real world?

Triangles and Pyramids

Because they have three sides, triangles, and particularly equilateral ones, share the symbolism of the number three, namely the unification of three separate elements or energies into a single,

powerful entity. As such, a triangle may represent a perfectly harmonized trinity of divinities; a graphic diagram of the underworld, mundane world, and the heavens; the human body, mind, and spirit; birth, life, and death; or, indeed, any other dynamic triple grouping. If your dream incorporated a triangular figure, it may alternatively have denoted three people who are somehow intimately linked in the waking world, such as you and your parents, or even a love triangle consisting of you, your partner, and a lover who has insinuated him- or herself into your relationship.

If you dreamed that you found yourself in an Egyptian setting, awed by the sight of the Great Pyramid, your unconscious may simply have been granting your waking wish to travel and see the wonders of the world. Alternatively, your dream

Opposite, center: Jung believed that mandalas offer each of us a means of achieving individuation, or self-understanding, a quest that you may unconsciously be contemplating if your dream highlighted this symbol. **Opposite, below:** If you are a Muslim who dreamed of looking up at the night sky and seeing a shining star enclosed within the arms of a shimmering crescent moon, was this Islamic symbol reminding you of your faith? **Top:** If your dreaming eye was drawn to a triangular arrangement of twigs, could it have represented an important trio of people in your waking world? **Above left:** Although a dream hexagram may denote the Jewish faith or Israel (or both), it has other symbolic associations, too.

pyramid may have been encouraging you to explore the structure of your own inner world and thus, eventually, to gain complete self-understanding. In the language of symbolism, the square base of a pyramid can denote your physical or unconscious foundations, with the four triangular sides (rising from their earthly base toward the heavenly, or spiritual, realm) signifying ever higher levels of con-

Above: If you dreamed of standing at the foot of a massive pyramid, could this dream structure have denoted the difficulties that you are facing in trying to reach the peak of your potential? **Right:** When trying to decode the meaning of a dream that was set within a city square, it's important to take the various symbolic significances associated with this shape into account. **Opposite, top:** If a multitude of squares formed a checkered pattern in your dream, could your unconscious have been commenting on your fluctuating fortunes, or "checkered" working or love life? **Opposite, center left:** In dreams, a cross shape can suggest a change of direction in the waking world. **Opposite, center right:** A dream swastika may have identified a real-life person's fascist tendencies. **Opposite, bottom:** You may have equated your dream cross with Christianity.

sciousness, and the apex of the pyramid representing the pinnacle of your conscious aspirations. The ancient Egyptians regarded the pyramids as representations of the cosmic mountain, or the universe in miniature. When this concept is translated into personal terms, a pyramid may therefore represent you and the "mountain" that you will need to ascend in order to achieve your highest ambition, which may be to gain spiritual enlightenment. This interpretation is echoed by the upward-pointing triangle (the symbol of the element of fire and the masculine principle), which can represent conscious aims, while the inverted triangle (the symbol of the element of water and the feminine force) points toward unconscious intuition. It is therefore important to note whether your dream triangle pointed upward or downward, because this

will tell you whether it would be better to channel your waking energies into furthering your conscious objectives or to turn inward and explore your unconscious mind.

Squares, Crosses, and Swastikas

The four-sided square is a symbol of the earth, of balance, solidity, stability, and orderliness. If you dreamed of a square—which may have manifested itself as a square room, a city square, a television screen, or a sidewalk or pavement stone, for instance— the reference may therefore have been to your own stable, dependable, and supportive personality. Rather more negatively perhaps, it may otherwise have been drawing your conscious attention to your "squareness," or your old-fashioned values and resistance to change.

Like the square, the cross is composed of two (or one) vertical and two (or one) horizontal lines, the former symbolizing aspirational, masculine tendencies, and the latter, receptive, feminine characteristics, which may have equal value, although one or the other may predominate. The four-armed cross can also represent the incorporation of four separate, but related, abstract concepts, such as the four cardinal points (north, south, east, and west) into one entity. If you dreamed of a cross, consider, too, whether it could have highlighted a choice that you must make in the waking world, or whether you have arrived at a metaphorical crossroads in life and are uncertain which direction will offer you the best future. The cross, or crucifix, on which Christ made the ultimate sacrifice, is the primary symbol of Christianity, so if

you are a Christian who dreamed of a cross, this symbol probably affirmed your faith, maybe highlighting your yearning for spiritual guidance, comfort, or protection. Alternatively, could it have represented a "cross," or painful burden, that you are having to bear in the waking world, such as caring for an older relative, even though it requires you to sacrifice your own desires?

If you dreamed of a swastika, or a hooked cross, you may immediately have connected it with Nazism or fascism when you awoke. And if the dream swastika was worn or carried by someone in your circle of acquaintances whom you know to harbor racist or extreme right-wing views, your unconscious may indeed have been underlining this link, perhaps

thereby warning you to steer clear of him or her. Yet the swastika has certain far more ancient—and positive—symbolic significances, which you may unconsciously, if not consciously, have recognized. "Swastika" is a Sanskrit word that means "wellbeing," and one of the many significances of this symbol to Hindus, Buddhists, and Jains is good fortune. More generally, when it is depicted as turning in a clockwise motion, the swastika represents solar or masculine generative vigor, and when it is portrayed revolving in a counterclockwise direction (when it is called the swavastika), it signifies lunar or feminine creative power. Could your unconscious therefore have summoned a swastika into dreamland to encourage you to give positive expression to your own dynamic or intuitive energy?

⅔ NUMBERS ⅔

Numbers can manifest themselves in dreams in a variety of ways. You may have dreamed of walking down a street lined with buildings when a particular house number caught your eye, for instance, or your attention may have been drawn to the combination of numbers on the license plate of the vehicle ahead as you were driving along a dream highway. Other dream scenarios that may have highlighted a particular number, or combination of numerals, include a date circled on a calendar or the arrival in the mail of a check for a specific sum of money. But do numbers have any meaning when they appear in dreams? Indeed, they sometimes do.

The memory is a database that stores all sorts of numbers of personal importance: house numbers, zip codes, telephone numbers, personal identification numbers, and appointment times, as well as the dates of birthdays and anniversaries, be they of weddings or of events of global significance, such as 6/6/1944 (D-Day) and 9/11/2001. By bringing a specific number to your dreaming notice, your unconscious may have been trying to prompt your conscious mind to recall something that happened when you were living in a house that bore a particular number; to dial a certain telephone number and make contact with a long-lost friend; to remind you of a numeric password that has slipped your waking mind; to keep the appointment scheduled for that time tomorrow; or to remember that your sister's birthday or your wedding anniversary, is imminent. And although you may have forgotten that you ever knew the date of D-Day, for instance, perhaps you learned it in school and it remains logged in your unconscious memory bank, and perhaps it surfaced in your dream to urge you to prepare for your own personal "D-Day," maybe the day on which you are moving house. Or perhaps your unconscious was using a form of symbolic shorthand when it summoned the numbers 9/11 into your dream to draw a parallel with the shock and devastation that you felt on that dreadful day of death and destruction and your similar reaction to the events that are currently rocking your waking world.

Mundane and Mystical Numbers

If you remain haunted by a number that was featured in your dream, it may have relevance to your waking world, but if its significance isn't immediately clear, checking your address book, diary, or even a publication that lists historical anniversaries may bring enlightenment. Remember, too, that your dream number may have referred to a grouping, be it of time (minutes, hours, days, months, years, or decades), people (the members of your family, for instance), or any other type of collective unit that is somehow important to you. You may

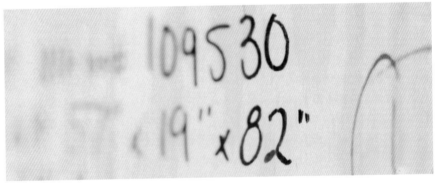

otherwise have a "lucky number," or else be consciously or unconsciously aware of one of the many systems of numerology. Numerology is the age-old study of numbers, which, many believe, influence human, earthly, and, indeed, cosmic life. Some of the significances with which certain numbers are credited—according to numerological principles established by the ancient Greek philosopher and mathematician Pythagoras, the Kabbalah (the ancient mystical tradition of Judaism), and the tarot divinatory system, among others—are outlined below and may help you to make sense of your dream.

Zero

Because it is linked in both shape and symbolism with seeds and eggs, zero signifies the potential inherent in the fertilized ovum, or embryo. Being circular in shape (or nearly so), it shares the circle's symbolic associations with the womb, enclosure, security, protection, eternity, and the void, or nonexistence. In the tarot, zero, or the unnumbered major arcana card, is the Fool, which in turn denotes the unconscious mind.

One and Two

According to the principles of Western numerology, odd numbers signify masculine, active powers, while even numbers denote feminine, passive energies. The number one is said to be imbued with masculine virility, vigor, and determination. It can also symbolize generative and creative potential, partly because it is the first (or source) of the numbers that follow, and partly because of its phallic shape. In addition, it may refer to the "number one" person in your life (usually you), isolation (being a single, unattached individual), or unity (being "at one" with another or others). In the tarot deck, one is also the number of the Juggler, or the

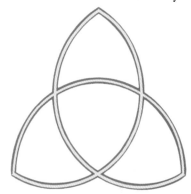

Magician, a major arcana card that symbolizes the will, or conscious mind, while in the Kabbalistic tree of life it is the sephira (or archetypal number of fundamental power) Keter, the divine crown and inspiration.

Two is a feminine number that signals a dual nature, the two sides of which may either be balanced or imbalanced—denoting, on the one hand, harmony, wholeness, and a coming-together (or marriage) or, on the other, division, opposition, and separation (or divorce). It may similarly signify equilibrium (as epitomized by the yin-yang symbol) and equanimity, or else ambivalence and indecision. The number of the tarot's High Priestess, the card of feminine intuition and insight, two is also the sephira Hokhmah, or wisdom, in the Kabbalistic tree of life.

Three and Four

Three is an important number in many religions because it represents a divine trinity, such as Hinduism's *Trimurti* (the Sanskrit for "having three forms"), which comprises Brahma (the creator), Krishna (the preserver), and Shiva (the destroyer); and Christianity's Holy Trinity of the Father (God), the Son (Christ),

and the Holy Spirit. In numerology, the number three can represent the basic family unit of father, mother, and, as a result of their union, child (which is why the number three can symbolize generative drive and the harmony of

three perfectly balanced, although inherently disparate, components). Its mystical powers of unification are additionally implied by such triads as the underworld, the earthly world, and the heavenly realm; the past, present, and future; and the body, mind, and soul. Three is the number of the Empress tarot card, which represents the feminine principles of fertility and nurture, also being that of the sephira Binah, or understanding, when it appears in the Kabbalistic tree of life.

Opposite: Could your unconscious have arranged these apparently random dream numbers to form a phone number, zip code, or numeric password that has relevance to your waking situation? **Above left:** Zero is a symbol of both nothingness and potential. **Left:** Was your unconscious telling you to look out for "number one," or yourself, with this dream image? **Above:** Three can represent a divine trio, as is signified by the triqueta, a symbol of Christianity's Holy Trinity.

Like the four-sided square, the number four denotes earthy solidity, practicality, and responsibility. It is a number that is replete with profound associations, too, notably the four phases of the moon; the four elements; the four seasons; the four times of day; the four cardinal points; the four Christian Gospels or Evangelists; the four aspects of the mind (intellect, emotion, sensation, and intuition); and the four members of the so-called "nuclear" family (father, mother, son, and daughter). These are all foursomes of distinct individual units that exist in perfect symmetry when unified). This is why four also implies order, harmony, and wholeness. It is the number of the Emperor—the epitome of masculine might and resolve—in the tarot deck of major arcana cards. Four is also the sephira Hesed in the Kabbalistic tree of life, denoting loving kindness or mercy.

Above: One of the number four's symbolic links is with the earth, from which spring "lucky" four-leafed clovers. **Top right:** The five digits of the hand contribute to five's symbolic significance as the number of humankind. **Above right:** Emphasizing seven's cyclical quality, the branches of the Jewish menorah represent the seven days of the week (as well as other sevenfold cosmic groupings).

Five and Six

Five is regarded as the number of humankind, for humans typically have five digits on each hand and foot, four limbs supplementing one head, and five senses. As the number of humanity, of a people who strive to transcend their mundane limitations to attain heavenly understanding, it suggests stability combined with dynamic, spiritual questing. It is therefore appropriate that five should be the number of the Pope, or the Hierophant, the tarot card that denotes spiritual authority and wisdom. In the Kabbalistic tree of life, five is furthermore the number associated with the sephira Gevurah (or Din), symbolizing bravery (or justice).

The beauty that arises from the integration and balance of two trinities is signified by the number six, and in the Kabbalistic tree of life six represents Tiferet, the sephira that similarly denotes the beauty inherent in perfect harmony. Through its amplification of the generative power of the number three, it is additionally a number associated with creation—and not only did God create the world in six days, according to Judeo–Christian belief, but six is the number of the Lover, or Lovers, a major arcana tarot card that signals an impending choice.

Seven and Eight

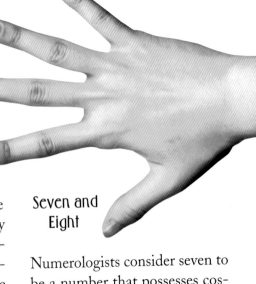

Numerologists consider seven to be a number that possesses cosmic, cyclical energy, not least because it was once believed that there were seven planets in the cosmos. Significantly, there are seven colors of the rainbow; seven days of the week (the seventh, Sunday, being the day that is sacred to God in Christianity); seven branches of the Jewish menorah; seven ages of man, or humankind; seven notes in the

musical scale; and, in antiquity, seven wonders of the world. If you dreamed of the number seven, also consider the possibility that it heralded the onset of the "seven-year itch," or an urge to be unfaithful to your partner after seven years of togetherness. As the number of the Chariot in tarot, seven can symbolize controlled drive and progress. Another of its symbolic associations is with victory and eternity, the qualities concentrated in Netzah, the seventh sephira in the Kabbalistic tree of life.

The number eight denotes perfect universal order, the existence of the material and the spiritual in total symmetry, as well as spiritual enlightenment (in many Eastern systems of mystical belief). And when it is placed on its side, eight becomes the mathematical symbol of infinity. In tarot, eight is the number of Justice, symbolizing impartiality in relation to others, while Kabbalism links this number with splendor, or the sephira Hod, in its symbolic tree of life.

Nine and Ten

Because it is the last single-digit number, nine can signify the reconciliation of all of the characteristics of the numbers that precede it, and hence completion. Pregnancy is usually of nine months' duration, so if

your waking mind is preoccupied with an unborn baby, this number may have great significance to you. Nine is the number of the Hermit in the tarot deck of major arcana cards and, as such, signifies solitude and introspection. Finally, as the number of the sephira Yesod in the Kabbalistic tree of life, nine denotes foundation.

According to Pythagorean theory, ten is the number of divine perfection that signifies the successful completion of one cycle and the start of another (as is reflected in the decimal system) through the union of the number one (the phallus) and zero (the womb). If you are Jewish or Christian and dreamed of this number, also consider whether your dream may have been referring to the Ten Commandments. Ten is synonymous with the tarot Wheel of Fortune, a card that promises change and opportunity (both good and bad), as well as with the sephira Malkut (kingdom) that is set at the bottom of the Kabbalistic tree of life.

Above: Nine is the number of completion, as is underlined by the emergence of fully formed babies into the world after nine months of gestation. **Below left:** Because it is said to unify heavenly and earthly matter, the number eight denotes cosmic equilibrium. If this number manifested itself in your dream, it may therefore have highlighted your desire to live in a "perfect world."

Double Figures

In the tarot, the significance of numbers does not stop at ten: the numbers eleven through twenty-one are each linked with a major arcana card. Eleven is associated with Strength (especially the power of the intellect); twelve is the number of the Hanged Man (signifying the sacrifice of egotistical urges); thirteen denotes Death (representing transition and rebirth); fourteen is associated with Temperance (symbolizing equilibrium); fifteen is the number of the Devil (signaling the need to resist temptation); sixteen's link is with the Lightning-struck Tower (promising freedom through adversity); seventeen represents the Star (suggesting renewed potential);

eighteen is the number of the moon (which warns of emotional confusion); nineteen denotes the sun (indicating attainment and happiness); twenty is associated with the (Last) Judgement, a card of assessment and new beginnings; while 21 represents the World, or Universe (symbolizing conclusion and unity).

Of all of the numbers between ten and twenty, twelve and thirteen are probably the most symbolically loaded. Twelve is significant because it is a unit by which we measure time (there being twelve hours between midnight and noon, and between noon and midnight, as well as twelve months in the year), while Christian tradition and Western superstition brand thirteen as unlucky because the thirteenth person present at the Last Supper was Judas, the betrayer of Christ. So, if the number twelve figured in your dream—perhaps in the form of the glowing, digital figures of a dream alarm clock—could it have been reflecting your sense of enjoying your brightest hour (the most successful time of your life), or a personal "high noon," or, alternatively, of enduring your darkest hour, or a "midnight of the soul," in the real world? Or if you dreamed of stopping at the thirteenth floor in an elevator, are you worried about falling victim to dangerous, unpredictable forces in waking life?

Finally, rather than sending an archetypal message, double-digit numbers may refer to your age, or the number of years that you have lived, when they appear in dreams. Certain of these staging posts that mark our progress along life's path are imbued with particular importance: as children, we may eagerly look forward to turning ten (thereby hitting double figures), to becoming teenagers

Left: If you dreamed of turning over the Hanged Man tarot card, whose number is twelve, your unconscious may have been urging your waking self to be less selfish or materialistic. **Below:** The numerals of a dream clock may have been drawing your conscious attention to the passing of time, and maybe also to your age. **Bottom:** If you are about to turn seventy in the real world, a dream that featured the number sixty-nine was probably highlighting your reluctance to enter a new decade.

on our thirteenth birthday, or else to attaining adulthood at sixteen, eighteen, or twenty-one. Thereafter, we may dread the prospect of "big" birthdays, such as becoming thirty or seventy, be it because we regret the inevitability of aging or because we fear that our days are rapidly dwindling. So if you are forty-nine and you dreamed of the number fifty, could it have referred to the half-century that you are about to notch up in the real world, and perhaps your anxiety about reaching this milestone?

TRAVEL AND JOURNEYS

When the unconscious sends us traveling in dreamland, it generally does so for one of two primary purposes. The first is to show us how easy or tough we are currently finding our journey along life's path. And the second is to urge us to take time out from our punishing or boring daily routines in order to reenergize our bodies, reinvigorate our minds, and revitalize our spirits, either by going on vacation or by adopting a more adventurous lifestyle. The dream scenario, together with your dreaming mood, should clarify which of these messages was being transmitted by your unconscious. A dream of walking, cycling, or driving along a dream highway, for instance, is likely to have been commenting on your progress through life. If your senses were stimulated as you appreciatively soaked up the sights, sounds, and smells of a foreign country in your dream, however, your unconscious was probably advising you to emulate the example set by your dreaming self and to book a vacation, or at least to expose yourself to fresh or "foreign" influences. But if you felt bewildered, or even threatened, by the alien environment in which you found yourself, your dream may have reflected your feeling of being out of place in your waking world.

When trying to decipher the meaning of any dream that portrayed you making a journey, it is important to take your mode of transport (be it your own two legs or a vehicle) into account, along with the pace at which you were moving, the direction in which you were traveling, whether you were journeying alone or with companions, the weather, your surroundings, any obstacles or points of transition that you encountered, and whether you were traveling light or were weighed down with baggage. All of these details, combined with your reaction to the events of your dream, will give you a better understanding of whether you are making good headway toward achieving your destiny in waking life.

Journeys Along the Path of Life

Did you dream that you were walking along a wide, straight road on a sunny day, keeping your destination in your sights as you strode forward vigorously, and with confidence? If so, the incidental symbols incorporated into your dream bode well for the future. The sunshine, for example, suggests a sense of optimism and wellbeing, while your straightforward route and constant view of your destination imply that you know where you are headed in life (and your goal may be to be happily married, to raise a family, to have a successful career, or all three). And—just as we often say that we are "standing on our own two feet" when we are leading an independent life, relying on no one

Left: A dream of pursuing a trail of footprints on a beach may have reflected your sense of following in someone's footsteps in the waking world, perhaps because you are taking the same career path as your father, for example.

but ourselves for support—so a dream in which you were walking effortlessly, energetically, and purposefully indicates that you are advancing effectively under your own steam, without anyone else's assistance, and are therefore in control of your destiny. Are you treading a lonely path through the waking world, however, and would you welcome the companionship of a like-minded fellow traveler to lighten your journey and, if necessary, to hearten and encourage you?

But perhaps the view ahead was hazy because your dream trail was enveloped in fog, or perhaps you could hardly discern anything because your journey took place on a pitch-black dream night. If your vision was obscured in any dream of traveling, the message is likely to have been that you have lost the focus that once enabled you to pursue your aims in a direct and clear-sighted manner, perhaps because emotions are clouding your conscious mind. And if your

Above: If the long shadows that fell across your way made the destination difficult to see, your unconscious may have been drawing a parallel with your vision of your future, which may currently be equally shadowy, or unclear. **Right:** In the lexicon of dreams, a flight of steep, crumbling steps can represent the difficulties that you are facing in gaining a firm foothold on a daunting career ladder in the real world.

dream trail was so overgrown that you struggled to push your way through the foliage that seemed to be closing in on you, an enormous rock or a treacherous hole suddenly appeared ahead of you, or if you were confronted by a dead end, your unconscious may have been drawing a parallel with the hindrances, obstacles, pitfalls, or impasses that are barring your way in your quest for success in waking life. Did your dreaming self persist in your efforts to clear a way ahead, sidestep the rock, jump over the hole, or turn and retrace your steps? If you managed to overcome the obstacle blocking your way in dreamland, it is likely that you will find a way of doing the same in real life. If you gave up and headed back the way you came in a disheartening dream scene, however, the implication is that you will be defeated by difficulties beyond your control and will therefore be unable to pursue your aims, or will "come to the end of the road." (But if you felt relieved as you beat a retreat in your dream, because you knew that you were returning to the warmth, safety, and familiarity of home, it may be that your unconscious was signaling that your domestic happiness is actually more important to you than the achievement of your intellectual or career goals.)

Did you dream that you were limping along a road in your dream, frustrated by your inability to move any faster? Sometimes our capacity to proceed swiftly and smoothly along life's path is hindered by the difficulties and delays inflicted on us by others (or even those of our own making). A dream limp may have implied that your freedom of movement is somehow being "crippled," "hobbled," or restricted in the real world, perhaps because your emotionally needy partner's demands on your time and attention are holding you back in the career stakes. Always consider how you were moving in a dream, and try to make a connection with your

attitude to your waking life at present; the parallel will usually be clear. If you were skipping or dancing, for example, are you feeling carefree and ebullient? Dragging your feet, on the other hand, may have signified reluctance; strutting, arrogance; running, being driven by fear or urgency; jumping, clearing obstacles or taking a short cut; tripping or stumbling, taking a wrong step or making a mistake; while crawling may have been implying humiliation, submissiveness, or else extreme difficulty. And if you were horrified to find that your legs wouldn't respond to your brain's commands, so that you couldn't move at all in an anxiety-saturated dream scene, your unconscious may have graphically depicted your sense of having come to an abrupt standstill in the waking world. Could this be because you are facing such a knotty dilemma in real life that you have become paralyzed with indecision?

Dream Directions

The direction in which you were moving in your dream can similarly send a clear message about your sense of purpose in pursuit of a goal in life, whether or not that target was visible, absent, or had assumed a symbolic guise. If you were walking along a straight, even road in the dream world, it is likely that you are following a direct, unproblematic route toward your objective. If the trail twisted and turned, or if you were wandering

Above: If you encountered a roadblock on your dream journey, your unconscious may have placed it in your path to represent an obstacle that has brought your progress through life to a similarly frustrating halt. Did you successfully bypass the dream road-block, or did a traffic policeman (an authority figure) order you back in line?

around aimlessly, however, your course is probably either proving maddeningly slow and indirect, or else it is unclear to you. And if you discovered, to your extreme annoyance, that you'd been going round in circles in your dream, do you feel that you are getting nowhere, despite your vigorous efforts to advance in life? Maybe you were even moving backward, in which case, could your unconscious have been reflecting your frustration because your position seems to have worsened or reversed in the waking world, or was it suggesting that you are backing off from a commitment that you've made (perhaps to yourself)?

Did you turn off the beaten track in your dream? If so, maybe you are being sidetracked, or diverted, from achieving your waking goal. Could your unconscious have been implying that you should try to get back on the right track? Or did your dream depict you "turning a corner"—in other words, successfully negotiating a tricky point in your life? Were you clambering up a dream hill or mountain and did you find it an uphill struggle? Or was gravity propelling you downhill, or maybe headlong down a slippery slope, with such velocity that you felt that you were losing control and heading for a fall? Remember, too, that other natural forces, such as powerful winds and turbulent seas, can push you in a direction that may not be of your own choosing in dreamland. In all such instances, try to link the circumstances of your dream with events in the waking world.

Perhaps you dreamed that you became increasingly uneasy on your dream journey as the realization began to dawn that you had lost your way (a metaphor for losing your sense of direction, or purpose, in life). If so, did you consult a compass, map, or atlas to try to work out your position and how best to reach your dream destination? In the real world, these navigational tools show us the course that we should chart. And in the terrain of dreamland, the direction indicated may refer to a life course, which you may already have mapped out or are alternatively negotiating in an ad hoc fashion, making choices only when a turning point presents itself. If the direction being shown by the needle of a dream compass was north, your unconscious may have been advising you to take an intellectual path, but because north also signifies a cold climate,

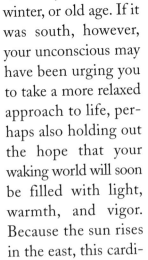

the reference may have been a chilling one, namely to darkness, winter, or old age. If it was south, however, your unconscious may have been urging you to take a more relaxed approach to life, perhaps also holding out the hope that your waking world will soon be filled with light, warmth, and vigor. Because the sun rises in the east, this cardinal point may have been directing you to step out on the road to spiritual renewal, while west, the direction of the setting sun, may have been telling you to accept that your energies are waning. Finally, a right-hand, or else upward, direction may have pointed toward taking a rational approach to the world around you, while a left-hand, or downward, bearing may have denoted turning inward and immersing yourself in your unconscious mind.

Modes of Transport and Single-person Vehicles

As well as describing a mode of transport or conveyance, the word "vehicle" can be interpreted as a medium of expression or achievement, a meaning that is particularly resonant in the language of dreams. In addition to expressing the manner in which we are powering our progress toward our goals, or what is driving our personalities, dream vehicles can tell us whether we are in control, whether we are being "driven" by someone else, or whether, indeed, we are completely out of control in our waking lives. When we jump onto a bike and pedal off down the road in waking life, for instance, we are powering and controlling our own movement, although we have to put more personal effort into getting ahead than if we were walking. A bicycle does, however, enable us to

cover greater distances, and if you dreamed of coasting rapidly along a smooth surface, having built up so much momentum that you hardly had to touch the pedals, the implication may have been that, thanks to your previous endeavors, you are currently advancing speedily and easily through this phase of your waking life.

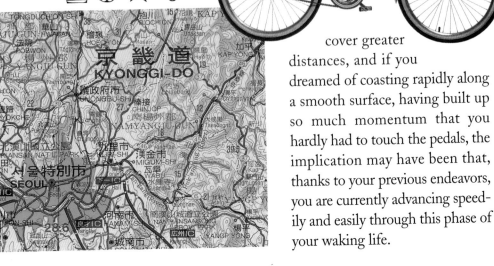

If you are male, a dream of mounting and then riding any vehicle, be it a bicycle, an animal, or a motorbike, may otherwise have been commenting on your sex drive. Did you feel comfortable in the dream saddle and did you forge ahead powerfully and confidently, or did you sit astride your mount precariously and have difficulty controlling it? The former scenario suggests that your conscious mind and sexual urges are working together harmoniously, while the latter may have expressed your sexual inhibitions or your sense of being at the mercy of your libido. And whatever your sex, if you dreamed of riding an animal, or of sitting in a cart and being pulled along by one, first try to decide what that creature symbolizes to you (a horse may represent your unconscious energies, for example) and then note whether the animal was doing your bidding, bucking against your control, or running away with you in dreamland. These considerations should indicate whether your unconscious is going along with, rebelling against, or ignoring the control that your conscious mind is exerting (or attempting to exert) over it.

Automobiles, Trucks, and Taxis

Some analysts assert that automobiles are, invariably, phallic symbols that denote thrusting masculine sexual energies in dreams, although other authorities consider this a simplistic interpretation. Indeed, if you dreamed of an automobile, it is important to pinpoint what this form of transport signifies to you in waking life. In the real world, automobiles are a personal (or familial) means of transport that provide independence of movement and access to distant opportunities, for example, so that your dream automobile may have represented your freedom to range far and wide, and in whichever direction you choose, in your journey along life's highway. If you actually own the automobile that featured in your dream, also think about why you selected it in real life (but if you don't, envisage yourself owning one and then ask yourself why you opted for that particular model). Was it the only vehicle that you could afford? Were you influenced by its reputation for reliability and safety? Did you need a large automobile in which to ferry your big family around, or a small one because you are single? Or was money no object, and were practical considerations irrelevant, so that you could treat yourself to your "dream" automobile? And was your primary purpose in choosing it, as well as picking out your preferred color, to project a certain image, or persona, so that others would immediately assume that the driver was sporty, quirky, or someone of wealth and stature, for instance? The answers to all of these questions should tell you more about your character, assertiveness, self-perceived image, status, and perhaps your sex appeal, and the driving force, or ambition, that

Opposite, top: An exit sign looming before you in dreamland may have been signaling the advisability of switching direction in waking life, perhaps by following an intellectual route (signified by an upward-pointing arrow). **Opposite, center:** A dream of riding a bicycle may have mirrored your sense of powering your own progress through the waking world. **Opposite, bottom:** If you dreamed of consulting a map after losing your way in a foreign country, the reference may have been to your waking efforts to get your bearings, perhaps because you have entered unknown territory, such as a new school or job. **Top:** In dreams, riding a horse can be a metaphor for the control that the conscious mind wields over unconscious urges. **Above and left:** Dream automobiles can symbolize the image that we hope to project to others, which may be sleek and wealthy (above) or rugged and powerful (left).

powers you through the waking world. If you were embarrassed to be seen in a rusty old wreck in a dream, however, could it have reflected your own feelings of inadequacy and self-disgust at present, perhaps because you have fallen on hard times in the real world? And if you dreamed of exultantly driving your friend's automobile, could the message have been that you admire his or her image so much that you long to appropriate it for yourself?

Were you a passenger in a dream automobile, or were you the driver? If someone else was at the controls, could the implication have been that the driver (did you know him or her?) is "taking you for a ride," or deceiving you, or else that you depend on that individual to make decisions for you? And are you happy to cede control of your waking hours to that particular dominating person, or is this occurring against your will, so that you are perhaps being "driven" to distraction? But if you were the dream driver, and if someone else

was in the vehicle with you, it is likely that you feel responsible for steering him or her in the right direction (probably one of your own choosing) in life. If, however, a passenger was infuriating you by peering over your shoulder and giving you unhelpful directions as you were driving along the streets of a dream city, could the reference have been to a "back-seat driver," or someone who is constantly trying to influence how you are living your life?

If a dream automobile's appearance can symbolize your persona, and the steering wheel your conscious, or controlling, mind, the engine and gas that fuels it can represent your inner power and energy. Did your dream depict you driving an automobile down an open road, cruising smoothly toward your destination? If so, you probably feel that you are in command of your waking circumstances, that you know exactly where you are going in life, are currently enjoying an easy "ride," and have enough stamina and energy to get you safely to your journey's end. But did your dream trip then start to go wrong? Perhaps you suddenly ran out of gas, in which case your unconscious may have been warning that you are neglecting your energy levels, the fundamental "fuel" that powers your progress, and that they are now on the verge of becoming so depleted that you are head-

ing for a breakdown (be it physical or emotional). Maybe you aren't eating healthily, or perhaps you aren't getting enough replenishing sleep. A dream of speeding, on the other hand, often implies that you are driving yourself at too fast a pace during your waking hours, maybe by trying to accomplish too much in too short a time. Are you living life "in the fast lane," in danger of losing your self-control, and are you consequently heading for a crash, a sudden collapse that will bring

Left: Dreams of driving at breakneck speeds sometimes warn dreamers that they have become so hyperactive in the real world that they are heading for disaster. **Above:** A dream of being stuck in traffic may have reflected your sense of having come to a frustrating standstill in the waking world due to a crowd of others cramping your style or limiting your freedom of movement. **Opposite, right:** The identity of your fellow travelers will usually give you a significant clue to the meaning of your dream if you spent it riding the subway. **Opposite, bottom:** Dream taxis can denote ultimately expensive shortcuts in our attempts to reach our destiny in life.

your progress to a dramatic halt in the real world? If so, perhaps you should apply the metaphorical brakes, or slow down, thereby regaining control of your waking circumstances. Indeed, if any part of your dream automobile malfunctioned, try to draw a parallel with your real-life situation. If a dream tire was punctured, for instance, has someone "deflated" you, or caused your self-esteem to plummet, by pricking your ego with a wounding verbal barb? Or if a faulty gas pedal resulted in you driving too fast or too slowly in your dream, are you living life at an exaggeratedly accelerated pace, or, alternatively, are you unable to summon the necessary "oomph" to make more rapid headway?

Were you driving a truck in your dream? Some of the dream symbolism of automobiles also applies to other motorized vehicles, but the function of the vehicle in the real world can have an important bearing on a dream's possible meaning. Trucks are generally used to transport large

quantities of commercial products or personal possessions from their source to their destination. Could your dream truck have hinted at changing your job, capitalizing on the fruits of your labor, or moving? But if your dreaming self knew that you were hauling a load of trash, and that you were on the way to dumping it, could your unconscious have been advising you to rid yourself of the accumulated possessions or emotional pressures that are complicating your progress and loading you down in waking life?

Did you dream of hailing, and then getting into, a taxi? If so, was the driver of the dream taxi one of your friends? Taxis usually offer a quick and direct means to our destination in real life, albeit at a price, and it follows that your intended goal, and especially the person who charged you your fare in your dream, may have had relevance to your waking situation. It may be, for example, that you are hoping to switch jobs in the real world, and that your friend is in a position to put in a good word for you with her company. She may be

offering you a shortcut to a new venture in life, but your dream may have been warning that she will require reimbursement (but not necessarily monetary payment) in return for the favor.

Public Transportation

Did you dream of getting on a bus, finding a seat, and then gazing out of the window at the passing scenery as your journey commenced? Although all forms of public transportation require us to purchase a ticket in order to get from A to B, this consideration is generally less significant in such dreams than both the implied surrender of our ability to control our individual freedom of movement and the identity of our fellow passengers. In the real world, most airplanes, trains,

buses, and passenger ships are owned by a corporate entity, which employs drivers, pilots, or captains to steer its vehicles to their destination, as well as conductors and stewards to ensure that passengers abide by company rules. If you recognized any of your coworkers on the dream bus, or, indeed, if you knew that you were traveling to work, it may therefore have been that your unconscious was referring to your career path. Could the bus have represented the organization for which you work; the driver, your manager; the conductor, your supervisor; and the other passengers, your fellow employees? If you think that this is so, were you content to sit quietly on the bus (that is, go along with company policy during your waking hours), did you argue with the conductor (thereby acting out your real-life resentment of the authority that your bosses wield over you), or even try to disembark (implying that you wish to leave your job)?

Trains travel on tracks, so if you dreamed of being a rail passenger, could the implication have been that you are unable to deviate from the course that others—maybe authority figures in your life, such as your parents—have set for you? Did your dream indicate that you are "on the straight and narrow," "on track," "on the right lines," or being carried along the correct route to your destiny? Or did it warn that your life is in danger of "derailing," or becoming dysfunctional? When interpreting a dream in which you were speeding ahead on a dream train, also note that Freudians associate trains with virility, or the penis, and railroad tunnels with the vagina. If you are a man who dreamed of being on a train that had broken down at the entrance to a tunnel, this dream situation may therefore have been commenting on your less than satisfactory sex life in the waking world.

Did you dream of presenting your travel documents at an airline's check-in desk prior to boarding an airplane? If so, were you traveling light or were you burdened with luggage? Although suitcases can simply denote travel in the symbolic language of dreams—and any travel-related dream scenario may merely have reflected your conscious anticipation of taking a vacation, or your desire to do so—an alternative interpretation is that they represent the emotional "baggage" that we all carry around in our heads. This is why it is important to take the luggage (or lack of it) that was

Opposite, top: In the language of dreams, trains and tracks can denote following a direct, unchanging course through your waking life. **Opposite, bottom:** If you dreamed of ascending to a breathtaking altitude in a cable car, your unconscious may have been expressing your conscious ambition to rise to exhilarating heights in your career. **Right:** According to Freudian theory, trains are phallic symbols, so if you are a man who dreamed of a steam train, was your unconscious telling you that your love life is "steamy"—or, perhaps, on the verge of "running out of steam"? **Below right:** A dream fighter plane may have been advising you to go on the intellectual attack during office hours.

accompanying you on your dream trip into account when considering your dream. Remember, too, that dream departures can imply bidding your old circumstances farewell and embarking on a new journey, or change of direction, in life (and perhaps into the great unknown), while dream arrivals often hint that you have either achieved your goal or that you envisage yourself doing so. So if you think that your dream portrayed you setting off on a new adventure in life, did it suggest that you have rid yourself of burdensome memories, problems, and preoccupations associated with your past? Or was the implication that these issues are still weighing you down and will continue to retard your progress in the future, wherever it is that you are headed? And if you are actually due to go on vacation soon, but dreamed that the check-in staff turned you

firmly away because there was a problem with your passport, could you be unconsciously aware that your passport is out of date? Otherwise, could the message have been that your ambitions are being frustrated, either by an authority figure's narrow mindedness or stubborn insistence on following the rules, or because you need to regularize or update a crucial detail of your current life before your unconscious (or conscious) mind will permit you to move on?

In the real world, airplanes enable us to transcend the delays and difficulties of land-based travel by transporting us swiftly through the air and then depositing us at our destination. And because air can symbolize

spiritual or cerebral aspirations, and the freedom within which to achieve them, if you dreamed of taking to the skies in an airplane, there are three interpretations to consider. Firstly, could your unconscious have been encouraging you to explore your spirituality or to rise above the limitations of daily life in order to concentrate on "higher" issues? Secondly, did it depict you on the fast track to a spectacularly successful career? Or, thirdly, was it advocating jetting off to an exotic location to enjoy a much-needed vacation?

Water-going vessels like boats and ships have similar symbolic significances in dreams, although, because they transport us over water, their meaning is usually concerned with the realm of the unconscious, with emotions and instincts. So if you dreamed that you were sailing the high seas as a passenger on an ocean liner, was your dream advising you to embark on a voyage of emotional self-discovery, to "anchor" yourself in a loving relationship, or to actually book the cruise that you've long been meaning to take in the waking world? Alternatively, whether you dreamed of being in the middle of a flight

Right: In the parallel universe of dreams, waiting at an airport can signify that you have entered a transitional phase in waking life.
Below: If you dreamed of being aboard a storm-buffeted ship, perhaps you are finding this stage of your journey through life an emotionally tempestuous experience.

or a sea crossing, your unconscious may have been commenting on the ease (or otherwise) of your current progress in life. Are you "flying high," or doing well, in the waking world? Do you feel that this phase of your existence is "plain sailing" (in other words, proceeding smoothly)? Are you being buffeted by turbulence (be it spiritual, intellectual, or emotional)? Or are you "up in the air," "lost at sea," or beset by uncertainty and confusion?

Points of Transition

If journeys in dreamland reflect how we are advancing in life, staging posts like airports, ports and harbors, railroad stations, and bus stops often represent transitional points in the cycle of our personal existence. So, too, do crossroads, tunnels, and bridges. If you saw yourself in a dream airport, walking resolutely toward a departure gate, did its number have any significance to you (maybe because it coincided with your present age, or perhaps because you regard it as being lucky in the real world)? If so, your unconscious may have conjured up this dream scene to hint that it is time that you waved farewell to this unsettled stage of your life and ventured off in a dif-

ferent direction (and perhaps a lucky break has already opened up for you). But if you dreamed of disembarking from a ship and stepping out onto the landing stage of a dream harbor, could the suggestion have been that you have actually embarked on a new phase in life, one in which your

future will be markedly different? Maybe your dream portrayed you standing bemused and confused in a railroad station, unsure of where you should be going, but surrounded by people rushing off to catch their trains. Or perhaps your dreaming self was standing at a bus stop, letting bus after bus pull away rather than jumping onto any of them. Dreams like these may have mirrored your waking desire to move on in life, along with your sense of uncertainty regarding where to go next. Was your dream warning that your indecision is putting you in danger of "missing the bus," or letting a potentially life-changing opportunity, or connection, pass you by?

If you were traveling on foot and arrived at a crossroads in dreamland, or were driving and found yourself negotiating a traffic circle, your unconscious was probably signaling that you have reached an important turning point in waking life, at which you must make a crucial decision. Did a dream signpost point you in a direction that you were tempted to take, or were you torn between two possible routes? (If the road signs bore any words, can you make a connection between them and a choice that you are facing in the real world?)

Maybe your dreaming self was driving along a highway when you noticed a sign offering you the option of turning off and driving through a tunnel beneath a mountain. If so, did you decide to enter the dream tunnel, or to carry on down the highway? If you chose the former option, your dream may have been highlighting your unconscious urge to depart from the route that you have been following in the waking world. And because mountains can denote towering challenges, and subterranean tunnels as passages through the earth symbolize the unconscious, could your dream have been indicating that you may be able to bypass the difficulties inherent in climbing to the peak of your ambitions by choosing to enter a transitional phase in your life? Furthermore, the inference may have been that, although spending a little time in the dream tunnel may expose you to all that your unconscious mind contains (basic urges, uncontrolled emotions, but also innate wisdom), perhaps this will act as a catalyst, enabling you to emerge with a clearer conscious sense of your direction in life.

In the real world, bridges are structures that span two otherwise disconnected points, thereby offering a shortcut between the

Below left: If you dreamed of approaching a border control, it is likely that you are hoping for a complete change of waking circumstances. If you were turned away in dreamland, however, the message may have been that you will not be able to move on until you have dealt with the unfinished issues that are holding you back. **Below:** In the language of dreams, bridges can represent links between the past and future, or else between opposite viewpoints.

two. Therefore, bridges represent points of transition in the lexicon of dreams, as well as a means of linking your past and potential future (which may have markedly different characteristics), or else of "bridging the gap" between your own opinions and someone else's opposing beliefs. So, if you dreamed of wondering whether to cross a bridge, could you see what was awaiting you on the other side? Be it a person, landscape, or cityscape, can you work out what he, she, or it represents in the context of your waking world? And is it something to which you'd like to commit, or that you ultimately feel has no place in your future?

MEDIA

We rely on radios, televisions, and newspapers to keep us informed of events that have occurred in the wider world and to advise us of likely future developments. When these media beam their messages into your dreams, their purpose may also be to inform you about your current circumstances—the difference being, however, that the source of the news that they carry is your own unconscious mind, not any external agency. Whether the news being imparted in your dream was good or bad, and whether it concerned domestic or foreign affairs, your unconscious was therefore almost certainly reporting on an aspect of your own personality or waking situation, of which your conscious mind may still be unaware. (For further insight into dreams that focus on means of communication, see the chapter on messages and communication.)

We also turn to the entertainment media—to the music and talk shows broadcast on the radio and to the soap operas and movies screened on the television—to entertain and divert us from the problems that beset our waking lives. And it may just be that snippets of what you heard or viewed the previous day worked themselves into the dramatic action of your dream, in which case their only significance may be as memories. Alternatively, your unconscious may have seized upon the plot of a film that you recently watched, or have appropriated a member of the cast, as a convenient vehicle with which to replay an event that occurred in your past or to act out a present preoccupation. (For more advice on entertainment-related dreams, consult the chapter on sports, games, and entertainment.)

Finally, while the written word can inform, enlighten, and stimulate the mind in both the real and dream worlds, and advertisements can mirror our aspirations, still and moving dream images may "paint a picture," provide a "snapshot," or otherwise reveal how you unconsciously perceive a facet of your waking life (or even yourself) at present. And if you were operating a camera or camcorder, or wielding a paintbrush in dreamland, the implication may have been either that you wish to place a fragment of your life and times on record, or that you would reap rich rewards from nurturing your talent as a photographer, cameraman, or artist.

Radio and Television

Although we can switch channels or turn off the TV set, we otherwise have no control over what we hear or see when listening to the radio or watching television in waking life. Furthermore, the nature and content of this one-way communication is controlled by a powerful authority, such as a media corporation. And when we listen to a news bulletin during our waking hours, we generally implicitly accept that the information being broadcast is the truth (because it is being reported by an authoritative source) and that it is significant (because that authority regards it as important enough to make public). Our waking reaction to a newscast also generally holds true in the parallel universe of dreams, but, in this instance, the broadcasting authority is the unconscious mind, perhaps acting on an intuition and perhaps urgently trying to transmit its message to its conscious counterpart. Did you dream that you were idly listening to the radio as you drove along in your automobile, when a newsflash suddenly made you stiffen and listen intently? If so, can you remember the news that grabbed your attention, and can you link it with your waking world? Remember that the message may have been coded, so that a gloomy economic forecast could have warned that you

Opposite: A dream in which you used a remote control to channel-surf may have portrayed your waking restlessness, perhaps because nothing seems to hold your interest for long in the real world, or else your conscious attempt to pinpoint an elusive intuition. **Left:** If you dreamed of sharing an exhilarating viewing experience with friends, your unconscious may have been compensating your waking self for your currently lonely and lackluster days. **Bottom right:** Dream radios can broadcast important messages from the unconscious.

may soon face a downturn in your personal finances; a war report may have referred to the strife that is about to break out between members of your family; and a story about a killing may have highlighted your own murderous feelings toward someone in waking life. But if you dreamed of adjusting a radio dial or zapping a television's remote control in order to find a particular station or channel, maybe your unconscious portrayed you trying to "tune in" to an intuitive feeling (whose presence you can sense, but whose message you are not yet receiving loud and clear).

As well as being instruments of communication that enable us to stay abreast of current affairs in the real world, radios provide entertainment and mental stimulation by broadcasting dramas, talk shows, and music. Televisions do, too—also offering us soap operas, quizzes, documentaries, and movies, while VCRs and DVD players allow us to record or view anything we want at our convenience. Did you dream of watching a televised discussion or movie, and if you did, can you recall its subject matter or course of events? Was it a faithful replay of a program or film that you actually saw last night, a variation on the theme, or else a figment of your sleeping imagination? If the same images that you watched before going to sleep played themselves out again before your dreaming eyes,

your unconscious may merely have been processing your memories of your real-life viewing experience. Another straightforward explanation for a dream like this is that your unconscious was providing you with an enjoyable diversion from the boredom or anxiety that pervades your days, by treating you to a feel-good fantasy. Alternatively, if you actually do spend your waking hours glued to the television, and your abiding memory of your dream is an unflattering image of yourself slumped, slack-jawed, and glassy-eyed in front of the screen, could your unconscious have been reproving you for having become a couch potato?

If you felt really involved with, or deeply affected by, a particular scene (which may, or may not, have been an exact rerun of the original) that was being played out on the dream television screen, however, it may just be that last night's viewing triggered a profound response in your unconscious mind. Did you identify with one of the characters, or with his

or her situation, perhaps because you once found yourself in similar circumstances, or else because you fear, or hope, that you may soon do so? If the actors in your dream were arguing furiously about how their young son should be disciplined, and you empathized with the cowering child, for instance, have you suppressed painful memories of being fought over, or threatened, by your own parents when you were small? (And if you were watching a video or DVD recording, the suggestion that the scene emanated from your own memory bank is redoubled.) Could your unconscious have screened this dream scene to force you to confront your unhappy memories, review them from an adult perspective, and come to terms with your childhood misery and fears? Or if you dreamed of wiping away a sentimental tear as you watched the heroine of a movie accepting her hero's marriage proposal, do you wish that your boyfriend would ask you to be his wife in real life? But if you dreamed of watching a talk show on anger management, but are certain that you've never seen a similar program during your waking hours, could your unconscious have conjured up this scenario both to draw your

conscious attention to your violent temper and to urge you seek the counsel of friends, family, or professionals for help in trying to control it?

The Written Word

Like books, newspapers and magazines are sources of knowledge. Yet because their contents are more ephemeral and quickly become outdated, because they contain a mixture of light- and heavyweight articles on all manner of issues, and because they are also interspersed with advertisements, they do not usually share books' symbolic association with wisdom in the language of dreams. The primary purpose of newspapers in the real world is to inform us of recent events and future trends, which is why dreaming of reading one of these daily or weekly publications usually has the same significance as a dream of hearing a radio or television news bulletin (see above). So if you dreamed that you were passing a newsstand when the sight of a newspaper headline caused you to stop in your tracks, its message may have relevance to your waking world. But if your dream depicted you scanning a newspaper column in search of a particular item, it may instead have re-

flected your conscious anticipation of receiving some important news in the real world, such as your exam results.

Another possible interpretation for a dream of flipping through the pages of a newspaper or magazine is that you have become bored with your life and that you are unconsciously looking for ways of incorporating more variety and interest into your waking hours. If, upon consideration, you believe this to be the case, and if you remember pausing in your dream to read a travel article whose theme was globe-trotting, for instance, could your unconscious have been advising your waking self to take time out of your day-to-day routine to see more of the world?

Left: If you are eagerly awaiting significant news during your waking hours, your unconscious may have mirrored your impatience by portraying you surveying the pages of a dream newspaper in search of a report revealing that vital news. **Above:** The unconscious may focus our dreaming vision on magazines to encourage us to build some entertaining diversions into our days.

Advertisements are designed to sell us products in the real world by tapping into our fantasies and aspirations, the implication being that if we buy the item in question then we will appear as glamorous as the models portrayed in their idealized images. If your dreaming self lingered over an advertisement promoting the object of your waking desire—a luxury automobile, for instance, or a pair of designer shoes—your dream was probably merely reflecting your waking obsession with owning it, and thereby impressing others. And if you are female and an advertisement for cosmetics that featured a woman's flawless face

held your dreaming attention, your unconscious could either have been mirroring your longing to look equally stunning, advising you to devote more attention to your appearance, or even urging you to completely transform your image, or persona, in real life.

Visual Images and Sound Recordings

Did you have a dream in which you took a photograph of your laughing children, who looked exactly as they do in waking life? If you did, your dream may have been responding to your sense that time is passing and your desire to retain a mental "snapshot" of your children as they are right now.

Indeed, paralleling their use in the real world as instruments with which to capture a moment in time, both cameras and camcorders can denote committing a mind's-eye image to memory when they appear in dreams. Are you currently spending your waking hours studying for an exam, and did

you dream of opening a textbook at a certain page and then taking a photograph of it? If you had a dream like this, your unconscious may have been expressing your wish to be blessed with a "photographic memory," or to be able to absorb information in precise detail for quick

Above left: In the language of dreams, magazine advertisements may reflect our conscious aspirations or unconscious yearnings or may otherwise set us an example to emulate. **Above:** Dream camcorders and cameras help us to commit mental images of the waking world to memory. **Left:** By giving you a pile of newspapers to browse through in dreamland, your unconscious may have been advising you to update your knowledge of recent events or to learn more about others' opinions in the real world.

and easy recall when you are actually taking the exam. In addition, when we look at photographs in the real world, we often see things that we were unaware of when the picture was taken. If you dreamed of taking a snapshot of an automobile that you are considering buying in real life, for example, the implication may have been that something important about the car has eluded your waking attention and that you should take a hard look at your prospective purchase before signing the paperwork that would make it your liability. A dream of recording the sounds around you with a cassette recorder may have similar interpretations, in that you may wish to remember the happy chatter that is currently filling your home or to be able to rewind and replay exactly what was said during the course of a college lecture or an important discussion with your boss about your promotion prospects.

But maybe you dreamed of examining a photograph of yourself and feeling upset because your features were so exaggerated

that you looked hideous. It is said that the camera never lies. In this instance, could the dream photograph have mirrored your own poor self-image, which may be totally out of perspective? Otherwise, could the dream have been telling you that your unpleasant waking behavior is causing others to perceive you as an ugly character?

If you dreamed of peering through a camera's viewfinder and becoming increasingly frustrated as you adjusted the lens because your subject remained out of focus, however, the implication may have been that you are not seeing something about that person or situation clearly, perhaps because your mind is so clouded with emotions that you have lost your "focus," or ability to discern the truth. But if you fitted a wide-angle lens to your dream camera, could the message have been that you should take a broader view of your current situation?

Recording tools like cameras and camcorders are also artists' accouterments, which enable us to express our creativity and produce beautiful or thought-provoking images. So if you dreamed of being happily absorbed in framing a camera shot or painting a picture, could the allusion have been to your talents in this

Left: A dream in which you took a snapshot of you and your partner brimming with happiness probably expressed your desire always to remember this wonderful time in your life. **Below:** Your unconscious may have drawn your dreaming attention to an artist's palette and paintbrush as a way of prompting you to explore your creative potential. **Below left:** The purpose of a dream of recording your thoughts on a Dictaphone may have been to ensure that you remembered them when you awoke. **Bottom:** If you were cast as a movie director in dreamland, was the allusion to controlling others in waking life or to directing the course of your own destiny?

field, which you may be neglecting during your waking hours? Remember, too, that every picture is said to tell a story, so also ask yourself what the image that you created in dreamland portrayed, whether you painted an accurate or a distorted picture of the subject, and whether your viewpoint is therefore equally objective or skewed.

SOUNDS

If a sound that your ears picked up in dreamland continued to resonate in your mind after you awoke, there are two possible explanations for this phenomenon. The first is that the sound was real and that your unconscious became aware of it and wove it into your dream. You can probably recall occasions when you were torn from your sleep by the insistent ringing of the telephone or doorbell, yet there may equally have been many more times when your conscious mind remained oblivious to these sounds and you kept sleeping. Even so, you may unconsciously have registered the intrusive sound of the doorbell, and responded to this real-life stimulus as you slept by opening a door in your dream. Alternatively, your unconscious may have incorporated the noise made by the doorbell into a different context in dreamland, so that maybe you dreamed that you were listening to a teacher in a classroom when the sound of the school bell brought the lesson to an end.

The second possible explanation is that the noise of the ringing doorbell was not caused by someone actually pressing the button, but that your unconscious instead re-created it in a dream in response to an emotional trigger. If you believe that this could be the case (perhaps because your home isn't equipped with a doorbell), the next step is to consider the purpose of this sound in the real world, to identify who, or what, initiated it in your dream, and then to make a symbolic link with your waking circumstances. Because doorbells alert us to the arrival of visitors who expect to be invited into our homes (themselves symbols of ourselves), or of door-to-door salespeople who hope to persuade us to buy their products, the dream doorbell may have been signaling that someone in your waking world wants to initiate direct person-to-person contact with you. So if you can remember who was requesting access to your home in this way in your dream, consider the possibility that your unconscious has detected that he or she wants something from you during your waking hours, and then try to pinpoint what that something may be.

In summary (having discounted an external source), identifying what a dream sound means to you in the real world, and subsequently drawing a parallel with your waking situation, may clarify the message from your unconscious.

Bells and Alarms

Did you dream that the ringing of a telephone urged you to pick up the receiver? If so, who was at the end of the dream line, and what did he or she say to you? In both the real and dream worlds, the ringing of a telephone or doorbell tells us that someone wishes to speak to us—something that we may already be

Left: If a telephone rang in your dream, you may be unconsciously aware that someone wants to make real-life contact with you.

Left: Whether or not it was known to you, if you were forced to listen to a disembodied voice telling you some uncomfortable home truths in dreamland, you may have been reprimanded by your conscience. Below: In both the real and dream worlds, alarms warn of a dangerous situation. Below left: Could the shrill ringing of a dream alarm clock have been sending your conscious self a "wake-up call," or have been alerting you to keep your wits about you?

uneasily aware and, indeed, trying to avoid during our waking hours. The unconscious may not permit us to ignore this uncomfortable truth forever, however. If you dreamed that you picked up the dream phone and that your ear was instantly assaulted by a barrage of angry reproaches from your friend for having stood her up recently, did you indeed fail to meet her as arranged, without a word of explanation in your waking world? If so, could your guilty conscience have caused the telephone to ring in your dream in order to encourage you to acknowledge your guilt, face up to its consequences, and apologize to your friend? Alternatively, maybe the telephone rang in dreamland, but no one responded when you answered it. If you had

this dream experience, could your dream have been metaphorically "ringing a bell," or prompting you to recall a memory that has been lurking in the shadows of your unconscious?

Indeed, we often rely on bells or alarms to act as reminders, usually to tell us that it's time to stop or start a certain activity in waking life. The ringing of an alarm clock signals the need to get out of bed and embark on a new day, for instance, while that of a kitchen timer informs us that a dish is cooked and is now ready to be removed from the heat, and that of a school bell may regulate a student's timetable. So if any of these bells resounded through your dream, your unconscious may have been prompting you either to turn over a new leaf and get up earlier; to

present the plan that you've been cooking up to a wider audience; or to learn a new life lesson in the real world.

Were you deafened in your dream by the shrieking of a fire, burglar, or car alarm? Just as real-life alarms warn of the imminent approach of extreme danger or a threat to our person or property, so, too, do their dreamland counterparts. So what set your internal alarm bells ringing? Perhaps you are already consciously aware that the faulty wiring in your home constitutes a fire hazard, that the lock on your front door is flimsy, or that your habit of leaving the keys handily in the ignition makes your automobile vulnerable to theft, but you haven't yet rectified the problem in the waking world. Could your unconscious have been trying to rouse you into taking urgent remedial action? Alternatively, was it alerting you to an overheated situation, an imminent invasion of your privacy, or a loss of control, and

consequently to a personal catastrophe that is about to befall your waking self unless you swiftly avert it? Other sounds that signal a clear warning in the real world include the whistles that are blown by police officers and referees, and the hostile growling or barking of angry dogs, any of which may have "called time" on an uneventful dream, heralding the start of a nightmare. Could the ear-shattering blast of a dream whistle have indicated that you are defying an authority figure or offending against the rules by which you live your waking life? Otherwise, was the allusion to "whistle blowing," or to informing on a transgression that has come to your waking notice? Or did the ominous growling or aggressive barking of the dog that your short-tempered boss was restraining on a leash in your dream reflect your intuitive sense that the dog's owner is about to unleash her pent-up anger on you in the real world, in the form of a vicious verbal attack?

If you had a dream in which you heard church bells pealing joyously or tolling sonorously, it is important to take any spiritual associations that this sound may arouse in your mind into account when considering the possible meaning of your dream. If you are

a Christian, for example, the sound of pealing bells may symbolize a baptism, a wedding, or a religious celebration in your personal lexicon of dreams, while tolling bells may denote a funeral. Are you actually anticipating attending such a church service in the near future, or did the sound of the bells underline the celebratory or despairing feelings that are flooding your mind at present?

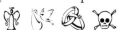

Knocking and Echoes

Did your dream portray you knocking on a friend's door? If so, is there a favor that you want to beg from him during your waking hours? Be it in the real or dream world, the significance of rapping on someone's door and ringing the doorbell are interchangeable (see above), so it may be that you are hoping to be invited into his inner sanctum—perhaps his actual home, or maybe the realm of his true personality or feelings. Or is there another reason why you require his attention? Is he ignoring your efforts to get through to him, or to make him understand how badly you need his help, in the waking world, for example? Or were you "knocking on wood" in

Above: A dream of knocking on someone's door suggests that you are anxious to be the focus of that individual's undivided attention in waking life. **Above left:** The ringing of church bells in dreamland usually gives expression to real-life feelings of joy or sadness, depending on whether the bells were pealing or tolling. **Left:** If the deafening wail of a police siren shattered a previously quiet dream, your unconscious may either have been warning that you are on the verge of committing a social offense or alerting you to an impending emergency in the waking world.

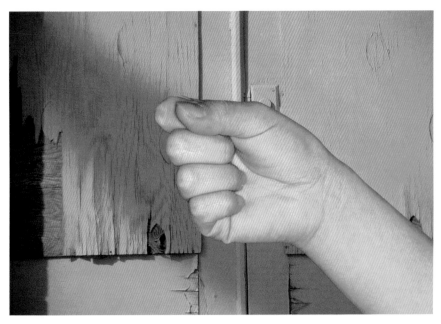

The Human Voice

If a noise made by a human voice—whether or not it was known to you—was the most striking aspect of your dream, it is vital to consider your dreaming reaction to that sound when thinking about what your dream may have meant. And when it comes to interpreting the symbolism of the sound itself, all you need do is to ask yourself what it signifies in the waking world. If the howls of your friend reverberated through your dream, for instance, causing your dreaming self to feel great distress, your unconscious was probably confirming the emotional torment that your friend's anguish is arousing within you during your waking hours. Similarly, if you woke with the sound of your own dream screams resonating in your mind, could they have expressed the fear or anger that you are experiencing in real life? Or were your yells a cry for help? And who caused you to scream in dreamland? Is it the same person who is terrifying or enraging you in the real world? Have you been suppressing powerful emotions

dreamland in an attempt to ward off a direct consequence of something that you've said, or done, that you superstitiously fear may have tempted fate to knock you back into line?

Was your lasting memory of a dream a disembodied spoken phrase that echoed through it, as though your dreaming self was caught in a loop that replayed the same words over and over again? If so, did you recognize the voice (was it yours?), and can you remember the words that were being repeated? The reason for these questions is that there are two probable interpretations of a dream like this, one that harks back to the past, and another that concerns the present (although both have implications for your future). If the voice belonged to your dead mother, and it replicated, word for word, the advice that she constantly gave you when she was alive, it may be that your

unconscious was trying to drum the truth of her counsel into your mind, to prevent you from behaving in a contrary manner. If, however, it was your voice that echoed within your dream, but rather than expressing your own thoughts, the words repeated a phrase that you associate with your friend, your dream may have contained an implicit warning that you are tending to "parrot," or unthinkingly repeat, her opinions. Is it time that you thought for yourself? Similarly, also consider whether your dream echo could have been evoking nostalgic memories of your past, or whether it could have signified that you have become stuck in a monotonous rut in waking life, from which you should try your utmost to break free in order to expose yourself to different viewpoints.

Opposite, top: Did your dream depict you knocking on wood, in a superstitious attempt to prevent bad luck from striking you during your waking hours? **Opposite, center:** If you are not actually a parent and were driven to distraction by a baby's incessant screaming in dreamland, it may be that your unconscious was drawing a parallel with the extreme irritation that someone's childish behavior is whipping up in your waking self. **Opposite, bottom:** Hearing a host of voices shortly before falling asleep is a common experience during the hypnagogic state.

which is why a dream voice—whoever it belonged to—can sometimes be said to be the voice of your conscience.

But did you awake perplexed, having had a dream in which everyone was talking in a foreign language? If so, could your dream have reflected your waking sense of being excluded from your social circle because

during your waking hours, and did venting them in such an emphatic manner in your dream at last give you a sense of release?

Perhaps the focus of your dream was a conversation, and maybe the message from your unconscious was unambiguous. If you dreamed that your wife was nagging you to start exercising regularly, for example, did your unconscious put these critical words into her mouth to tell you that you really do need to safeguard your health in this way? Indeed, in the language of dreams, your sleeping mind's choice of words often communicates a truth of which you are unconsciously aware, but consciously prefer to disregard,

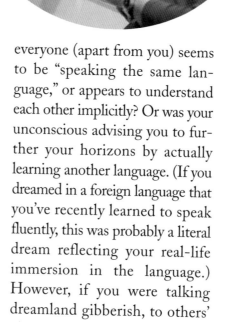

everyone (apart from you) seems to be "speaking the same language," or appears to understand each other implicitly? Or was your unconscious advising you to further your horizons by actually learning another language. (If you dreamed in a foreign language that you've recently learned to speak fluently, this was probably a literal dream reflecting your real-life immersion in the language.) However, if you were talking dreamland gibberish, to others' obvious mystification, did your

dream mirror your self-perceived inability to communicate effectively with others in the real world? But if you were unable to understand what your friend was saying in your dream because she was speaking so quietly, could the implication have been that she is having difficulty connecting with you in the real world, perhaps because you are unreceptive to her point of view? If you heard a number of voices whispering in your dream, however, do you fear that others are gossiping, or spreading rumors, about you behind your back, or else intriguing against you or keeping something a secret from your waking self?

Above: A dream of seeing someone whispering into another person's ear may mean that you feel excluded from their close relationship in the real world. **Above left:** If you overheard a group of real-life colleagues talking together in dreamland, are you worried that they are gossiping about you during office hours, or was your unconscious emphasizing your sense of being excluded from their circle? **Left:** In the language of dreams, cheering often articulates ecstatic or triumphant feelings.

Below right: If your waking hours are miserable, but you exploded with hilarity in your dream, your dreaming self may have been urging your conscious self to discover the therapeutic power of laughter. **Bottom right:** A dream that incorporated the enchanting sound of exquisite violin music may have been highlighting the romantic feelings that have been aroused in you in waking life. **Below:** Dreams in which we are singing can reflect our emotional state, which may be elated or gloomy.

Was your dream filled with the sound of laughter? If so, and you are finding your waking world fun, your unconscious was probably just reflecting your current pleasure in life. But, if your real life is fraught with anxiety, your unconscious may instead have been telling you to lighten up. Some dreams that feature laughter can be more complex, however, and in such instances mulling over your dreaming response to hearing laughter can speak volumes about your waking world. A dream of feeling elated because you'd told a joke that made your friends roar with delighted laughter may, for instance, have suggested that you long to be popular and to bask in the approval of your social circle,

perhaps because you are feeling overlooked and unappreciated in real life. (A dream of being applauded with ecstatic claps and cheers sends a similar, wish-fulfillment message.) Or if, in a

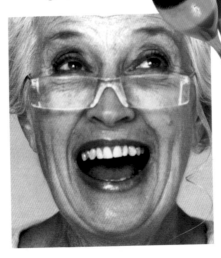

humiliating dream scene, you saw yourself burst into tears before turning and fleeing from the mockery of your coworkers, the sound of their derisive laughter still resounding in your ears, have you been made to feel a "laughing stock" during office hours, maybe because your colleagues constantly ridicule your ideas? Alternatively, perhaps you dreamed that you were trying to make your teenage son accept the importance of going to bed before midnight, and were infuriated when he simply laughed in your face. Could this dream have mirrored your son's real-life contempt for the values that you hold dear, or did your unconscious disguise the archetypal trickster as your son in an attempt to make you rethink the worth of those values?

Music and Instruments

Music is one of the most powerful expressive vehicles available to us. Through music, composers are able to convey nuances of feeling that are impossible to put into words, thereby sometimes moving their audiences to shed tears of joy or sadness. As in the real world, so in the realm of the sleep—so that if you heard, or made, music in dreamland, a beautiful melody may have expressed your sense of inner harmony, or of being "in tune" with those who surround you in the waking world. Alternatively, a cacophony of harsh, clashing notes may have reflected your emotional discord or feeling of being "out of tune" with your friends and family. Did you dream of sitting in a

flower-filled garden, listening with pleasure to the birdsong trilling forth from the trees around you? A dream like this may have mirrored the sweetness of your waking hours, perhaps because you've recently had some wonderful news. But if you dreamed of wincing as you heard your child sawing at a violin, and of trying hard to resist the temptation to cover your ears to shut out the appalling caterwauling that she was producing, was your unconscious mirroring the intolerable effect that her constant whining is having on you in the real world? 🕊️ ⚽

The type of music that permeated your dream may have had significance, too, especially if it was not the sort of sound that is your preferred listening during your waking hours. If you are a lapsed Christian who dreamed of being deafened by thunderous organ music, for example, could your dream have been highlighting your unconscious fear of having offended your religion's spiritual authorities by disregarding their teachings? If you

are a lover of classical music in the real world, but you woke up with the words of a pop song running maddeningly through your head, it may, of course, have been that you heard the song on the radio yesterday and you can't dislodge it from your mind. Alternatively, could your unconscious have retrieved the song from the depths of your memory bank because it expresses so perfectly how you are feeling at present? And if you would never think of attending a classical concert in the waking world, but your dream portrayed you doing just that, and—what's more, enjoying it—could your unconscious have been telling you not to dismiss other people's "classical" (or establishment values) or old-fashioned tastes, because if you heard them out, they might just "strike a chord" with you, or evoke your sympathy and understanding?

Above: A dream of listening raptly to an orchestra playing an evocative piece of classical music, when you actually only listen to popular music in waking life, may have been advising you to open your ears to older people's viewpoints. **Left:** If you dreamed of walking over to a jukebox and selecting a particular number, you may unconsciously have chosen that song to express how you are currently feeling. **Below:** Dream drums can exhort us to pay attention to something or someone or to keep in step, or conform with, others during our waking hours.

Remember that if you were passively listening to music in your dream, the reference was likely to have been to your emotional reaction to your waking circumstances. If you were actively making music in a dream scene, however, bear in mind the possibility that the allusion was to the emotions with which you are currently suffused, and that your unconscious may have depicted you playing a particular instrument in an attempt either to encourage or discourage self-expression. So did you dream of banging a drum? If you did, ask yourself whether you are seeking others' undivided attention in the real world, whether you long to make people march to the sound of your "drum" (or to follow your lead), whether you are trying to "drum up" support for a waking venture, or whether the reference was to the sense of responsibility that you are desperately trying to "drum into" your son's head. But if you were clashing a pair of cymbals in your dream, was your dream depicting the furious "clash" of contrary opinions that

you and your wife have recently had in the real world? Or if you raised a trumpet to your lips and blasted out a triumphant fanfare, have you been "blowing your own trumpet," or bragging loudly about your success, during your waking hours?

Another consideration to take into account when trying to decode a dream that featured a musical instrument is the sexual symbolism associated with some. A flute can be interpreted as a phallic symbol, for instance, while the curvaceous bodies of violins, cellos, and guitars resemble the curves of the female torso. So if you dreamed of any of these instruments, was your dream an erotic one?

Finally, if you do, or did, actually play the self-same instrument with which you produced breathtaking music in your dream, don't discount the possibility that your unconscious was simply encouraging you to nurture your real-life talent.

Left: Could a dream of coaxing melodious music from a piano's black-and-white keys have been advising you to work on harmonizing your "black-and-white," or extreme, opinions? **Below left:** According to Freudian theory, guitars can symbolize a woman's body, so if you are a man whose dream transformed you into a strutting rock star and a master of the electric guitar, could the reference have been to your "electric," or exciting, love life? **Bottom:** Dreams of singing the blues can convey real-life "blues," or feelings of depression.

MESSAGES AND COMMUNICATION

Although every dream is, in a sense, a message, or an internal memo from your unconscious to your conscious mind, some dream communications are far from explicit. Even when we consciously accept that an animal or a building, for example, was probably conveying a message when it appeared in a dream, we may still find it difficult to think outside the box, or to tune into the unconscious mind's wave length and thus grasp what it was trying to tell us. So when the unconscious summons modes of communication, such as letters, e-mails, and telephones, into dreamland, it may be because it intuitively understands that this is the best chance of forcing our rational selves to recognize that these symbols are transmitting a message. Whether we actually get that message, however, is another matter.

When trying to interpret the meaning of any dream in which you received or sent a message, first consider whether the communication made a clear reference, one that you instantly understood, to something about your waking life. Then (and particularly if the message was confusing) think about what you associate with the dream messenger—if there was one—and how that may pertain to your waking situation. For example, if you regard people who deliver mail as impartial go-betweens who carry welcome news, bills, or junk mail, you may be able to link a dream mailman with a person who is acting as an intermediary in your waking life. The next issue to mull over is the form that the communication took, and what it signifies to your waking self. A written missive, such as a letter, memo, fax, or e-mail, may imply formally putting something "in writing" or "on the record," for instance, while a telephone conversation may suggest a more informal approach to making contact. Or was the communication coded or even telepathic, implying either a lack of understanding or an extremely close connection? Considering all of these aspects of your dream, along with its context and any other symbols that were incorporated into it, may help to clarify the message from your unconscious. Finally, note that while all of the chapters in this book deal with messages in one form or another, you may find consulting the chapters on the media and sounds especially enlightening.

Written Messages

Did you dream of leaning over a blank sheet of paper, pen in hand, as you mused about what to write? An unsullied piece of paper offers an opportunity to make a fresh start, and the pen a means with which to express your thoughts. So, do you remember whether you were about to write a letter or the opening line of a novel in this dream scene? If your dreaming intention was to compose a letter to your sister, from whom you regret having become estranged in the real world, your unconscious may have been prompting you to initiate contact with her in reality, in the hope of renewing your relationship. But if you enjoy writing, and you secretly believe that you have a bestseller in you, was your dream encouraging you to put pen to paper, open the floodgates to your imagination, and get your masterwork written? The message implicit in writing in dreamland may, therefore, have been that you feel an urge to communicate with someone in particular, or else with a wider audience. A dream of watching a cursor blinking away at the top of a blank word-processing document may have held a similar message—although, if you associate computers with your working life, maybe the reference was to communicating with a business associate or else to starting a long overdue task.

Left: A dream pen may be encouraging you to express your ideas or to convey your thoughts in the real world. **Above:** In the lexicon of dreams, a blank piece of paper represents a fresh start in waking life.

Perhaps you dreamed that you opened the door to the mailman, except that rather than being the person who regularly delivers your mail in the waking world, the dream mailman was your father, who handed you an envelope that bore your brother's handwriting. Maybe you then dreamed of opening the envelope, reading the letter, and learning that your brother wanted to borrow money from you. If so, mailman aside, was your dream a relatively faithful reflection of your waking situation, in that you are financially secure, but your brother is chronically short of money? If this is the case, your dream may have reflected your conscious or unconscious anticipation of receiving a similar request from your sibling in real life, with your father playing the role of a medi-

ator between the two of you. Alternatively, and particularly if your brother has no financial worries, could your dream have suggested that you unconsciously recognize, perhaps because your

Above: If you furrowed your brow in concentration as you tapped away at a computer's keyboard in an industrious dream scene, was your unconscious advising you to follow your dreaming self's example in catching up with your correspondence in the waking world? **Below left:** A dream of receiving a postcard or letter from someone you know suggests that you are unconsciously aware of that person's desire to communicate with you in real life.

father keeps dropping subtle hints in the real world, that your brother is in need of your help (but not necessarily your money) and that you should turn your waking attention to this issue? Considering the appearance of any handwriting that featured in your dream can also be revealing—and even more so if you are aware of the principles of graphology (the study of handwriting, principally as a means of analyzing character). Continuing

this dream theme, there may have been nothing out of the ordinary about your brother's script, but if it appeared shaky, could your unconscious have been stressing his real-life vulnerability? And if any words were capitalized or underlined, did they "underline," or emphasize, the crux of your dream's message? (While his or her handwriting can divulge your current perception of the writer of a dream letter, a typewritten or word-processed communication implies that you and the sender have an impersonal connection.)

As well as protecting their contents from damage when in transit and, through their addresses, ensuring that letters arrive at their correct destinations, envelopes are symbols of mystery in waking life—we can hazard an informed guess at what they contain, but we can never be sure until we have opened them. As in the real world, so in the world of dreams,

if you dreamed of holding an envelope in your hand, you probably wondered whether it bore good or bad news. If you are expecting your exam results, or the verdict on your performance in a recent job interview, to be mailed to you in real life, your unconscious was probably mirroring your waking anxiety about failing. Did you then open the envelope with shaking hands in your dream? If so, did its contents

send you into a fever of ecstasy or the depths of despair? Whether the news was the best or the worst in dreamland, don't read too much into it, because your unconscious was probably just fulfilling your waking wishes, echoing your deepest fears, or otherwise preparing you for how you may feel when that all-important envelope arrives in reality. Your dream may come true during your waking hours, but equally, it may not. Perhaps you were thrilled when you recognized an old friend's handwriting on a dream envelope. A dream like this may simply have been an unconscious expression of your desire to hear from that person again. But if you're in

Left: If your dreaming self received a love letter from someone whom your waking self considers just a friend, could you have unconsciously sensed that person's romantic interest in you? **Center:** When they arrive in dreamland, both packages and envelopes can bring unexpected news. **Below left:** Just as Queen Elizabeth I of England's signature suggests an intricate personality, so dream handwriting can convey crucial information about your perception of the writer's state of mind. **Below:** If you dreamed of sorting through your mail in search of a specific envelope, are you anticipating receiving important news in the real world?

overdraft in waking life and, with a shudder of dread, you dreamed of picking up an envelope bearing the logo of your bank, and then immediately stuffing it unopened into a drawer, it is likely that the message from your unconscious was a warning. In this case, out of sight is not out of mind—or out of your unconscious mind, at least—so that, while you may be consciously choosing to ignore your increasingly dire financial situation, your unconscious may continue to plague you with a dream of this nature until you confront, and deal with, the problem in the waking world.

Left: A dream of mailing a postcard to your family describing your wonderful vacation may have been encouraging you do the same in the real world. Alternatively, could your unconscious have been pointing out that it's been a long time since you communicated with the folks back home? **Below left:** If you dreamed of being deluged with e-mails, all of which required an immediate response, do you feel overwhelmed by the demands and deadlines that others are imposing on you during your waking hours? **Bottom:** Dream address books may list those to whom you are close in waking life, but also those from whom you have grown apart. **Opposite:** Whether you used a telephone or a pair of cans as a means of dream communication, was your unconscious telling you to make your feelings clear to a certain person, or simply to initiate contact with him or her in the real world?

Unlike letters, electronic communications such as e-mails and faxes reach their intended recipients without needing to be enclosed in an envelope, and, what's more, they can be sent and received virtually instantaneously. Although the message inherent in a dream of composing, sending, or receiving a dream e-mail or fax is likely to parallel that implied by writing, mailing, or receiving a letter in dreamland, urgency may be the crucial difference. But then, immediacy is not always a desirable quality. For instance, perhaps you dreamed that you sat at your computer in your office, fuming with rage at your boss's latest demand, started typing out your feelings of fury, immediately felt a sense of release, but then realized to your horror that you'd been using your e-mail program, had automatically clicked the "send" button, and had somehow transmitted your message to everyone in your address book. If you had a dream like this, you must still have been cringing when you awoke—but what was the message inherent in your dream? Your unconscious was probably warning you to keep your temper on a tight leash and to consciously restrain your tendency to act impulsively, because such behavior may have disastrous and widesprea repercussions in

waking life. A dream of e-mailing a memo to your coworkers announcing that you are intending to quit smoking and asking them to be supportive, may, however, have expressed your desire to "go on record," or to publicly state your intention (an action that would, of course, make it more difficult for your weak-willed self to sabotage your own efforts to kick your habit).

Maybe the approach of winter in the real world triggered a dream in which you were going through your address book (be it electronic or traditional) and deleting or crossing through the names of people to whom you'd decided not to send holiday greetings this year, while placing a check next to the lucky ones. In this case, you were probably unconsciously sorting the people in your waking life into those with whom you wish to break contact and those who remain important to you. So, did your dream send your conscious self any surprising messages about someone in your extended family or social circle, for instance?

Verbal Communication

Like e-mails and faxes, telephones—and particularly, the cell phones that we carry around with us—enable us to communicate instantly with others, and them with us. The message of a dream in which you picked up the telephone to call your sister, or answered a call from her, is almost certainly that she is on your mind (whether you are intending to phone her in the waking world or are, instead, avoiding speaking with her). But when you got through to your sister, did she drone on and on about herself without pausing for breath, so that you found it impossible to get a word in edgewise and eventually slammed down the receiver? Becoming simultaneously bored and infuriated by a one-sided dream conversation like this may have confirmed your waking sense of grievance with a sister who actually does appear so uninterested in you that you long to sever contact with her. Alternatively, was your unconscious trying to tell you to become more assertive and to interrupt your sister, or to sharpen up your communication skills and tell her how hurtful you find her attitude toward you, thereby possibly gaining her respect and setting your waking relationship on a more equal footing? Another possible interpretation to consider is that, by arousing such extreme annoyance in your dreaming self, your unconscious was drawing your conscious attention to your own tendency to monopolize your waking conversations.

Depending on the context, dreaming of making a phone call may sometimes remind us of the urgent need to set up a meeting or appointment before it's too late. For example, perhaps you made a mental note to apply for a job that was advertised in the newspaper in the waking world. Although the closing date for applications has slipped your conscious mind, your unconscious has remembered that the deadline is tomorrow and so has depicted your dream self calling the number given in the advertisement, in order to prompt your waking self to do the same in the morning.

But maybe you dialed your mother's number in a dream and then became increasingly frustrated as the phone rang and rang, but she didn't pick up. If so, have you been anxiously trying to communicate an important truth about yourself to her during your waking hours, and do you feel that she is unreceptive to your viewpoint? Or did your dream reflect your real-life worries about your mother's health and safety, perhaps because she is growing old, lives on her own in a faraway town, and you fear that if she had a mishap in the home there'd be no one there to assist her? Indeed, in an emergency situation, such as when we are confronted by an uncontrollable fire or a major traffic accident, the first thing that we typically do is call 911. And if you dreamed of making a panic-stricken call to the emergency services, could your unconscious have been highlighting your fear that a disaster (but not necessarily an actual fire or automobile crash) has devastated your waking world, or may soon do so, and that you are frantic for help?

Coded and Telepathic Messages

In the real world, codes are used either to keep sensitive information secret from outsiders or enemies or, in the case of systems like shorthand or Morse code, to convey information as briefly and speedily as possible. Any dream in which you sent or received a coded communication that you could decipher may, therefore, have been advocating the need for secrecy, brevity, or speed when communicating with a certain someone in waking life. But if you were unable to understand a note that a friend passed you because it was written in code, or else in a language with which you are not familiar, the implication was probably that you are currently finding the workings of her mind incomprehensible.

Left: If you called the emergency services in a panic-stricken dream scene, could your unconscious have been warning that a catastrophe is about to befall you, or was it urging you to seek professional help because you can no longer cope with an aspect of your waking life? Above and below: If you received a dream message in binary code (above) or Morse code (below) from someone you know in waking life, did you understand the communication? If so, your unconscious may have been underlining the need for secretiveness or speed in your dealings with that person in the real world. But if the meaning of the message was a mystery, are you finding it equally difficult to understand what the sender is trying to tell you?

This page: When two people have an exceptionally close connection in the waking world (below), one may unwittingly transmit his or her real-life distress to the other in a dream. A dream of asking a psychic (left) to channel the spirit of a departed loved one probably reflected your desire to be in touch with him or her again, however.

There is one form of communication between two people that requires no messenger, pen and ink, or telephone line, and that is telepathy (or thought transference). Although this phenomenon is both scientifically inexplicable and unproven, psychologists generally acknowledge its existence and there is also much anecdotal evidence to support it (and perhaps you have even experienced it yourself). If you dreamed of your much-loved brother desperately clutching at his chest, accompanied by a strong sense that he was in acute distress, and then, after you awoke, you received news that he'd actually had a heart attack during the night, your brother may well have communicated his pain to you telepathically. Indeed, it is believed that telepathy typically occurs spontaneously between two people whose relationship is characterized by its emotional closeness at a time when one is undergoing a crisis, although the "sender" may be unaware of transmitting his or her extreme emotional reaction to the "receiver." Another (albeit very rare and controversial) example of dream-time telepathy is prearranged mutual, or shared, dreaming, which may occur after two people have consciously agreed to meet up with each other in dreamland, or else to dream of the same scenario. If, however, you are mourning the death of your husband in the real world and you dreamed of conversing happily with him in a dream, either directly or through a medium, you are likely to have experienced a wish-fulfillment or comforting, compensatory dream, or else one that reflected your enduring sense of emotional connection with your husband. ☠

MAGIC

If magic was the theme of your dream, it is important to bear in mind your waking attitude toward witches, wizards, and their mysterious arts, when trying to work out what the dream could have meant. Do you associate those who inhabit the realm of magic with malevolence, danger, and dark supernatural powers, as exemplified by the popular perception of Halloween as a night when humans are vulnerable to the forces of evil? Are you influenced by Wicca, and do you therefore believe that the form of witchcraft that its followers practice harnesses the energies of nature for benevolent purposes? Or has your opinion been swayed by your reading or viewing of the *Harry Potter* or *Lord of the Rings* books or movies, so that you believe that magic can be used with either good or evil intent, but that righteousness will eventually prevail? Whatever your viewpoint, remember that it may color your interpretation of your dream.

Whether or not you consciously believe in magic, fairy tales probably introduced you to its concepts in childhood—that is, at an age when you unthinkingly accepted the existence of the supernatural. Although your conscious, adult mind may now dismiss the idea that there is a parallel world of the occult, vestiges of your childhood beliefs may endure in your unconscious mind, surfacing in dreams as a metaphor for emotions or phenomena to which you have been exposed, but that you cannot explain or understand. You may, for instance, have intuitively recognized that someone secretly wishes you harm in the real world, in which case your unconscious may have portrayed him or her as a malicious witch or warlock. Or maybe you cannot shake off the feeling that you have been cursed because your waking life is plagued by bad luck, and your dream depicted the person whom you have unconsciously identified as the cause of your woes sticking pins into a doll that looked just like you. But if your dreaming mind cast someone known to you as a sorcerer or sorceress, do not assume that he or she really does have supernatural abilities. Indeed, the only conclusion that you can draw from your dream is that you regard him or her as having the wish, or power, to help or harm you.

Witches and Magicians

Perhaps you dreamed that you, your boyfriend's mother, and your own mother were together when you made a remark that set off a blazing row, and then you suddenly noticed that your mother was clothed in the long, white robes of

Right: A wicked witch in your dream may represent a threatening older woman in the waking world whom you have unconsciously identified with the archetypal terrible mother.
Opposite: A dream in which a woman you know was transformed into a witch—complete with pointed hat, black cat, and broomstick—may simply have meant that she arouses feelings of uneasiness or mistrust in you.

T.H.TOWNSEND 1911

Left: Not all sorceresses are malevolent. If a woman of your acquaintance delivered oracles in a trancelike state in dreamland your unconscious may have been observing that you consider her a source of uncanny wisdom. **Below:** A coven of witches can denote a powerful cabal of real-life women in the symbolism of dreams.

a priestess, your boyfriend's mother had exchanged her everyday outfit for the black garb of a witch, and that sparks of phosphorus were flying from their fingertips. A dream like this may have portrayed your sense of being the helpless bystander in a real-life battle of wills between your protective mother and your aggressive potential mother-in-law—women who both have the power to influence your life, although one has your best interests at heart and the other, you feel, would like nothing better than to destroy you. Your unconscious portrayal of your boyfriend's mother as a wicked witch may be clichéd, but nevertheless has dual archetypal significance, as does the depiction of your mother as both a formidable protector and a force for good. Would it surprise you to know that these characterizations correspond to a fusion of the mother/priestess and the terrible-mother/witch archetypes? Do you regard your mother as a source of wisdom, someone who intuitively understands you and who unfailingly offers you, and everyone she knows, illuminating, selfless advice? Have you unconsciously identified your boyfriend's mother as a poisonous, fault-finding manipulator, a woman who has an uncanny ability to play on your weaknesses, with devastating consequences for your self-confidence? Indeed, if any woman of your acquaintance—be it your grandmother, stepmother, aunt, cousin, sister, boss, coworker, or friend—was transformed into a sorceress in dreamland, ask yourself whether your dream was drawing a parallel between her character and treatment of you in the waking world and the qualities and actions attributed to the benevolent archetypal priestess or the malevolent archetypal witch.

In times past, a justified fear of discovery and persecution caused witches to convene only rarely, in the dead of night, and at an isolated location, in covens that were traditionally said to number thirteen (which Christianity brands a treacherous number). If you dreamed of stumbling into an eerie dream scene in which you were confronted by a coven of witches, did you recognize the sisterhood's members? If you did, it may be that you suspect them of being in secret solidarity in the real world, intensifying their individual powers by working together to promote a collective aim, either benign or malign (which is why it's important to note whether they were practicing white or black magic in your dream).

Maybe you had a dream in which your real-life boss—a charismatic man who has recently joined your company—gathered the members of your team together and told you that he wanted you to burn a rival business down to the ground because this would earn him a promotion, a demand that you thought so preposterous that you burst out laughing. And perhaps your dream then turned into a scene reminiscent of a horror movie when you realized that your coworkers were nodding like robots and that your boss had morphed into a demonic figure whose

glowing red eyes were boring accusingly into you. By immersing you in a nightmare scenario like this, your dreaming mind was almost certainly expressing your unconscious impression of your new boss as a man with evil ambitions, who abuses his power over others by brainwashing his staff into carrying out his dastardly plans. Furthermore, it is likely that you have unconsciously identified him with the archetypal figure of the black magician, a self-obsessed megalomaniac with devilish skills of sorcery, who will stop at nothing to further his aims to control and dominate others, accumulate unimaginable wealth, and be revered for his grandiose status. In the archetypal language of dreams, the black magician's counterpart is the high priest, who—although equally able to mind-read, mesmerize, control, and channel apparently supernatural forces—rarely demonstrates his extraordinary abilities and prefers to live apart from others, and seemingly on a higher, more spiritual, plane. You may sometimes encounter the high priest in dreamland when

Above: If your dream portrayed your real-life boss in an eerie, evil light, could your unconscious have cast him as the archetypal black magician to emphasize your waking suspicion that his ulterior motives are sinister? **Top right and right:** Whether he materialized in your dream as a witch doctor or shaman (top right), or else as a magician or archetypal high-priest figure (right), if an older man whom you respect in the real world gave your dreaming self some sage advice, your waking self would probably be wise to heed it.

your dreaming self is in urgent need of guidance, or even of rescuing from the clutches of a dangerous person. The high priest of your dreams may appear in the guise of an older man of your waking acquaintance whose integrity, impartiality, and insightful wisdom commands your awe and respect, and who may be someone—maybe your grandfather or perhaps your school principal—whom you regard as a mentor. 🎭

However, there is yet another type of magician whom you may have encountered in a dream scene, namely, a conjuror, someone who performs tricks that owe little, if anything, to magic, but everything to sleight of hand. Perhaps you dreamed of being in the audience at a talent show, when, to your amazement, a charming someone whom you've recently befriended in the real world walked into the spotlight, doffed his tall hat, and then extracted a white rabbit from it, to rapturous applause. You may still be smiling at the memory, but will the most likely interpretation of your dream wipe the smile from your face? Consider this: could your unconscious have been warning that your new friend is a confidence trickster, someone who creates the illusion of being trustworthy and accomplished, but is actually a deceiver, a manipulator, and perhaps even an out-and-out swindler? 🎭 ⚽

Magical Rituals and Paraphernalia

Maybe you are a single man who dreamed of watching the young woman whom you have started to date in the real world leaning over a cauldron and muttering strange-sounding words while adding handfuls of herbs to the bubbling brew. If you had a dream like this, could your unconscious have been implying that you find this woman "bewitching," or enchanting, and that you are so helplessly attracted to her that it is as though she has cast a spell on you? (And you may be interested to know that cauldrons symbolize the womb in the lexicon of dreams.) If you are a woman in an established relationship, maybe you had a weird dream that was jam-packed with magical references. Perhaps you were standing in a magic circle facing your husband or boyfriend who was wearing a wizard's flowing black robes and intoning an incantation, when he raised his wand, pointed it at you, and discharged a bolt of fiery energy, which promptly bounced off the invisible force field that enclosed you and rebounded on him, causing his wand to flop down limply and causing the once commanding wizard to throw a childish tantrum. Could your dream have portrayed your "disenchantment" with the man whom you once admired, and your sense that your own growing inner strength is causing the strategies that he once used to control you to backfire on him, so that you

now see him as the peevish person that he really is? If this interpretation rings true, the knowledge that wands can be considered as both phallic symbols and conductors of powerful energies, while magic circles denote protection, may add a deeper layer of meaning to your dream. (Indeed, when trying to make sense of any dream that featured the paraphernalia of magic, bear in mind that pentagrams and hexagrams are symbols of defense against outside forces, that a broomstick's significance may also lie in its phallic shape, as well as its ability to enable its rider to take flight, and that such creatures as black cats, toads, owls, bats, and all manner of imps and monsters can be cast as witches' familiars, or aiders and abettors.) But if, in a thrilling dream scene, you discovered that you had magical powers and instantly used them to make your pesky little brother disappear in a puff of smoke, do you wish that you could "magic" him, and his constant pestering, out of your waking hours, at least for a while?

If, in the real world, nothing is going right for you, your latest setback may have triggered a dream that apparently explained why you seem to be jinxed. For instance, you may have dreamed of looking through a keyhole and

freezing with shock at the sight of your closest friend, whose skin had now assumed an acid-green hue, holding a miniature version of you in her hands as she intoned the chilling words of a hex dooming you to failure and misery. Although a dream like this implies that your so-called "friend" is really invoking supernatural powers with which to curse you, this explanation is highly improbable. It is far more likely that you have unconsciously detected your friend's jealousy of you (which may be why your dreaming mind depicted her with green skin), and that her barely concealed *schadenfreude*, or pleasure in your misfortune, has made you suspect that she is somehow responsible for your troubles. Spells need not always be cast for malevolent purposes in dreamland, however. For example, if you are expecting a child in reality, perhaps you dreamed that your newborn baby was being baptized, and that an

ethereal godmother held it in her arms and promised that it would always enjoy health, happiness, and good fortune. Could your dream have expressed your hope that your child will lead a "charmed" existence, whether or not you recognized the good fairy as an influential woman who actually has the power to smooth his or her path through life in the real world?

Opposite, far left: By depicting someone in your social circle as a slick conjuror, your unconscious may have been warning your waking self not to be taken in by his showman's trickery. Opposite, above right and bottom right, and this page, left: In the parallel universe of dreams, a cauldron (opposite, above right) can denote both the womb and mystical powers of regeneration, while a magic circle (opposite, bottom right) provides protection from evil forces, and a hex sign (left) wards off witchery. Above: If your dreaming self stumbled across a toad, traditionally branded a familiar of witches, could your unconscious have been reflecting your sense that its mistress, whom you may not yet have identified, has placed a curse on you? Above left: In dreams, good fairies can represent female benefactors in the waking world.

MONSTERS AND MYTHICAL CREATURES

Monsters may only be figments of the imagination, but if you have ever had to comfort a child who has woken screaming from a nightmare, you will know that they have the power to scare young dreamers out of their wits. Freakish beings seem to haunt children's dreams more often than they do adults', and there is a straightforward explanation for this. Not only are children regularly exposed to fairy tales, stories, and illustrations that include monsters (and usually malevolent ones) among their cast of characters, but children's immature, inexperienced perspective makes it difficult for them to separate fact from fantasy, so that they often believe that such fiends really exist. (And if you have noticed that a certain bedtime story that you read or tell your child regularly gives him or her nightmares, perhaps it would be best to drop it from your repertoire.) Although horror movies sometimes similarly prompt us to have nightmares of supernatural bogeymen as adults, identifying the trigger is, perhaps, less important than asking why your unconscious should have subjected you to a monstrous experience in dreamland, especially if it terrified you.

Most dream analysts agree that the unconscious dreams up monsters—after all, imaginary beings—to represent deep-rooted fears, ugly emotions, "monstrous" urges (either your own or another person's), painful, unresolved experiences, phobias, or problematic situations, whose cause we may not consciously recognize or understand, but that are nevertheless so threatening that we suppress them during our waking hours. A child's unconscious fear of being separated from his parents may, for instance, be expressed by a nightmare in which he is torn from his mother's arms by a hideous creature, which may, or may not, have the face of someone whom he considers hostile. Similarly, a woman's dread of being overpowered by a predatory man's lust may take the form of an attack by a dream werewolf. Such nightmares may be recurring, and if they are it is crucial to try to work out what the monster symbolizes. Identification is the first step toward understanding our fears, which makes them less frightening and consequently easier to confront, come to terms with, and maybe ultimately to banish. Remember, too, that not all of the emotions or instincts represented by dream monsters are unnatural or evil, and that their manifestation in dreamland simply means that they are struggling for self-expression, even if you are unable to give them a "face," or identify them, in waking life.

Mythical Creatures

The human mind has characterized inexplicable or irrational energies or fears as monsters for millennia, and it may be that your unconscious borrowed the grotesque creature that appeared to your dreaming self from the annals of mythology or folklore because it so closely embodied your unconscious feelings. If so, and you are familiar with the myth of which it is a part, details of the tale may help you to work out what the monster represents to you personally, as well as how to overcome it or else integrate it into your waking life. Above all, remember that its appearance, powers, and intentions will have provided important clues, both to the nature of your "monster" and how best either to neutralize it or to channel its energies.

Certain mythical creatures were believed to inhabit the sky, earth, underworld, or sea—realms that all have symbolic significance in

Opposite: The unicorn can symbolize purity of spirit or enlightenment when it canters into dreamland, but because it is a horned creature that is said to have an affinity for virgins, its appearance in dreams may otherwise have erotic significance. **Left:** If you dreamed of riding a winged horse, such as the celebrated Pegasus of Greek mythology, your unconscious may have been advising you to harness your instinctive drives in your quest for conscious illumination. **Below:** In the language of dreams, dragons can variously denote good fortune, evil, or a hostile individual (typically an older woman) in the waking world.

subtext to a dream that featured a unicorn, for not only was it said that it could only be tamed by a virgin, but its horn can be interpreted as being a phallic symbol.

The dragon, a winged serpent, is a mythical beast to whom complex symbolism is attributed, and if it flew into your dream, your interpretation may be colored by your cultural heritage. In Chinese belief, the dragon is one of the creatures of the Chinese zodiac, the year of the dragon being said

their own right in both mythology and dreams. The sky, or air, is said to be the province of freedom and spiritual or intellectual transcendence, for example, so if you had a dream in which you mounted a winged horse like the Pegasus of Greek myth in order to escape a ravening pursuer, your unconscious may have been urging you to soar above the mundane problems that are besetting your waking life by harnessing the unconscious instincts that drive you (represented by the horse's body) to the intellectual or spiritual potential inherent in your conscious mind (symbolized by its wings). Another celebrated mythical horse is the unicorn, whose snow-white coat emphasizes its traditional association with purity and goodness. Be aware, however, that there may have been a sexual

to bestow energy, enthusiasm, and charisma. This fabulous being is also revered as a bringer of good fortune, happiness, and children, as well as a protector against malignant forces. By contrast, Christianity brands the dragon the embodiment of Satan, an evil creature that must be slain by a saintly hero, while Jungian theory deems it a form taken by the terrible-mother archetype (a personification that we echo when we refer to ferociously fierce women as "dragons"), who must similarly be rendered powerless before true freedom can be attained. So if you share the Chinese view of dragons, your unconscious may have been trying to inspire optimism by summoning it into your dream, the suggestion possibly being that your waking life will soon be enriched and your ambition given wings. If you are influenced by the Western view of dragons, however, the implication may have been that a hostile authority figure—perhaps a vicious older woman, or maybe someone whom you unconsciously regard as an evil-doer—is threatening to overwhelm you and that it is time to muster the courage to fight back in the waking world. Dragons were also said to be the guardians of treasure, so could your unconscious have been telling you that you will have to overcome

a formidable obstacle in your quest for self-enrichment, be it material, spiritual, or emotional? On consideration—and especially if your dreaming self did not react to it fearfully—you may otherwise equate your dream dragon with the snake's positive associations, on the one hand as a symbol of latent vital energy or, on the other, as an agent of spiritual transcendence, a message that may have been underlined if the dragon breathed fire (a symbol of purification and transformation) over you in dreamland. If so, did your dream highlight your unconscious desire to undergo a dynamic process of inner renewal? A dream of watching a phoenix immolate itself on its fiery death pyre and then arise renewed from the ashes, as recounted in Arabian myth, may likewise have expressed your yearning to put the past behind you and to be "reborn" as a new person. 🜍 🜏 🜎 🜊 🜛

The bodies of mythological hybrid beings were thought to be composed of two or more animal species, and whether or not you identified the man with the bull's head who lumbered through your dream as being the Minotaur of Greek myth, for instance, working out what each of its physical characteristics means to you in isolation, and then in combination, may help you to identify

the nature of your "beast." Did you actually dream of the man-eating, subterranean-dwelling Minotaur? If so, you may decide that the coupling of a human body with a bull's head points toward a man in your life who is governed by his unconscious instincts, especially his mindless lust, who is easily enraged, and who therefore presents a dangerous threat to you (especially if you are a woman, although the knowledge that the Minotaur consumed human flesh may add an extra edge to a man's dream, too). Otherwise, could your unconscious have summoned the Minotaur into your dream to draw your waking attention to your own "bullheadedness," that

Above: Because the Minotaur of Greek mythology fed on young men and women, its appearance in dreams can reflect an all-consuming fear that is lurking in the depths of the unconscious. It may alternatively represent a man who is driven by uncontrollable sexual urges in the real world. **Left:** If you dreamed of witnessing the fiery death and rebirth of a phoenix, do you wish that you could make a fresh start in life?

is, your stubborn, or even stupid, approach to a waking situation? Other creatures from the realm of Greek mythology that combined human characteristics with those of animals include centaurs, who had the body and legs of a horse, from which rose the torso, arms, and head of a man. If you dreamed of a centaur, you may conclude that it represented the fusion of the horse's strength, stamina, and drive with a human's intellect and skills, and, as a result, perhaps the seamless union of the unconscious and conscious minds, a target that your dream may have been advising you to aim for, particularly if the dream centaur was holding a bow and arrow. The centaur, or archer, is also the symbol of Sagittarius, so could your dream alternatively have been referring to someone of your acquaintance who was born under this zodiacal sign?

Did you dream of the Sphinx, or else of a multiheaded monster such as the serpentlike Hydra? If so, are you currently feeling defeated by a crucial conundrum that is blocking your progress during your waking hours? The reason for this question is that you may unconsciously have remembered that the Sphinx of Greek myth (a creature with a woman's head and a lion's body) killed any-

one who failed to answer her riddle correctly, and may therefore have conjured the Sphinx into your dream to represent the enigma that is baffling you. (And if you remember Oedipus's solution, could it hold the key to solving your problem?) The Hydra was notable for its nine heads, each of which, when hacked off, was instantly replaced by two new ones,

so if you dreamed of battling against this nightmarish creature, could your dream have portrayed your sense of struggling to take one step forward, only to find that you have instead moved two steps backward, or did it symbolize the drastic multiplication of the problems that are blighting your waking hours?

Mermaids and sirens may have particular significance when they figure in men's dreams because both mythology and folklore warn that these hybrids of the female form bring heartbreak at best, and annihilation, at worst, to members of the masculine sex. As the French legend of Mélusine tells, the beautiful, flowing-haired, fish-tailed mermaid is,

Below left: In the lexicon of dreams, the fearsome, multiheaded Hydra can signify the persistent problems, or ever-escalating difficulties, against which you may feel that you are battling in vain in waking life. **Below:** If you are a man who was utterly enchanted when a mermaid materialized in your dream, could she have represented your anima, or else a bewitching real-life woman to whom you are hopelessly attracted, but despair of ever making yours?

however, regarded as being more benign than her siren sisters because she is capable of feeling real affection for men, even if she cannot ultimately be sustained by love alone when out of her element, water. If you are a male dreamer, were you captivated by the appearance of an elusive mermaid in an oceanic dream scene, and did you swim after her, only to hear the tantalizing echo of her laughter as she yet again slipped from your hands? If so, did she

Above: She may not display a pair of fishes' tails when the siren enters a man's dream, but her powerful, "come-hither" sexual allure, coupled with her air of mystery, signals that a dangerous temptress may be circling the dreamer and preparing to pounce in the waking world. **Right:** The dreaming mind may send a giant lumbering into dreamland to represent either a real-life difficulty of "gigantic" proportions or a formidable person.

have the face of a woman to whom you are deeply attracted in real life, someone who seems willing enough to flirt with you, but deftly eludes your attempts to form a real connection with her? Or was the mermaid your anima, the feminine part of your personality, who, by leading you ever farther into the sea, was encouraging you to explore the depths of your own emotions? According to Greek myth, sirens were sea nymphs whose enticing songs lured sailors toward the rocks on which they sat, thereby deliberately causing ships to be wrecked and their victims to drown. So potent is this myth that the word "siren" is today used to describe both a heartless, treacherous, yet irresistibly seduc-

tive, woman and a wailing warning signal that alerts all within earshot to danger. So if you are a man who dreamed of being tempted to follow a beckoning vamp, or of being melted by the sweet-talking flattery of a stunning woman who has caught your waking attention, could your dream have been warning that a honeytrap has been set for you, and that unless you recognize your perilous situation and overcome your instinctive urge to succumb to enticement, you will pass the point of no return and expose yourself to blackmail, emotional devastation, or even physical harm? Was your dream siren the archetypal huntress, a sexually aggressive woman who has set your internal alarm bells ringing?

Fairy-tale Monsters

Fairy tales and their modern-day spin-offs, horror films, are populated by all types of monsters, many of whom are said to be governed by bestial urges that compel them to prey on vulnerable humans. Are you a woman, and did you dream of being hunted down by a werewolf, a creature that is human by day, but that is transformed into a predatory wolf by night? If so, your unconscious may have been warning that an apparently harmless man in your social circle is actually a dangerous sexual predator who may pounce on you at any moment. While werewolves are believed to have a particular preference for young women, vampires, their fanged fellow fiends of the night, are opportunistic killers who take

their sustenance—human blood— wherever they find it. Not only is no man, woman, or child safe from their bloodlust, but vampires themselves can assume any form. Whatever your sex or age, if you had a nightmare in which someone you know came too close for comfort before baring a set of needle-sharp fangs and directing them at your neck, could your dream have been reflecting your sense that that person is intent on "bleeding you dry"? Your dream is unlikely to have been alerting you to a literal vampire in your life, but instead to a parasitical someone

who is feeding off your energy, sapping your vitality (blood being a symbol of the life force), or else sponging off your finances and therefore thriving at your expense.

Maybe you dreamed of running as fast as your legs could carry you from a roaring ogre, a hideous, gigantic, manlike being who seemed intent on devouring you. If you had a nightmare like this, is your male boss, or else an older man who has authority over you, currently making your waking life a misery with his deliberate cruelty? If so, it may just be that you unconsciously equate that person with the archetypal ogre, the father figure turned bad, which is why your unconscious characterized him as this menacing fairy-tale tyrant in dreamland. Not all giants are ogres, however, and maybe you dreamed of being rescued from the ogre's clutches by a gentle giant, perhaps another

influential figure in your life who you look up to because of his or her moral strength and regard as a potential protector. Either way, in the lexicon of dreams, any towering monster can represent something that poses a gigantic problem to your waking self or else someone whose power over you makes you feel small and helpless.

Elves, fairies, gnomes, imps, and goblins are all miniature beings from the realm of fantasy who possess magical powers, which they may use either benevolently, to help humans, or mischievously, to wreak havoc. So if a fairy godmother appeared to you while you were sleeping, and, with a wave of her wand and a sprinkling of fairy dust, transformed your dream world into one of beauty, happiness, and riches, did you have a wish-fulfillment dream? Or if you dreamed that a band of tittering imps were causing mayhem in your home, do you unconsciously suspect that, in the absence of any plausible real-life explanation, supernatural forces beyond your control are inflicting mishap after mishap on your domestic life at present?

Top left: If you came across an appealing-looking fairy in dreamland, did your dreaming mind spirit it into your sleep in response to your unconscious longing to receive a little magical help in coping with your hectic waking life? **Left:** A dream werewolf can alert a female dreamer to the danger posed by a potential male seducer in the real world.

Right: In the symbolism of dreams, fairies can hint at your own latent powers of transformation, so if your eyes were captivated by a vision of a host of ethereal fairies dancing gracefully in a moonlit dream scene, was your unconscious encouraging you to discover your inner "magical" potential? **Below:** If a crowd of hyperactive imps caused chaos in your dream, are your waking hours currently so blighted with irritating problems that you feel as though you have been targeted by a gang of these mischievous pests?

Ghosts, Succubi, and Incubi

Did a shadowy figure materialize in your dream, an apparition which, although without substance, somehow reminded you of someone? If so, and you felt no fear because the ghostly presence resembled a loved one who has died, it is likely that that person has either been in your thoughts or that something that happened, or someone whom you encountered, the previous day triggered a vague memory of that individual, such as a character quirk or piece of advice that he or she once gave you. Alternatively, and particularly if you shrank from the phantom in your dream, could the specter have represented a source of guilt, maybe someone whom you once wronged, a ghost from your past that is still haunting your conscience, despite your conscious efforts to push it to the back of your waking mind?

Perhaps you woke up sweating with fear, having had a nightmare experience while you were sleeping, not exactly a dream, but more a sense that an implacable force was crushing your chest, causing you to struggle to breathe and preventing you from moving. If so, and you are female, you may have suffered an incubus attack, or, if you are male, a succubus attack. In more puritanical times, when sexual pleasure was frowned upon, women who had erotic

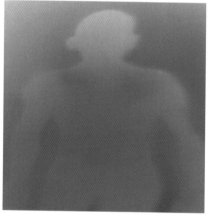

Top left: Dream leprechauns may either highlight mischief-making in the real world or hint that a hoard of treasure is within the dreamer's reach. (The allusion may not have been to material wealth, but to emotional or spiritual riches.) **Above and right:** One reason why a ghostly figure may have haunted your dream is that the day's events evoked an intangible memory of a departed loved one. Another is that your unconscious was pointing out an uncomfortable truth that your conscious mind has worked hard to suppress, just as the ghost of his father appeared to Shakespeare's Hamlet to tell him something that he may unconsciously already have known, namely that his father was murdered by Hamlet's new stepfather.

dreams were said to have been visited by male demons (incubi), while sexually voracious female fiends (succubi) were thought to target slumbering men, these malevolent spirits pinning down and paralyzing their sleeping victims in order to have their wicked way with them. Although the words "incubus" and "succubus" are still used today to describe the sensation of a weight pressing down on your chest, accompanied by a feeling of dread and an inability to move while you are sleeping, they are no longer applied to sexual dreams, which are, of course, perfectly normal. And while the cause of these distressing dreams remains unclear, dream experts have ruled demons out of the picture, instead believing that they may be prompted by temporary breathing difficulties combined with sleep paralysis, a condition that we all experience while sleeping, but rarely become aware of.

SOCIAL, FAMILY, AND WORK GATHERINGS

When your unconscious brings you together with other people for a common purpose in the parallel universe of dreams—be it to celebrate a special occasion or catch up with family, to network or have fun, to discuss a work issue, or simply to be among like-minded spirits—it often does so to pass comment on the nature of your interaction with those with whom you are in contact in waking life.

Did you dream of getting together with your family, attending a party or enjoying a meal in a restaurant in the company of friends, participating in a work-related meeting or conference, being a member of a gang or club, or even of being a face in the crowd? If so, the individuals who surrounded you, your dreaming reaction to their presence, and the events that occurred during the course of your dream all send significant messages about your personal likes and dislikes, your self-perceived status within your family, social, or professional circle, your self-confidence, your insecurities, and your individuality.

Although such dreams generally reflect your conscious feelings about the people whom you regularly encounter in waking life, your unconscious may sometimes surprise you, either by portraying them behaving uncharacteristically or by evoking an unexpectedly powerful emotional response to a certain individual or social situation in your dreaming self. If you are puzzled about what your dream could have meant, this chapter may give you the key to its interpretation, but you may also find consulting the chapters on family and people helpful.

Family Occasions

Anticipation, nostalgia, or wish fulfillment could all explain why you experienced a dream in which you were happily celebrating a set-piece festive occasion in the bosom of your family, just as you do whenever there is a birthday, anniversary, religious festival, or national holiday to be commemorated in the real world. Are you looking forward to meeting up with your family in the near future, for example? Did your dream recall an outstandingly happy event in your past that you wish that you could relive, or do you long for the joy, comfort, and security that comes from being surrounded by affectionate loved ones?

Yet occasions like these can sometimes be highly stressful—especially if our participation is prompted by a sense of duty rather than by the enjoyment that we derive from being in the company of our kin—and the mood can often sour, at best, and become explosive, at worst, under the twin pressures of having to pretend to get along with people whom we have resented since childhood and, what's more, appear as though we are relishing the experience. Perhaps you woke boiling with rage from a dream in which your family had gathered at your home to celebrate your birthday, but, instead of lavishing gifts and attention on you, your parents criticized your housekeeping, your brother bragged about how much more successful he was than you, and your sister made snide comments about your appearance. Whether or not your dream accurately reflected your parents' and siblings' tendency to put you down rather than bolster your self-esteem in waking life, your unconscious may have been highlighting the unresolved grudges that you have probably held against your family since your earliest years. Do you chafe under the authority that you perceive your parents as wielding over you, even if they rarely try to exert it now

your life a misery at school by taunting and belittling you, was your dream reflecting your unconscious desire to arouse their respect or envy, thereby settling old scores? If your waking life seems to have become a social wasteland—perhaps because you are working such long hours that your friends have fallen by the wayside—and were thrilled to receive an invitation to a party from a group of real-life pals in your dream, however, was your dream telling you that it is high time that you revitalized your social life to give your currently one-dimensional existence an enjoyable extra dimension? And could your unconscious have been warning that, although your neglected friends are still hoping to tempt you from your desk in waking life, they won't persist in their efforts if you decline their invitations for much longer?

that you are an adult, for example? Do you feel that your relationship with your brother and sister is marred by sibling rivalry? Alternatively—and particularly if the members of your family are loving, supportive, and nonjudgmental in the real world—by putting disparaging words into their mouths, was your dreaming mind expressing your unconscious feelings of inadequacy because, having measured yourself against the examples set by your parents, brother, and sister, you feel that you are failing to meet the high standards that you expect of yourself?

Social Events

Did you dream of addressing invitations to a party that your dreaming self was planning? If so, can you remember whose presence you were requesting and the reason for the celebration? It may have been, for instance, that you were inviting old school friends, with whom you have lost touch since your mutual schooldays, to a class reunion in dreamland. If so, have those people and days been on your waking mind recently, and could your unconscious have been encouraging you to make contact with them in the real world for a nostalgic get-together? But if you were inviting your former classmates to celebrate a spectacular success that your dreaming self had achieved, and they actually made

Opposite, above, and below: Chilled champagne, piñatas, and brightly colored decorations are all symbols of celebration that may emphasize an elated waking mood when they appear in dreamland. **Top:** If your real-life relationship with your family members is argumentative, but they showered you with gift's on your dreaming self's birthday, you may have had a wish-fulfillment dream.

Whatever it is that they are celebrating, parties give people the opportunity to mingle, be it to get to know one another socially, to network, or simply to have fun in a relaxed atmosphere. So if you were giving a party in your dream, could it therefore have reflected your desire to widen your social circle, to forge new business contacts, or to let your hair down among friends? Acting as a host or hostess in dreamland also implies that you have numerous acquaintances and social confidence, which may be a quality that you already possess, but if the very thought of throwing a party makes your waking self shudder with horror, was your dream temporarily fulfilling your conscious longing to be more popular, self-assured, and socially adept, or else hinting that you have the potential to connect easily with others if only you could overcome your timidity? By depicting us at dream parties, the unconscious signals how well we tend to deal with groups of people, so that a dream

of circulating self-confidently among your fellow guests will have sent a far more positive message than one in which you headed straight for a shadowy corner, tried your utmost to look

nonchalant in your solitary state, and froze with nervousness when anyone showed signs of approaching you. (And if you really are a social wallflower because you suffer from crippling shyness, could your dream have been suggesting that you are missing out on an enriching element of life, and would counseling help you to overcome your apprehension in social situations?)

If you found yourself enjoying an animated conversation with someone whom you actually know at a dream party, your unconscious was probably either confirming the pleasure that you derive from his or her company in the real world or else indicating that you would like to get to know that person better. But if you dreamed that someone of your acquaintance in waking life gate-crashed a party that you were attending, made a beeline for you, and then pestered and insulted you, did this dream scene express your exasperated sense of being targeted, stalked, or persecuted by him or her during your waking hours? Or did it highlight your perception of that person as being a "party pooper," or someone who persistently seems to spoil your fun?

If you dreamed of reveling in a festive meal at a restaurant, the nature of the occasion, your fellow diners, and your dreaming mood will similarly all have relevance to your waking relationships. By setting your dream celebration in a restaurant, your unconscious may additionally have been implying that you and the people with whom you were sharing the dream meal either sustain each other emotionally or that you wish that this were the case. And if wine was served with the dream meal, the reference may have been to relaxing together, while champagne may have denoted a real-life cause for mutual celebration. But if you cook for your family day in and day out in the real world, maybe the message was simply that you long to be relieved of your daily duties once in a while and to be treated to a gourmet meal occasionally. If you had difficulty selecting a dish from a dream menu, however, your unconscious may have been transmitting an entirely different message, particularly if you have reached a transitional point in your life or are puzzling over a complex prob-

lem in the real world. In this case, could your dream have been reflecting your waking indecision in the face of a number of equally tempting opportunities or options?

Meetings and Conferences

If you have a job in the real world, it is likely that meetings are a regular feature of your waking hours. Real-life meetings have many purposes—to report on progress, to enable opinions to be exchanged, or to try to reach a collective decision on future company strategy, for instance—but when the unconscious mind convenes a meeting in dreamland, it is usually to comment on your perception of, and relationship with, those who work alongside you. Any such dream will generally confirm your conscious opinion of your boss, for example, who may have dominated the dream meeting in as authoritative a manner as he or she does during office hours. But what could it have meant if you were shocked in your dream when a colleague, who normally agrees with you and whose intellect you don't rate very highly,

turned to face you and then delivered a vehement, withering speech that demolished your own contribution to the dream meeting? Could your unconscious have been warning your conscious self that it has detected that that person is harboring feelings of hostility toward you and, what's more, that you should regard him or her as a competent, ruthless, and formidable rival in your struggle to further your career?

Opposite, top: A dream in which you sparkled with confidence as you flirted vivaciously with someone whom you know in real life may have highlighted your unconscious attraction to that person. **Opposite, center:** If you dreamed of having a fantastic time at a New Year's party, but are too shy to attend such an event in the real world, could your unconscious have been encouraging you to resolve to overcome your inhibitions? **Opposite, bottom:** When wine imbues your dreaming self with the feel-good factor, your unconscious may be advocating unwinding among friends in waking life. **Above:** If you find your boss forbidding during your working hours, your dream may have confirmed your conscious reaction to her. **Left:** Dream menus can point toward a multitude of tempting choices in the real world.

If you are actually due to address a conference in real life and dreamed of standing on a podium, stuttering and stammering your way through your presentation before eventually drying up completely and leaving the stage feeling humiliated, your unconscious was probably merely mirroring your anxiety about your performance in your forthcoming ordeal. Remember that real-life conferences are forums that facilitate the sharing and exchange of professional knowledge, so that if you dreamed of participating in such an event, was your unconscious advising you to open your mind to your colleagues' viewpoints during your working hours? But if you dreamed of addressing an audience on your professional area of expertise and it wasn't until your voice was drowned out by boos and jeers that you realized that you were at the wrong venue and were delivering your lecture to a convention of science-fiction fans, could the message have been that you are either targeting the wrong listeners (perhaps your teenage children) when enthusing about your pet obsession in waking life, or that your single-mindedness is irritating those who do not share your intellectual passion (maybe your friends and family)? If, on the other hand, your words were heard with rapt interest in dreamland, your unconscious may have been encouraging you to share your opinions with others, the implication being that they are worth hearing and will therefore command attention in the real world, too. 🃟 🔔 ⚽

Gangs, Clubs, and Crowds

Wanting to be accepted and liked, and included in a close-knit circle of sympathetic soul mates, is a fundamental human urge. This desire to fit in with others is why many people look back with fondness on their childhood if they were a member of a gang, or else recall their school years with pain because they were the target of a group of bullies whose collective purpose seemed to be making those outside the charmed circle feel like misfits and freaks. Similar feelings of being buoyed up and empowered by the support of like-minded individuals—perhaps a club of which you are a member—or otherwise of feeling vulnerable and excluded by a group of people whose presence is inescapable in the waking world, often surface in dreams as a literal reflection of waking reality. If

you dreamed of being one of the "in crowd" and, secure in the knowledge that your friends were egging you on, of taunting a helpless old woman, but then of being overcome by remorse, for instance, was your unconscious urging you to detach yourself from a callous group mentality, to think for yourself, and to listen to the voice of your conscience? But if you dreamed of being the victim of a vicious attack by a band of children who had the faces of your coworkers in the waking world, was your unconscious mirroring your sense of being persecuted by a clique at work that seems to have ganged up on you? Alternatively, if you dreamed of being in seventh heaven when, quite by chance, you encountered a group of strangers who shared your waking enthusiasm for family history, could your unconscious have been encouraging you to join a genealogical society in the real world? Or if, during your waking hours, you are trying to ignore the undeniable fact that you have gained too much weight, and you dreamed of standing on a pair of weighing scales in a public venue and of hearing the cheers of the people around you ringing in your ears when it was announced that you had lost ten pounds, was your unconscious telling you that you would receive vital emotional support—and maybe also a svelte figure—if you joined a weight-watchers' club?

Did you dream that you were part of a huge, excited crowd that had gathered in a sporting arena to await the arrival of your favorite sports team or rock star? If so, did you feel a sense of euphoric solidarity with those who surrounded you? A dream of feeling at one with the crowd may have been emphasizing the security that you derive from being among people who are on the same wave length as you in waking life. If, however, your dreaming self then realized in a sudden moment of clarity that those around you were cheering for an appallingly inept team or a painfully tuneless singer, your unconscious may have been urging you to break free of the accepted mindset—be it the collective opinions of your

family, friends, coworkers, or society at large—and to remain true to your personal beliefs, even if your nonconformist stance makes you unpopular in real life. Finally, if you dreamed of being in the middle of a crowd of people who were jostling you, prodding you, and hemming you in, could your unconscious have summoned up this oppressive dream scene to represent the numerous problems that are "crowding in" on you during your waking hours?

Opposite, top: If you are nervous about the prospect of giving a presentation in waking life, your unconscious may have been trying to boost your confidence by portraying you performing impressively in a similar dream situation. **Opposite, bottom:** Dream cliques can reflect your conscious sense of either feeling like a social misfit or reveling in your popularity in the real world. **Above left:** If your dreaming self was transformed into a cheerleader, your unconscious may have been highlighting the euphoria that your waking self derives from feeling as one with those around you. **Below:** In the symbolism of the unconscious, crowds can signify a dreamer's oppressive waking circumstances.

? PUZZLES AND MYSTERIES ?

Although it may not always seem like it when your head is in conflict with your heart, your conscious and unconscious minds are united in their overriding priority, which is what's ultimately best for you. So if you consciously feel defeated by a quandary that you are facing in the waking world, your unconscious may step in to help by sending you a problem-solving dream. The trouble is, because your conscious and unconscious minds don't always speak the same language, you may either not recognize the clues that your unconscious gave you, or else have such difficulty deciphering your dream that you end up feeling even more mystified. When trying to interpret the meaning of a dream that you are sure was concerned with your real-life dilemma, it's therefore important to try to suspend the usual rational thought processes of your conscious mind and instead to adopt the intuitive mindset of the unconscious. If you dreamed of a lightning flash, or of a light bulb suddenly turning itself on, for example, rather than focusing on the phenomenon itself, ask yourself what effect it had. And if "illumination" came to mind, then consider whether the bolt of lightning or light bulb illuminated something in your dream that may hold the key to solving your waking problem. Otherwise, could your unconscious have used this symbol as a metaphor for the flash of illumination that will soon enlighten you (if it hadn't already done so when you awoke)?

Our waking selves are sometimes unaware of being confused, particularly when we are preoccupied with dealing with the pressing minutiae of our day-to-day lives. It may be that you have lost your sense of purpose in the real world, for instance, but are so busy coping with your daily duties that you have not consciously realized this. It is unlikely, however, that your fundamental confusion has escaped your unconscious mind, which is, after all, the realm of emotion and intuition. A dream may have depicted you trying to navigate your way out of a maze in an attempt to make you consciously aware of your lack of direction in the waking world. (And it may even have shown you a way of getting back on the right track in your dream, although whether you consciously understood the allusion is, again, another matter.)

Whether you are trying to solve a real-life conundrum or to make sense of a puzzling dream, this chapter may help you to see the light.

Knots and Closed Containers

Did you dream of tying a knot in a handkerchief? If so, and you are

aware of the old practice of doing just that to remind yourself not to forget something, your dream could have been prompting you to remember to carry out an important task when you awoke. Alternatively, if you are mulling over the pros and cons of marriage in real life and are familiar with the expression "tying the knot," was your unconscious advising you that "getting hitched," or married,

would be the right decision? But if you became ever more frustrated when attempting to straighten out a tangled electrical cable in your dream, only to find that your efforts had created yet more knots, was your unconscious observing that you are "tying yourself in knots," or that you alone are responsible for the increasingly stressful muddle that is blighting your waking hours?

Maybe you dreamed that a mysterious parcel bound with string arrived in the mail and that you couldn't cut the twine because you'd mislaid your scissors and were instead forced to fiddle with the knots that secured it. If you had a dream like this, did you manage to loosen the knots, remove the string, and open the package, or was your lasting memory of your dream an image of yourself breaking a fingernail and storming off in a huff? In this dream, the knots may have represented the "knotty," or extremely complicated, problems that are preventing you from gaining access to hidden, or secret, knowledge (symbolized by the package). Depending on what transpired in the dream, your unconscious may therefore have been hinting that you will either solve these problems or that they will defeat you (perhaps because you are being too impatient). If you are consciously seeking the answer to a baffling question during your waking hours and dreamed of opening the dream package, what did you find inside, and can you equate it with your conundrum? Maybe you are about to leave school and are pondering which career path to follow—perhaps you are torn between accountancy and archeology—but have received such conflicting advice from your parents and teachers that you are now thoroughly confused. If so, and your dream package contained a calculator, could the message from your unconscious have been that accountancy is the career for you?

If your waking life appears untroubled by quandaries or hindrances, however, and you were unable to open the mystery parcel

in dreamland, it may be that your unconscious was trying to highlight an aspect of your personality that you are consciously denying, in which case the appearance of the dream package may have provided clues about its nature. If it was gift-wrapped, for instance, could the reference have been to a "gift," or talent, that you have repressed in waking life, perhaps because you consider it irrelevant to your career? If you think that this may be the case, could the implication have been that you should try your utmost to access it because incorporating it into your waking world would prove surprisingly life-enhancing? A dream treasure chest may have posed a related question: are potential riches—perhaps life-enriching emotions—lying within you, just waiting for you to retrieve, reveal, and revel in?

Locks and Keys

Keys are often used as symbols of freedom in waking life: they are commonly depicted on coming-of-age cards, for instance, while on passing their driving tests, a lucky few are presented with keys to automobiles that will give them the freedom to drive wherever they please. Keys are symbols of home-ownership, too, as well as of home security (and few real-life situations are more stressful than when we lose or forget our keys and find ourselves locked out of our homes), yet we also give our house keys to people whom we trust. Jailers furthermore carry

Opposite, left: If you tied a knot around your finger in dreamland, was your unconscious trying to tell you not to forget to carry out an important task the next day? **Opposite, right:** An exasperating dream of trying to separate a pair of tangled cables may have paralleled your unsuccessful efforts to unravel a "knotty" problem in the real world. **Top left:** If your dreaming self despaired of ever untangling a mass of entwined fishing nets, could your unconscious have conjured up this dream image to represent a complex emotional entanglement from which you are struggling to extricate yourself in waking life? **Above left:** Boxes and chests can represent the dreamer in the symbolic language of the unconscious.

will have to look elsewhere before finally "unlocking," or releasing, the insight that will help you to make sense of your conundrum? Finally, according to Freudian theory, keys are phallic symbols, while locks can signify the vagina, so if you dreamed of a key being inserted into a lock, could this dream image have had erotic significance?

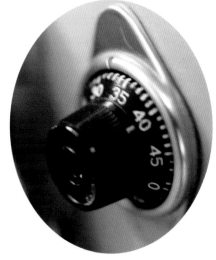

bunches of keys, so that they can additionally be symbols of confinement. As in the real world, so in the dream world, and if a key featured in your dream, your unconscious may have been either highlighting any of these real-life scenarios (or their symbolic associations) or reflecting your waking wishes or fears, depending on your current circumstances.

There is another possible interpretation to consider if your dreaming vision homed in on a key, however. Could it have represented the "key" to, or explana-

tion for, a puzzle that is pre-occupying your conscious mind at present? If you think that this could be so, did the dream key fit, and open, a dream lock (which may have represented the crucial obstacle that is barring your access to the knowledge that lies beyond it)? Was the dream lock set in a cupboard or box (both of which can denote the self, and their contents hidden inner qualities, be they latent or repressed) or a door (a symbol of transition and opportunities)? What was revealed when the key opened the lock in dreamland, and can you relate your discovery to your waking problem or emotional quandary? But if the key was not a match for the lock in your dream, could the suggestion have been that you

Mazes and Labyrinths

Did you dream of wandering through a maze of corridors in dreamland? If so, were you searching for something, trying to find your way out, or hopelessly lost, not knowing whether you were com-

Above, right, and far right: Dream keys (above and right) may sometimes enable your dreaming self to unlock a conundrum—which may be symbolized by a padlock (far right)—that your conscious mind has failed to solve. **Above, far right:** If you dreamed of chancing upon the correct combination of numbers with which to open a safe, could those numbers somehow help you to crack a problem in the waking world?

ing or going or what you were aiming for? The reason for this question is that mazes and labyrinths can symbolize a tortuous quest for knowledge or freedom on the one hand, or merely mirror the general confusion that is fogging your sense of purpose in waking life on the other. If your dreaming self was trying to pinpoint the location of an item that you were certain was awaiting you around every corner, for example, it may be that your dream portrayed you hunting for the answer to a problem that is perplexing your waking mind, or perhaps for something that you have lost in the real world. Dream

labyrinths can, however, represent the unconscious mind, especially when they are depicted as being a network of underground tunnels. So, if you were creeping ever deeper into the bowels of the earth in your dream, the implication may have been that you are trying to locate a deeply buried emotion, memory, or intuition, whose presence you have sensed, but that has not yet surfaced in your conscious mind. Did you find the object of your quest in your dream, and did you then awake feeling somehow enlightened or fulfilled? Alternatively, did you encounter a ferocious monster, which chased

you away before you could discover the precious item for which you were searching? If so, could the monster have represented a dreadful memory or fear that you will have to confront and overcome before you can gain access to the treasure that lies within you?

Below: The unconscious may depict you trapped in a dream maze when your conscious self can see no way out of a muddled waking situation. A dream in which you enlisted the aid of a ladder to find your way out of the maze may have been advocating taking a rational overview of the real-life problem.

Secrets, Riddles, and Crosswords

Are you keeping a troubling or guilty secret in real life, and did you dream of sharing it with your best friend and immediately feeling as though an immense burden had been lifted from your shoulders? If so, your unconscious may have been encouraging you to do the same during your waking hours, probably because your secret is weighing so heavily on your mind that you are unable to think of anything else. Or did you dream of betraying your sister's confidence by telling her boyfriend that she had misgivings

If you were trying to locate an exit from the dream maze, the reference may alternatively have been to an emotional entanglement or a complex situation in which you are inextricably involved that is inhibiting your freedom of action during your waking hours. Did you succeed in finding a way out in your dream? If so, the suggestion may have been that you will eventually manage to break free in waking life, too. But if you dreamed of becoming exasperated to the point of tears because whichever path you took, you always ended up in the same place, could your unconscious have been reflecting your sense of "going around in circles," or of never getting any further, or of making a breakthrough, one that would take you in a fruitful new direction in the real world? Remember that tunnels can denote transition, while entrances signify opportunities, so could your unconscious have been implying that you are in such a confusing, in-between stage of life that you have become overwhelmed by bewildering emotions, and that your inability to think rationally is furthermore preventing you from making the right choices?

Above left: If you are feeling so overwhelmed by conflicting emotions during your waking hours, your unconscious may mirror your emotional confusion by setting your dream in a labyrinthine scenario, complete with signs pointing you in contradictory directions. **Below:** A dream of opening the lid of an enigmatic dream crate may have hinted at a startling real-life revelation.

about him, in doing so repeating the exact words that she used when pouring out her feelings to you after swearing you to secrecy in the real world? If her boyfriend consequently broke up with her in dreamland and left your sister sobbing with grief, could your unconscious have been warning you to keep this important secret to yourself because there would be terrible repercussions if you revealed all?

Did you wake up with a riddle posed by a dream character running through your mind, and are you currently feeling confounded by a "poser," or apparently insoluble question, during your waking hours? If so, it may just be that you have unconsciously found the solution, which your dream was communicating to your conscious self. If the meaning of both the dream and real-life riddles continue to elude you, however, it is possible that you are taking an

overly intellectual approach to trying to solve them and that you will be more successful if you bring your intuition into play. If you are able to tap into the problem-solving powers of your unconscious mind, the answer may appear blindingly obvious in retrospect. Consider, for example, the fabled riddle of the Sphinx of Greek mythology: "What goes on four feet, on two feet, and three,

Bottom left: If you were unable to locate the final piece of a jigsaw puzzle in an infuriating dream scene, could your unconscious have been drawing a parallel with your search for a piece of elusive information that would enable you to make sense of a waking enigma? **Below left:** A dream in which you played the role of a detective may have been advising you to focus on getting to the bottom of a real-life mystery. **Below:** When the unconscious depicts us puzzling over crosswords, it may be trying to give our conscious minds a clue that will help us to solve a puzzle in the real world, and maybe that clue is to think intuitively.

but the more feet it goes on, the weaker it will be?" Oedipus triumphed over the Sphinx by answering "man," who typically crawls on all fours as a baby, walks on two feet when mature, and supports his feet with a cane in old age, images that the dreaming mind may faithfully re-create, but may fail to communicate to its conscious counterpart when using words. So try to think laterally, rather than rationally, when mulling over the meaning of your dream riddle. Similarly, if you were flummoxed by a dream crossword clue, also consider the possibility that your powers of intuition, rather than your knowledge of vocabulary, hold the key to its solution, so that if you are able to channel your instincts, you may suddenly gain a conscious insight into a waking conundrum.

SPORTS, GAMES, AND ENTERTAINMENT

If your favorite pastime in the real world is participating in a sport, playing chess or cards, taking the stage as an amateur actor or musician, dancing, or any other form of entertainment, and you dreamed of doing exactly that in dreamland, your unconscious may have been sending you one of three primary messages. It may firstly merely have been reflecting your conscious preoccupation with your hobby, perhaps also highlighting your anxieties about your performance, demonstrating how you could become more accomplished, or even fulfilling your hopes for stardom. Secondly, it may have been encouraging you to indulge in the activity that gives you pleasure, particularly if you've been so busy dealing with the demands on your time and attention that you have neglected the pursuit of that pleasure in waking life. Always consider your dream in light of these two interpretations before seeking an alternative explanation.

The third possible meaning is more profound, but may be especially pertinent if your dream depicted you engaged in a leisure occupation that plays no part in your waking hours. It is often said that life is "a game," or that the world's "a stage," and it may just have been that your unconscious was passing comment on your current approach to living your life and your consequent success. If you were playing baseball, for example, the reference may have been to how well you are interacting with the people whom you regard as being "on your side" in real life, or to how effectively you are outwitting your rivals. Similarly, a dream of playing chess may have been concerned with the intellectual competition that you are facing in the real world. And if you were performing on stage in front of an audience in dreamland, your unconscious may have screened this scene to show you how convincingly you are playing the role that you have chosen to project to the waking world. Dreams of circus acts, on the other hand, often graphically portray how you are currently feeling, which may be like a puppet on a string or as though you are on a rollercoaster ride. The parallel between the dream scenario and your waking life should usually be clear, but if you are struggling to make sense of your dream, this chapter may enlighten you.

Sporting Scenarios

Did you dream that you had been transformed into a Super Bowl quarterback, and that you deftly evaded a vicious onslaught from the defensive rush before passing

the ball effortlessly to your wide receiver for a game-winning touchdown just before time expired? If so, wish fulfillment apart, your unconscious may have been reliving a real-life office triumph, in which you martialed your team of coworkers brilliantly and skillfully outmanouvered your counterparts in a rival firm, thereby enabling your company to win a crucial contract. Indeed, most dreams in which you were playing a team game reflect how effectively you are performing within a group situation in waking life, maybe among your

friends or family, but more usually in relation to your colleagues (if you have a job). So if you dreamed of playing baseball, soccer, hockey, or volleyball, for

Opposite: Dreams of playing ball games like football (left) and volleyball (right) tend to reflect how harmoniously we are interacting with those who surround us in our day-to-day lives, as well as how successfully we are dealing with the challenges that confront us in the waking world. **Left:** A dream of hitting a hole in one may have been drawing a parallel with an "ace," or spectacular, achievement that you have recently pulled off in the real world, or hope to. **Below:** If you dreamed that you lost a game of tennis because your racket's strings broke, can you make a connection with a vital, but unreliable, professional tool—such as an outdated or defective computer—that is causing your waking self to lose your competitive edge?

instance, are you interacting in dynamic harmony with your fellows? Are you the linchpin that holds everyone together, or do you envy another person's star quality? Are you letting the side down by being lazy or clumsy, or do you blame someone else for being the weakest link that consistently undermines your team's collective efforts? Do you play fairly, are you a "good sport," and remain cheerful when you lose, or do you cheat or foul others and throw a tantrum when things don't go your way? Do you respect referees' authority, automatically argue with them, or try to hoodwink them? Are you—individually or collectively—fending off the forces that are opposing you, or are you being obstructed or brought down by their superior strength or mental agility? What is the goal for which you are aiming? And is your team consistently triumphant, erratically successful, or an also-ran? The answers to all of these questions may prove illuminating when considered in the context of your career or personal life.

If you dreamed of being an individual competitor in a game of tennis or golf, your unconscious was probably drawing a parallel with your self-sufficiency, or sense of relying upon no one but yourself to forge your way through life. Who was your opponent in dreamland? Was it someone against whom you are battling for supremacy in the waking world (perhaps an arch rival at work), and who was the dream victor? Did you serve an ace or hit a hole in one in your dream? If so, your unconscious may have been commending you on your outstanding performance in the real world. But if you missed shot after shot, or putt after putt, in a frustrating dream scene, was your unconscious warning that your current lack of application or dedication is causing your skills, be they professional or intellectual, to become rusty, and that unless you focus on sharpening them during your waking hours and become more self-disciplined, you may end up being a loser in the game of life? Or did you perform badly in your dream because your racket or club was faulty or antiquated? In this case, your unconscious may have been advising you to update the tools of your trade because they are handicapping your progress in waking life. And if you dreamed of boxing, wrestling, or practicing a martial art, such as kick-boxing, karate, or judo, your dream may have had unambiguously hostile or defensive undertones (was your dream opponent someone you know?), although your unconscious may alternatively have been urging you to control your aggression in a disciplined manner in real life.

A dream of performing on an athletics track may similarly have shone a spotlight on your performance against those with whom you are competing in the real world, when your unconscious may have portrayed you streaking ahead of the rest of the pack or stumbling at the first hurdle and seeing the others leave you far behind. Whether you were running, cycling, skating, or skiing, if you were powering your own sporting progress in dreamland, and particularly if there was no one against whom to measure your success, your unconscious may otherwise have been drawing a parallel with how adeptly you are controlling your

efforts to get ahead, and how smoothly and rapidly you are advancing toward your goal in waking life. If you dreamed of cycling along a bumpy road, for instance, was the suggestion that you have hit a difficult patch in the waking world? Or if you dreamed of lacing up a pair of ice skates or rollerblades, was your unconscious urging you to "put your skates on," or to make a concerted effort to increase your rate of progress? But if you dreamed of skiing down a treacherous trail, losing a ski pole, and then tumbling headlong down the slope, could your unconscious have been warning that you are on the verge of losing control of your real-life situation and that you are heading for disaster?

Did your dream depict you working out in a gym? If so, your unconscious may have been urging you to safeguard your health by incorporating a regular exercise routine into your waking hours. If you don't think that this explanation applies, however, could your dreaming mind have been encouraging you to build up your strength (not necessarily physical, but perhaps intellectual or emotional), or else could it have been making a link with how you are feeling in the real

world? If you were running on a treadmill in the dream gym, for instance, was your unconscious implying that your waking life has become dreary and repetitive and is being marred by your sense of getting nowhere? Or if you were lifting weights in dreamland, could they have represented the heavy burden that you have shouldered in the waking world? And if a dream fitness instructor was yelling at your exhausted, sweat-drenched, dreaming self to perform fifty more reps when you were already on the point of collapse, do you feel that you are being pushed beyond your limit, perhaps by someone who has authority over you, during your waking hours?

Above: If your dream depicted you preparing to set off on a run, could your unconscious have been alluding to your waking sense of needing to get ahead, or on the fast track, in your career? **Above left:** A dream in which you were practicing a martial art may have been advocating adopting a more calculated or self-disciplined approach in your battle to neutralize the threat that a real-life professional rival is posing to your cherished waking ambitions. **Left:** If your unconscious portrayed you as an ice skater who was wobbling precariously across a frozen lake in dreamland, could it have done so in order to highlight your lack of confidence in negotiating your way through a slippery situation in which you have recently found yourself in the waking world?

Games and Gamesmanship

In the parallel universe of dreams, the playing of board and card games usually denotes how well we are rising to a particular challenge in the real world, or, more generally, how successfully we are directing the various pieces, or components of our lives, or are playing the hands that fate has dealt us, by implication often in comparison with a real-life rival or our peers. Because little physical exertion is required, dreams of this nature typically highlight our intellectual performance, our ability to formulate and execute a master plan, along with our quick- or slow-witted reaction to unexpected setbacks. So if you dreamed of playing chess, who was sitting across the chessboard from you? Was he or she someone against whom you have pitted your wits in the real world? Had you masterminded a winning strategy, and was the game going to plan in your dream, or did your opponent throw your scheme into disarray with his or her unexpected tactics? Were you playing an offensive or defensive game in dreamland, and, whichever it was, did it win you victory? Your response to all of these queries may tell you more about your current approach to waking life. Consider, too, whether the color of your pieces was significant, and whether the pieces themselves could have represented certain people in your waking world. If you were controlling the white chess pieces in the dream game, for instance, do you associate yourself with benevolence, and your opponent, whose pieces were black, with malevolence? Could the king have represented your partner, the center of your world, but someone who needs defending at present in waking life? Or does another meaning for the word "pawn," that is, someone who is being manipulated by another, have relevance to your waking situation?

Maybe you had a dream of playing cards with your friends, but that a previously fun game suddenly turned sour when you accused one of the players of cheating. If so, could your unconscious have been trying to tell you that that person is deceiving you in real life, too? A card game can be likened to the game of life, so if you were feeling quietly smug because you held all of the aces in the dream game, was your unconscious reflecting your sense of having a powerful advantage in the real world, of which those around you are as yet unaware because you are "holding your cards close to your chest," or being secretive?

Left: If you dreamed of winning a game of poker by triumphantly flourishing a royal flush, it may be that you are feeling smugly certain that you will soon be in a position to outdo those against whom you are competing in waking life. **Below left:** By literally demonstrating the "domino effect" in dreamland, your unconscious may have been warning that an action that you are contemplating taking in the real world may have widespread repercussions. **Below:** Superstitious dreamers may believe that the ace of spades prophesies disaster and death when it appears in their dreams.

Indeed, there are many colloquial expressions associated with cards that your unconscious may have expressed literally. Did you "play your cards right," or implement your game plan successfully in dreamland, and, if you did, should you be doing the same in waking life? (If you were bluffing convincingly during a dream game of poker, for example, was your dreaming self setting your waking self an example to follow, for instance?) Did you "lay your cards on the table," or reveal your intentions to your fellow players, and, if so, was your unconscious advising you to come clean with those around you in the real world? If your dreaming self had an "ace up your sleeve," are you biding your time before bringing your secret weapon into play in waking life? And if you focused on a particular playing card in your dream, could it have symbolized a person, or

dice have been associated with fate for millennia. So if your unconscious depicted you rolling a die and desperately willing it to show a six (a symbol of victory) in a tense dream scene, did it reflect your sense that your destiny is in the hands of fate, that the direction that your future is about to take is out of your conscious control, or that you are "dicing with death," or taking a dangerous risk in real life? Any dream in which you were gambling may similarly have been warning that you are considering

Top left: In the symbolism of dreams, chess can refer to the game of life, with the white pieces denoting goodness, and the white king representing a real-life male authority figure (albeit someone whose freedom of action is limited) who is currently vulnerable to attack, and who must therefore be protected by those on his side. **Above:** Dice can symbolize the unpredictability of fate when they are thrown in dreams. **Right:** If you bought a ticket to a show in dreamland, was your unconscious urging you do to the same during your waking hours in order to enjoy some much-needed diversion?

risking everything for which you have worked in the waking world on a chance—perhaps by investing in a tempting, but shady, business venture—and that the odds may be stacked against you. Alternatively, and especially if your bet won you a fortune in dreamland, could your unconscious have been encouraging you to set aside your natural caution and take a chance on someone or something—but not necessarily the lottery, the roulette wheel, or a horse race—because your stake (and the reference may have been to an emotional rather than a financial investment) has the potential to reap you rich rewards in the real world?

Acting, Music-making, and Dancing

Although a dream of watching a romantic movie or thought-provoking play may have been encouraging you to seek out love or intellectual stimulation in the real world, it may otherwise have been signaling that all is not what it seems in waking life. Did you dream of settling yourself in a theater seat, of waiting with excited anticipation for the play to start, and then, when the curtains parted to reveal the actors, of being astonished to see that the

quality, that has relevance to you at this point in your life? Hearts can denote love, so could a dream queen of hearts have represented your mother, for example? Associations vary, but the suit of diamonds may have highlighted your aspirations, clubs may have pointed toward your finances, and spades may have warned of obstacles in your path. But if you cut the pack and were confronted by a joker in what seemed a significant dream moment, was your unconscious trying to draw your attention to the archetypal trickster, or to someone whose mischievous behavior is playing havoc with your waking circumstances?

The winning of certain games, notably those played with dice, depends entirely on chance, which is one of the reasons why

Above: If you watched members of your family perform a play in dreamland, could your unconscious have been trying to tell your conscious self that they are secretly engaged in hoodwinking, or deceiving, you in waking life? **Below right:** By depicting you acting on a dream stage, your unconscious may have been demonstrating how successfully you are projecting your chosen persona to your real-life "audience."

cast consisted of your friends and family? If so, remember that the business of theaters (as well as of movie theaters) is illusion, and that by sending you a dream like this your unconscious may have been alerting you to a charade or a drama that those around you are performing in the waking world. So ask yourself, could those around you be colluding in acting out a pretence for your benefit in real life? Maybe your birthday is approaching, for example, and you are feeling annoyed that no one has offered to throw you a party. If this is the case, could your unconscious have been hinting that some feverish party-planning has actually been going on behind the

scenes, and that your friends are simply acting as though they have forgotten your big day in order to surprise you?

But if you dreamed that you were acting on stage, how did the audience react to your performance? We all tend to role-play during our waking hours, or to project a persona that isn't always faithful to our real selves, in order to make ourselves more appealing to our target audience, so maybe your unconscious was commenting on how appreciatively your performance is being received by those who surround you during your waking hours. Remember that the part that you were playing, and the scene in which you were acting, may have had a parallel with a certain crucial waking situation. Were you such a compelling actor in your dream that you had your rapt audience eating out of your

hand, suggesting that you are being equally convincing in real life? Or was your act so wooden or false that you were heckled and booed, when your unconscious may have been telling you that the image that you are projecting appears ludicrously artificial or unconvincing? If you dreamed that you were unwilling to take center stage and that you had to be pushed into the spotlight, could your unconscious have been mirroring your reluctance to "put on an act," and to blithely pretend that you are something that you are not, on the one hand, or your dislike of being the center of attention in waking life, on the other? Did you forget your lines in your dream and need to be prompted? If so, you may currently be suffering from a crisis of confidence in the real world—perhaps because you feel unprepared or under-rehearsed for a role that you are playing or are about to assume— and are unconsciously aware that you must rely on someone else's help if you are to pass yourself off as being competent enough to act the part. Your dream may also have implied that life is not a dress rehearsal, that you only have one chance to make a success of your performance on the world stage, and that it is therefore important to "get your act together," or to organize yourself effectively, in waking life.

Was your dream played out against an orchestral setting? If so, were you conducting the orchestra, or did your dream depict you as one of the musicians? It may be that the dream orchestra represented a community of which you are a part in the waking world, which is why your position in relation to the other musicians in the dream scene may have been significant. If you wield authority over others in real life, a dream of conducting an entire orchestra may have reflected how successfully you are exerting control over your charges, or are "orchestrating," or organizing, your collective efforts, for instance. So did your talent as a conductor enable you all to make sweet music together in the dream concert hall (suggesting that you are an inspiring leader and gifted coordinator), or was the sound that you produced painfully discordant (implying that your management skills are inadequate)? But if your dream cast you as a member of the violin section, could the reference have been to your sense of "playing second fiddle," or of playing a minor role in a communal environment in waking life, perhaps as a junior member of your department at work? Ask yourself, too, whether you were in or out of tune in relation to the rest of the orchestra in your dream, and therefore whether you are blending harmoniously with your friends or colleagues or conflicting with them during your waking hours. A dream of singing in a choir may also have had any of these meanings, but if you were a soloist in dreamland, your unconscious may have been mirroring your feeling of being in the limelight during your waking hours. Depending on the events that unfolded as you gave your recital in the dream, your unconscious may consequently have been reflecting your anxiety about your performance in a forthcoming real-life situation in which you will be the focus of public attention, or else have been boosting your confidence by fulfilling your desire to impress your audience.

If you dreamed that you were dancing in dreamland, were you dancing alone, with a partner, or with others? A dream of dancing on your own may have been expressing waking feelings of joyfulness, although if you had your eye on an attractive someone in the dream scene and were hoping that your sensuous moves would attract his or her admiration so that you'd soon be dancing cheek to cheek, your dream may have had erotic overtones. If your dream portrayed you ballroom dancing, however, who was your partner, and did you dance so fluently together that it

was as though you were one person? In this case, your dream may have been highlighting someone who is actually, or who you long to be, your partner in real life, be it your spouse, business partner, or best friend. So did your dream mirror your sense of being "in step" with that person, or of working in blissful unison during your waking hours? Perhaps you dreamed that you were line-dancing with members of your family in a country-music scene. If so, your unconscious may have been either reflecting your tendency to conform with the common "line," that is, to accept your family's collective opinion, or else your habit of "stepping out of line," or of failing to conform to the behavior that your loved ones expect of you in waking life. So were you dancing "in line" with those around you, or were you "out of step" with them, in your dream?

Entertaining Diversions

Did you wake from a bizarre dream in which you were performing a circus act? If you did, your unconscious may have been drawing a telling parallel with your reaction to your waking circumstances (which may be exceptionally testing at present), also mirroring either your sense of rising successfully to meet life's challenges or your fear of being unable to master your current situation. Remember, too, that the reaction of the dream audience is likely to have been significant, because it may have denoted that your efforts are either being regarded with approval by those in your waking circle or that they are failing to impress. So if your unconscious portrayed you as a juggler in your dream, was it referring to the many commitments that you are having to "juggle," or actively manage, during your waking hours? And if you

think that the dream balls could have represented your waking obligations, did you let any of the balls drop in your dream, or were you able to keep them all in the air? Maybe you were walking a tightrope or performing acrobatics in dreamland. If so, do you feel that you are having to "tread a fine line," or to maintain an acute sense of balance in tricky waking situation, or that your mental agility and skills are being tested to their limits in the real world? But if you were dressed as a clown in a dream circus

Opposite, top: If you dreamed of making melodious music with your friends, it is likely that your relationship with them is similarly harmonious in the real world. **Opposite, bottom:** Could a dream in which you became an elegant and accomplished ballet dancer have mirrored your sense of performing equally impressively during your waking hours? **Above:** A dream in which your unconscious portrayed someone you know as a clown may have been trying to tell you that that person is actually concealing feelings of extreme sadness. **Left:** If you found yourself keeping in perfect step with your real-life partner as you danced the tango together in an erotically charged dream scene, was the allusion to your spine-tingling sexual compatibility?

Right: A stomach-churning fairground ride in dreamland can point toward a sickeningly unstable waking situation. **Below:** In conjuring a ventriloquist's dummy into your dream, could the message from your unconscious have been that someone is putting words into your mouth, or trying to control what you say, in real life?

ring, and were sporting a huge, painted-on smile, do you feel that you are under pressure to present a cheerful front to others during your waking hours, when you are actually feeling terrible? (This explanation may also be pertinent if someone you know was transformed into a clown in your dream, is that person concealing his or her fundamental unhappiness by putting on a brave face? Otherwise, consider whether the dream clown could have been a manifestation of the archetypal trickster, whose jokes and jibes may have been making a penetrating point about how you perceive yourself.) When trying to interpret a dream that featured a clown, also ask yourself whether your unconscious was referring to a "clown" or "joker," that is, to someone who is clumsy, rude, irritating, or idiotic in waking life (and it may even be you). Finally, do not dismiss the possibility that any dream that focused on a chaotic circus scene may have been observing that your waking world resembles a "circus," or has become wildly disorganized.

Your unconscious may similarly have been commenting on your response to waking life if it conjured up a dream in which you took a fairground ride or paused to watch a sideshow. If you dreamed of becoming dizzier and dizzier as you hurtled up and down a rollercoaster's tracks, for instance, are you feeling sickened by the dramatic emotional ups and downs to which you have been subjected in the real world lately, and are you longing to recover your equilibrium by grounding yourself in mundane reality? If you were spinning around on a carousel, did this dream experience mirror your sense of "going around in circles," or of making no progress during

your waking hours, or else of your life currently resembling a "merry-go-round," or a whirl of social activity? But if you dreamed of swaying gently in a carriage at the top of a Ferris wheel, and of trying to spot your friends far below, was your unconscious suggesting that they are only a small part of your waking world, and that you should take an overview of your situation at this stage of your life? Alternatively, maybe you were drawn to a puppet show that was being acted out in a dream fairground. If so, was your unconscious warning that you are under the total control of a dominant personality during your waking hours, or was it suggesting that you are the one who is manipulating other people's actions, or "pulling their strings"?

EROTICA

If you had an explicitly sexual dream, you are likely to have woken either glowing with delight and trying to retain the ecstatic feelings that your dream aroused in you or squirming with disgust and anxious to forget your sordid encounter in dreamland as quickly as possible. Because the sexual urge is so powerful we rarely react neutrally to erotic dreams, either when our sleeping selves are experiencing them or when our waking selves look back on them. Sexual desire is a basic drive that prompts humans, along with other members of the animal kingdom, to set the mechanics of breeding in motion in order to produce offspring, thereby ensuring that our genes survive our deaths by living on in the next generation. Indeed, so convinced was Freud that the libido wields an overwhelming influence over our programming that he tellingly named the group of unconscious instincts—notably hedonism, self-preservation, and procreation—that he identified as governing the life instinct "eros," after the ancient Greek god of erotic love. Our built-in sexual urge is thus a fundamental component of the unconscious mind, the part of the psyche from which dreams emanate, which is why it is hardly surprising that it so often finds an outlet in dreams.

But if sexual desire is such a natural, healthy instinct, why do we sometimes awake from an erotic dream feeling repelled and contaminated? Freud's explanation was that the conscious mind has become conditioned by social conventions to consider sex an uncivilized, bestial, and distasteful act. According to Freud, the conscious mind consequently represses, or censors, certain sexual images and feelings expressed by the unconscious because it deems them unacceptable, much as a movie censor rules that certain "obscene" scenes should be edited out of a film prior to its public release. It is a form of denial that may even prevail while we are sleeping, particularly if we are highly sexually repressed. Freudian doctrine holds that we may unconsciously summon up visual metaphors for the sexual organs (long, rigid objects like guns and towering erections to represent the penis, for example, and holes and receptacles to symbolize the vagina and womb) and the sex act (such as a train entering a tunnel or a key being inserted into a lock), because facing the real thing would make us feel intolerably guilty or "dirty."

Modern analysts acknowledge that it is important to take the Freudian viewpoint into account when interpreting erotic dreams, but alternative theories are considered equally valid, depending on the individual dreamer and his or her dream experience.

Passionate Encounters

There are a number of reasons why you may have dreamed of having sex, or of viewing pornographic images, ranging from the straightforward to the complex, and sometimes a mixture of both.

If you are a teenager, you may be reassured to know that adolescents frequently have erotic dreams, partly because the onset of puberty causes sex hormones to flood the body, and partly because this is a time when sexual curiosity is first awakened. Such dreams therefore usually result from natural physiological stimuli coupled with a normal waking preoccupation with what it would be like to make love.

Left: Although some people look back on their erotic dreams with delight, others consider them so disgusting that they try to banish them from their memories.

Sexual deprivation or frustration is another reason why many people experience erotic dreams. Remember that the sexual drive is a strong one, so that if your sex life has dwindled to nothing in the waking world, it may be compelled to find release in dreamland. Similarly, if you are in an unsatisfying sexual relationship that has left you feeling unfulfilled and unhappy, your unconscious may respond to your yearnings and compensate you with a mind-blowing dream of you with the sexiest partner imaginable. Indeed, your dreams may even give you an enlightening insight into your true sexual compatibility and leanings.

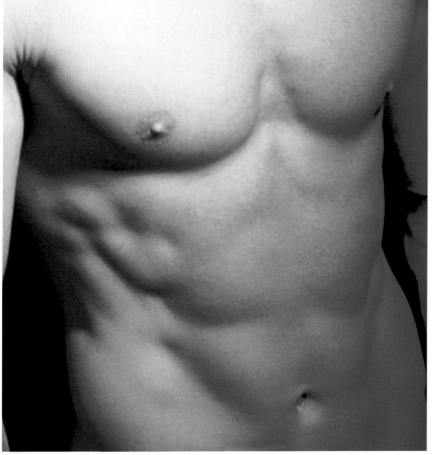

Above: We sometimes experience erotic dreams when boredom has crept into a real-life sexual relationship. **Left:** If you are a woman who suffers from low self-esteem, your unconscious may have been trying to boost your sense of worth by depicting your ideal man making love to you in a steamy dream scene.

If you dreamed of making love to someone to whom you are strongly attracted in the real world, your unconscious was probably fulfilling your waking wishes, especially if it seems improbable that you will actually end up in bed with him or her. It may alternatively be that you are feeling unattractive, unlovable, overlooked, or neglected and that your unconscious was boosting your self-esteem by portraying you as being the object of desire of someone—perhaps a movie or rock star, or maybe the hottest person in your school or work-place—whom countless people lust after in the waking world.

If you don't think that any of the above expla-nations apply, there is a far more abstract Jungian explana-tion to consider when trying to make sense of a dream of mak-ing love to someone whom you felt was your soul mate, whether your dream lover was a person you know or a stranger. Could your unconscious have depicted your union with your anima, or the feminine aspects of your char-acter if you are a man, or your animus, the masculine traits that lie within you if you are a woman—in other words, with your "other half"? Could your dream have symbolized the com-plete integration of your mascu-line or feminine qualities into your personality, a union that may either already have occurred or that your unconscious was urg-ing you to strive for? Whether or not this interpretation strikes a chord with you, remember, too, that sex can be an act of procre-ation, so that your dream may have been referring to the fruit-ful use of your creative powers (although not necessarily to your fertility).

Troubling Sexual Dreams

It's important to accept that the desire to have sex is a healthy human urge, and that your dreams allow you to give rein to this drive, as well as to indulge in all manner of erotic experi-mentation, in an environment in which no actual psycho-logical or physi-cal harm can be inflicted on anyone.

If you woke troubled from a sexual encounter in dreamland with someone whom your waking self considers an inappropriate sexual partner, or from a distressingly graphic, violent, or "abnormal" experience, be assured that there is often a nonsexual expla-nation for such a dream. If you find your dream particularly disturbing, however, and especially if it repeatedly recurs, consider seeking profes-sional counseling.

Maybe you are a mar-ried man who dreamed of being in bed with your friend's wife, a woman you like but would never sleep with in the real world—partly because you could not betray your friend's trust and partly because you have no intention of being unfaithful to your own wife—and are having

Left: If you are male and dreamed that a woman to whom you are attracted in real life lured you into her bed, but then cruelly rejected you, your unconscious may have been warning that your heart will be broken if you succumb to her charms in waking life. **Below:** If your dream portrayed you sleeping with someone who is sexually off-limits in real life, and you now feel ashamed, remember that the message from your unconscious may not have been that you desire that person. It may just be that you would like to enjoy a close emotional connection with him or her.

feelings of irrational remorse. Why would your unconscious have por-trayed you actively enjoying this guilt-inducing scenario? Well, it may be that you are consciously repressing your feelings of physical attraction to her, and that your dream fulfilled the fantasy that you are pushing to the back of your

mind during your waking hours but cannot totally banish from your thoughts. Alternatively, perhaps you find her intriguing and would like to become more intimate with her, not sexually, but to get to know her better or to establish a closer relationship. Also mull over the possibility that your dream betrayal of your friendship could have symbolized your feelings of shame because you have been disloyal to your friend in waking life. But if you felt worse about your own dream infidelity, maybe you are feeling ashamed about having betrayed your wife's faith in you in some way.

If you are a man who dreamed of being spurned by a contemptuous woman after she'd led you on and had had her way with you, and you are drawn to her sexual magnetism in waking life, could your unconscious have been emphasizing her archetypal huntress qualities, thereby advising you to steer clear of her because emotional devastation beckons if you succumb to temptation? Similarly, if you are a woman who dreamed of being bedded and then abandoned by a man whose devil-may-care attitude attracts you in real life, could your unconscious have been warning that he's someone who

will love and leave you—in other words, that he is an archetypal wastrel?

Incest is one of society's great taboos, and if you had a dream in which you slept with your sister, you probably awoke feeling utterly appalled, in which case you'll be relieved to learn that it is highly unlikely that your unconscious was highlighting your sexual attraction to her. Instead, is it possible that you and your sister are unhealthily, or claustrophobically, close or dependent on one another, be it emotionally or practically? Another point to bear in mind when trying to interpret any

Opposite, top: The purpose of the unconscious in sending a woman a dream in which she shared an erotic interlude with a man with whom she longs to have a relationship in the waking world, only for her dream lover to up and leave immediately thereafter, was probably to warn that the best she could hope for from such a liaison would be the occasional one-night stand. Opposite, bottom: A cherry can denote virginity in the symbolic language of dreams. Right and below: Dreams of being sexually harassed or assaulted often highlight feelings of being violated by a real-life abuse of authority (but not necessarily sexual), or else of being victimized by a dominating personality.

dream that depicted you making love with someone who plays a major, but platonic, part in your everyday life is that your unconscious may merely have been reflecting your waking preoccupation with him or her at the same time as you became sexually aroused in your sleep. So if you dreamed of being turned on by your unattractive boss, it may not have been a cause-and-effect dream phenomenon, but rather a coincidence.

If you dreamed of losing your virginity and are actually a virgin in real life, your dream may have mirrored your conscious anticipation of, or worries about, doing just that in the waking world, thereby perhaps giving you an opportunity to experience how you would feel. If you are no longer a virgin, however, by sending you a dream like this, could your unconscious have been referring to your recent loss of "innocence," or to your disillusionment in the real world, perhaps because a person whom you once thought could do no wrong has been exposed as a scheming manipulator?

A dream of being sexually assaulted was probably awful, and if your dream re-created an attack that actually happened to you in real life, you are almost certainly still feeling traumatized by your violation and haven't yet come to terms with what happened. (If this is indeed the case, counseling may help you to resolve your feelings of guilt, pain, or anger, thereby enabling you to achieve closure.) Otherwise, did you know the dream aggressor, and is he or she a domineering person, someone who exerts power (maybe emotional) or authority over you, or else a person with whom you have "locked horns" in the wak-ing world? If so, by depicting your sexual subjugation, your unconscious may have been stressing your sense of having no choice but to submit unwillingly to his or her control on the one hand, or your fear of being humiliated because you sense that your "opponent" is close to winning your power struggle on the other. Also consider the possibility that you have detected—unconsciously, if not consciously—that that individual poses a real sexual danger to you.

Maybe you are heterosexual but had a deeply unsettling dream of being in bed with a friend of the same sex. If so, and if you enjoyed the dream interlude, it may be that

Above: Same-sex erotic encounters in dream-land can indulge suppressed feelings of sexual curiosity, but may otherwise merely denote an intense emotional relationship. **Below:** If you dreamed of feeling degraded when your real-life sexual partner treated you like an object, rather than an individual, was your dream portraying a truth that you unconsciously recognize, but can't consciously face up to?

force you to be more understanding and broad-minded?

If you are a man who dreamed of visiting a prostitute and are finding your sex life unsatisfying in the real world, it may be that you are considering, either consciously or unconsciously, relieving your sexual tension by doing the same in waking life, perhaps because you feel that this would enable you to avoid making an emotional commitment or disrupting your family life. If you are a woman who dreamed of working as a prostitute and found it a positive experience, maybe you are unconsciously craving an element of sexual danger or adventure in waking life, or else the satisfaction that you would derive from wielding power over men. But if being cast in the role of a prostitute in dreamland made you feel violated and disgusted, do you feel that your real-life partner is emotionally disconnected from you and is just using you for sex? Whatever your sex, if your unconscious depicted you as an unwilling prostitute, do you feel that you have "prostituted" yourself or "sold out" recently in waking life?

you are indeed sexually attracted to other members of your sex (and perhaps especially to your friend), but have repressed this inclination because your socially conditioned conscious mind recoils from the very thought. In this case, your dream may have been fulfilling your unconscious fantasies, perhaps also encouraging you to come out of the closet in real life. Some psychologists believe that we are all "bi-curious" at some level; a dream like this may have given you the opportunity to make an experimental foray in order to explore your emotional reactions to the experience in the safe environment of dreamland. If you are sure that you are straight, however, perhaps your dream was only emphasizing the warm and intimate relationship that you enjoy with your friend. Another possible explanation, especially if you felt guilty about your dream betrayal of your significant other, is that your conscience is troubling you because you feel closer to your friend than you do to your partner. But if you are emphatically homophobic during your waking hours, could your unconscious have been trying to

KEEPING A DREAM DIARY

Keeping a dream diary can be a most rewarding exercise. Night after night, the unconscious sends us off on bizarre adventures, floods us with intense feelings, exposes us to horrors that can do us no harm, and highlights crucial aspects of our characters. No movie director could be more inventive, and no movie library more extensive, than your own unconscious mind and the variety of dramas that it screens, while no psychologist is capable of giving you a more penetrating insight into your personality. Yet because we rarely make a conscious effort to remember, record, or understand our dreams, we are wasting a vital opportunity to learn more about ourselves and consequently to take steps to transform our waking lives for the better.

Whether you document only one dream a week or write up the dream, or dreams, that you have every night, keeping a dream diary will not only preserve the dreams that your unique, unconscious mind has generated, but will enable you to keep track of your experiences in dreamland and thus also of your state of mind. Consulting your dream diary will furthermore enable you to discern the patterns that underlie your dreams, to recognize your emotional reaction to certain situations, and then take conscious steps either to improve your waking circumstances or to face them more positively. If you work regular office hours in the waking world, and an examination of your dream diary reveals that you repeatedly have nightmares in the small hours of Monday morning, for instance, your journal may at last have enabled your conscious self to grasp what you have unconsciously known for some time, that is, that you find your working hours "a nightmare." Based on the advice from your unconscious, you may then either decide to leave your job or find a way of actively controlling, rather than passively suffering, its challenges.

Your Dream Diary

Before starting to document your dreams, you will need to equip yourself with the necessary tools to station permanently by your bedside with which to record their details as soon as you awake. You can choose from either a batch of photocopied pages of the blank dream diary on pages 394 to 395 or a notebook, along with a ballpoint pen or pencil and a flashlight, or else a Dictaphone or cassette recorder. Each of these recording methods has its advantages, depending on your nighttime circumstances. If you have a bedfellow, writing down the details of your dream by flashlight (turning on a bedside light would probably disrupt both his or her sleep and your unconscious mindset) has the virtue of quietness. If you sleep alone, however, you may prefer to dictate the details of your dreams into a Dictaphone or cassette recorder, although you will then have to transcribe your spoken words into a written dream diary in order to study them (which you may also need to do if you chose the notebook option). Advice on how to set out, and keep, your dream diary is given below.

Once you have recorded, and perhaps also analyzed, your dream on paper, you may find that you are left with a mass of scribbles and doodles that is difficult to decipher. If so, consider copying your dreamwork into a second journal to keep as a neater, more permanent, ongoing record to which you will find it easier to refer when trying to identify recurring patterns. (If you have filled in the photocopied pages of the dream journal given here, which you could then file in chronological order in a ring binder, you may find this additional step unnecessary, although note that the transcription process can often give you further insight into the meaning of your dreams.) This "official" dream journal could take the form of a large, hardback notebook or word-processed computer files, and the advantage of using a computer is that you can run an automatic search

for key words or dates when trying to link one dream with another. If you decide to keep both a rough and an "official" dream diary in tandem, don't throw your original notes away, however, because there may be occasions when you want to compare them with your "official" diary in order to check a detail.

Whatever form your dream diary takes, it's best to allocate two pages to each dream, one containing a list of headings (see below) alongside which to insert the appropriate information—if you are using a notebook, set aside its left-hand pages for this purpose—and the other a blank page—to which you should devote the notebook's facing, right-hand pages—on which to write your interpretation of your dream.

Remembering Your Dreams

You have, no doubt, already found that your dreams tend to disappear from your memory almost as soon as you get up. When your conscious mind takes control of your body again, it is so busy focusing on the day ahead that it tunes out, and then swiftly erases, your unconscious recollection of the events that occurred in dreamland the previous night. Although tantalizing echoes of your dream may still linger in your mind, or be triggered during the day, echoes do not provide sufficient material with which to work when exploring your dreams in depth, which is why it's important to try to remain in the frame of mind that prompted your dreams in the first place when you are recording them.

Opposite and above: If you decide that writing down your dreams would be the best way of recording them, you'll need some paper or a notebook, a pen or pencil, and a flashlight.
Left: If you dread the prospect of returning to school or work after a weekend of freedom, your dream diary may show that you are regularly plagued by anxiety dreams shortly before waking up on Monday mornings.

Although simply becoming interested in your dreams will stimulate your powers of recollection, there are two useful methods that you could use in conjunction with each other to help you to remember your dreams long enough to log them accurately. First, you could try programming your unconscious mind to recall your dreams using autosuggestion, maybe by saying to yourself, "I will remember my dream when I wake up" just before dropping off to sleep, a technique that often successfully enlists the aid of your unconscious. Second, as soon as you are aware of having become conscious during the night or early morning, lie still and let your mind drift until you are immersed in the memory of your dream. Now is the point at which you should slowly, but immediately, reach for your flashlight, pen, and dream diary, or else your Dictaphone, and start recording your dream.

Recording Your Dreams

As soon as your pen is poised, or your Dictaphone is switched on, let the words flow, whether they escape from your unconscious mind in a torrent or in only a few key words or phrases that describe the theme of the dream or your dreaming mood. Work as quickly as you can, and try not to let any conscious thoughts intrude as you place your dream on record, because even pausing to try to think of an apt word can frequently cause the memory of your dream to

fade frustratingly rapidly. And if you find it easier to sketch, rather than verbally describe, an aspect of your dream, then do so. If possible, also write down the time at which you awoke, because if you end up documenting a series of dreams that night, the order in which they occurred may be significant. Once you have committed your dream to paper or tape, you can then either return to dreamland or get out of bed and start your day, safe in the knowledge that you have captured the essence of your dream and will consequently be able to expand on your narrative and decipher its meaning later in the day.

When you return to your dreamwork (preferably on the same day, while there is still a chance that you can recall your dream, and in a quiet place where you won't be distracted), write up your dream as fully as you can from your original notes—ideally preserving its immediacy by using the present tense—also re-creating any drawings that you may have made. There are certain additional details that you should always log, notably the *day and date* on which the dream occurred, along with the *time* when it ended, if you wrote it down. The combination of these details with your description of your dream will enable you to compare your dream diary with a calendar to see if you can discern whether any specific events in the real world prompted your dream, or gave rise to a dreaming pattern, and, if you think that they did, to learn to understand your emotional response to these trigger situations. For this reason, too, it is important to record the *atmosphere* that pervaded your dream (threatening, wet, or sunny, for example), along with your dreaming self's *mood* (such as scared or relaxed). You should also *number* your dreams in the order in which you had them, starting with "1" for the first dream, followed by "2" for the next, and so on.

Having completed the bare bones of a page in your dream diary, writing down significant elements of your dream under separate headings may both help you to decode your dream and highlight potentially recurring themes or symbols for future reference. The dream diary on pages 394 to 395 suggests that you write down the *time* in which the dream was set (day or night, the season, the past, present, or future, for instance); any *colors* that caught your dreaming attention; whether *movement* was an important aspect of your dream (were you running, climbing, flying, falling, or undertaking a journey, for example?); the *setting*, any *people, animals, buildings, objects, signs,* or *symbols* (road signs, vehicles, or shapes, for instance) that featured in your dream; and any *words* or *puns* that your dream may have contained.

Further information that it is always helpful to record is *what happened yesterday, how you were feeling yesterday,* and *a possible trigger for the dream* because these details may help you to pinpoint your unconscious response to real-life events. You may also find that giving your dream a *title* or theme ("Dancing With my Dog Daisy," for example), and deciding on its *type* (such as a nightmare or a recurring or wish-fulfillment dream), proves useful when looking for patterns in your dreams, and if you believe that you have identified any, you could record the numbers of the relevant dreams under another heading entitled *possible link with dream number(s)*.

Remember, however, that the format of this dream diary is only a guide, so don't feel obliged to enter information under every heading if nothing springs to mind. And you may even prefer to devise a different list of headings that is better tailored to the nature of your dreams.

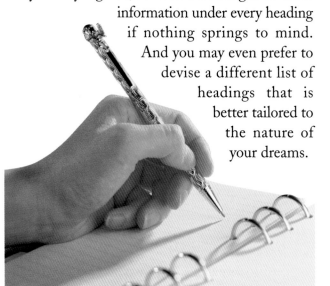

Analyzing Your Dreams

By filling in a page of your dream diary in this way, you have now created both a record of your dream and one of the best starting points for its analysis. Using the right-hand page of your notebook, or a new page of your computer file, jot down your thoughts about the meaning of your dream. You should find the pages of this book illuminating when pondering the various elements of your dream, and further potentially useful tools include dictionaries and encyclopedias, free and direct association, or describing your dream to, and maybe discussing it with, someone else. Above all, however, remember to try to think as intuitively as possible because this way you'll be tapping into your unconscious (after all, the source of your dream). And when you think that you have found a likely explanation for anything that seemed significant in your dream, try to explain why you have reached your conclusion because this will help you to understand the symbolic language that is personal to you (if you dreamed of a cat, for example, and you are feline-phobic, write down your dislike of these creatures).

When you have finished, sit back and consider the message that you believe your unconscious was sending you before entering it at the bottom of the page. Does it make perfect sense in the context of your waking world? Alternatively, has it startled you and made you think about changing an aspect of your life? But don't be discouraged if the meaning of your dream eludes you. Not only will you find that the interpretation process becomes easier with practice, but your dream diary may later reveal that your baffling dream is one of a sequence of similar dreams that has either yet to unfold or whose meaning you have not yet grasped.

Opposite, top: On waking, try not to let any conscious thoughts disrupt your mindset before you have recorded the details of your dream. Your ability to remember the dream will fade rapidly as your waking frame of mind asserts itself. **Left:** You could transcribe your initial notes into an "official" dream diary and compare this with your calendar, which may help you to discover whether a real-life event or pattern in your routine triggered your dream.

MY DREAM DIARY

Day and Date .... **Time** .... **Number** ....

Dream Title ....
Type of Dream ....

Atmosphere ....
My Dreaming Mood ....

Narrative of Events ....

....

....

....

....

....

....

....

Time ....
Colors ....
Movement ....
Setting ....

People ....

Animals ....
Buildings ....
Objects ....
Other Significant Signs or Symbols ....
Words or Puns ....

What Happened Yesterday ....

How I was Feeling Yesterday ....

A Possible Trigger for the Dream ....

....

Possible Link with Dream Number(s) ....

....

MY DREAM DIARY

Interpretation

Possible Message ....
....
....
....
....

BIBLIOGRAPHY

Adler, Alfred, *What Life Should Mean to You*, George Allen & Unwin, London, 1980.

Beaton, Annelie, *Dictionary of Dreams*, Caxton Editions, London, 2000.

Chetwynd, Tom, *Dictionary of Symbols*, The Aquarian Press, London, 1982.

Crisp, Tony, *Dreams and Dreaming*, London House, London, 1999.

Dee, Nerys, *Understanding Dreams*, Thorsons, London, 2000.

Francis, Valerie, *Illustrated Guide to Dreams*, Bison Books Limited, London, 1995.

Freud, Sigmund, *The Interpretation of Dreams*, Wordsworth Editions Limited, Ware, 1997.

Gibson, Clare, *Signs and Symbols*, Saraband Inc., Rowayton, 1996.

Gibson, Clare, *The Ultimate Birthday Book*, Saraband Inc., Rowayton, 1998.

Gregory, Richard L. (Ed.), *The Oxford Companion To The Mind*, Oxford University Press, Oxford, 1987.

Hadfield, J.A., *Dreams and Nightmares*, Penguin Books, Harmondsworth, 1954.

Jones, Richard M., *The New Psychology of Dreaming*, Penguin Books, Harmondsworth, 1978.

C. G. Jung, Four Archetypes: *Mother, Rebirth, Spirit, Trickster*, Routledge & Kegan Paul, London & Henley, 1972.

C. G. Jung, *Jung: Selected Writings*, Fontana Press, London, 1983.

McLeish, Kenneth Ed., *Bloomsbury Guide to Human Thought*, Bloomsbury Publishing Limited, London, 1993.

Millidge, Judith, *Dream Symbols*, Saraband Inc., Rowayton, 1998.

Parker, Julia, and Parker, Derek, *Thecomplete Book of Dreams*, Dorling Kindersley Limited, London, 1998.

Powell, Rosalind, *Dream Therapy*, Hermes House, London, 2002.

Understanding Dreams, HarperCollins Publishers, Glasgow, 1999.

ACKNOWLEDGMENTS AND PHOTO CREDITS

The publisher would like to thank all those who assisted in the production of this book, including those listed on page 5, Kerry Ryan for the index, and Paula Reel for the illustration. Grateful acknowledgment is also made to the following individuals and institutions for permission to reproduce illustrations and photographs: **© 2002 Arttoday.com, Inc.:** 6, 13, 15, 16, 17, 85, 87b, 88t, 100t, 109t, 140, 145t, 146t, 151tr, 153b, 171, 173bl&tr, 174r, 180b, 184c, 185t&r, 187, 188tl, 189b, 193t&b, 195tr, 201t&b, 203tl, 204t, 208 (all except cl), 209tl&r, 210tl, 212 (all), 213tr, 214tr, 215 (both), 216b, 217b, 219b, 220t&b, 221br, 222tr&cl, 223, 224t&bl, 225br, 226l, 228 (all), 229tl&bl, 235br, 236c, 239t, 248t, 254tr, 255b, 258t, 263b, 265t, 271, 275t, 276t&c, 277t&bl, 279, 280t, 283both, 284t, 285tl, 287b, 288 (both), 292t, 294, 295, 296tl, 297tl&b, 299b, 300b, 301b, 304 (all except tr), 305t, 309t, 310 (both), 311tl&br, 312, 313tl&b, 314t&bl, 315t, 316tr&b, 317, 318 (both), 319, 320bl, 321 (all), 322b, 323 (both), 324 (both), 325t, 326t, 327r, 328, 329 (both), 330b, 331 (all), 332t&cl, 333, 334tl, 335 (all), 336 (all), 337 (all), 338 (all), 339t&br, 340t&b, 341 (both), 342 (both), 343 (all except tl), 344c, 345 (all except c), 346tr&b, 347 (all), 348, 351t (both), 352tr, 353t, 355b, 359t, 360b, 361c&b, 364t&c, 365 (both), 366 (both), 367 (both), 368 (both), 369 (both), 370 (all), 371, 372 (both), 373l&r, 374 (both), 375b, 376t&b, 377b, 378b, 379 (both), 380t, 381 (both), 382 (both), 384t, 385 (both), 386 (both), 387b, 388t; **AKG, London:** 25, 27, 28b, 30, 33; **© Theo Allofs:** 168b; **© Larry Angier:** 52–3, 86; **© Mary Liz Austin:** 211; **Author's Collection:** 36, 42b, 216t; **The Bettmann Archive:** 24r, 140b; **Bibliothèque Nationale, Paris:** 83tl, 94br, 101b, 102b, 350b; **© Kindra Clineff:** 167l; **© Comstock, Inc.:** 1–5, 52l, 57r, 58b, 59tl&r, 60 (both), 66t, 73t, 75 (both), 77, 83r, 84tr&bl, 110l, 112tr, 121 (all except bl), 123r, 124tl&c, 126tl, 131r, 142tl, 156c (both), 157 (all), 158l (both), 159l, 160t (both), 163l, 167t&b, 169 (all), 170 (all except cl & bl), 172 (all except br), 175 (all except tl), 176c&b, 179c, 188tr, 194, 195c, 199b, 206r, 213b, 214br, 217tl, 219t, 224c, 225c, 247t, 250t, 263r, 267, 268bl, 269c&b, 270bl, 272c, 276b, 296tr, 298c, 302 (all), 303 (all), 304tr, 305b, 306 (all), 307c&b, 309c, 311tl&cl, 315b, 320br, 332cr, 334b&tr, 339l, 343t, 344b, 345c, 362 (both), 363c&b, 364b, 377t&c, 383; **© Ed Cooper:** 56, 70; **© Corbis Corporation:** 22, 32b, 96b, 97t, 100b, 146c&b, 147b, 148c&b, 149t, 150 (all), 151b, 152, 161t, 177b, 179b, 180c, 181 (both), 182 (all), 183t, 184t, 188b&r, 189c, 190t&b, 191 (both) & bl, 192tl, 193c, 196c, 197b, 198b, 199t, 200 (both), 201cr, 202t&b, 205t, 209c, 221cr, 230 (all), 231 (both), 232, 235bl, 237l, 238 (all), 240t, 245t&br, 246t, 248b, 251, 252 (all), 253 (both), 254tl, 255t&c, 256b, 257t, 259 (both), 260 (both), 261, 262 (both), 264 (both), 274r, 278t, 280b, 281 (both), 284b, 285tr&b, 384b, 388b; **Corel Stock Photo Library:** 24l; **© Terry Donnelly:** 218, 226–7, 270t; **© Nikki Fesak:** 74t, 177t, 178c, 179t; **© Carolyn Fox:** 90, 119; **The Granger Collection:** 44t; **© Rudi Holnsteiner:** 249; **Idaho State Historical Society:** 40 (#60-13926); **John Fitzgerald Kennedy Library (by Mark Shaw, Whitehouse):** 44b; **© Balthazar Korab:** 166b; **Library of Congress, Prints and Photographs Division:** 65, 71, 74b, 78b, 79t, 86br, 87t, 88b, 91, 92 (both), 103, 105b, 106b, 109b, 110r, 112b, 114l&b, 115, 116, 117t&b, 118l&b, 120t, 121bl, 124b, 125t, 126b, 130, 131b, 132 (both), 133t&bl, 134l, 135 (both), 138, 140t, 141t, 142t&bl, 144 (all), 147t, 148t, 149b, 151tl, 153t, 155 (both), 156tr&b, 158tr, 159r, 161b, 170bl, 175tl, 178b, 180t, 185bl, 186b, 192b, 196b, 198t, 203bl&r, 204b, 207, 208cl, 209br, 210tr, 214tl, 216c, 217tr, 222tl, 225tl, 229tr, 233tr&b, 234t, 236b, 237r, 239b (both), 240b, 241 (both), 242, 243 (all), 250b, 254b, 256t, 257t, 265b, 266 (both), 268t, 270c, 273t, 274l, 282 (both), 289, 290, 300c, 301t, 326b, 330t, 349, 350t, 353c, 358b, 360t; **Montana Historical Society, Helena:** 129; **National Archives:** 21, 63t, 66r, 67b, 80, 81b, 82, 96t, 98, 99, 102t, 247b, 258b; **Nebraska State Historical Society—Solomon D. Butcher Collection:** 38b; **© Chuck Pefley:** 168t; **Penguin/Corbis-Bettman:** 63b; **Peter Palmquist Collection:** 35b, 38t, 49; **© PhotoDisc, Inc.:** 18 (both), 19 (all), 20 (both), 24c, 29b, 34 (both), 35t, 37, 39 (both), 41 (both), 42t, 45 (both), 46 (all), 47 (all), 48 (both), 50t, 54, 55 (both), 57l, 58t, 59b, 62, 66b, 67t, 68, 69, 72, 73b, 79b, 81t, 83b, 86c, 89, 97t, 104b, 105t, 106t, 107, 112tl, 113t, 117l, 118t, 120c, 123l, 124tr, 125b, 126tr, 128, 136t, 137, 141b, 142cr, 145b, 154, 160b, 163r, 166t, 170cl, 172br, 173tl&br, 174t&bl, 176t, 210b, 233tl, 234b, 235t, 236tl, 244, 245bl, 246b, 272br, 273t, 286, 287t, 291, 292b, 293, 296b, 298t&b, 299t, 320t, 322t, 325b, 327l, 332b, 340c, 344t, 346tl, 351b, 352tl, 357b, 361t, 363t, 373c, 375t, 376c, 378t&c, 380b, 387t, 389; **Planet Art:** 11, 26, 28t, 29t, 50b, 61, 76, 78t, 101t, 104t, 108, 111, 113b, 114t, 134r, 278b; **© David Rago:** 268br, 269t; **© Paula Reel:** 178t; **© Paul Rocheleau:** 164b, 165; **Saraband Image Library:** 8, 14, 23, 32l&t, 51, 64, 84tl&c, 93, 127, 139t, 183c, 184b, 186t, 189c, 190c, 191br, 192tr, 195t, 196t, 197t, 199c, 201cr, 202c, 204c, 205b, 206c&b, 209bl, 213c (both) & tl, 214bl, 220c, 221bl&tl, 222tl&cr, 224br, 225tr, 270br, 272tl, 275b, 277c&br, 278c, 297tr, 300t, 307t, 308b, 309b, 311cr, 313tr, 314br, 316tl, 352b, 354, 355, 356 (both), 357t, 358t, 359b; **State Historical Society of Iowa, Iowa City:** 139b; **© John Sylvester:** 164t; **© Graeme Teague:** 94tl; **Wyoming State Museum—Division of Cultural Resources:** 136b; **© Charles J. Ziga:** 9, 31, 43, 95, 162, 229br, 308t, 353b.

INDEX

abandonment 85–6
abduction 102–3
Aboriginal belief 9
abortion 109–10
abysses 240, 283
accidents 102, 107
accountants 47
acorns 209
acting 161, 378–9
address books 344
adolescence 33 *see also* teenagers
adoption 40, **114**
affection 96–7 *see also* love, positive emotions
aggression *see* violence
aging 37, 120, 145, 147, 149, 209, 216, 269, 270, 272, 281, 300, 316
air 244–250
airplanes 63, 107, **247–48**, 324–5
airports **324–5**, 326
alarms 236, **334–5**
albatrosses 193
alcohol 34, 138, 144, 172, 364
aliens 42–4
ambition and success 54–61, 247–8, 250, 282, 300, 321, 325
ambushes 102–3
amphibians 199
angels 28
anger 27, 37, 41, **62–3**, 75, 77–84, 101–2, 110, 117, 121, 178, 182, 204, 232, 233–4, 236, 305
animals 71–2, 101–2, 133, **177–86**, 321 *see also individual animals*
anniversaries 269, 312
anxiety and frustration 68–76, 110, 112, 113, 138, 152, 257–8, 267, 269, 316, 346 *see also* fear
apnea 244
applause 57, 60, **338**
apples 223–5
Aquarius 278
archery 277
archetypes 18–24, 39, 306:
    amazon 21, 178;
    anima/animus **19–20**, 37, 42, 44, 120, 125, 358, 385;
    black magician **23**, 351;
    father **22**, 137–8, 140, 277;
    feminine/masculine 20–4;
    hero/heroine 277; high priest/wise old man 22, **23**, 37, 139, 147, 191, 351–2;
    huntress **21**, 40, 101, 179, 183, 277, 358, 385; mother **20**, 140, 178, 180, 184, 196,

251, 283–4, 350; Mother Earth 20; ogre **22**, 40, 101, 138, 359; persona **18**, 75, 160, 208, 219, 287, 321, 322; priestess/wise old woman **22**, 37, 39, 116, 147, 191, 350; prince 22, 39, 40; princess 21, 178; shadow **19**, 42, 62, 65, 72; siren **21**, 39, 40, 179, 277 ; terrible mother **21**, 40, 101, 179, 196, 205, 240, 283–4, 348, 350, 356; trickster **24**, 94, 121, 185, 277, 338, 378; villain **23**, 101; warrior **23**, 277; wastrel 22, 39, 386; witch 22, 179, 350
arguments *see* conflict
Aries 181, **277–8**
Aristotle 10
armies 81–2
arms (limbs) 151
arrows 84
artists 46, 58, 332
ashes 235–6
astral bodies 274–8
astrology 276–8 *see also signs of the zodiac*
athletics 54–5, **376**
atlases 320
attaché case 159
attack 99–104
attics 170
auditions 68–9
authority figures 100, 120, **137–42**, 262, 296, 298, 324
automobiles 75, 107, **321–3**
avalanches 266
babies 108–15, 151, 237, 253, 275
backs 150
baldness 147
balloons 250
bananas 224
bankruptcy 92
baptisms 115, 335
barking 335
baseball 58, 374–5
basement 169
bathrooms 170
bats **186**, 353
battles 81–2
bayonets 82–4
beaches **280**, 317
beards 147
bears 71, **183–4**
beauty 146, 160, 217, 285, 314
bedrooms 170
beds 170
beef 175–6
beer 172
bees 216

beetles 201–2
beggars 45–6
bells 333–5
belts 156
bereavement 86–9 *see also* death
bicycles 35–6, 320–1
billfolds 159
binary code 346
birdcages 187–8
birds 187–193, 246, 271, 339
birth 108–15, 132, 255
birthdays 59, 122, **269**, 316
bisexuality 388–9
bishops *see* spiritual authorities
black 260, 305, 351
blackbirds 191–2
blackmail 105
blemishes 145–6
blindness 148
blood 102, 144–5, 153
blouses 156
blushing 146
boats 251–2, 325–6
bodily functions 153
body, the 143–53
body art 161
bombs 82–4, 233
bones 144
bonfires 231
bookkeepers 47
books **292**, 297
border controls 327
bosses 138, 298, 300, 365 *see also* authority figures
boulders 285
bouquets 59–60, **217–22**
boxes 369, 370
boxing 375–6
boxing gloves 159
bracelets 160
bravery 93–4
bread 175
breasts 151, 224
breathing 244–6
breezes 261
bridges 253, **327**
brooms **170**, 353
brothers 38–9, 137 *see also* family members, siblings
budgerigars 192–3
buds 208, 215–6
bugs 201–2
buildings **286–94**
bullets 82–4
bulls 102, 133, **180–1**, 302
bullying 22, 34, 103, 117, 133, 297
burglaries 105, 166
burials 135–6
buried alive, being 241
buses 74–5, **323–4**

bus stops 326–7
butterflies 200–1
buttocks 153
buttons 156
cable cars 325
cables 368, 369
cakes 176
calendars 268–9
camels 183
cameras 331–2
canals 255
Cancer (astrology) 196, **278**
cancer (disease) 143
candles 32, 201, 231
candy 175
cannon 82–4
canyons 283
Capricorn 278
cards 377–8
carousel 382
cars *see* automobiles
cassette recorders 332
castles 287–8
caterpillars 200–1
cathartic dreams 13
Catherine wheels 307
cats **177–9**, 353
cauldrons 352
caves/caverns 243, 284
celebrations and achievements 57–8, 269, 362, 364–5
celebrities 44
cellars 169
cellos 340
cell phones 345–6
cemeteries 135–6
centaurs 357
chairs 169
chalices 32
chameleons 199
champagne **172**, 365
charity 94–6
chasms 240, 283
cheating *see* deceit
checks 300
cheering 337
cheerleaders 120, 367
cherries 225
cherubs 306
chess 377
chest, the (body) 150–1
chests (box) 369
chewing 149
chicken (food) 176
chickens (animal) 193
childhood 89, **116–22**, 296
children 107, 116–18, 171, 367 *see also* family members
chimneys 167
choirs 380
choking 150
chores 97–8

christenings 115
Christmas 269–70
Christmas trees 212
chrysanthemums 222
churches 290–1
circles 307
circuses 381–2
cities/**cityscapes 286–94**
clairvoyants 273
class reunions 363
classrooms 295–8 *see also schools*
cleanliness 153
cliffs 69, 281–2
climbing 54–7, 240, 282
cloaks 158–9
clocks **267–8**, 316, 334
clothing and adornments 75, 142, **154–62**, 170, 231
clouds 260
clowns 381–2 *see also* archetypes: trickster
clubs 366–7
coats 158–9
cobwebs 170, 206
cockerels 193
cockroaches 201
coded messages 346
coffee 172
coffins 136
cold 264–5, 320
colleges 139, 154–5, 297–8 *see also* schools
colors 154–5, 284, **301–11**
colors and shapes 301–11
comets 276
communication 341–7
compasses 320
compensatory dreams 13
computers 75, **299–300**, 342
conception 108–9
conferences 366
confinement 52, 73–4, 136, 141, 240
conflict 77–84, 99, 133, 261
congregations 32
conjurors 352
constipation 153
contact lenses 148
contentment **48**
contrary dreams 13
cooking 173, 231
copying 63
corridors 169
cosmetics 18, 161
costumes 159–60
courthouses 293
cowards 42
cows 180
crabs 196, 278
crashing 322
cradles 110
cranes (bird) 190

cremations 135–6
crime 66, **104–6**, 133–4, 138, 141
crocodiles 199
crops 226
crosses 311
crossroads 326–7
crosswords 373
crowds 76, 366–7
crowns 59, 157
crucifixes 311
crustaceans 196–7
crutches 144
crying 67, 117, 138, 199
cuckoos 192
cucumbers 228
daggers 82–4
daisies 222
dams 255–6
dancing 380–1
dandelions 221
darkness 270–1
dates (fruit) 225
dates (days) 312, 316
daughters see family members
dawn 270, 274
day **270–1**, 301
deafness 148
death 67, 86–9, **129–36**, 190, 221, 268, 274, 277
debts 92 see also money
deceit 66, 104
defecation 153
deities see spiritual authorities
Dement, William 6
demons 29
dentists 69
depression 67, 241, 260, 304
deserts 265, **280–1**
desserts 176
detectives 373
devils 29
diaries 268–9
dice 378
diets 174–5
digging 238–9
disasters 107, 265–6, 276, 283, 346, 376
discipline 35, 46, 134, 137
diseases 143–6 see also illness
disguises 18, 199
disobedience 78–9
diving 257
divorce 127–8, 149, 236, 266
doctors **47**, 69, 142, 294
dogs 133, **177–9**, 335
dolls 117, **121**
dominoes 377
doorbells 333–4
doors **167–8**, 335
dots 307
dragons 355–6
drapes 168
dream types 13–17
Dreamtime, the 9

drifters 45–6, 250
drinks/drinking 34, 35, 41, 138, 171–2, 251, 269, 364–5
drowning 258
drums 339, 340
ducks 193
dungeons 75
DVDs 329–30
earrings 160
ears 148
earth 237–42, 278
earthquakes 265–6
Easter 269–70
eating 145, 149, **173–4**
echoes 336
eclipses 275
eggs 189, 193, 175–6, 306, 308
ego, the 11
elves 359
e-mails 344
embers 235–6
embracing 96–7
engagements 123–4
envelopes 342–3
envy see jealousy
erotica 19, 27, 50, 65, 102, 151, 157, 171, 174, 180, 181, 184, 231, 232, 243, 246, 255, 264, 302, 321, 324, 340, 370, **383–9**
escape see freedom
evening 270–1
exams 57, **68–9**, 145, 174, 267, 296
executions 66, 133–5
explosions 233, 265
extended family 39–40
eyes 147–8, 276
fabrics 155–6
faces 18, 146
facial hair 147
factories 299
fairgrounds 382
fairies/fairy tales 18, 353, **359–60**
fall (season) 271
falling 57, 69–71, 240, 241, 248, 282
false awakenings 13
fame 44, 60
family members 33–40, 130, 314
family occasions 130, 270, 362–3
farewells 89
farmyard animals 179–82
fashion 154–61
fastenings 156
father figures 137–8
fatherhood 108–14
fathers 22, **33–7**, 78, 109, 137, 150, 362
fathers-in-law 39–40
fatness 174–5
faxes 344
fear **63–4**, 99, 118, 124, 145, 152, 206, 252, 343: of being

pursued 71–2, 285; of death 132; of exams/tests 68–7; of falling 69–71
feathers 188
feces 153
feet 152–3
fertility 108, 112, 185, 195, 199, 209, 214, 225, 237, 254, 268, 275, 385
fever 143–4
fighting 77–8, 80–4
fingerprints 107
fingers 151
fire 107, 136, **230–6**, 265, 278
fired, being 86, 134, 138, 234, 266
firefighters 234–5
fireworks 232
fishing **194–5**, 251
fishing nets 369
fish, reptiles, and amphibians 175, **194–9**, 251, 254, 278 see also fire
flames 32 see also fire
flies 202–3
floating 248, 257–8
flooding 254, 256
flowers 59–60, 208, **215–22**, 285 see also individual flowers
flying 52, 63, 107, 188, 246–8, 326
fog 260
food and drink 169, **171–6**, 364–5 see also fruits and vegetables
food poisoning 175
football 374–5
footprints 317
foreigners 44
foreign languages 298, 337, 346
forests 210–1, 253
forgeries 104
forgetting see memory
fortresses 287–8
fostering 114
fountains 255
fraud 104
freckles 145
freedom 52, 76, 145, 158, 188, 200–1, 247, 261, 323
Freud, Sigmund 10–12, 83
Freudian theory **10–12**, 198, 246, 288, 289, 324, 340, 370
friends 41–2, 51, 103, 104, 122, 178, 270, 364, 366
frigidity 257, 263, 264, 284
frogs 199
frost 263
fruit and vegetables 174, **223–9**
frustration **68–76**, 138, 229, 318–9, 325, 372, 375
funerals 37, 86, **135**
furniture 169
future events 273

gambling 378
games 121, 377
gangs 366–7
gardens/gardening 131, **163–6**, 219, 237–9
gatherings **362–73**: family 362–3; meetings and conferences 365–6; social events 363–65
Gemini 278
gems 60, 160–1
genitalia 149, 151–2, 159, 226, 324
Gestalt theory 12
ghosts 130–1, **361**
giants 359
gifts 59–60
glaciers 265
globes 297
gloves 159
goddesses **25–7**, 275
gods **25–7**, 139 see also religion
gold (color) 303
gold (precious metal) 60
goldfish 194
golf 375
gorges 283
gossiping 148, 337
graduation ceremonies 57
grandparents 37, 116
graves/graveyards 135–6, 240
gray 301, 306
grief 67, 86–9, **129–36**
growling 335
guilt **65–6**, 104–5, 110, 134, 141, 145, 146, 152, 157, 388
guitars 340
guns 82–4
gurus see spiritual authorities
gyms 376
gypsies 45–6
hail 261
hair 146–7
hallways 169
hamsters 177
handbags 159
hands 151
handkerchiefs 368
handwriting 342–3
happiness see positive emotions
harbors 326–7
hats and headgear 156
hawks 190
heads 146
heads of state 140
health 47, 69, 142, 142, 143–53, 299
hearing 32, 148
heart, the 150–1, 268
hearths 230
heat 230–6, 260, 264–5, 274, 302
heaven 31
height 153
hell 31, 279

herbs 229
hexagrams **309**, 353
hills 55, **281–2**, 319
hobbies 97–8
hobos see drifters
hockey 374–5
holes 240–2, 318
holidays 269–70
holly 212–3
home, the 163–70
homesickness 89–90
honey 176
honeybees 204
horses **179–80**, 321
horseshoes 180, 306
hospitals 47, 69, **294**
hostility 62, 99, 241, 335
hot-air balloons 248
hotels 248
houses 163–70
howling 336
hunger 173–4
hurdles see obstacles
hurricanes 262
ice 256–7
icebergs 257
illness 47, 129, 132, **143–53**, 294, 304
imprisonment **73–4**, 141, 293–4 see also confinement
imps 353, 359
incest 387
incontinence 153
incubated dreams 13
individuality/identity 32, 33, 34, 38, 40, 63, 72, 138, 142, 181, 239, 245, 299
infidelity 65, 127–8, 152, 158, 225 **385–6**
injuries 102, **144–6**, 294
in-laws 40
insects 200–6 see also individual insects
inspirational dreams 14
instruments 340
interviews 68–9
invisibility 153
islands 279–80
itching **146**, 155, 156
ivy 212–3
jackets 158–9
jealousy 27, 51, 64–5, 102, 105, 126, 148, 153
jewelry 160
jewels 60
jigsaws 373
jokes 338
journeys 317–27
joy 48, 232, 282, 338, 380
judges see authority figures
jugglers 381
jukeboxes 339
jumping 54, 57
Jung, Carl **10–12**, 129, 207, 308
Jungian theory **10–12**, 286, 307, 308, 356, 385

jungles 281
Jupiter 277–8
juries 141
Kabbalism 312–6
karate 375–6
keys 167, 369–70
killing 132–3
kindergarten 121
kings **44–5**, 59, 140
kissing 96–7
kitchens **169**, 173
kites 250
kittens 177–9
knees 152
knives **82–4**, 132, 135
knocking 335–6
knots 368–9
labyrinths 307, **370–2**
ladders **55–6**, 371
ladybugs 201
lakes 253
lambs 181
lamps 169
landscapes 279–85
lateness 74–5, 267
laughter 338
lawyers 47
learning 297–8
leaves 208–9
lectures/lecturers **297–8**, 366
legs 152
lemons 225
Leo 278
lessons 297–8
letters 341–3
Libra 278
libraries 292
lies 104
lifeboats/life rafts 252, 258
lifeguards 94
light 243, 259, 270–1, 274, 306
lighthouses 289
lightning 262
lingerie 157–8
lions 182–3
lips 96–7, 149
literal dreams 14
locks 167, 370
loneliness 88–9, 279
loss 85–92: abandonment 85–6; bankruptcy 92; bereavement 86–9, 305; debts 92; farewells 89; homesickness 89–90; loneliness 88–9; losing something 91–2; lost, getting 91, **320**, 371; lottery, winning the 60
lotuses 221
louses 203
love 25, 34, 39, 50–2, 59, 107, 114, 123, 127, 150, 160, 171, 219, 231, 302, 385 *see also* erotica, family members, marriage, people, positive emotions
lovers, fantasy 50, 65, 127–8

lucid dreams 14
luggage 324–5
machinery malfunctions 75
magazines 330–1
magic 348–53
maids 47
mail delivery 342, 369
maize 226
make up 161
malnutrition 175
maple trees 213
maps 320
marathons 55
marriage 123–8, 368 *see also* weddings
Mars 277, 278
martial arts 375–6
martyrdom 135
masks 18, 75, 159–60
massage 96–7
matadors 181
matches 231
mazes 307, **370–2**
meat 175–6
medals 59
media 328–32
meetings 365
memory/memory loss 69, 117, 270, 297, 299, 330, 331, 336
menus 365
Mercury 277–8
mermaids 357–8
messages and communication 28, 277, 297, 328, **341–7**
meteors 276
mice 186
military hardware 82–4
milk 151, 171
Minotaur 356–7
mint 228–9
mirrors 146, 170
miscarriages 109–10
mist 248, **260**
mistletoe 214, 275
moles (animal) 186
moles (skin) 145
mollusks 196–7
money 60, 92, 131, 150, 189, 195, 300, 378
monkeys 184–5
monks *see* spiritual authorities
monsters and mythical creatures 64, 71, 72, 353, **354–61**, 371
moon 252, **274–5**, 308, 316
morse code 346
mosques 290–1
mosquitoes 203
Mother Earth 237
motherhood 108–14 *see also* babies, children, fertility
mothers 20–1, **33–7**, 78, 171
mothers-in-law 39–40
moths 200–1

motorbikes 321
mountains 55, **281–3**, 319, 327
mouths 149
movie theaters **292**, 378–9
mud 239–40
mullahs *see* spiritual authorities
murder 37, 41, 105, 141, **132–3**, 329
museums 292–3
music **338–40**, 380
mustaches 147
mutiny *see* rebellion
mutual dreams 14, 347
mysteries 368–73
mythical creatures 354–61
nakedness 75–6
naming ceremonies 115
natural phenomena 259–66
necklaces 160
necks 150
neckties 157
negative actions 99–107
negative emotions 62–7
Neptune 277–8
nests 188–9
newspapers 330–1
New Year **269–70**, 365
night **270–1**, 301
nightdresses 157
nightmares 14 *see also* anxiety, fear, *etc.*
night terrors 14
noses 148
nostalgia 37, **89–91**, 116, 121, 131–2, 139–40, 163, 212, 272–3, 295–8, 336, 362
N.R.E.M. (non-rapid-eye-movement) sleep 7
nudity **75–6**, 151
numbers 312–6
numerology 312–6
nuns *see* spiritual authorities
nurses **47**, 294
nuts 209, **226**
oases 280–1
obesity 174–5
obstacles/obstructions 54, 72, 282, 285, 318, 376
occupations 46–7
oceans 195–7, **251–2**, 280
octopuses 197
offices *see* work
ogres 359
olive trees 213
onions 229
orange (color) 303
oranges (fruit) **225**, 303
orchards 223
orchestras 339, **380**
orphans 40
out-of-body experiences 15, 246
overalls 158–9
owls **190–1**, 271, 353
oxen 180–1
oxygen 245, 246

oysters 196, 174
packages 343
padlocks 370
pains 143–51
painting 332
pajamas 157
palm trees 213
panic *see* fear
pants 157–8
paper 341–3
parachutes 248–9
paralysis 68, **72–3**, 268, 319
parcels 369
parenthood 108–14
parents 20–2, **33–7**, 38, 78, 85
parks 285
parrots 192–3
parties 122, 160, 245, **363–5**, 379
passports 325
past events 272 *see also* aging, nostalgia
past-life dreams 15
pay 300
peace 34, 189, 212, 253, 279, 304
peacocks 191
pebbles 284
Pegasus 355
penises 152 *see also* phallic symbols
penitentiaries 293–4
pens 341
pensions 300
pentagrams **309**, 353
people 41–7
pepper 176
pets 177–9
phallic symbols 57, **83–4**, 102, 157, 184, 195, 198, 214, 216, 224, 232, 289, 313, 321, 340, 353, 370
phobias 63, 69, 205, 258
phoenix 356
photographs 331–2
physiological dreams 15
pianos 340
pigeons 187, 189
pigs 182, 239
pilots 142
pimples 145
pine cones/trees 214
Pisces 195, 278
places of worship 290–1
planets 276–8
Pluto 277–8
poker 105, **377**
police 141–2
pollution 245
ponds 253–4
popcorn 176
popes *see* spiritual authorities
poppies 222
pork 175
porters 47
ports 326

positive actions 93–8
positive emotions 48–53
postcards 342, 345
potatoes 229
powerlessness 32, 69, 73, 100, 103, 104, 117, 138, 152, 240, 322
precipices 281–2
pregnancy 108–9, 145, 255
precognitive dreams 15
premonitory dreams 273
presentations **68–9**, 365–6
presidents 140
priestesses *see* spiritual authorities
priests *see* spiritual authorities
prime ministers 140
prisons 73–4, 141, **293–4**
prizes 59
problem-solving dreams 16
professional authorities 142
professors 139
prophets *see* spiritual authorities
prostitutes 389
psychic powers **273**, 347
public transport 323–6
punishment 66, **104–6**, 133–4, 137, 141
puppet shows 382
puppies 177–9
purses 159
pursuit 64, **71–2**, 285
puzzles and mysteries 368–73
pyramids 309–10
Pythagoras/Pythagorean theory 312, 315
queens **44–5**, 59, 140
rabbis *see* spiritual authorities
rabbits 185
racing 54, 55
radio 328–9
railroad stations 326–7
rain 260–1
rainbows 262–3, 302
rainforests 281
rape 103–4, 388
rats 186
ravens 191
ravines 283
reading 32
rebellion 37, 78–9, 100, 118, 179
recreational activities 97–8
recurring dreams 16
recklessness 41
red 302
redundancy 86
referees **140**, 375
rejection 52, 64–5, 76, 124
religion and spirituality 6, 7, 10, **25–32**, 134, 180, 189, 212–4, 263, 304, 311

religious ceremonies and accouterments 32, 115
R.E.M. (rapid-eye-movement) sleep 7, 73
reptiles 197–9
rescue 93–4, 258
reservoirs 256
restaurants 174, **364–5**
restraints 73–4
retirement 132
rice 174, 226
riddles 373
rings 123–4, 160
rivers 252–3
roads 318–9
robbery 105
rocks 285
rollerblades 376
rollercoasters 382
romance 50, 125, 127, 231, 232, 261, 262, 280
roofs 166–7
roses 217, **220–1**
royalty **44–5**, 59, 140
running **54–5**, 74, 376
sacrifice 124, 133–5, 315
sacred places 290–1
sadness 67, 136, 338
safes 370
safety-valve dreams 16
Sagittarius 278
sailboats 251–2
saints 28
salads 174
salaries 300
salespeople 47
salt 176
sand 280–1
Saturn 277–8
satyrs 23
scans 144
scars 145
schools 34, 57, 118, 121–2, 139, **295–300**
scientists 47
scissors 170
Scorpio 206, **278**
scorpions 206
screaming 113, 336–7
seas 195–7, **251–2**, 257–8, 280
searching 92
seashells 307
secrets 239, 372–3
seeds 209, **215–6**, 223, 225, 237–8
self-image 154–5
servants 47
sewing 98, **155**
sexual assault 103–4, 388
sexual dreams *see* erotica
sexual organs *see* genitalia
shamen 351
shapes 284, 306–11
sharks 195
sheep 181
shells 196–7

ships 279, 325–6
shirts 156–7
shock 129
shoes 158
shopping 291–2
shorthand 346
shoulders 150
siblings 38–9, 130–1, 362
sickness 47, 129, **143–53**, 294
sidewalks 287
singing 380
sirens (mythological) 357–8
sirens (signal) 335
sisters 38–9 *see also* siblings
skates/skating 256, **376**
skeletons 144
skiing 376
skin 145–6
skulls 144, 161
sky, the 303
skyscrapers 289
sleep 6–8
smells 148
smog 245
smoke **235–6**, 245
smothering *see* suffocation
snails 196–7
snakes 197–8
snow 264
soccer 58, **374–5**
social, family, and work gatherings 362–73
socks 158
sofas 169
soil *see* earth
soldiers 46, 58, 81–2, 141–2
songs 338–9
sons *see* family members
sorceresses 350
sores 146
sounds 333–40
spades 238
speaking: 32, 44, 334, 336, 337, 366: inability to speak 74, 168
spears 84
spectacles 148
spells, magic 348–53
Sphinx, the **357**, 373
spiders 63, **205–6**
spirals 307
spiritual authorities 23, **25–32**, 138–9
spirituality *see* religion
sporting arenas 292
sports, games, and entertainment 54–9, 140, **374–82**
spring (season) 215, 272
springs 254
squares 310
stairs 55–7, 170
starfish 195
stars (celestial) 276
stars (shapes) 195, 309
stealing 105, 106

stepparents 39–40
stillbirths 109–10
stings 204–5
stocktaking 300
stones 284
stopwatches 267
stores 291–2
storks 191
storms 166, 258, 262
straitjackets 72
strangers 42–4, 100
streams 252–3
streets 286–7
strongholds 287–8
stuttering 69, 366
succubi 361
suffocation 42, 143, 150, 155, 244–5, 296
sugar 176
suicide 132
suitcases 324–5
summer 202, 272
sun 259–60, **274–5**
sunbathing 259–60, 280
sunburn 260
sunflowers 216, 221
sunshine **259–60**, 301
superego, the 11
superheroes/heroines 93–4
supreme being, the **27**, 139
swans 193
swastikas 311
swimming **257–8**, 280
swimming pools 257
swimwear 157–8
swine 182
swords 82–3
synagogues 290–1
tadpoles 199
tarot cards 312–6
taste 149
tattoos 161
Taurus 181, 278
taxes 28
taxis 323
tea 172
teachers 64, 120, 122, 139, **296–8** *see also* authority figures, schools
tears *see* crying
teenagers 99, 114 **118–21**, 138, 149, 383
teeth 69, **149**
telepathic dreams/powers 17, 273, **347**
telephones 333–4, **345–6**
telescopes 276
television 328–30
temperature (weather) 264–5
temples 290–1
temptation 65–6
tenderness 50–2
tennis 375
tests 68–9
textbooks 298
Thanksgiving 269–70

theaters **292**, 378–9
thinness 174–5
thirst 171
threats 29
throats 150
thunder 262
ties 157
tigers 183
time and the seasons 267–73
toads **199**, 353
toilets 153
tornadoes 262
tortoises 199
touching 96–7
towers 288–9
towns 286
toys 117, **121**
trains 74–5, **324**
transportation 74–5, **320–6**
trapped, being *see* confinement
travel and journeys 158, 317–27
treadmills 376
treasure 60
trees 207–14, 223–6, 313–5 *see also individual trees*
triangles 309
tridents 277
trophies 59
trucks 323
trumpets 340
tunnels 243, **327**, 371
turkeys 190
tutors 297–8
umbrellas 159
umpires 140
unfaithfulness 127–8
unicorns 355
uniforms 140–1
universities 297–8
Uranus 277–8
urine 153
vaginas 243
vagrants *see* drifters
valleys 283
vampires 63, **358–9**
vases 219
VCRs 329–30
vegetables 223–9 *see also individual vegetables*
veils 160
Venus 277–8
vertigo 69–71
villages 286
vinegar 176
violence/aggression 72, 77–84, **99–104**, 278, 335, 385
violins 340, 380
virginity 387
Virgo 278
visibility 153
vision 147–8
voices 336–7 *see also* speaking

volcanoes 265
volleyball 374–5
vomiting 143
vultures 191
wages 300
waiters 47
walls 167
wands 352–3
war 81–2
warehouses 300
warmth 265
washing 153, 170
wasps 204
watches **267–8**, 273
water 171, 195–7, 219, 235 **251–8**, 260–1, 263, 277, 278, 280, 307
waterfalls 255
waves 252
wealth 60 *see also* money
weaponry **82–4**, 102
weather and natural phenomena 259–66
webs 206
weddings 50, **124–7**, 305, 335
weight gain/loss 174–5, 244, 367
weights 376
wells 254
werewolves 72, 358
whales 196
wheat 226
whirlpools 254, 307
whirlwinds 262
whispering 337
whistles 335
white 305–6, 351
wild boar 182
wildflowers **219**, 285
windows 167–8
winds 261–2
wine 169, **172**, 365
winter 215, 272
wish-fulfillment dreams 17
witch doctors 351
witches 348–51
wizards 352–3
wolves 184
woods 210–1
woodworm 201–2ß
work and workplaces 46–7, 75, **298–300**, 365–6
work gatherings 365–6
wounds 102, 144–6
wreaths 219
wrestling 375–6
wrinkles 145
writing 58, 60, 297, 341–3
x-rays 144
yin-yang symbols 307
zebras 183
zippers 156
zodiac, the 276–8
zoos 182

KEY TO THE FIFTY DREAM THEMES

These pages provide the key to the fifty chapters in this book. First look up your dream in the index. For related interpretations, use these symbolic icons to follow up the cross references you will find throughout the book.

 Ambition and Success
54–61

 Marriage
123–128

 Negative Emotions
62–67

 Death
129–136

 Anxiety and Frustration
68–76

 Authority Figures
137–142

 Conflict
77–84

 The Body
143–153

 The Archetypes
18–24

 Loss
85–92

 Clothing and Adornments
154–161

 Religion and Spirituality
25–32

 Positive Actions
93–98

 The Home
162–170

 Family Members
33–40

 Negative Actions
99–107

 Food and Drink
171–176

 People
41–47

 Birth
108–115

 Animals
177–186

 Positive Emotions
48–53

 Childhood
116–122

 Birds
187–193